T0144116

DEEP LEARNING AND IoT IN HEALTHCARE SYSTEMS

Paradigms and Applications

DEEP LEARNING AND IoT IN HEALTHCARE SYSTEMS

Paradigms and Applications

Edited by
Krishna Kant Singh, PhD
Akansha Singh, PhD
Jenn-Wei Lin, PhD
Ahmed A. Elngar, PhD

First edition published 2022

Apple Academic Press Inc.
1265 Goldenrod Circle, NE,
Palm Bay, FL 32905 USA
4164 Lakeshore Road, Burlington,
ON, L7L 1A4 Canada

CRC Press
6000 Broken Sound Parkway NW,
Suite 300, Boca Raton, FL 33487-2742 USA
2 Park Square, Milton Park,
Abingdon, Oxon, OX14 4RN UK

© 2022 Apple Academic Press, Inc.

Apple Academic Press exclusively co-publishes with CRC Press, an imprint of Taylor & Francis Group, LLC

Reasonable efforts have been made to publish reliable data and information, but the authors, editors, and publisher cannot assume responsibility for the validity of all materials or the consequences of their use. The authors, editors, and publishers have attempted to trace the copyright holders of all material reproduced in this publication and apologize to copyright holders if permission to publish in this form has not been obtained. If any copyright material has not been acknowledged, please write and let us know so we may rectify in any future reprint.

Except as permitted under U.S. Copyright Law, no part of this book may be reprinted, reproduced, transmitted, or utilized in any form by any electronic, mechanical, or other means, now known or hereafter invented, including photocopying, microfilming, and recording, or in any information storage or retrieval system, without written permission from the publishers.

For permission to photocopy or use material electronically from this work, access www.copyright.com or contact the Copyright Clearance Center, Inc. (CCC), 222 Rosewood Drive, Danvers, MA 01923, 978-750-8400. For works that are not available on CCC please contact mpkbookspermissions@tandf.co.uk

Trademark notice: Product or corporate names may be trademarks or registered trademarks and are used only for identification and explanation without intent to infringe.

Library and Archives Canada Cataloguing in Publication

Title: Deep learning and IoT in healthcare systems : paradigms and applications / edited by Krishna Kant Singh, PhD, Akansha Singh, PhD, Jenn-Wei Lin, PhD, Ahmed A. Elngar, PhD.

Names: Singh, Krishna Kant (Telecommunications professor), editor. | Singh, Akansha, editor. | Lin, Jenn-Wei, editor. | Elngar, Ahmed A., editor.

Description: First edition. | Includes bibliographical references and index.

Identifiers: Canadiana (print) 20210176210 | Canadiana (ebook) 20210176296 | ISBN 9781771889322 (hardcover) | ISBN 9781774638118 (softcover) | ISBN 9781003055082 (PDF)

Subjects: LCSH: Medical care—Data processing. | LCSH: Internet of things. | LCSH: Machine learning.

Classification: LCC R855.3 .D47 2022 | DDC 610.285—dc23

Library of Congress Cataloging-in-Publication Data

Names: Singh, Krishna Kant (Telecommunications professor) editor. | Singh, Akansha, editor. | Lin, Jenn-Wei, editor. | Elngar, Ahmed A., editor.

Title: Deep learning and Iot in healthcare systems : paradigms and applications / edited by Krishna Kant Singh, PhD, Akansha Singh, PhD, Jenn-Wei Lin, PhD, Ahmed A. Elngar, PhD.

Description: First edition. | Palm Bay, FL : Apple Academic Press, 2021. | Includes bibliographical references and index. | Summary: "This new volume discusses the applications and challenges of deep learning and the internet of things for applications in healthcare. It describes deep learning techniques along with IoT used by practitioners and researchers worldwide. The authors look at the role and impact that deep learning and the IoT plays in healthcare systems, such as the convergence of IoT and deep learning to enable things to communicate, share information, and coordinate decisions. The book includes deep feedforward networks, regularization, optimization algorithms, convolutional networks, sequence modeling, and practical methodology. Chapters look at assistive devices in healthcare, alerting and detection devices, energy efficiency in using IoT, data mining for gathering health information for individuals with autism, IoT for mobile applications, and more. The text offers mathematical and conceptual background that presents the latest technology as well as a selection of case studies. Deep Learning and IoT in Healthcare Systems: Paradigms and Applications provides an abundance of valuable and useful information for advanced students, scholars and researchers, and industry professionals working with healthcare systems backed by IoT and deep learning techniques"-- Provided by publisher.

Identifiers: LCCN 2021014038 (print) | LCCN 2021014039 (ebook) | ISBN 9781771889322 (hardback) | ISBN 9781774638118 (paperback) | ISBN 9781003055082 (ebook)

Subjects: Medical informatics. | Medical care--Data processing.

Classification: LCC R858 .D46 2021 (print) | LCC R858 (ebook) | DDC 610.285--dc23

LC record available at https://lccn.loc.gov/2021014038
LC ebook record available at https://lccn.loc.gov/2021014039

ISBN: 978-1-77188-932-2 (hbk)
ISBN: 978-1-77463-811-8 (pbk)
ISBN: 978-1-00305-508-2 (ebk)

About the Editors

Krishna Kant Singh, PhD, is a Professor in Computer Science and Engineering, Faculty of Engineering & Technology, Jain (Deemed-to-be University), Bengaluru, India. He has wide teaching and research experience. He has authored more than 50 research papers in Scopus- and SCIE-indexed journals of repute. He has also authored 25 technical books. He is also an associate editor of the *Journal of Intelligent & Fuzzy Systems, IEEE ACCESS* (SCIE), and a guest editor of *Open Computer Science*. He is also member of editorial board of *Applied Computing & Geoscience* (Elsevier). Dr. Singh has acquired BTech, MTech, and PhD (IIT Roorkee) degrees in the area of image processing and remote sensing.

Akansha Singh, PhD, is an Associate Professor in the Department of Computer Science and Engineering, ASET, Amity University, Noida, India. She has to her credit more than 40 research papers, 20 books, and numerous conference papers. She has been the editor for books on emerging topics with publishers like Elsevier, Taylor and Francis, Wiley, etc. Dr. Singh has served as a reviewer and technical committee member for multiple conferences and journals of high repute. She is also the Associate Editor *for IEEE Access* journal, which is an SCI journal with impact factor of 4.018. Dr. Singh has also undertaken a government-funded project as a principal investigator. Her research areas include image processing, remote sensing, IoT, and machine learning. She holds BTech, MTech, and PhD degrees in Computer Science, with her PhD from IIT Roorkee in the area of image processing and machine learning.

Jenn-Wei Lin, PhD, is currently a full professor with the Department of Computer Science and Information Engineering, Fu Jen Catholic University, Taiwan. Prior to that, he was a Researcher with Chunghwa Telecom Co., Ltd., Taoyuan, Taiwan, from 1993 to 2001. His current research interests include cloud computing, mobile computing and networks, distributed systems, and fault-tolerant computing. Dr. Lin received his MS degree in computer and information science from National Chiao Tung University, Hsinchu, Taiwan, and his PhD degree in electrical engineering from National Taiwan University, Taipei, Taiwan.

Ahmed A. Elngar, PhD, is the Founder and Head of Scientific Innovation Research Group (SIRG) and Assistant Professor of Computer Science at the Faculty of Computers and Artificial Intelligence, Beni-Suef University, Beni-Suef, Egypt, where he is also a Director of the Technological and Informatics Studies Center (TISC), Faculty of Computers and Information. Dr. Elngar has more than 25 scientific research papers published in prestigious international journals and over five books covering such diverse topics as data mining, intelligent systems, social networks, and smart environment. Dr. Elngar is a collaborative researcher. He is a member of the Egyptian Mathematical Society (EMS) and the International Rough Set Society (IRSS). His other research areas include Internet of Things (IoT), network security, intrusion detection, machine learning, data mining, artificial intelligence, big data, authentication, cryptology, healthcare systems, and automation systems. He is an editor and reviewer of many international journals. Dr. Elngar has won several awards, including the Young Researcher in Computer Science Engineering from the Global Outreach Education Summit and Awards 2019, in Delhi, India. He also received Best Young Researcher Award (Male) (under 40 years), Global Education and Corporate Leadership Awards (GECL—2018). Also, he hold the intellectual property rights called "ElDahshan Authentication Protocol," from the Information Technology Industry Development Agency (ITIDA), Technical Report, 2016. Dr. Elngar participates in many activities in the community and in environmental services, include organizing workshops hosted by universities in almost all the governorates of Egypt. He has also organized a workshop on smartphone techniques and their role in the development of visually impaired skills in various walks of life. Dr. Elngar received his PhD from the Faculty of Computers and Artificial Intelligence, Computer Science Department, Beni-Suef University, Egypt.

Contents

Contributors

Reshu Agarwal
Amity Institute of Information and Technology, Amity University Noida, Uttar Pradesh, India

Rajeev Agrawal
G. L. Bajaj Institute of Technology and Management, Greater Noida, Uttar Pradesh

Abhineet Anand
Chitkara University Institute of Engineering and Technology, Chitkara University, Punjab, India

Pratik Bhattacharjee
Department of Computer Science & Engineering, Brainware University, Barasat, Kolkata

Suparna Biswas
Maulana Abul Kalam Azad University of Technology, West Bengal, India

Pushpa Choudhary
Department of Information Technology, G. L. Bajaj Institute of Technology and Management, Greater Noida, Uttar Pradesh, India

Subhadip Chowdhury
DSMS Group of Institutions, West Bengal University of Health Sciences, West Bengal, India

C. Deepa
Department of Computer Science and Engineering, KIT- Kalaignarkarunanidhi Institute of Technology, Coimbatore, Tamil Nadu, India

Ritam Dutta
Surendra Institute of Engineering and Management, MAKAUT, West Bengal, India

Ahmed A Elngar
Faculty of Computers & Artificial Intelligence, Beni-Suef university, Beni Suef City, Egypt

R. Indrakumari
SCSE, Galgotias University, Greater Noida, Uttar Pradesh

Shylaja Vinaykumar Karatangi
Electronics and Communication Engineering, G.L. Bajaj Institute of Technology and Management, Greater Noida, Uttar Pradesh, India

Harleen Kaur
Guru Nanak Dev University, Amritsar, Punjab, India

Latika Kharb
JIMS, Sector 5, Rohini, Delhi 110085, India

Manavalan
Central Drugs Standard Control Organization, Puducherry

K. K. Mishra
Department of Information Technology, G. L. Bajaj Institute of Technology and Management, Greater Noida, Uttar Pradesh, India

Sai Prasad Mishra
SCSE, Galgotias University, Greater Noida, Uttar Pradesh

Om Prakash
Electronics and Communication Engineering, St. Marry College of Engineering, Hyderabad, Telangana, India

Amrita Rai
Electronics and Communication Engineering, G.L. Bajaj Institute of Technology and Management, Greater Noida, Uttar Pradesh, India

Subrata Sahana
SCSE, Galgotias University, Greater Noida, Uttar Pradesh

Vikram Sandhu
Guru Nanak Dev University, Amritsar, Punjab, India

Amit Sehgal
Sharda University, Plot No 32–34, Knowledge Park 3, Greater Noida, Uttar Pradesh 201310, India

T. L. Singal
Chitkara University, Rajpura Campus, Punjab, India

Arun Kumar Singh
Department of Information Technology, G. L. Bajaj Institute of Technology and Management, Greater Noida, Uttar Pradesh, India

Prateek Singh
Department of Information Technology, Amity University, Noida, India

Rashbir Singh
Department of Information Technology, Amity University, Noida, India

Sonia Singla
University of Leicester, United Kingdom

Sweta Sneha
Healthcare Management & Informatics, Information Systems, Michael J. Coles College of Business, Kennesaw State University, Kennesaw, GA, USA

Rishabh Kumar Srivastava
SCSE, Galgotias University, Greater Noida, Uttar Pradesh

Subba
Sri Manakula Vinayagar Engineering College, Puducherry

K. Tharageswari
Department of Computer Science and Engineering, Karpagam Academy of Higher Education, Coimbatore, Tamil Nadu, India

Ashish Tripathi
Department of Information Technology, G. L. Bajaj Institute of Technology and Management, Greater Noida, Uttar Pradesh, India

Prem Chand Vashist
Department of Information Technology, G. L. Bajaj Institute of Technology and Management, Greater Noida, Uttar Pradesh, India

Abbreviations

AACs	alternative communication devices
AAL	ambient-assisted living
AD	Alzheimer's disease
ADL	activities of daily living
ADR	adverse drug reaction
AI	artificial intelligence
ALS	amyotrophic lateral sclerosis
AMR	adaptive multihop routing
ANN	artificial neural network
AODV	ad-hoc on-demand distance vector
AP	access point
ASD	autism spectrum disorder
ASIC	application-specific integrated circuit
AT	assistive technology
ATIA	Assistive Technology Industry Association
BAN	body area network
BITs	behavioral intervention technologies
CAE	contractive autoencoder
CALM	campaign against living miserably
CBR	community-based rehabilitation
CDMA	code-division multiple access
CH	community healthcare
CHI	children health information
CHS	complete healthcare system
CIS	computer integrated system
CNNs	convolutional neural networks
CT	computed tomography
CV	cardiovascular
CVDs	cardiovascular diseases
DBM	deep Boltzmann machine
DBNs	deep belief networks
DCNNs	deep convolutional neural structures
DL	deep learning
DLL	data link layer

DNNs	deep neural networks
DPI	direct physical interface
DSP	digital signal processing
ECP	embedded context prediction
EGC	embedded gateway configuration
EH	energy harvesting
EHR	electronic health record
EHRs	electronic health records
EMH	indirect emergency healthcare
EMRS	electronic medical record system
FDS	fall detection systems
GANs	generative adversarial networks
GATE	Global Collaboration on Assistive Technology
GDM	gestational diabetes mellitus
GDP	gross domestic product
GPS	global positioning system
GUI	graphical user interface
HBR	heartbeat rate
HER	electronic health record
HR	heart rate
ICT	information and communication technology
IDDM	insulin-dependent diabetes mellitus
IEP	individualized education plan
IIT	intensive insulin therapy
IoMT	Internet of medical things
IoT	Internet of things
IR	infrared
KNN	K-nearest neighbor
LAN	local area network
M2M	machine-to-machine
MAC	medium access control
MAN	metropolitan area network
MCI	mild cognitive impairment
MEMS	microelectromechanical system
m-IoT	Internet of m-health thing
ML	machine learning
MRI	magnetic resonance imaging
NC	normal cognitive
NEMS	nano-electromechanical systems

NHTSA	National Highway Traffic Safety Administration
NOD	Nottingham Obstacle Detectors
OCR	optical character recognition
OS	operating system
OVO	one-versus-one
PAN	personal area network
PCA	principal components analysis
PD	Parkinson's disease
PET	positron emission tomography
PSAPs	personal sound amplification products
RBD	rapid eye movement sleep behavior disorder
RBMs	restricted Boltzmann machines
RFID	radio-frequency identification
RNNs	recurrent neural networks
ROC	receiver operating characteristic
RPL	routing protocol for low power
RPS	rotation/second
RREQ	route request
RSSI	received signal strength indicator
SALSA	Southern Arizona Limb Salvage Alliance
SMA	semantic medical access
SNP	single-nucleotide polymorphism
SNR	signal-to-noise ratio
SVM	support vector machine
T1D	type-1 diabetes
T2D	type-2 diabetes
TA	temporal abstraction
TB	tuberculosis
TDMA	time-division multiple access
UPNs	unsupervised pretrained networks
VAE	variation autoencoder
WAN	wide area network
WBAN	wireless body area network
WBN	wireless BAN
WDA	wearable device access
WHO	World Health Organization
WPAN	wireless personal area network
WSN	wireless sensor network

Preface

This edited book, *Deep Learning and IoT in Healthcare Systems: Paradigms and Applications,* is intended to discuss the applications and challenges of deep learning and Internet of Things for healthcare applications. The major objective of this book is to provide a platform for presenting IoT-enabled healthcare techniques.

The text offers mathematical and conceptual background presenting the latest technology. It describes deep learning techniques along with IoT used by practitioners and researchers worldwide. The book includes deep feedforward networks, regularization, optimization algorithms, convolutional networks, sequence modeling, and practical methodology, and it also presents the concepts of IoT. IoT is the set of technologies that make traditional devices into smart devices. IoT finds its application in almost all areas and connects devices to a network for sharing and analysis of data. Finally, the book offers research perspectives, covering the convergence of deep learning and IoT. It also presents the application of these technologies in the development of healthcare frameworks.

This book is an attempt by the authors to present the most relevant topics in IoT, deep learning, and their applications in healthcare applications. Today, IoT is one of the fastest growing fields, and it is being widely used in a variety of industries. One of the major applications of IoT is in remote healthcare monitoring systems. IoT-based systems are developed by a combination of various techniques such as wireless communication, sensor technology, and, most importantly, data processing. Deep learning is being recognized as one of the most efficient techniques in data processing. The convergence of IoT and deep learning enables things to communicate, share information, and coordinate decisions.

Recently, IoT-based applications in the medical field have drawn substantial attention of researchers and technologists. In this book, an overview of present technologies that support IoT-based applications is presented. Secondly, the techniques of deep learning are presented in a lucid and illustrative manner. The book also discusses the latest design and development of IoT-based healthcare systems. Finally, the book suggests scenarios where IoT and deep learning can be applied.

This book is an amalgamation of theory, mathematics, and examples of the discussed technologies. It will be relevant for all levels of students studying computer science or electronics. The target audience includes students, teachers, as well as industry people.

This book will provide the recent paradigms of deep learning and IoT for healthcare applications. Readers will get a deep insight into the fundamentals of deep learning and IoT individually. Thereafter, the convergence of deep learning and IoT is presented. The application of these two fields in healthcare industry is also presented.

CHAPTER 1

Deep Learning for Healthcare

C. DEEPA[1*] and K. THARAGESWARI[2]

*[1]Department of Computer Science and Engineering,
KIT—Kalaignarkarunanidhi Institute of Technology, Coimbatore,
Tamil Nadu, India*

*[2]Department of Computer Science and Engineering,
Karpagam Academy of Higher Education, Coimbatore, Tamil Nadu, India*

[*]Corresponding author. E-mail: deepachinnaiyan@gmail.com

ABSTRACT

Deep learning is a subfield of machine learning (ML) that offers flexibility and understanding of concepts by learning to represent the universe as a nested hierarchy of concepts. These concepts are connected to each other by means of elements called neurons or neural network. In human brains, high-level information is connected by means of connections called synapses or elements called neurons. Nowadays, huge volume of data is being processed in hospital and clinics, wherein the handling of these data gives a tough time in predicting diseases and symptoms to the patients. The electronic system records and the information is collected in these records are mixed up. So with the help of a standard analytic method it is impossible to analyze each and every value and data that we obtain. In order to overcome these problems, conventional techniques of ML are used. In this, the computer systems are trained to predict and prescribe the medicines to the patients. In drug discovery and predicting the drugs to every individual their day-to-day activities are noted and with the help of the genomic activity and the data available for each person will be prescribed with a different dosage of drug according to the genomes and their activities. The algorithm used for the prediction of diseases is deep convolution neural network that trains the system and provides a test report and pattern recognition is used to distinguish the images obtained from the CT, X-ray, and MRI techniques and provide a report for certain types of tumors.

1.1 INTRODUCTION

Deep learning is a subfield of artificial intelligence (AI) pointing in achieving its goal toward phoney intelligence. It relies upon the neural framework and duplicates the human brain. It achieves phenomenal power and versatility in thoughts by making sense of how to address the world as a settled chain of significance. Deep learning enables mathematical models made up of various layers of preparation to learn data portrayals with multiple reflective aspects. All such techniques have considerably improved its cutting edge of discourse acknowledgement, visible item acknowledgement, identification of the object, and various fields such as tranquillize disclosure and bioinformatics. Insubstantial information metrics discover a perplexing framework by using the calculation of backpropagation to show how a system could alter its internal variables that are used to record the representation from the previous layer in each layer. Deep convolutional networks have made progress in the handling of videos, images, speech, and sound, while intermittent networks have shed more light on, for instance, information and speech (LeCun et al., 2015). In light of a portion of the deficiencies of AI, and the huge advancement in the hypothetical and mechanical capacities available to us today, profound learning has risen and is quickly growing as a standout among the most energizing areas of science. It is used in advanced, for example, self-driving vehicles, picture acknowledgement on web-based life stages, and content interpretation from one language to another. Deep learning is an AI subfield committed to creating calculations that clarify and, what is more, realize high and low dimensions of reflections of information that customary AI calculations regularly cannot. The models in profound learning are regularly enlivened by numerous sources of learning, for example, amusement hypothesis and neuroscience, and a large number of the models frequently impersonate the fundamental structure of the human sensory system. As the field progresses, numerous scientists imagine an existence where programming is not so hardcoded as it frequently needs to be today, considering a progressively powerful, summed up answer for tackling issues. The design of deep learning models is often with the ultimate objective of having layers of nondirect units that process data, or neurons, and different layers of data deliberation procedures in these models.

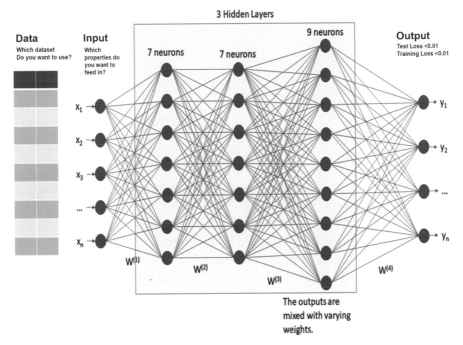

FIGURE 1.1 Deep neural network.

1.2 ARCHITECTURE USED

Deep learning architecture plays a vital role in designing the parameters and activities based on some of the specified industries. They are classified in different types such as

- unsupervised pretrained networks (UPNs),
- convolutional neural networks (CNNs),
- recurrent neural networks, and
- recursive neural networks.

1.2.1 UNSUPERVISED PRETRAINED NETWORKS (UPNS)

Generative adversarial networks (GANs) are a situation of a scheme that uses unsupervised networks to find out how two models can be prepared in parallel. A main aspect of GANs (and all-inclusive generative designs) is the means by which they use a parameter check that is essentially smaller than that typical for the measurement of the data on which the system is being prepared. UPN is further subdivided into three major concepts. They are

- GANs,
- Autoencoders, and
- Deep belief networks (DBNs).

1.2.1.1   AUTO ENCODERS

An autoencoder is a cognitive system with three layers: a layer of information, a layer of encoding, and a layer of interpretation. The scheme is ready to replicate its data sources, enabling the shrouded layer to attempt to adapt large portrayals of the sources of information. An autoencoder cognitive system is an unattended calculation of ML that uses backpropagation, considering objective characteristics to be equal to data sources. An autoencoder seems to be ready to attempt to replicate their contribution to their output. Beneath, it also has a shrouded layer depicting a code used to communicate with the data. Autoencoders relate to a family of neural networks but also are strongly linked to principal components analysis (PCA). Some of the key autoencoder facts are as follows:

- This is an uncontrolled PCA-like ML algorithm.
- It mitigates the function with the same objective as PCA.
- It is a neural network.
- The target output of the neural network is its input.

Although autoencoders are comparable to PCA, their autoencoders are often more versatile than PCA. Autoencoders can portray liners in encoding as well as nonlinear transformation, but PCA may only transform linearly. Because of its network representation, autoencoders could be linked to create a deep learning network. Autoencoder types are

- denoising autoencoder,
- sparse autoencoder,
- variation autoencoder (VAE), and
- contractive autoencoder (CAE).

1.2.1.2   DBN

DBNs consist of restricted Boltzmann machines (RBMs) layers for all the pretrain stages, followed by a feedforward network for the fine-tuning stage.

In the segments that pursue, we clarify increasingly about how DBNs exploit RBMs for all the more likely model preparing information.

1.3   HIGHLIGHT EXTRACTION WITH RBM LAYERS

RBMs are used to separate more elevated highlights from vectors of crude information. To provide it, we have to fix the hidden unit loads and states with the final goal of creating something close to the first data parameter when we show a data record to the RBM and ask the RBM to replicate the record. Hinton discusses this impact as far as how machines long for information.

The essential motivation behind RBMs with regard to profound learning and DBNs is to become familiar with these more elevated highlights of a dataset in unmonitored style of preparation. It was discovered that we should prepare stronger neural systems by allowing RBMs to continually adapt bigger quantity of highlights using highlights from a reduced RBM pretrain layer as a contribution to a higher quantity of RBM pretrain layer.

1.3.1   *GENERATIVE ADVERSARIAL NETWORK (GAN)*

Studying such features in an unmonitored manner is regarded to be DBNs' pretraining period. Every shrouded layer of an RBM throughout the pretrain phase requires the propagation of the data dynamically to progressively complicated highlights. These highlights of a higher demand are dynamically consolidated for exquisite mechanized component design in nonlinear methods. The note network would be the GAN. It has been shown that GANs are quite skilled at synthesizing fresh pictures based on other pictures of practice. This notion can be extended to model other fields such as

- video and
- sound (Patterson and Gibson, 2017).

GANs are an instance of such a network using unmonitored learning to simultaneously train two models. The major aspect of GANs is how they use a variable count that is considerably smaller than usual to regard to an amount of information upon which we train the network. The entire network is compelled to portray the training information effectively, creating it more efficiently to generate information comparable to the training information.

1.3.2 TRAINING OF GENERATIONAL DESIGNS, UNMONITORED LEARNING, AND GANS

If we had a large corpus of training images (such as the ImageNet dataset), we could build a generative neural network that outputs images (as opposed to classifications). We would consider these generated output images to be samples from the model. The generative model in GANs generates such images, while a secondary "discriminator" network tries to classify these generated images. This secondary discriminator network attempts to classify the output images as real or synthetic. When we have a big collection of training pictures (like the ImageNet datasets), we may create a neural generative network that produces pictures (as compared to categories). We would consider such output pictures produced as model samples. Such pictures are produced by the conceptual system in GANs, while a supplementary network of "discriminatory" attempts to identify such pictures. Such a supplementary discriminator network tries to identify as true or synthetic the output pictures. We would like to update its variables while training GANs so that the network produces more credible output pictures depending on the dataset. The aim is to create images sufficiently realistic to fool its discriminator network to a point that it does not differentiate between actual and the synthetic input information.

1.3.3 CNN

CNN's goal is to know through convolutions to include greater-request data. With images and efficiently top image grouping rivalries, they are suitable to resist acknowledgment. They could recognize faces, individuals, signs of the street and countless visual data components. CNN covers the content inquiry by means of optical character recognition, yet it is equally useful as distinct printed units when assessing words. They are also fantastic when it comes to breaking down noise. One of the simple reasons why and how the globe perceives the strength of deep learning is the viability of CNN in image recognition. CNNs power significant machine vision developments with evident apps for auto-driving cars, robots, drones, and visually impaired therapy.

1.3.4 RECURRENT NETWORK OF NEURAL

It is a part of a group of neural feedforward systems. In their ability to send information after several time steps, they are not always the same as the other feedforward technologies. Traditionally, such networks have also been hard to train, but, more recently, research advancements have rendered them more accessible to practitioners. These networks bring every vector from an input vector series and model it one at a moment. This enables its system to maintain status while modeling every vector input around the input vector window. Recurrent networks of neural are a characteristic of modeling the time dimension.

1.3.5   RECURSIVE NETWORK OF NEURAL

It can handle the input of a variable length. The main distinction is that in the training data sets, recurrent networks of neural can describe the hierarchical structures. Images usually have a scene with many objects. Decoding images are often an interesting problem area, but it is nontrivial. This deconstruction's recursive nature forces us not only to define the items throughout the scene but also to identify how well the items connect to an image. These networks can retrieve almost all granular frameworks and greater-level hierarchical systems in data sets like pictures or phrases. Recursive neural network applications include

* decomposition of the image scene,
* natural language processing, and
* transcription of audio to text.

1.4   HOW DID DEEP LEARNING IN HEALTHCARE DEVELOP?

As healthcare frameworks in established countries change toward an esteem-based, constant focused model of consideration conveyance, we encounter fresh complexities identified with enhancing the structure as well as managers of medicinal services conveyance; for example, enhancing the incorporation in processes to consideration of patient-focused endless disease conveyance by managers (Jiang et al., 2017).

Man-made consciousness and AI can possibly be the impetus for change of healthcare frameworks to improve proficiency and viability, make headroom for all inclusive healthcare inclusion, and to improve results (Panch et al., 2018). The healthcare system itself contains two central information-processing errands: first, screening and finding, which is the sequence of instances based on history and examination, and, second, therapy and observation, which involves organizing, doing, and monitoring a multistep process to express a potential outcome. The fundamental form of such processes over the spaces of well-being structure and the consideration schemes provide speculation age, testing of theory, and exercise. AI may enhance speculative age and hypothesis testing tasks within a well-being structure by revealing newly hidden trends in data and then along such lines will have the capacity for important effects at both the individualized level and the structure level (Panch et al., 2018).

Similarly, the ML algorithm has used the current statistical significance records and techniques to understand the available information. This allows a clear perspective of the information on healthcare, processes ML models to be integrated with many factors and generalized across a much wider range of data types, and can generate outcomes in more complicated circumstances (Henglin et al., 2017). These arrangements are in different zones, commonly in emergency clinic as opposed to the network setting, and in most instances depend on single-focus data, with suggestions for reproducibility (Johnson et al., 2017) and generalizability (Celi et al., 2014). Be that as it may, the fast pace of advancement of AI proceeds with both inside human services and all the more extensively over all data, preparing undertakings in the public arena (Brynjolfsson and Mcafee, 2018).

1.5   ARTIFICIAL INTELLIGENCE BENEFITS IN HEALTHCARE

ML is a technology that is progressing rapidly. While there are interesting technical breakthroughs to come, as with any fresh technique, there will be not only technical difficulties that restrict the implementation of ML to health but also a lack of a receptive framework for implementation and dissemination. Among other things, a responsive framework for AI needs the accessibility of curated information, an adequate legislative environment, legal measures to protect the freedoms of people, clear laws on accountability, and the ability to handle strategy change to allow the suitable implementation of ML. AI is the technology that propels rapidly.

While there are critical specialized jumps to come forward, with respect to any new innovation, there will not simply be specialized difficulties that limit the use of AI in healthcare but rather the nonattendance with an open setting for their reception and dispersion. A responsive setting for AI needs, along with others, accessibility of sourced information, an empowering administrative condition, legitimate arrangements to protect natives' rights, clear principles on responsibility, and ability to oversee key changes to empower proper presentation and use of AI. Some of the benefits are:

1. curation of data,
2. trust and data management,
3. working with the technology industries,
4. accountability, and
5. capacity for managing strategic change

1.6 APPLICATIONS OF HEALTHCARE IN MACHINE LEARNING

Some of the main fields in which machine learning apps are available for healthcare are

- identification of the diseases,
- customized medicines,
- discovery of drugs,
- manufacturing of drugs,
- research on clinical trials,
- radiography,
- digital medical records,
- predictions of epidemic outbreak, and
- operational robotics (Puneet Mathur 2018).

1.6.1 DISCOVERY OF DRUGS

The development of drugs is not an easy method. Before a drug is introduced into the sector, it requires a substantial quantity of studies, testing, time, and financial investment. The price of marketing a fresh drug is estimated to be as high as USD 2.6 billion. Data science may exploit multiple sets of unorganized and organized biomedical information across multiple fields from various exams, therapy outcomes, studies, social media, etc. Using efficient mathematical algorithms, it can then generate a model on how the drug could communicate to body enzymes and estimate the success rate. The simulation may accelerate the process by making the original screening adequate to assess the drug effectiveness potential. This not only means an enormous decrease in drug development costs and time but also minimizes failure hazards. Methods in data science can be integrated into studies with genomic information that can provide precise ideas into genetic defects resulting from particular drugs and illnesses.

1.6.2   WEARABLE DEVICES

Wearable devices have become rapidly ubiquitous. In addition to creating a cool accessory, people are motivated to manage their own health. They record significant health measurements such as heart rate, blood pressure, the pattern of sleep and pulse, etc. Wearable devices are a wonderful help, especially for the elderly. It assists family members to remain up-to-date on the health of the patient and learn instantly in emergencies to the medical employees. Wearable devices are linked to the mobile device and generate significantly and save into the cloud volumes of patient information that can be accessed if necessary. Data scientists will analyze the above raw data from wearable devices using AI, bigdata, and ML to predict significant ideas. They may observe differences in patient health through sophisticated analytical models and identify a disease or a related symptom. This enables physicians to predict and provide preventive care for a probable health problem.

1.6.3   DIAGNOSTICS

Diagnosis is a crucial component of a treatment cycle of patients as it defines the nature of the therapy to be given. However, diagnosis is far from ideal even in this 21st century. The 2018 BBC reports disclosed that around 40,000–80,000 fatalities result in diagnosis defects in the United States alone. While there are huge amounts of information that can be used to carry out efficient experiments, most current models are unable to do so. Analysts can use in-depth learning methods through data science to process comprehensive clinical and laboratories records to make a faster and more efficient diagnosis. Analysis of data may enable them to identify early indications of a problem and allow physicians to provide patients with healthcare as well as improved therapy. In addition, medical scientists can use this information to diagnose early-stage chronic diseases and diagnose therapy alternatives that have demonstrated records of achievement. Healing of ailments like cancer and heart diseases can be essential.

1.6.4   PUBLIC HEALTH SECTOR

Most healthcare organizations, in an attempt to enhance general public wellness, have begun to exploit data analytics. Huge amounts of dispersed healthcare information are available from multiple sources such as Google

Maps, websites, social media, and wearable devices. The above information poses a serious threat to knowing a particular geography in the public health. It can be analyzed by data researchers to develop heat maps related to parameters such as population, health problems, geographic medical outcomes of individuals, etc. The above assessment enables them to recognize the symptoms from an impending health problem within this region, enabling them to become familiar with the accessibility of medical services within this region. It also enables them to define the reasons why individuals are unable to choose therapy. Healthcare professionals could use the results to adopt preventive measures for the region's current or potential health problem.

1.6.5 REDUCED COSTS FOR HEALTHCARE

Only with time do healthcare expenses appear to rise, and this demonstrates to be an impact factor in providing a superior patient care. However, this can also be tackled with analytics and BI instruments. Data researchers may analyze data billing and clinical system information related to charging and variables classifications. It enables them to dig down to the room utilization trends and the resources needed to meet patient requirements, thus helping to define potential regions of operational holes and loss of income. Providers can use information science to improve the supply chain and review maintenance schedules for machinery to avoid unforeseen breakdowns. It can assist them know how low expenses can be maintained. To use analytics, patient recovery and discharge planning protocols can also be monitored appropriately to reduce readmission rates. In summary, such information-driven regulations may make space for decreased operating expenses, resulting in lower healthcare expenses for patients with enhanced fulfillment. In enhancing care service as well as patient experience, this will also be essential.

1.6.6 OPTIMUM RESOURCING

Healthcare demands will only improve, and at any specified stage in time, suppliers may find it difficult to have sufficient medical employees for patient care. Any shift in the patient stream will always impact systems, such as emergency care units and ICUs, functioning in an inflexible timeline. The labor costs will be increased by more than necessary employees. An inadequate amount of employees, on the other hand, may decide to work overtime and reach a burnout phase. Can you hold the optimal staff at your disposal? The solution lies with data analytics. This can estimate variations in patient visits over the years depend on historical information and create a pattern in personnel distribution based on previous entry rates. It would provide suppliers with a concept of whether the center will need what level of employees. Thus, appropriate and timely allocation of beds, employees, and other necessary resources can be made to patients.

Obviously, in relation to evolving patient care, information helps healthcare companies to tackle resource management problems, insufficient medical employees, and high cost of therapy. Also, it empowers patients by disseminating consciousness between them and engaging them in the process of treatment.

1.7   DEVELOPMENT CYCLE OF MACHINE LEARNING

Before we begin to see AI and applying forecast models to the different informational collections, we might want to convey a disclaimer to the pursuer's consideration that none of the information that is being utilized in the activities has a place with any of my customers or from genuine patients in reality. Any similarity to any informational collection around the globe is simply an occurrence. Neither the writer nor the distributor of this book assumes any liability of the validness or security of this informational index. The motivation behind distributing this therapeutic informational index is to influence the reader to see how to apply AI on a social insurance informational collection in the creation condition. This informational index cannot be utilized for some other reason, for example, clinical preliminaries or any creation or business-related exercises electronically or something else (Puneet Mathur 2018).

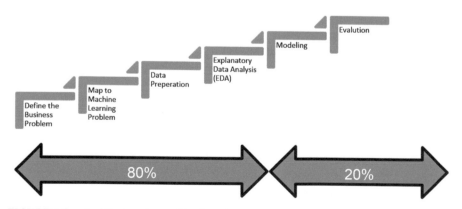

FIGURE 1.2   Architecture in machine learning.

1.7.1 DEFINITION OF BUSINESS PROBLEM

A problem statement or a requirement is obtained from the client and given to the business people in order to make a clarification in the problem statement.

1.7.2 MAPPING OF THE ML ALGORITHM

After identifying the business problem, mapping is carried out for the ML problem in which a particular algorithm is selected to define the data. The data is separated as training and test data. The system or machine is trained to process the data and segregate it according to the problem statement.

1.7.3 DATA PREPARATION

An analytic sandbox is created to perform the entire analytics required for the business statement or the project. This takes place in different stages, for example, extract the data, load the data, and then transform the data for processing.

1.7.4 EXPLANATORY DATA ANALYSIS

The measurable and imagining investigation is performed to discover the anomalies or mistakes in the information that has been readied, which at that point waitlist the prescient display of the information that is kept for use.

1.7.5 MODELING

After preparation of the data and shortlisting of the predictive model for the project, several algorithms have experimented so that we could find the best-suited algorithm for this project and an optimal model that gives the best result and then finally create a feedback loop for the model. We can use different techniques such as classification, association, and clustering to model the system.

1.7.6 EVALUATION

In this phase, a detailed study is done to check whether the business problem and modeled study of the project that is done are the same according to the stakeholders.

1.8 PREDICTION OF DISEASES USING THE ML ALGORITHM

The diagnosis of diseases revolves around the same process as mentioned in the ML architecture. This follows particular criteria such as data selection, feature selection which includes data preprocessing, model training and evolution of the data that are available. (Beysolow II, 2017). Classification of automatic heartbeat is a significant method to help physicians recognize epidural heartbeats in the long-term Holter ECG monitoring. In order to enhance the efficiency of heartbeat assessment on ECG information, we suggest an illness-specific feature method of selecting by defining an ideal feature subset. To assess this technique, an experiment comprising three steps will also be performed. First, all characteristics are listed as calculated in the decreasing order of a one-versus-one (OVO) *F*-scores. Second, such rated characteristics are incorporated into the validation system and parameterized. Finally, an analytical application used for this study is descriptive analytics, which uses raw data units. To view and understand complex information in large data sets, visual analytics is used. Patient stratification is a method that is used to divide a large set of data into smaller units and provide personalized support to the patients, and with this data from stratification, predictive analysis is done (Zang et al., 2014).

1.9 CASE STUDIES: HEALTHCARE AND DEEP LEARNING

Health care and deep learning will be a conjoint word in the near future. There are several case studies performed in order to explain the working model of deep learning and healthcare analysis. Nowadays, there are several functionalities in the medical domain that are processed with the help of AI and deep learning techniques. Some of the major studies that are performed in these domains are cancer detection, heartbeat functionality, working of lungs, that is, pulmonary detection, genomics and personalized medicine, and so on. In this section, we would look into pulmonary detection for tuberculosis (TB) with deep learning techniques.

1.9.1 CASE STUDY I

Aim

To evaluate the viability of deep convolutional neural structures (DCNNs) of chest radiographic identification of TB.

Materials and Techniques

In this investigation, four de-identified HIPAA-consistent data sets have been used, which were excluded out of a study conducted by an organizational audit committee consisting of 1007 posteroanterior chest X-rays. The data sets included authorization (17.1%), preparation (68.0%), and testing (14.9%). Two distinctive DCNNs, GoogLeNet and AlexNet, were used to organize the images as an aspiratory TB appearance or as a noise. Used on ImageNet were both untrained and educated systems, and development was done with various preprocessing technologies (Krizhevsky et al., 2017; Szegedy et al., 2015). Sessions on the greatest-performing computations were conducted. A free council-certified cardiology physician indiscriminately decoded the photos for circumstances where the optimization algorithms were in inconsistency to evaluate a prospective radiologist-enlarged job cycle. The DeLong method which is used to predict the heart attack risk a detailed assessment is done for a collector working mark bends (Jaeger et al., 2014), and regions below the bend (AUCs) were used to assess model implementation.

Results

The AlexNet and GoogleNet use a classification system which had its AUC as 0.99, which is made possible with the help of DCNN algorithm. The AUCs of both the systems concerned were much more popular than those for the untrained systems ($P = 0.001$). Extending its data set further increased the accuracy (P is 0.03 and 0.02 for AlexNet and GoogleNet, respectively). In 13 of 150 experiments, the DCNNs used to have a difference that was indiscriminately assessed by a cardiology physician who efficiently interpreted each one of the 13 cases (100%). This radiologist-widened methodology resulted in 97.3% affectability and 100% explicitness (Lakhani and Sundaram, 2014).

With DCNNs, deep learning can exactly group TB with an AUC of 0.99 in chest radiology. In cases where there would be a contradiction among all the algorithms, radiologist-enlarged methods further enhanced the accuracy (Lakhani and Sundaram, 2014).

1.9.2   *CASE STUDY II: PREDICTION OF BREAST CANCER USING ML TECHNIQUES*

Predicting any illnesses is a not a simple assignment, as the work behind it is a tedious task, and it requires abnormal state of expense to discover a specific disease. To reach a resolution, one must be extremely secure with the patient's history and his/her genome information in order to give them an exact prescription. Prediction of bosom malignancy information utilizes many AI calculations in discovering the state of the patient and the disease. For this think-about situation, we have used strategic relapse in discovering the earnestness of the malady. To begin with the procedure, we have to initially bring the information into the machine. At that point, the machine will expel the invalid information from the data set and reshaping of the information will be completed. Inspection of the information will be done by checking the highlights of the informational collection (Table 1.1).

The features of the data vary from the diagnosis stage to texture, radius, perimeter, smoothness, concavity, and so on. Correlation of data has to be found out and removed from the data set. The data with correlation shows a difference in prediction and diagnosis processes. Different correlation techniques have been used to find out the worst case, standard errors (SEs), and mean variations.

After finding the correlation process, the relationship between the data is found with the same correlated values to it. Finding out the relationship between each variable is more important in the diagnosis process.

The likeness of the factors is discovered utilizing the ggcorr plot with increasingly exact and accurately. Then comes the utilization of the PCA procedure in discovering the plot against the informational collection and arrives at a resolution dependent on the outcomes and the result from it.

An excessive number of factors can cause such issues underneath:

- expanded PC throughput,
- too mind boggling perception issues,
- reduction in proficiency by including factors that have no impact on the investigation,
- make information understanding troublesome, and
- the ggcorr plot above, high relationship worth methods and it has "multicollinearity" between factors.

We use one principle part for model improvement by reducing the factors with a high relationship. When deciding the number of foremost parts, we utilize the aggregate commitment rate or a screen plot and the past advance of the primary segment where the eigenvalue bend lies evenly. PCA uses institutionalized information so it can keep away from information contortion brought about by scale distinction. In the results of PCA, if the cumulative proportion is 85% or above, it can be determined by the number of principal components. For example, if the cumulative proportion of PC4 is 88.7, then the sum of proportion of PC1–PC4 is 88.7%.

TABLE 1.1 Inspection of Data with Features

Diagnosis	Radius_ mean	Texture_ mean	Perimeter_ mean	Area_ mean	Smoothness_ mean	Compactness_ mean	Concavity_ mean	Concave points means
Malignant	17.99	10.38	122.80	1001.0	0.11840	0.27760	0.3001	0.14710
Malignant	20.57	17.77	132.90	1326.0	0.08474	0.07864	0.0869	0.07017
Malignant	19.69	21.25	130.00	1203.0	0.10960	0.15990	0.1974	0.12790
Malignant	11.42	20.38	77.58	386.1	0.14250	0.28390	0.2414	0.10520
Malignant	20.29	14.34	135.10	1297.0	0.10030	0.13280	0.1980	0.10430
Malignant	12.45	15.70	82.57	477.1	0.12780	0.17000	0.1578	0.08089

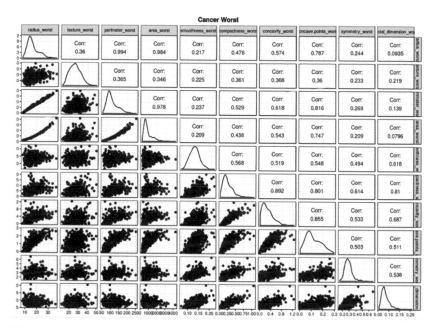

FIGURE 1.3   Correlation in the worst case.

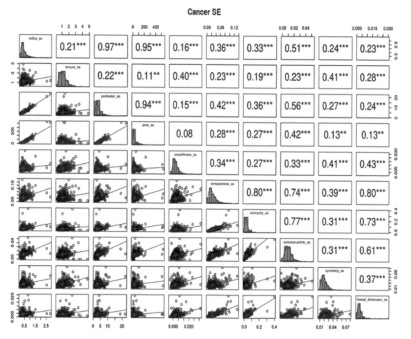

FIGURE 1.4   Correlation with SE.

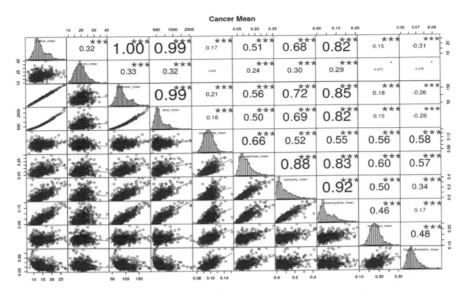

FIGURE 1.5   Correlation with mean data function.

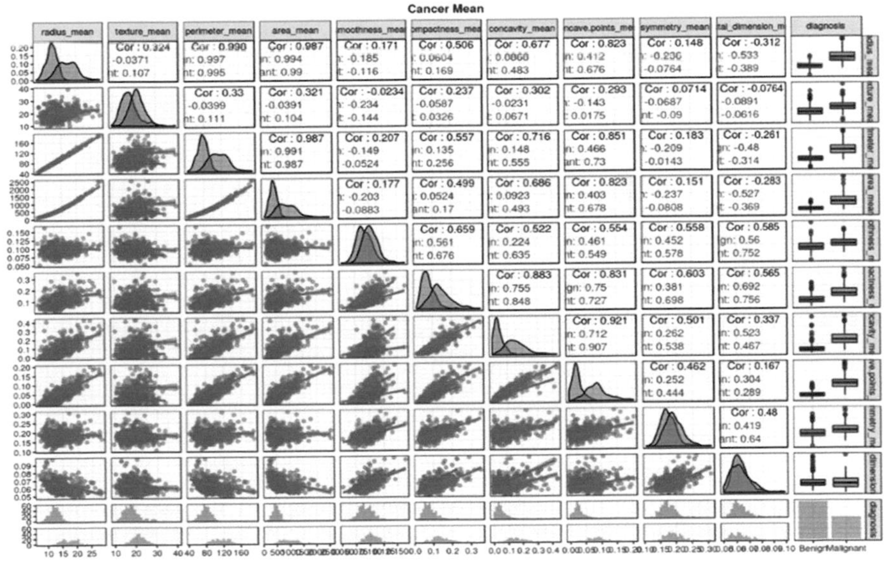

FIGURE 1.6   Finding the relationship for the cancer data variables.

Finally, PCA variables are got for all the scenarios that includes mean, SE, and worst cases.

The cumulative proportion from PC1 to PC6 is about 88.7%. (above 85%)

It means that PC1~PC6 can explain 88.7% of the whole data.

```
## Importance of components:
##                          PC1     PC2     PC3      PC4      PC5      PC6
## Standard deviation     3.6444 2.3857 1.67867 1.40735 1.28403 1.09880
## Proportion of Variance 0.4427 0.1897 0.09393 0.06602 0.05496 0.04025
## Cumulative Proportion  0.4427 0.6324 0.72636 0.79239 0.84734 0.88759
##                          PC7     PC8    PC9    PC10    PC11    PC12
## Standard deviation     0.82172 0.69037 0.6457 0.59219 0.5421 0.51104
## Proportion of Variance 0.02251 0.01589 0.0139 0.01169 0.0098 0.00871
## Cumulative Proportion  0.91010 0.92598 0.9399 0.95157 0.9614 0.97007
##                          PC13    PC14    PC15    PC16    PC17    PC18
## Standard deviation     0.49128 0.39624 0.30681 0.28260 0.24372 0.22939
## Proportion of Variance 0.00805 0.00523 0.00314 0.00266 0.00198 0.00175
## Cumulative Proportion  0.97812 0.98335 0.98649 0.98915 0.99113 0.99288
##                          PC19    PC20   PC21    PC22    PC23    PC24
## Standard deviation     0.22244 0.17652 0.1731 0.16565 0.15602 0.1344
## Proportion of Variance 0.00165 0.00104 0.0010 0.00091 0.00081 0.0006
## Cumulative Proportion  0.99453 0.99557 0.9966 0.99749 0.99830 0.9989
##                          PC25    PC26    PC27    PC28    PC29    PC30
## Standard deviation     0.12442 0.09043 0.08307 0.03987 0.02736 0.01153
## Proportion of Variance 0.00052 0.00027 0.00023 0.00005 0.00002 0.00000
## Cumulative Proportion  0.99942 0.99969 0.99992 0.99997 1.00000 1.00000
```

FIGURE 1.7   Cumulative proportion.

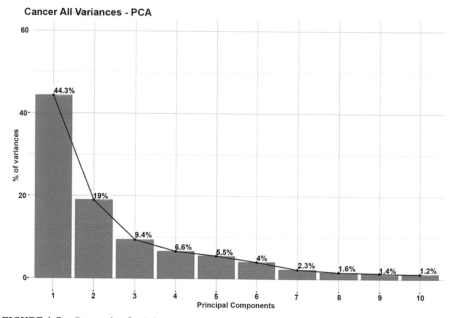

FIGURE 1.8   Scree plot for PCA.

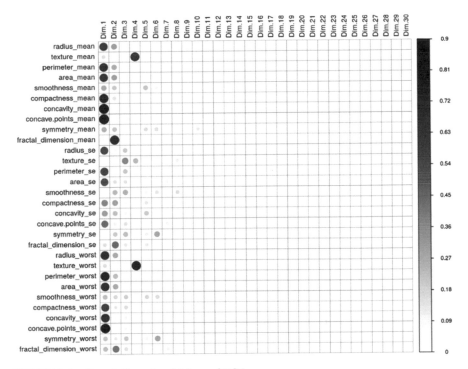

FIGURE 1.9 Correlation of variables and PCA.

The correlation between the variables and PCA is determined. Contribution of each of the variables is found out using the PCA values.

Finally, we determined the PCA values by choosing a particular ML algorithm and start proceeding with the test and training data and then the decision is made with the appropriate algorithm and their working conditions. By following all the steps in ML modeling, a final radar visualization is provided so that the difference or prediction between malignant and benign cancer data is produced.

Finally, with the following set of graphs, predictions can be made possible for identifying the cancer status.

1.10 CONCLUSION

A robust model has been made in well-being segment area to foresee and give a superior answer for the general population so that the death rate of the general population would be diminished, and with this model, cost adequacy

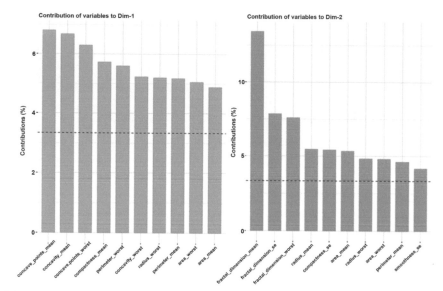

FIGURE 1.10   Contribution of variable.

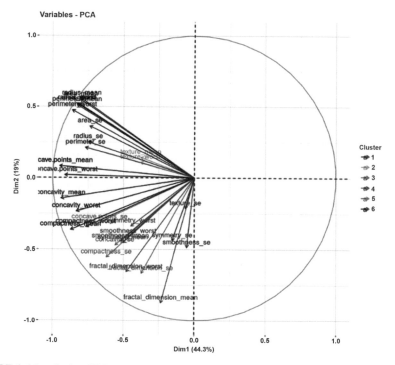

FIGURE 1.11   Optimal PCA.

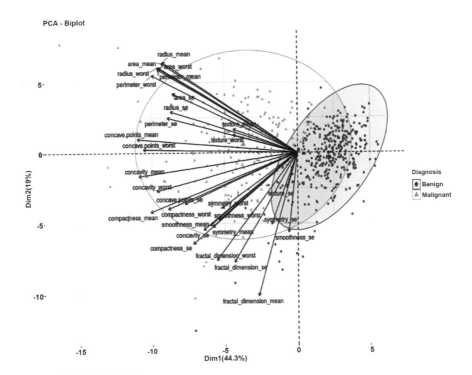

FIGURE 1.12   PCA biplot.

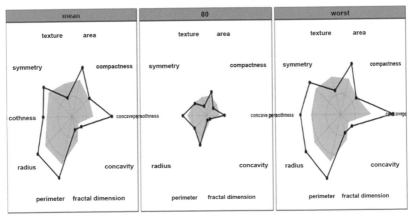

FIGURE 1.13   Radar plot for Benign cancer data.

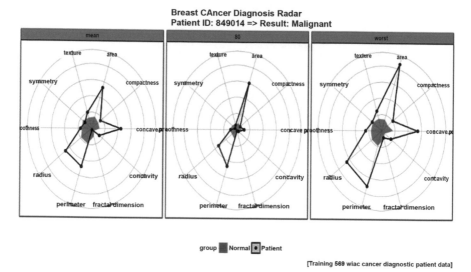

FIGURE 1.14   Radar plot for malignant cancer data.

has been executed, remembering that this system can be utilized for all groups of individuals. A detailed view of deep learning and healthcare that depicts the working, modeling, and evaluation of the process is discussed. The techniques focused are the emerging techniques and methodologies in the healthcare analysis in data science.

KEYWORDS

- **artificial intelligence**
- **machine learning**
- **deep learning**
- **neural networks**
- **convolution network**

REFERENCES

Beysolow II T. (2017). Introduction to Deep Learning Using R: A Step-by-Step Guide to Learning and Implementing Deep Learning Models Using R. Apress.

Brynjolfsson E., & Mcafee A.N. (2018). The business of artificial intelligence. Harv Bus Rev. 24, 2017. Available: https://hbr.org/cover-story/2017/07/the-business-of-artificial-intelligence. Accessed: 28 September 2018.

Celi L.A., Moseley E., Moses C., Ryan P., Somai M., Stone D., & Tang K. (2014). From pharmacovigilance to clinical care optimization. Big Data, 2(3), 134–141. Medline:26576325 doi:10.1089/big.2014.0008.

Henglin M., Stein G., Hushcha P.V., Snoek J., Wiltschko A.B., & Cheng S. (2017). Machine learning approaches in cardiovascular imaging. Circul Cardiovasc Imag, 10(10), 1–9. Medline:28956772 doi:10.1161/CIRCIMAGING.117.005614.

Jaeger S., Karargyris A., Candemir S., Folio L., Siegelman J., Callaghan F., Zhiyun X., Palaniappan K., Singh R.K., Antani S., Thoma G., Yi-Xiang W., Pu-Xuan L., & McDonald C.J. (2014). Automatic tuberculosis screening using chest radiographs. IEEE Trans Med Imag, 33(2):233–245, doi: 10.1109/TMI.2013.2284099.

Jiang F., Jiang Y., Zhi H., Dong Y., Li H., Ma S., Wang Y., Dong Q., Shen H., & Wang Y. (2017). Artificial intelligence in healthcare: past, present and future. Stroke Vasc Neurol, 2(4), 230–243.

Johnson A.E., Pollard T.J., & Mark R.G. (2017). Reproducibility in critical care: a mortality prediction case study. In: Proceedings of the 2nd Machine Learning for Healthcare Conference, 68, 361–376.

Krizhevsky A., Sutskever I., & Hinton G.E. (2017). ImageNet classification with deep convolutional neural networks. Commun ACM, 60(6), 84–90.

Lakhani P., & Baskaran S. (2017). Deep learning at chest radiography: automated classification of pulmonary tuberculosis by using convolutional neural networks. Radiology, 284(2), 574–582.

LeCun Y., Bengio Y., & Hinton G. (2015). Deep learning. Nature, 521(7553), 436–444.

Panch T., Szolovits P., & Atun R. (2018). Artificial intelligence, machine learning and health systems. J Glob Health, 8(2).

Patterson J., & Gibson A. (2017). Deep Learning: A Practitioner's Approach. O'Reilly Media.

Mathur P. (2018). Machine Learning Applications Using Python: Cases Studies from Healthcare, Retail and Finance. Apress.

Gupta R. (2019). Top six use cases of data science in healthcare. Available: https://bigdata-madesimple.com/top-6-use-cases-of-data-science-in-healthcare/

Szegedy C., Liu W., Jia Y., Sermanet P., Reed S., Anguleov D., Erhan D., Vanhoucke & Rabinovich A. (2015). Going deeper with convolutions. In: Proceedings of the IEEE Conference on Computer Vision and Pattern Recognition (CVPR), IEEE, 1–9.

Zhang Z., Dong J., Luo X., Choi K. S., & Wu X. (2014). Heart-beat classification using diseases specific feature selection. Comput Biol Med, 46, 79–89.

CHAPTER 2

Role of AI in Healthcare

SONIA SINGLA

Independent Researcher, Birmingham, UK, E-mail: ssoniyaster@gmail.com

ABSTRACT

The Internet of things (IoT) has various applications in therapeutic organizations, from checking of remote sharp sensors to healing gadget blends. It helps in keeping patients verified, in any case, to improve their health by allowing authorities to pass on their thoughts. Human organizations' IoT can in like way help by enabling patients to contribute greater essentialness by collaborating with their experts. Regardless, restorative organizations' IoT is not without its obstacles. The quantity of information they gather can be a test for remedial office IT to coordinate.

Around more than 30 million peoples are affected with diabetes in the United States. Directing diabetes conventionally incorporates a guarantee to a sound lifestyle, routine checking of glucose levels, and adherence to a medication schedule. Today, artificial intelligence (AI) is employed with an ultimate objective to improve the individual fulfillment for diabetics. Man-made reasoning has a huge amount of potential to improve various domains of our lives. Diabetes treatment has a lot of manifestations. The AI system will help restricting some of them just by thinking about an undeniably exact treatment. At the end of the day, the count would determine the exact portion, guaranteeing that the patient is not taking an exorbitant measure of medication, which could cause negative side effects. Modernized thinking is giving direction that could help more than 30 million Americans encountering diabetes. That advice is starting from estimations expected to assist people with diabetes to sufficiently control their glucose levels.

Keeping those measurements as low as possible moderate a couple of disarrays related to the diabetes, as shown by the American Diabetes Association. These traps can hurt the eyes, kidneys, and nerves. These chapter is to get account of the role of AI and machine learning in the treatment of diabetes and other nontransferable infection. Noncommunicating diseases join an extent of unending conditions, including harmful development, diabetes, cardiovascular diseases (CVDs), hypertension, similar to Alzheimer's and various dementias.

2.1   WHAT IS ARTIFICIAL INTELLIGENCE?

AI is a piece of programming building that expects to make savvy machines. It has transformed into a crucial bit of the development business. Research related to man-made thinking is concentrated. The inside issues of man-made cognizance fuse programming PCs for explicit attributes, for instance,

- to learn,
- to think,
- reasoning,
- observation
- to arrange, and
- controlling and moving objects.

Data building is a highlight of AI investigation. Machines can routinely act and react like individuals just if they have unlimited information relating to the world. Man-made cognizance must approach objects, characterizations, properties, and relations between all of them to execute getting the hang of structuring. Beginning sound judgment, thinking and basic intuition control in machines is an irksome and dull task. Simulated intelligence is also a highlight of AI. Learning with no kind of supervision requires an ability to recognize structures in floods of wellsprings of information, while learning with enough supervision incorporates portrayal and numerical backslides. Request chooses the characterization an article has a spot with, and backslide oversees obtaining a ton of numerical data or yield points of reference, thus discovering limits enabling the time of proper yields from information sources. Logical assessment of AI counts and their introduction is a well-portrayed piece of speculative programming building every now and again suggested as computational learning theory.

2.2   AI IN DIABETES

Diabetes mellitus, for the most part known as diabetes, is a metabolic disorder that causes high glucose. The effect of diabetes leads to insufficient insulin in body or inability to use the insulin being made. Untreated high glucose from diabetes can hurt nerves, eyes, kidneys, and various organs of the human beings. There are a few different sorts of diabetes:

Type 1 diabetes is an insusceptible framework infirmity. The safe system strikes and smashes cells in the pancreas where insulin is made. It is foggy what causes this ambush. About 10% of people have this type of diabetes.

Type 2 diabetes happens when your body ends up impenetrable to insulin, and sugar forms in your blood.

Prediabetes happens when your glucose is higher than run of the mill; anyway, it is not adequately high for an assurance of type 2 diabetes.

Gestational diabetes is high glucose during pregnancy. Insulin-blocking hormones made by the placenta cause this sort of diabetes (www.health-line.com).

The diabetes crisis in the United States cannot be misrepresented. The numbers are horrendous: beginning at 2012, around 9.3% of Americans had diabetes, and more than 86 million were prediabetic.

All things considered, diabetes prompts in any occasion 243,000 passings yearly, and type 1 and 2 diabetes record for a totaled yearly direct therapeutic cost of $176 billion in the United States, as a result of diabetic disarrays and related crisis facility affirmations. Principal in turning away these affirmations and debilitating burdens is the control of blood glucose levels, shirking of dangerous lows (routinely suggested as hypoglycemic events). While various relationship over all organizations are using AI to help comprehend the heavy slide of data made by the countless number of devices accessible for use, the social protection division has an exceptional opportunity to use AI for the most significant of causes, improving patient outcomes for people who experience the evil impacts of diabetes and, finally, saving lives. For an instance of how AI has been shown to improve diabetes patients' outcomes, look not any more remote than a continuous observational fundamental held at the Diabetes Clinic in the Netherlands, one of Europe's driving diabetes offices. The Diabetes Clinic's progressing observational fundamental used a structure based on a self-streamlining AI. The system, called Rhythm, gauges and administers blood glucose measurements of people with diabetes, in the perspective of nonprominent biometric sensors and AI. By using redid blood glucose desire models that changed in accordance with all of the eight patients who checked out the observational fundamental, the masters controlling the starter found that in seven of the eight patients, the Rhythm system alone cultivated a 20% extension in time in range and a 9% decline in unsafe lows—both key estimations for diabetes patients—stood out from

Diabetes' starting at now suitable, high-contact approach. The observational fundamental of Rhythm showed that the Diabetes Clinic had an alternative to not simply coordinate the blood glucose control results it, as of late, achieved through standard human checking but truly upgrade them. Thus expecting an automated, AI-fueled system can improve—than the Diabetes Clinic's authorities at controlling blood glucose levels, we should have the choice to achieve the office's low diabetes hospitalization rates inside the general open of diabetics. Despite diminishing the amount of possibly dangerous extraordinary scenes related to diabetes, this would result in $67 billion per year cost venture reserves. Finally, extrapolating the results achieved by Rhythm over the general US people would astoundingly influence our overall population's prosperity. This primer not only centers a way ahead for keeping an eye on the stunning size of diabetes in the United States but also traces how much the restorative administrations division—and patients in all cases—stay to get from man-made mental ability. In all honesty, the assurance that AI advancement shows up in human administrations is inciting an impact of endeavor: courses of action to social protection related to AI associations are growing year by year since 2011 and financing bounced from $64 million in 2013 to a colossal $358 million in 2014.

There is important work to be done to improve the aftereffects of diabetes patients in the United States; anyway, AI has, in any occasion, enormous potential to help with a critical piece of the diligent work. Everything considered that is the certifiable certification of AI: to take the world-changing contemplations that the human character is prepared for envisioning and apply those musings at a scale that nobody, yet machines, can reach (www.information-age.com).

Diabetes mellitus is a significant unending affliction, impacting up to 3% of the masses in the industrialized countries. Insulin-dependent diabetes mellitus (IDDM) patients need exogenous insulin implantations to oversee blood glucose assimilation. It has been shown (*Journal of Medicine, 1993*) that intensive insulin therapy (IIT), involving 3–4 imbuements reliably, or the use of subcutaneous insulin siphons, is the best technique to adjust blood glucose and, along these lines, to lessen or defer IDDM challenges; the unconventionality in the development of treatment and high costs are the certain drawbacks. Research focus results and the recorded and moreover anamnestic data are verified, additionally, to finally change the patient's therapeutic perspective. Diabetic patients the board is plainly an eccentric endeavor; how to alter the focal points beginning from IIT with its impediments includes talk, that incorporates social and good considerations

(Lasker, 1993). It has been maintained that the usage of current advances of information developments and decision sincerely steady systems may improve cost-reasonability of IIT, by diminishing the amount of periodical control visits, while extending the patient/specialist correspondence rate. A couple of gadgets and cautioning systems for therapeutic game plan assessment are now available, both on a well-ordered and on a visit-by-visit premise (Lehmann and Deutsch, 1995), and for some of them, the capacity of giving authentic decisions has been demonstrated probably (Andreassen et al., 1994). The exponential advancement in the openness and the usage of media transmission organizations pushes toward the blend of such instruments in a framework's organization condition to give long-expel help to seeing, similar to the long-separate checking ability to the specialist (Gomez et al., 1992). The usage of fitting AI techniques, for instance, data-based systems, intelligent data analysis, and case-based reasoning, may redesign the structure of the general organization: it should be possible to allow the customers abusing an astute work territory for a periodic treatment examination and update (Montani, 2019).

By virtue of an appropriated system, the nearness of an around the world shared cosmology is fundamental to ensure the probability of correspondence between the building portions: the way of thinking goes about as the standard expressing to which all of the modules insinuate while exchanging information and is used to choose the direct of the whole structure. The T-IDDM theory is secured in a learning base made using an edge system (Andreassen et al., 1994) that reinforces diverse heritage and formed spaces. It is dealt with logical arrangements, which depict substances (for instance, patients, explore office views), events (for instance, checking data estimation), reflections (for instance, hyperglycemia), drugs, supportive shows, and so forth. Since spaces are made, we in like manner expected to define a chain of significance for classes addressing types (for instance, the class of numerical characteristics and the one of fixed-length strings). Types are applied classes: no events are produced using them; anyway, they are used to store information required by the case openings. We use the database chiefly as a conclusive instrument to depict the space theory, while we misuse a social database to manage the certified data. The structure of the database tables, similar to the bearings to store and recuperate the data, is delivered normally dependent on the cosmology information. An SQL interface, prepared to get the request steer to the database, and moreover to reestablish the resulting data, ensures the correspondence between the customer and the data document (Montani, 2019). The data accumulated by patients during home-watching, and sent through the PU-MU affiliation, are time-ventured and secured a couple of times (from three to four) for multiple days. To allow a fitting comprehension of the data, we have subdivided the 24-h regular term into a great deal of consecutive noncovering time cuts, concentrated on the period of dinners or insulin implantations; each datum is consequently identified with a given time cut. The MU manhandles the home-checking information through a great deal of mechanical assemblies to picture and to separate the accumulated data. Data examination ranges from a ton of real methodologies, for instance, the extraction of the step-by-step typical estimation of the blood glucose level, the step-by-step insulin need, and the amount of authentic hypoglycemic events in an offered time allotment, to progressively complex sorts of reflections. An interesting portrayal of the course of longitudinal data is obtained through the temporal abstraction (TA) framework. The basic rule of TA systems is to move from a period point to an interval-based depiction of the data. Given a progression of time-ventured data (events), the neighboring discernments that offer a normal part are totaled into between times (scenes). In more detail, two crucial classes of reflections can be portrayed: basic thoughts for perceiving predefined plans in a univariate time game plan and complex consultations for discovering specific momentary associations between scenes, similarly with respect to examining multivariate models (Fang, et al., 2018). Central considerations remove states (for instance, low, ordinary, high characteristics) or examples (augmentation, reduction, or stationary plans) from a one-dimensional time course of action. Complex considerations examine for specific short-lived associations between scenes that can be delivered from a crucial reflection or from other complex thoughts. This kind of TA can be manhandled to expel multidimensional models or to recognize one-dimensional instances of complex shapes. Intensive cases of the usage of TA methodologies to checking data for diabetic patients can be found in Fulmer et al. (2018).

Youth weight treatment is an astounding human administration target requiring educating and supporting individuals for characterizing self-care destinations, basic intuition to recognize hindrances to achieve these goals, and updates or reassurances to perform concentrated works on sustaining or therapeutic information (Fulmer et al., 2018) and managing enthusiastic responses to conflicting pieces of life. Robotizing these strategies offers ensure for scaling exhibited practical interventions to greater gatherings of spectators. This would reduce intervention costs per part and expand reach. Impressive undertakings have been associated with automating behavior change strategies (Brand et al., 2016) for weighing the board when all is said is done (Bardus et al., 2016) and among children and adolescents explicitly (Brand et al., 2016). Most of these developments helped projects and applications that, in any case, have not had the perfect ramifications for body game plan results or intervening practices (Brand et al., 2016). Man-made mental ability (AI) with significant learning offers strategies for extending interventions by means of automating transport for on-demand get to and overhauling the ampleness as the system reliably learns (Ramesh et al., 2004). Stephens and partners are the first to make and report a versatile direct chatbot, named Tess, using AI to improve the undertakings of specialists meaning to kid chunkiness (Stephens et al., 2019). We acclaim their undertakings to widen chatbots in the pediatric field. Chatbots have been used with an arrangement of prosperity-related practices (e.g., physical development (Kramer et al., 2019), mental well-being (Hoermann et al., 2017), medicate adherence, wretchedness, and pressure) to express empathy and compassion. This, in any case, is the essential application to weigh the pediatric board. Tess is expected to operationalize cognitive behavior therapy, motivational interviewing, and behavioral activation and to fill in as a partner to typical treatment. Texts were made and attested by mental prosperity specialists and changed in accordance with a patient's sentiments and concerns. Tess was proposed to self-gain from customer affiliations subjected to responses to end-of-session requests. This work addresses a noteworthy and imaginative consequent stage in the movement of prosperity preparing for weighing the administrators among youth.

Given the early frustrations with applications, in any case, careful assessment must be associated with these new undertakings. Stephens et al. report a feasibility feature demonstrating tolerant responsibility, saw backing, and target progression. These outcomes are basic to represent, yet future research ought to survey Tess's dedication as a pediatric weight the board instrument in a totally powered randomized controlled starter.

Mediations are thought to work by influencing key mediating factors, changes that affect the proximal (social) and distal (body structure) outcomes (Baranowski and Lytle, 2015). To increase Tess's possible ampleness on distal outcomes, beginning evaluations may wish to gauge, refine, and streamline its impact on widely appealing key outcomes of patients (e.g., distress and uneasiness) and psychosocial interceding factors (for instance, self-suitability and result expectations). Such research could serve to prepare Tess to enhance its influence on variables while in transit to needed outcomes and, along these lines, limit the dissatisfaction of changing proximal and distal outcomes and insist theoretical subtleties of direct change.

Simulated intelligence in AI normally requires figuring and a colossal game plan of points of reference, all of which are explained (e.g., right/ off-base and acceptable/unacceptable). Tess's basic getting ready was not presented. Its proposed learning (remarks) from keen sessions relied on customer responses to a request on "settlement" close to the completion of a correspondence. Given the social alluring nature of response likely in an inconsistent provider calm coordinated effort, it is hazy whether the remarks correctly give significant information on the settlement of the messages expected to extensively update correspondence among Tess and the customer. It is moreover cloudy what shields are set up to neutralize blunder of information given by the customer or to verify against Tess going off-substance and radiating base or potentially frightful information. Future progression and refinement of Tess will most likely require remarks of wise progressions by specialists and a mindful assessment of systems and response counts to ensure that shields are set up to help assurance in content commitment and accuracy.

Concerns have been raised about extreme use (Van den Eijnden et al., 2018) and ill-advised introduction (Pediatrics, 2016) of media by adolescents. No composing has appeared on child usage of chatbots. Unfaltering by the biggest measure of alarm, encouraging families to develop an age-fitting family use plan that sets standards and assistants correspondence around family media use (Pediatrics, 2016) including chatbots would be valuable. Given the present proposals concerning screen media use among children and youngsters and its potential effect on forcefulness-related practices, for instance, rest (Carter, et al., 2016) and dietary confirmation (Marsh et al., 2013), everything considered, gatekeepers will require a type of oversight or possibly consideration in their adolescent's associations with chatbots.

Tess' discourses with patients were driven in any case, anyway separate from, the treatment given by the prosperity capable. It remains to be seen whether issues, contemplations, and concerns passed on to Tess by the customer, yet not conferred to the going to the master or parent, may obstruct the thought given, or its sufficiency. Perhaps, Tess can be changed to give outstanding learning to the capable and the parent around the completion of a customer session. Additionally, it is not clear what may happen if perils of self-hurt were conferred to Tess, yet not instantly offered an explanation to a reliable social affair. Finally, a wide age run was locked in with the uncovered assessment (9-year olds). Nine and eighteen year olds are at different developmental stages and have liberally special self-care aptitudes, correspondence needs, and styles. Emotional examination of the exchanges by part age could give understanding of how Tess could be specifically crafted to age and related complexities to light up the future with respect to chatbots for children (Thompson and Baranowski, 2019)

Behavioral intervention technologies (BITs) are stand-out ways to deal with the benefits of development and mind research to address changing prosperity needs through various media, including Internet mediations, convenient applications, and PC diversions. BITs present a couple of potential favorable circumstances, including extended spread and accessibility, cost ampleness, extended duty, and decreased disfavor, especially among youth.

A lead training chatbot, Tess, addresses different parts of social prosperity, for instance, distress and strain. Open all day, every day, Tess passes on changed integrative assistance, psychoeducation, and interventions through brief exchanges by methods for existing correspondence channels (i.e., short messenger service [SMS]). This examination overviewed the feasibility of joining Tess in direct managing of adolescent patients (n = 23; mean age = 15.20 years; age range = 9.78–18.54 years; 57% female), adjusting to weigh the board and prediabetic reactions. Tess associates with patients by methods for a favored procedure for correspondence (SMS substance educating) in individualized exchanges to propel treatment adherence, direct change, and all-in-all prosperity. Pre-grown-up patients' nitty-gritty experience positive headway toward their goals 81% of the time. The 4123 messages exchanged and patients representing comfort assessments (96% of the time) demonstrate that youngsters attracted to and saw this chatbot as steady. These results highlight the credibility and bit of leeway of assistance through automated thinking, unequivocally in a pediatric setting, which could be scaled to serve greater social events of patients. As an associate to clinicians, Tess can continue with the therapeutic association outside accessible time while keeping up patient's satisfaction. Due to the capacity of Tess for steady learning, future accentuations may have additional features to grow the customer experience (Stephens et al., 2019).

Regardless of our sincere endeavors, pediatric heaviness remains a huge general restorative issue. Through a wide variety of approaches to manage the area this condition has been utilized to, a few have gained significant ground. Advancement is continuously being researched as a worthwhile and open system for passing on lead interventions. Stephens and accomplices report the likelihood of using a lead preparing social chatbot, Tess, to grow a multicomponent pediatric weight intervention for adolescents. We take a gander at the advantages and drawbacks of this system. Although social chatbots offer an intriguing, what is more, novel procedure for propelling constant assistance, critical issues and decisions must be meticulously considered during the structure stage to help ensure a secured area for a vulnerable populace (Stephens et al., 2019).

2.3 ROLE OF AI IN CARDIOVASCULAR DISEASES

CVD (where C, coronary, cardiomyopathy, congenital; V, vascular; D, disease), as the term appears, is a heart and vein ailment and one of the genuine explanations behind mortality in India and around the globe. Very few people think about that the usage of tobacco, alcohol use, overweight; weight and inadequate eating routine with high proportion of salt relate to hypertension, which is known as high blood pressure and is the major risky component related with coronary supply course ailments. It is moreover one of the huge explanations behind the death of women in European countries and is continuously essential in increasingly prepared women as they enter menopause (EIWH). Generally, impacts in India are a result of poverty, nonappearance of learning, treatment workplaces, and early start of ailment that has affected both urban and rural zones. Melancholy and uneasiness are seen to be typical among progressively settled women and increasingly young woman are in penchant for smoking, fast sustenance, and alcohol usage in European countries, which is of high risk of coronary conductor illness. About 52% people fails horrendously in India at age under 70 years due to CVD (ISSN 2250-3153), and examination done in 1995–1996 and 2004 shows that most noteworthy examples of people in the restorative center stay has extended for diabetes, trailed by wounds, and coronary ailments and illnesses in 2004 (Engelgau et al., 2019)

2.3.1 ORDINARINESS AND MORTALITY OF CARDIOVASCULAR CONTAMINATION

From September 2015 to July 2016, cross-sectional data shows the greater part of women was 56% than men and power rate of diabetes 9%, for hypertension regularity rate was 22%, for hypercholesterolemia inescapability rate of 20%, and prevalence rate for past and current smokers about 14% and 4% (Marbaniang et al., 2017). In 2016, research done on urban zone of Varanasi shows that the transcendence rate of hypertension was 32.9% and mean systolic and diastolic BP were 124.25 ± 15.05 mm Hg and 83.45 ± 9.49 mm Hg, respectively. Men were progressively impacted than women

(Singh et al., 2017). The inescapability rate of hypertension among adults (>20 years) was 159 per thousand for both urban and rural regions in 1995. In May to October 2012, a huge segment of the patients in Odisha primary social protection focus were encountering respiratory (17%) and cardiovascular affliction (10.2%) (Swain et al., 2017). In 2012–2014 assessment, data accumulated from 400 urban and 400 rural houses from western India reveals the nonappearance of guidance for prescription use; generally, medications used were for cardiovascular affliction without drug and expiry dates and not authentic portion being taken (Mirza and Ganguly, 2016). In 2010–2012, in Vellore, a cross-sectional assessment done by the Rose Angina Survey and electrocardiography found that the inescapability rate for coronary heart infection was 3.4% in rural men, 7.3 % in urban men, 7.4% in rural women, and 13.4% in urban women, high among women than male as suggested by the transcendence rate determined between 1991 and 1994 (Oommen et al., 2016). In 2010–2012, cross-sectional outline exhibits that the transcendence rate extended in urban and rural than 1991–1994. The use of alcohol, overweight, raised circulatory strain, and smoking has put urban Delhi people at a high risk of cardiovascular diseases than those in rural Delhi. The mean weight document in the urban region was seen to be 24.4–26.0 kg/m^2 and 20.2–23.0 kg/m^2 in the rural region; the systolic circulatory strain in the urban region was seen to be 121.2–129.8 mm Hg and about 114.9–123.1 mm Hg in the rural region; and the diastolic heartbeat strain in the urban region was seen to be 74.3–83.9 mm Hg and about 73.1–82.3 mmHg in the nation (Kaufman et al., 2016). The impact of high peril leads by diabetes, hypertension, and smoking between the age of 35 and 70 years, and nonattendance of treatment is critical explanation behind deaths in India (Khetan et al., 2017).

In the near future, man-made mental ability frameworks, for instance, AI, significant learning, and abstract enrolling, may expect a fundamental employment in the improvement of cardiovascular (CV) drugs to support precision CV medicine. Clinical thought starting at now faces businesslike challenges identifying with cost diminishes in shirking and treatment, negligible exertion sufficiency, overutilization, lacking patient thought, and high readmission and demise rates. Beneficial associations among specialists and data scientists are relied upon to enable clinically significant mechanized and perceptive data assessment. Until this point in time, gigantic data, for instance, "omics" data, human gut microbiome sequencing, online life, and cardiovascular imaging, are exorbitantly colossal and heterogeneous, and change too quickly, to be secured, inspected, and used. Mimicked insights can mishandle colossal data and be used in frontline relentless thoughts. Without a doubt, CVDs are flighty and heterogeneous in nature, as they are realized by various innate, biological (e.g., air pollution), and leading (e.g., diet and gut microbiome) factors. At present, significantly more movements ought to be made to envision absolute and reasonable results, instead of studying a clear score structure or standard CV chance components.

Man-made knowledge frameworks have been applied in cardiovascular medication to examine novel genotypes and phenotypes in existing afflictions, improve the idea of patient thought, achieve cost reasonability, and decline readmission and death rates. In the past decade, a couple of AI techniques have been used for CVD examination and conjecture. Each examination requires some degree of appreciation of the issue, the extent that cardiovascular medicine and estimations, to apply the perfect AI count. As soon as possible, AI will bring about an adjustment in the context toward precision CV drugs. The capacity of AI in CV remedies is tremendous; however, the carelessness of the challenges may overshadow its potential clinical effects (Krittanawong et al., 2017).

2.4   ROLE OF AI IN MENTAL WELL-BEING

Schizophrenia is a veritable and profound established neurodevelopmental disorder that impacts how an individual thinks, feels, and behaves. People with schizophrenia may experience hallucinations, cluttered talk or behavior, and obstructed mental limitations. They may hear voices or see things that are not there. They may believe that different people are examining their cerebrums, controlling their thoughts, or plotting to hurt them. These practices can be frightening and troubling to people with schizophrenia and make them pulled back or very incited. It can moreover be frightening and troubling to the community around them. People with schizophrenia may talk about abnormal or astounding musings for a portion of the time, which can make it difficult to carry on an exchange. They may sit for a serious long time without moving or talking. Occasionally, people with schizophrenia seem, by all accounts, to be perfectly fine until they talk about what they are thinking about. "Productive" reactions are insinuated as useful because the indications are additional practices not generally seen in sound people. For specific people, these signs travel all over. For other individuals, the symptoms become stable after some time. These symptoms can be, not kidding—yet at various events—, unnoticeable. Positive symptoms include:

Pipedreams: When an individual see, hears, smells, tastes, or feels things that are not veritable. Hearing voices is standard for people with schizophrenia. People who hear voices may hear them for a long time before family or buddies see an issue.

Fantasies: When an individual trusts things that are not substantial. For example, an individual may believe that people on the radio and TV are talking truly to the individual being referred to. At times, individuals who have likes may believe that they are in danger or that others are endeavoring to hurt them.

Thought issues: When an individual has points of view that are odd or peculiar. People with figured issues may have trouble dealing with their contemplations. An individual will stop talking during a thought or make up words that have no significance.

Advancement issues: When an individual shows odd body improvement. An individual may repeat certain developments over and over—this is called stereotype. At the other unprecedented times, an individual may stop moving or talking for quite a while, which is a remarkable condition called mental stun.

2.4.1 NEGATIVE SYMPTOMS

"Negative" symptoms include social withdrawal, inconvenience showing up, or inconvenience working consistently. People with antagonistic symptoms may require help with normal errands. Negative indications include

- talking in a dull voice,
- showing outward appearance, for instance, a smile or glare,
- having inconvenience experiencing fulfillment,
- having inconvenience organizing and remaining with a development, for instance, looking for nourishment, and
- talking besides no to different people, despite when it is noteworthy.

These symptoms are more truly to be seen as a component of schizophrenia and can be mistaken for wretchedness or various conditions.

2.4.2 EMOTIONAL REACTIONS

Emotional reactions are hard to see; in any case, they can make it hard for people to have a business or to manage themselves. The element of mental limit is a champion among the best pointers of a person's ability to improve how they work. As often as possible, these symptoms are perceived exactly when express tests are performed. Abstract reactions incorporate (www. nimh.nih.gov)

- trouble getting ready information to choose,
- issues using information following learning it, and
- inconvenience in centering.

The utilization of significant learning with unaided features for gigantic data examination holds vital potential for perceiving novel genotypes and phenotypes in heterogeneous CV infirmities, for instance, Bragada issue, HFpEF, Takotsubo cardiomyopathy, white-coat hypertension, HTN, pneumonic hypertension, familial AF, and metabolic issues. In addition, the improvement of AI applications and precision drug stages will support precision CV medicine. Afterward, emotional PCs, for instance, IBM Watson, will be standard in social protection workplaces and help specialists with their fundamental initiatives and desires for patient outcomes. Various advance organizations, for instance, IBM, Apple, and Google, are placing seriously in human administration assessment to energize precision tranquilization. We believe that AI would not replace specialists; nonetheless, it is noteworthy that specialists acknowledge how to use AI sufficiently to deliver their hypotheses, perform colossal data examination, and streamline AI applications in clinical practice to facilitate the time of precision CV medicne. Regardless, mindlessness of the challenges of AI may command the impact of AI on CV medicine. Computer-based intelligence, significant learning, and mental preparing are promising and can change how medication is bored, yet specialists ought to be set up for the cutting-edge AI period (Krittanawong et al., 2017).

Pete Trainor is a kind advocate of Us Ai, an item architect having some mastery over man-made cognizance. Trainor and his group have made SU, which he calls an "add-on bot" that could continue running in existing talk applications, for instance, Facebook Messenger and Twitter Direct Messages. "Various mental prosperity philanthropies or social occasions starting at now have a sort of assistance instrument on their locales," Trainor explains. "SU can be snared onto these instruments to help recognize 'trigger' words or articulations, which can alert the master on the furthest edge and after that triage a reaction or offer up substance and associations. SU has been set up to see 'desire', and it utilizes AI to organize language against different conditions or conditions."

SU, due to dispatch one year from now, is being made using directions from the Campaign Against Living Miserably (CALM). Specifically, Trainor says, "SU scans for lost reason; that could be a job adversity or a division, for example. Troublesome vernacular is also hailed, for example when someone feels that their family would be in a perfect circumstance without them."

SU, Trainor says, is being made considering the "staggering" inescapability of male suicide. "Suicide is the best foe of men developed under 45. Suicide can happen so quickly, so the idea is to use AI to recognize those crises shows and stall out in a terrible circumstance essentially quicker. Reckless ideation may make over some unclear time period, anyway when someone contacts a consideration gathering like CALM, the exhibit itself can happen in only minutes, so driving someone up in a line of calls could be a help."

Similarly, as seeing emergency conditions, SU can in like manner be used to go-to individuals toward master help. "SU jumps on watchwords, so if the program on a magnanimity's visit mechanical assembly, for example, made sense of how to perceive that an individual was ex-military and encountering PTSD, by then it could control them to an ace altruism that dealt with that, like Help for Heroes."

Dr. Paul Tiffin and Dr. Lewis Paton, both from the Department of Health Sciences at the University of York, starting late drove an assessment into the odds and challenges related to using mechanized thinking to treat mental health issues. Paton says advancement can "increase access to mental assistance," and that "guided personal development is an earlier framework for treating mental prosperity issues." Where this as of late included using books and exercises, Paton perceives that applications made responsive by AI "may be better than tolerating no treatment in any way shape or form." He raises, regardless, that "motorized and online medications do will by and large have higher dropout rates diverged from those that incorporate a human."

What precisely degree can a machine's bits of information into mental health really be trusted? Tiffin says that since clinicians "often need to override a computerized decision," machines are "saw even more antagonistically for submitting blunders" than individuals are. The precision of a machine's encounters, he says, depends upon the points of reference the system has been set up to get it. "There are well-seen conditions where computations have wound up being uneven in view of the general population that gave the arrangement data."

Given the wide range and complexities of mental prosperity conditions, the availability of good getting ready data could be an imperative issue for any planner of this advancement. "Medicines subject to social benchmarks, those that urge people to put more vitality in activities they find pleasurable just as satisfying," Tiffin says, "credit themselves to robotization. That is because they are commonly unsophisticated and rely upon 'right here and now'." However, medications that "incorporate delving into the patient's past in order to appreciate their present inconveniences would be generously harder for a dishonestly savvy system to ever duplicate."

Paton believes the whole deal occupation of AI in treating mental well-being issues should incorporate a "blend of both veritable and counterfeit counselors' time." While there is apparently an understanding of the enthusiastic health organization that distinctive issues snappier would be useful, there remain inquiries over the advancement's ability to isolate between signs, to break down and to impersonate the compassion that patients regard in human teachers. Holly says her experience of Woebot proposes that it could be a useful transient fix, yet Sally Brown alerts that such development, in any case huge in its own way, should "not be viewed as a response for unending understaffing or underfunding" (Krittanawong et al., 2017).

Symbol therapy (AT), an inventive experiential philosophy, engages patients to make an image of their persecutor (the voice in their sound-related verbal mental excursions) and empowers them to manage their signs while resisting their sentiments of fear head-on. Bantering with these images furthermore moves control from the image to the patient.

Makers of the randomized outwardly impeded examination said that image treatment diminished pipedreams on a very basic level following 12 weeks (half of the customary treatment extend) and had a logically critical effect on facilitating various signs of schizophrenia. Every so often, it has been even used to absolutely stop seizures all around.

2.5   ROLE OF AI IN PARKINSON DISEASE

Parkinson's disease (PD) is a condition wherein parts of the cerebrum become persistently hurt over various years.

The three major signs of PD are

- programmed shaking of explicit bits of the body (tremor),
- moderate improvement, and
- firm and fearless muscles.

A person with PD can in like manner experience a wide extent of other physical and mental signs. These include: pity and anxiety, parity issues (this may grow the chances of a fall), loss of sentiment of smell (anosmia), issues resting (a dozing issue), and memory issues.

Man-made thinking is an empowering zone of advancement in the voyage to improve the lives of people with PD.

Shortening assessment times would be a valuable improvement for people with PD and prosperity specialists alike—with less time spent on examinations, they would no doubt contribute more vitality discussing things like the impact of PD on people's regular day-to-day existences and the sufficiency of drugs.

Assortment of prevalence with gender reveals that the event rate amidst 70–79 years was enduring with data, in some it indicates increased events in males. Over 80+ years, there was extended recurrence in males; however, there was a decrease event rate in females (Hirsch et al., 2015). Sex-based refinement was noted between ages 60–69 and 70–79 years. Meta-assessment performed by Xu et al. showed higher estrogen development in females, which prompts higher dopamine levels. Male diligence has higher danger than that of female and has earlier start than women. Analysis performed on males and females has showed increased rate in the two individuals with age; at any rate, it was higher in males of all age groups in ranges of 60–69 and 70–79 years and adjust at age over 80 years (Hirsch et al., 2016).

Some studies reveal that the high estrogen found in females was responsible for less risk. The study was done on PD to know, all things considered, the impact of sickness on age, sex, and geographic area, for instance, Asia, Africa, South America, and Europe/North America/Australia. A meta-examination shows an increase in rate of PD infection with age as it was found to be lower being around 41 at the age of 40–49 years, 107 with an increase in age to 50–59 years and 1903 in age above 80 years (Pringsheim et al., 2014).

PD recurrence was studied in 588 cases to know the impact of contamination on age, sex, and ethnicity. Data from KPMCP and Bay Area Metropolitan communicates that the disease increases with ages above 60 years, is more in men than women, higher in Hispanic than non-Hispanic whites, less in Asians, and the lowest in Blacks (about 10.2, 95% CI: 6.4, 14.0) (Eeden et al., 2003). At the age of 60 years, no refinement was found in individuals, at any rate; sexual direction differentiates with regard to recurrence of PD and appears to differentiate by ethnicity (Alves et al., 2008).

The power rate for PD was found in 44 patients of age less than 50 years; moreover, it was found to be high in patients of age 75 years. The assessment done similarly shows that males have higher recurrence rate than females and it is high in Nile valley of upper Egypt when compared to the other Arabian countries (Khedr et al., 2015).

The examination was done in Benghazi, in north-eastern part of Libya on 163 patients, of which 87 were male patients and 76 were female patients. The start of disease was the same in both male and female patients. The inescapability rates were 32.5 and 30.3 per 100,000 for male and female patients, respectively.

The rate increased with age and was higher in the two sexes at the age of 70 years (Ashok et al., 2013). The examination was done in Al Kharga area of Egypt to assess the inescapability of PD closely and personally for age under 40 years with 62,583 individuals in years 2005 and 2009. Around 15,482 individuals were of age under 40 years and 49 individuals in these groups admitted to have PD. The normality rate was seen to be the same in men; however, in women, it increased with age and was high in rural zones when compared with that in urban domains (Tallawy et al., 2013).

The rate of regularity and event rate were much higher at age under 60, and nine assessments reported their augmentations with age at any rate; in six examinations, it showed a decline in the rate of power. The observed assortment can be a result of conditions and inherited factors and a direct result of differences in methodologies for case ascertainment, decisive criteria, or age dispersal in study populations (Campenhausen et al., 2005).

The assessment demonstrates that the event rate increases with age and decreases at the age of 89 years and is most common among Hispanics, followed by non-Hispanic Whites, Asians, and Blacks. It is higher in males than females in the beginning, but the refinement decreases with increasing age owing to the high mortality rates in elderly (Widrefelt et al., 2011).

PD was contemplated from 557 patients from rural and urban regions of north Karnataka; the results showed that PD starts at increasingly settled age, advances with age, is more in men than women, and is found more in people with no family parentage of PD as it used to be thought in earlier way that it is found more in persons having family heritage (Kadakol et al., 2012).

An examination was done by a gateway survey on 140 people, and among these, 46 people had encountered the evil impacts of PD; the results exhibited that the regularity rate increases with age and is more in men than women (Bharuch et al., 1988).

The examination was done on 382 patients in 2004–2015, in South Central India, Telangana State, shows that the onset of sickness is 60 years and is more in males as compared to females living in common domains. In India and Asia, PD is low as compared to other countries. (Jha, and Chaudhary, 2017).

An examination was done in 13 African countries from 1944 to 2004 by using Medline, INASP, and African Journal Online databases. The results exhibit that the prevalence and incidence rate of PD increases with age and is found more in men than women living in rural areas as compared to urban areas. Augmentation in PD transcendence is for all intents and purposes two-fold, which needs to be additionally inspected by the assessments (Liu et al., 2016).

The ordinariness of PD in specific examinations exhibits that it increases with age, and a couple of assessments show a decrease beyond 80 years, which can be a direct result of incorrect diagnosis differing survival time, and lower response rate. Future research is required to be done in China as only two assessments shows rate data (Zou et al., 2015).

The 22 assessments done show that male and female extent increases with age, is assessed to be extended by 0.05 and 0.14 in 10 years, and is for all intents and purposes equivalent in age under 50; anyway, it is on numerous occasions more in males when compared to females of age more than 80 years (Moisan et al., 2017). PD in males and females was essentially similar, yet high risk is found in males (De Lau et al., 2004).

2.5.1   SPREAD OF THE AILMENT WITH AGE AND THE ONSET OF DISEASE:

Numerous investigations analyze that the early start of the disease is 40 or 41 years, and, a couple of studies indicate that it starts at about 30 years. It is found to increase with age and in specific examinations it advances toward getting to be steady at the age of 80 years, while in specific examinations, it augments above 80 years (Widrefelt et al., 2011).

2.5.2   INESCAPABILITY AND INCIDENCE RATES

Around 1601 cases were from North America, Europe, and Australia and fairly less 646 from Asia was represented Parkinson's ailment have been shown to be less ordinary in Asian countries and to go from 15 for each 100,000 to 12,500 for each 100,000, and the event of PD from 15 for each 100,000 to 328 for each 100,000. The purpose of the assessment was to measure the normality and 10-year rate of PD in the Australian social context. PD expresses inescapability rates of 0.48% in individuals of 60–69 years, 0.82% for individuals of 70–79 years, and 0.56% in individuals above 80 years or settles afterward. No PD case was represented for individual under 60 years, which shows that the PD rate increases with age and become stable above 80 years (Mehta et al., 2007). The epidemiological research in a country like India with various ethnic races studies characteristic perils for PD. Due to refinement in ethnic innate characteristics, PD is dynamically regular in Caucasians than non-Caucasians, lower among non-Whites (Saudi Arabia, China, Japan, African-Americans, and Indian non-Parsis) than Whites (USA, Europe, Australia) (Muthane et al., 2007). The assessment done on Arab countries suggests that the recurrence of PD is not as high as that found in people of other countries. The transcendence of PD among Arabs (27–43 for every 100,000 persons) is higher than in Black Africans (Nigeria 10 for every 100,000, Ethiopia 7 for every 100,000, and China 18 for every 100,000). It is much lower from that of made countries (more than 100 for every 100,000) (Benamer et al., 2010). The assessment done suggests that PD in Arab countries is seen to resemble the estimation of 27 for every 100,000 in Saudi Arabia, at any rate; in specific assessments, it has been represented different rates. One assessment conducted in Irbid, Jordan, has uncovered an inescapability rate of 37.4 per 100,000; however, a subsequent report suggests an inescapability rate of 31.4 per 100,000 and a third report showed an inescapability rate of 43 for every 100,000. The PD prevalence rate was found to be 557.4 per 100,000 in Egyptian area of Assiut, a rate that is significantly higher than the past rate. In Saudi Arabia, a screening of 98 PD patients for PD-causing pathogenic changes in 2015 found 76 cases in males and 22 cases in females when compared to the past record in 1993–1998. The report suggests that biological exposures and innate beauty care products, which are assorted among Middle-East countries can be the explanation behind the low inescapability of PD (27 for each 100,000) and power rate uncovered by most assessments on Arab (overwhelmingly North African) people (31.4–557.4 per 100,000). The qualification explained by the makers is that their examination populations were usually provincial when compared with examination populations in urban areas (Yasser et al., 2011). The assessment suggests that the PD increases with age, and the ordinary age for the start of PD is 60 years. People living in rural regions have higher danger of exposure to pesticides. The disease is increasingly plausible n made countries. Folks are progressively effective when diverged from females and explanations behind these are not known (Ayano, 2016). Around 24 articles were found by looking for Medline and Embase, where the event of PD was seen to be about 4.5 per 100,000 man and the normality rate was 27–43 for every 100,000 individuals. PD in Arabs was not exactly equivalent to others and was seen to contribute by 7% as a purpose behind dementia in Arabs. The inescapability of PD in Arabs (27–43 for every 100,000 individuals) is higher than that found in Black Africans (Nigeria 10 for every 100,000, Ethiopia 7 for every 100,000, and Togo 20 for every 100,000) and Chinese (18 for every 100,000).

Going through door to door was done in some investigations and some reviewed by prosperity capable which is generally not equivalent to network-based chase as in approach to gateway diagram less people is verified and inescapability of PD is high in such cases which can be a result of different reasons yet it prompts mistake of data generally in nation zones (Zhang and Roman, 1993).

Medline and Embase databases were used generally in research to assemble the data, nearby disseminated papers and review papers were dismissed, and simply book references were taken into idea to mull over the epidemiology of PD around the globe; at any rate, the explored papers from PubMed and organizations included were not taken into account, and in some review research papers, the strategies were simply excluded.

The condition in which caregiver live and improvement required among them yet was not found much information which is of high concern issue (Szeto et al., 2016).

A couple of examinations shows qualification in start of sickness, reasons saw to be that of family lineage concern which ought to be see more in detail, what condition, inherited and other key components have work in start of infirmity earlier as the examination done in Karnataka from common and urban domains exhibits the affliction more in patients with no family parentage. In essentially all assessments it has been found that the affliction is found more in zones with current locale and in commonplace areas when diverged from urban zones and it is of major concerned issue for what it's value found more in made countries which means where the all-inclusive community lives longer, is it because of mechanical reason or usage of more pesticides or as a result of ethnicity ought to be tended. In specific assessments the prevalence of PD of Beijing and Shanghai was found like that of western countries, and that of prevalence of PD in North Africa was found like European countries however in various examinations Prevalence in China was found not actually Western countries and that of eastern and western African countries not as much as that of Western Countries (Clarke et al., 2016) which exhibits that more research is required to be done to know the explanation for refinement in detail as social orders from different establishment is sweeping taking everything together countries and can be the noteworthy purpose behind it or the examinations was limited to provincial regions as diverged from urban zones. Folks are seen to be more fruitful than females; at any rate the extent is for all intents and purposes proportionate as it increases with age where further examinations is ought to have been pondered the qualification and what are the parts that makes folks more effective than females and whether the reasons is relied upon to high estrogen closeness which is up 'til now obscure (Liu et al., 2016).

2.5.3   PARENTAL FIGURES OF PD

An assessment was done on 166 patients to find a relationship between PD patients with normal cognitive (NC) function and PD with mild cognitive impairment (MCI). High impact on assets was being found in parental figures of PD-NC patients when compared to PD-MCI patients and lower measurement of QoL was represented in PD-MCI patients concerning physical prosperity. Results give the idea that there is a need for the leading body of parental figure inconvenience, as on starting occasions of scholarly handicap, PD-MCI watchmen have suffered bundles of hopelessness. An examination was done on 72 patients to review individual fulfillment and care of patients suffering with PD. Results exhibit that a part of the patients were satisfied and welcomed by explicit focus and restorative orderly guides; further research is required that considers on physiotherapy, language preparing, support direction, and social authorities' work in the administration of PD (Clarke et al., 2016).

Physiotherapy can help patients encountering PD with joint contractures to have better improvement in walking, swimming, and other physical activities. Various exercises, for instance, tai chai, are recommended by NINDS-sponsored clinical fundamental. Word-related and diet treatment can help in the improvement of ailment. Anxiety and depression were general findings in the survey done on parental figures (Eloise et al., 2011).

Levodopa remains the most dominant drug for controlling PD reactions, yet it relates to basic challenges, for instance, the "wearing off" sway, levodopa-incited dyskinesias, and other motor complexities. Catechol-*o*-methyl-transferase inhibitors, dopamine agonists, and nondopaminergic treatment are elective medicines in the organization of PD and may be used cooperatively with levodopa or one another. The neurosurgical treatment, focusing on significant cerebrum prompting, is reviewed rapidly. Regardless of the way, this review has tried to include the most recent advancements in the treatment of PD; it is basic to observe that new medicines are not better than the developed standard treatment and that the treatment options must be individualized and modified to the necessities of each individual patient (Jankovic and Aguilar, 2008).

The Oxford Parkinson's Disease Center, driven by Consultant Neurologist Professor Michele Hu and Adjacent Professor Richard Wade-Martins, is making amazing strolls forward on various fronts in the fight to appreciate this condition. Mostly, they have been allowed a five-year study from the NIHR Oxford Biomedical Research Center to examine the association between PD and a rest condition known as rapid eye movement sleep behavior disorder (RBD). In RBD, the turn that ordinarily turns off advancement during rest is imperfect, making people move or shout while dozing.

Rest issues are interesting for sensory system experts since they can be an early marker of issues with the tangible framework. Michele and her partners are particularly focusing on the association between RBD and PD because various people with PD are thought to encounter the evil impacts of RBD as well. A person who continues to develop PD may have RBD for quite a while before the issues begin with their improvement when they are cognizant. So, may it be possible to use RBD as a sort of "biomarker" for PD?

The underlying advancement for the assessment gathering is to invite people who are now coming into office for an NHS rest concentrate to wear some new unit. The annual equipment fuses a development sensor worn on the wrist, a heartbeat and oxygen sensor worn on a fingertip, and a rest watching device worn on the head, chest, or midsection.

Michele and group in the Oxford Institute of Biomedical Engineering will "train" PC counts to precisely interpret the data that the wearable unit assembles. This data collection needs to choose people from over the United Kingdom who have either RBD or PD to wear the rest watching device at home for two- or three-night times at customary intervals (www. neuroscience.ox.ac.uk).

Kind, Europe's largest private AI association, is collaborating with Parkinson's UK and The Cure Parkinson's Trust, two UK philanthropies, to repurpose three existing prescriptions and recognize two novel medicine centers to treat PD. The planned exertion underscores the creation and different usages of AI in medicine disclosure. Considerate AI items use a computational method known as a five-layer neural framework to make models that can anticipate the blood–brain barrier and various properties of potential drug candidates. The item's judgment is constantly revived and improved using AI figuring and contribution from experienced biomedical customers (Labiotech). Parkinson AI is a smartphone app that gives an exceptional and adequately accessible response for self-diagnosing and following PD symptoms using its cutting-edge AI. Parkinson AI utilizes a smartphone's compass, gyroscope, and accelerometer sensors to deal with a number of fundamental tests on the patient. Parkinson AI's diet and exercise plans help with stifling the disease after some time. Parkinson AI helps track and separate the development of PD constantly (step-by-step, month-to-month per year). Parkinson AI adequately helps the patient in engaging against PD while also self-diagnosing signs of the disease using smartphone's sensors with its exceedingly forefront machine learning (ML) computations. PD findings on a smartphone are

- track disease development,
- diet plans, and
- simple exercise routine.

Making a record on Parkinson AI by downloading it from Google Play Store or Apple App Store is excessively basic and takes no longer than a minute. Parkinson AI requires the customer to poise only three fundamental tests, which can be performed on any forefront smartphone—tremor, posture, and finger tap tests—using its cutting-edge AI technique. Parkinson AI's prohibitive ML figuring thus describes the customer as a PD-tolerant or a controlled subject by assessing the power and repetition of signs with a degree of precision. Customers can moreover pursue illness development by coordinating these tests at regular time intervals. Parkinson AI's diet and exercise plans help with impeding PD after some time (www.parkinsonai.com).

They sourced data accumulated during the mPower clinical starter, a large scale, mobile phone-based examination of PD that had 1853 customers that give measurement information and possible prior master discoveries of the disease. It also mentioned the customers a complete list of tests planned to measure improvement, talk, finger capacity, and spatial memory handicaps.

A portable test required the users to keep their phone in their pocket, walk around, turn, and recollect their methods. A voice examination mentioned that they state "aaaah" into their phone's microphones. A tapping test then required them again to tap, and the last test—a memory test—prepared them to go over a list of pictures appearing on a cross section. In the wake of prehandling, the list ended up with 300, 250, 400, and 25 tests for measurement of walk, voice, tapping, and memory tests, respectively.

The results empowered into perceptive models—unequivocally convolutional neural framework for the walk, voice, and tapping test and a discontinuous neural framework with bidirectional long transient memory for the memory test (www.venturebeat.com).

2.6 ROLE OF AI IN DEMENTIA

The word "dementia" delineates a great deal of signs that may be associated with memory loss and difficulties with memory, basic reasoning, or language.

A person with dementia may in like manner experience changes in their perspective or behavior.

Dementia is caused when the psyche is hurt by diseases, like Alzheimer's disease or strokes. Alzheimer's disease is the most outstanding explanation behind dementia but not the only one. The symptoms that someone with dementia experiences will depend upon the parts of the cerebrum that are hurt and the disease that is causing dementia (www.alzheimers.org.uk).

An assessment conducted by the Alzheimer's Association predicts that the Medicare spending on AD is fundamentally increased to $189 billion in 2015, and by mid-century, the cost of treating AD paid by Medicare and Medicaid combined will exceed $1 trillion annually.

A huge gathering of abstract aides, characteristic sensors, video and sound advancements, and advanced composed sensor systems are a work in advancement to screen the prosperity, security, and success of mentally weak persons. Progressive improvement of these headways can improve the idea of care and individual fulfillment of the elderly and family parental figures and delay or thwart the prerequisite for institutional care (i.e., nursing homes).

The number of increasingly settled Americans suffering from Alzheimer's disease and related dementias will essentially increase to 13 million by 2050, as such increased will leads to increase in therapy and care taker. An approach to manage this rising crisis is the progression and utilization of smart assistive advances that make up for the physical and scholarly inadequacies of progressively prepared adults with dementia and, consequently, decrease their inconvenience. The makers coordinated a wide range of building, structuring, and remedial databases to develop savvy scholarly contraptions, physiologic and characteristic sensors, and advanced facilitated sensors that may find future applications in dementia care. An overview of the enduring composition reveals a stunning focus on the physical impairment of progressive young individuals with usually nonprogressive, anoxic, and frightful personality wounds, with a couple of clinical assessments expressly incorporating individuals with dementia. The limits, characteristics, and confinements of each development are trailed by an outline of research methodology limitations that must be overcome to achieve a quantifiable headway to meet the social protection needs of developing America (Barucha et al., 2009).

For predicting dementia, AI cases appear to fall into four critical orders:

Talk monitoring: Companies are using AI to look at talk guides to perceive and screen dementia development.

Restorative image analysis: Companies are making programs using AI to examine breaking down of breadths in the mind to help foresee the start of dementia.

Visual indicators: Companies are getting ready counts to study eye advancement guides to follow and compare the scholarly limit and cerebrum development.

Genetic analysis: Companies are using AI to analyze inherited data to predict the start of dementia.

A leading man-made thinking (AI) PC test can help recognize whether individuals are in the first place of dementia.

Through a movement of request with an instinctive on-screen image, a PC program organized by examiners from Osaka University and Nara Institute of Science and Technology can see whether responses given by individuals show abstract issues.

The reason behind the assessments was to search for direct choices as opposed to the therapeutic imaging used by medicinal centers to characterize the ailment, particularly as the rate of the disease increased. Examiners also expected to cut down the chance of people getting the opportunity to be familiar with being represented a comparative game plan of request by masters choosing if someone is showing up of dementia. Through estimations, the program assesses the look, delay in responses, sound, the degree of activity words and things used, and voice verbalization and audits. These computations relied upon features of talk, language, and appearances from recorded trades with more seasoned individuals, some of whom had been resolved to have dementia notwithstanding other, sound individuals. By virtue of man-made thinking that empowers machines to learn without being adjusted, PCs had the alternative to perceive individuals with dementia from strong controls at a rate of 90% by methods for six requests. Every request took a couple of minutes. Senior maker Takashi Kudo expressed, "If this development is also made, it will end up possible to know whether a more seasoned individual is to start with times of dementia through talks with PC images at home once per day."

"It will ask them to search for helpful help, provoking early end."

The necessity for early mediation is crushing, as someone in general makes dementia predictable. Alzheimer's Disease International, which looks the overall event of dementia – which is an umbrella term for a social affair of symptoms—states that around 50 million people had the disease in 2017.

This number tends to increase altogether, accomplishing 75 million out of 2030 and 131.5 million out of 2050. Research has showed that many individuals with dementia have not been officially investigated, underlining the necessity for less troublesome, progressively accessible ways to deal with to decide whether someone is affected. Almost about 40,000 individuals under the age of 65 years in the United Kingdom have dementia according to the Alzheimer's Society. While there is no fix treatment, drugs can help patients having dynamic existences and manage their symptoms.

KEYWORDS

- **artificial intelligence**
- **healthcare**
- **machine learning**
- **mental wellness**
- **cardio vascular**

REFERENCES

Alves, G., Forsaa, B.E., Pedersen, F.K., Gjerstad, D.M., & Larsen, P.J. (2008). Epidemiology of Parkinson's disease. Journal of Neurology, 5(1), 18–32.

Andreassen, S., et al. (1994). A probabilistic approach to glucose prediction and insulin dose adjustment: description of metabolic model and pilot evaluation study. Computer Methods and Programs in Biomedicine, 41, 153–165.

Ashok, P.P., Radhakrishnan, K., Sridharan, R. and Mousa, E.M. Epidemiology of Parkinson's disease in Benghazi, North-East Libya. Clinical Neurology and Neurosurgery, 88(2), 109–113.

Ayano, G. (2016). Parkinson's disease: a concise overview of etiology, epidemiology, diagnosis, comorbidity and management. Journal of Neurological Disorders, 4(1), 298–300.

Baranowski, T., & Lytle, L. (2015). Should the IDEFICS outcomes have been expected? Obesity Reviews, 16(Suppl. 2), S162–S172. https://doi.org/10.1111/obr.12359

Bardus, M., van Beurden, S.B., Smith, J.R., & Abraham, C. (2016). A review and content analysis of engagement, functionality, aesthetics, information quality, and change techniques in the most popular commercial apps for weight management. The International Journal of Behavioral Nutrition and Physical Activity, 13, 35. https://doi.org/10.1186/s12966-016-03599

Benamer, S.T.H., Silva, D.R., Siddiqui, A.K., & Grosset, G.D. (2010). Parkinson's disease in Arabs: A systematic review. Movement Disorder, 23(9), 1205–1210.

Benevolent AI is Putting AI to Work to Treat Parkinson's Disease in the UK. (n.d.). Retrieved June 2, 2019, from https://labiotech.eu/medical/benevolent-ai-parkinsons-disease/

Bharucha, E.N., Bharucha, P.E., & Bharucha, E.A. (1988). Prevalence of Parkinson's disease in the Parsi community of Bombay, India. Achieves of Neurology, 45(12), 1321–1323.

Bharucha, A.J., Anand, V., Forlizzi, J., Dew, M.A., Reynolds, C.F., Stevens, S., & Wactlar, H. (2009). Intelligent assistive technology applications to dementia care: current capabilities, limitations, and future challenges. The American Journal of Geriatric Psychiatry, 17(2), 88–104. https://doi.org/10.1097/JGP.0b013e318187dde5

Brand, L., Beltran, A., Hughes, S., O'Connor, T., Baranowski, J., Nicklas, T., … Baranowski, T. (2016). Assessing feedback in a mobile videogame. Games for Health Journal, 5(3), 203–208. https://doi.org/10.1089/g4h.2015.0056

Campenhausen, V.S., Bornschein, B., Wick, R., Botzel, K., Sampaio, C., Poewe, W., Oertel, W., Siebert, U., Berger, K., & Dodel, R. (2005). Prevalence and incidence of Parkinson's disease in Europe. European Neurophyscopharmacology, 15(1), 473–490

Carter, B., Rees, P., Hale, L., Bhattacharjee, D., & Paradkar, M.S. (2016). Association between portable screen-based media device access or use and sleep outcomes: a systematic review and meta-analysis. JAMA Pediatrics, 170(12), 1202–1208. https://doi.org/10.1001/jamapediatrics.2016.2341

Clarke, C., Zobkiw, R., & Gullaksen, E. (1995). Quality of life and care in Parkinson's disease. The British Journal of Clinical Practice, 49(6), 288–293.

Council on Communications and Media. (2016). Media use in school-aged children and adolescents. Pediatrics, 138(5), e20162592.

Diabetes: Symptoms, Causes, Treatment, Prevention, and More. (n.d.). Retrieved June 1, 2019, from https://www.healthline.com/health/diabetes#symptoms.

De Lau, L.M., Giesbergen, P.C., de Rijk, M.C., Hofman, A., Koudstaal, P.J., Breteler, M.M. (2004). Incidence of Parkinsonism and Parkinson disease in a general population: the Rotterdam Study. Neurology, 63, 1240–1244.

Eeden, D.V.K.S., Tanner, M.C., Bernstein, L.A., Fross, D.R., Leimpeter, A., Bloch, A.D., & Nelson, M.L. (2003). Incidence of Parkinson's disease: variation by age, gender, and race/ethnicity. American Journal of Epidemiology, 11(1), 1015–1022.

Eloise, H.T., Naismith, L.S., Pereira, M., & Lewis, G.J.S. Quality of life in Parkinson's disease caregivers: the contribution of personality traits. BioMed Research International, 1(1), 1–10.

Engelgau, M. M., Karan, A., & Mahal, A. (2012). The Economic impact of Non-communicable Diseases on households in India. Globalization and Health, 8, 9. https://doi.org/10.1186/1744-8603-8-9

Fang, K.Y., Bjering, H., & Ginige, A. (2018). Adherence, avatars and where to from here. Studies in Health Technology and Informatics, 252, 45–50.

Fulmer, R., Joerin, A., Gentile, B., Lakerink, L., & Rauws, M. (2018). Using psychological artificial intelligence (Tess) to relieve symptoms of depression and anxiety: randomized controlled trial. JMIR Mental Health, 5(4), e64. https://doi.org/10.2196/mental.9782

Ferrara, P., Corsello, G., Ianniello, F., Sbordone, A., Ehrich, J., Giardino, I., & Pettoello-Mantovani, M. (2017). Internet addiction: starting the debate on health and well-being of children overexposed to digital media. The Journal of Pediatrics, 191, 280–281.e1. https://doi.org/10.1016/j.jpeds.2017.09.054

Gomez, E.J., et al. (1992). A telemedicine distributed decision-support system for diabetes management, Proceedings of the 14th Annual International Conference of the IEEE Engineering in Medicine and Biological Society, 1238–1239.

Hirsch, L., Jette, N., Frolkis, A., Steeves, T., & Pringsheim, T. (2016). The incidence of Parkinson's disease: a systematic review and meta-analysis. Neuroepidemiology, 46(4), 292–300. https://doi.org/10.1159/000445751

Hoermann, S., McCabe, K.L., Milne, D.N., & Calvo, R.A. (2017). Application of synchronous text-based dialogue systems in mental health interventions: systematic review. Journal of Medical Internet Research, 19(8), e267. https://doi.org/10.2196/jmir.7023

How AI can improve patient outcomes for type 1 and 2 diabetes. (n.d.). Retrieved June 1, 2019, from https://www.information-age.com/ai-can-improve-patient-zoutcomes-type-1–2 diabetes-123467505/

How it Works—ParkinsonAI. (n.d.). Retrieved June 2, 2019, from https://www.parkinsonai.com/how-it-works.

Jankovic, J., & Aguilar, L.G. (2008). Current approaches to the treatment of Parkinson's disease. Neuropsychiatric Disease and Treatment, 4(4), 743–757.

Jha, K.P., & Chaudhary, N. (2017). Epidemiology of Parkinson's disease in south central India–a longitudinal cohort study. IAIM, 4(7), 8–17.

Kadakol, G.S., Kulkarni, S.S., Kulkarni, B.B., Kulkarni, S.S, Bhaskar, L.V.K.S., Wali, G.M., Datta, N., Hiremath, S.V., & Gai, P.B. (2012). Parkinson's disease in North Karnataka. Antrocom Online Journal of Anthropology, 8(1), 1973–2880.

Kaufman, J.D., Spalt, E.W., Curl, C.L., Hajat, A., Jones, M.R., Kim, S.-Y., ... Adar, S.D. (2016). Advances in understanding air pollution and CVD. Global Heart, 11(3), 343–352. https://doi.org/10.1016/j.gheart.2016.07.004

Kramer, J.-N., Künzler, F., Mishra, V., Presset, B., Kotz, D., Smith, S., ... Kowatsch, T. (2019). Investigating intervention components and exploring states of receptivity for a smartphone app to promote physical activity: protocol of a microrandomized trial. JMIR Research Protocols, 8(1), e11540. https://doi.org/10.2196/11540

Khedr, E., Fawi, G., Muhammad, A., & Zaki, F.A. (2015). Prevalence of Parkinsonism and Parkinson's disease in Qena governorate/Egypt: a cross-sectional community-based survey. Neurological Research, 37(7), 1–10.

Khetan, A., Zullo, M., Hejjaji, V., Barbhaya, D., Agarwal, S., Gupta, R., ... Josephson, R. (2017). Prevalence and pattern of cardiovascular risk factors in a population in India. Heart Asia, 9(2), e010931. https://doi.org/10.1136/heartasia-2017-010931

Krittanawong, C., Zhang, H., Wang, Z., Aydar, M., & Kitai, T. (2017). Artificial intelligence in precision cardiovascular medicine. Journal of the American College of Cardiology, 69(21), 2657–2664. https://doi.org/10.1016/j.jacc.2017.03.571

Lasker R.D. (1993). The diabetes control and complication trial. Implications for policy and practice. The New England Journal of Medicine, 329, 1035–1036.

Lehmann E.D., & Deutsch T. (1995). Application of computers in diabetes care – a review (I and II). Medical Informatics, 20, 281–329.

Liu, C.C., Li, Y.C., Lee, C.P., & Sun, Y. (2016). Variations in incidence and prevalence of Parkinson's disease in Taiwan: a population-based nationwide study. Parkinson's Disease, 1(1), 1–8.

Marbaniang, I.P., Kadam, D., Suman, R., Gupte, N., Salvi, S., Patil, S., ... Mave, V. (2017). Cardiovascular risk in an HIV-infected population in India. Heart Asia, 9(2), e010893. https://doi.org/10.1136/heartasia-2017-010893

Marsh, S., Ni Mhurchu, C., & Maddison, R. (2013). The non-advertising effects of screen-based sedentary activities on acute eating behaviours in children, adolescents, and young adults. A systematic review. Appetite, 71, 259–273. https://doi.org/10.1016/j.appet.2013.08.017

Mehta, P., Kifley, A., Wang, J.J., Rochtchia, E., Mitchell, P., & Sue, M.C. (2007). Population prevalence and incidence of Parkinson's disease in an Australian community. Internal Medicine Journal, 37(1), 812–814.

Moisan, F., Kab, S., Mohammed, F., Canonico, M., Quintin, C., Carcaillon, L., Nicolau, J., Duport, N., Singh, A., Boussac, M., & Elbaz, A. (2017). Parkinson disease male-to-female ratios increase with age: French nationwide study and meta-analysis. Movement Disorders, 87(1), 952–957.

Montani, S. (2019). Artificial intelligence techniques for diabetes management: the TIDDM project. Proceedings of the 14th European Conference on Artificial Intelligence (ECAI), Berlin, Germany, August 20–25, 2000.

Mirza, N., & Ganguly, B. (2016). Utilization of medicines available at home by general population of rural and urban set up of western India. Journal of Clinical and Diagnostic Research, 10(8), FC05–FC09. https://doi.org/10.7860/JCDR/2016/20600.8298

Muthane, U.B., Ragothaman, M., & Gururaj, G. (2007). Epidemiology of Parkinson's disease and movement disorders in India: problems and possibilities. The Journal of the Association of Physicians of India, 55(1), 719–724.

NIMH . (n.d.). Schizophrenia. Retrieved June 1, 2019, from https://www.nimh.nih.gov/health/publications/schizophrenia/index.shtml.

Oommen A.M., Abraham V.J., George K., & Jose V.J. (2016). Prevalence of coronary heart disease in rural and urban Vellore: a repeat cross-sectional survey. Indian Heart Journal, 68(4), 473–479. https://doi.org/10.1016/j.ihj.2015.11.015

Oxford Neuroscience. (n.d.). The role of AI in spotting the onset of Parkinson's disease. Retrieved June 2, 2019, from https://www.neuroscience.ox.ac.uk/news/the-role-of-ai-in-spotting-the-onset-of-parkinson2019s-disease.

Pringsheim, T., Jette, N., Frolkis, A., & Steeves, T. (2014). The prevalence of Parkinson's disease: a systematic review and meta-analysis. Movement Disorders, 29(13), 1583–1586.

Quelly, S. B., Norris, A. E., & DiPietro, J. L. (2016). Impact of mobile apps to combat obesity in children and adolescents: A systematic literature review. Journal for specialists in Pediatric Nursing: JSPN, 21(1), 5–17. https://doi.org/10.1111/jspn.12134

Ramesh, A.N., Kambhampati, C., Monson, J.R.T., & Drew, P.J. (2004). Artificial intelligence in medicine. Annals of the Royal College of Surgeons of England, 86(5), 334–338. https://doi.org/10.1308/147870804290

Rivera, J., McPherson, A., Hamilton, J., Birken, C., Coons, M., Iyer, S., … Stinson, J. (2016). Mobile apps for weight management: a scoping review. JMIR mHealth and uHealth, 4(3), e87. https://doi.org/10.2196/mhealth.5115

Singh, S., Shankar, R., & Singh, G.P. (2017). Prevalence and associated risk factors of hypertension: a cross-sectional study in urban Varanasi. International Journal of Hypertension, 2017, 5491838. https://doi.org/10.1155/2017/5491838

Stephens T.N., Joerin A., Rauws M., & Werk L.N. (2019) Feasibility of pediatric obesity and prediabetes treatment support through Tess, the AI behavioral coaching chatbot. Translational Behavioral Medicine, 9 (3), 443–450

Stephens, T.N., Joerin, A., Rauws, M., & Werk, L.N. (2019). Feasibility of pediatric obesity and prediabetes treatment support through Tess, the AI behavioral coaching chatbot. Translational Behavioral Medicine, 9(3), 440–447. https://doi.org/10.1093/tbm/ibz043

Swain, S., Pati, S., & Pati, S. (2017). A chart review of morbidity patterns among adult patients attending primary care setting in urban Odisha, India: an international classification of primary care experience. Journal of Family Medicine and Primary Care, 6(2), 316–322. https://doi.org/10.4103/2249-4863.220029

Szeto, J., Mowszowski, L., Gilat, M., Walton, C., Naismith, S., & Lewis, S. (2016). Mild Cognitive impairment in Parkinson's disease: impact on caregiver outcomes. Journal of Parkinson's Disease, 6(3), 589–596.

Tallawy, E.N.H., Farghaly, M.W., Shehata, A.G., Rageh, A.T., Hakeem, A.M.N., Mohammed, A.A.H., & Badry, R. (2013). Prevalence of Parkinson's disease and other types of Parkinsonism in Al Kharga district, Egypt. Neuropsychiatric Disease and Treatment, 9(1), 1821–1826.

Thompson, D., & Baranowski, T. (2019). Chatbots as extenders of pediatric obesity intervention: an invited commentary on "Feasibility of Pediatric Obesity & Pre-Diabetes Treatment Support through Tess, the AI Behavioral Coaching Chatbot". Translational Behavioral Medicine, 9(3), 448–450. https://doi.org/10.1093/tbm/ibz065

The Diabetes Control and Complication Trial Research Group (1993). The effect of intensive treatment of diabetes on the development and progression of long-term complications in insulin-dependent diabetes mellitus. The New England Journal of Medicine, 329, 977–986.

Van den Eijnden, R., Koning, I., Doornwaard, S., van Gurp, F., & Ter Bogt, T. (2018). The impact of heavy and disordered use of games and social media on adolescents' psychological, social, and school functioning. Journal of Behavioral Addictions, 7(3), 697–706. https://doi.org/10.1556/2006.7.2018.65

VentureBeat. (n.d.). Google unveils 3 accessibility projects that help people with disabilities. Retrieved June 2, 2019, from https://venturebeat.com/2019/05/07/google-ai-accessibility-project-euphonia-diva-live-relay/

What is Artificial Intelligence (AI)? - Definition from Techopedia. (n.d.). Retrieved June 1, 2019, from https://www.techopedia.com/definition/190/artificial-intelligence-ai.

What is dementia? | Alzheimer's Society. (n.d.). Retrieved June 2, 2019, from https://www.alzheimers.org.uk/about-dementia/types-dementia/what-dementia.

Widrefelt, K., Adami, O.H., Cole, P., Trichopoulos, D., & Mandel, J. Epidemiology and etiology of Parkinson's disease: a review of the evidence. European Journal of Epidemiology, 26(1), S1–S58.

Yasser, A., MacAskill, M., Anderson, T., & Benamer, H. (2017). Parkinson's disease in the Gulf countries: an updated review. European Neurology, 74(1), 222–225.

Zhang, X.Z., & Roman, C.G. (1993). Worldwide occurrence of Parkinson's disease: an updated review. Neuroepidemiology, 12(1), 195–208.

Zou, M.Y., Liu, J., Tian, Y.Z., Lu, D., & Zhou, Y.Y. (2015). Systematic review of the prevalence and incidence of Parkinson's disease in the People's Republic of China. Neuropsychiatric Disease Treatment, 11(1), 1467–1472.

## CHAPTER 3

Case Studies: Healthcare and Deep Learning

ASHISH TRIPATHI[1*], ARUN KUMAR SINGH[1], K. K. MISHRA[2], PUSHPA CHOUDHARY[1], and PREM CHAND VASHIST[1]

[1]*Department of Information Technology, G. L. Bajaj Institute of Technology and Management, Greater Noida, India*

[2]*Department of Computer Science & Engineering, Motilal Nehru National Institute of Technology, Allahabad, India*

Corresponding author. E-mail: ashish.mnnit44@gmail.com

ABSTRACT

As the size of the medical data is increasing day by day, the traditional techniques of data analysis are becoming inefficient to provide accurate and valid information on time. Therefore, to overcome the limitations of the traditional techniques, deep understanding and analysis capabilities are required to detect and diagnose the disease in the early stage. In recent years, several artificially intelligent techniques have been developed for the analysis of different diseases, such as cancer, diabetes, Alzheimer's diseases, and lots more. In this context, deep learning techniques are playing a significant role in analyzing the medical dataset for faster detection and diagnosis of diseases. In this way, these techniques are helping medical research and practitioners working in the healthcare industry. This chapter presents the role of deep learning techniques in the healthcare system. The role of deep learning has been discussed in the analysis and support in clinical decisions and diagnosis of medical images. A tabular detail of the various deep learning techniques applied in the healthcare system has been shown. In the end, we have presented the case study of cancer, diabetes, and Alzheimer's diseases.

3.1 INTRODUCTION

In the current era, healthcare requires technology-enabled smart techniques to manage and analyze abundant biomedical data to ensure the correct measurement of diseases and also recommend the right treatment to the right patient at the right time (Collins and Varmus, 2015). For this, complete information containing several aspects of patient's data is required.

In health-care system, the availability of the huge amount of medical data presents ample opportunities and challenges for biomedical researchers to ensure the availability of better treatment to the patient at minimum cost with improved efficiency. In this context, exploring the association among all the information obtained from different data sets plays a significant role in developing reliable techniques based on machine learning (ML). Previously, it had been tried to build joint knowledge base based on linking multiple data sources with the aim to do predictive analysis and discovery of diseases, and to provide the best treatment for them (Xu et al., 2014; Chen et al., 2015; Wang et al., 2014).

Although, existing deep learning techniques show good result on extracting real-time and valid information with accuracy from medical data set, but still these techniques have not been applied widely on the available medical dataset to get the expected outcome (Bellazzi and Zupan, 2008).

In reality, it has been found that the full use of data is still a big challenge due to its high & multidimensional nature, heterogeneity, temporal dependency and, irregularity (Hripcsak and Albers, 2012; Jensen et al., 2012). Also, it becomes more complicated when the same data is represented in different ways at different places across the data and cause of conflict and inconsistency in decision making (Mohan et al., 2011). In this contest, a continuous effort and innovative techniques are required, which automatically discover the knowledge from the heterogeneous and novel data to ensure the quality of diagnosis in terms of timeliness and accuracy (Bengio et al., 2013).

In recent years, a dramatic growth has been found in the application of deep learning due to massive growth in new datasets and need of computational power (LeCun et al., 2015). Like other domains, healthcare and medicine require deep learning models to process the huge amount of data being generated as well as use of medical devices and digital record system on a large scale (Russakovsky et al., 2015; Hirschberg and Manning, 2015; Hinton et al., 2012; Cireşan et al., 2013).

Deep learning methods could be more appropriate for solving healthcare problems by using its different inbuilt features such as end-to-end learning,

learning with multiple levels of representation, good in exploring the high-dimensional data, and capable of handling complex and heterogeneous data. Unlike traditional ML, deep learning does not require human intervention to guide machines, thus no concern of human error and thus it improves accuracy (LeCun et al., 2015; Miotto et al., 2017).

In recent studies, various capabilities of advanced deep learning techniques have been mentioned such as learning from complex and unstructured data (Miotto et al., 2017; Wei et al., 2017), image recognition using deep convolutional neural networks (CNNs), and text categorization by deep belief networks. Major applications of deep learning in medical diagnosis are health informatics, biomedicine (Mamoshina et al., 2016), magnetic resonance imaging (MRI) and CT scans, and ECG (Kumar et al., 015; Pyakillya et al., 2017), and all these are useful in the diagnosis of severe diseases like cancer, heart disease, and brain tumor. Medical applications such as classification, detection, localization, registration, segmentation, image reconstruction, post-processing, and regression are some specific uses of deep learning in medical field.

Deep learning gives better performance in heterogeneous environment as it learns from raw data as compared to ML and other traditional techniques, and its hidden layers support it to learn abstractions from the given inputs (Miotto et al., 2017). The basis of deep learning is the working capability of neural network that applies general purpose learning procedures to learn from data.

3.2 BACKGROUND AND RELATED WORK

3.2.1 PRESENT SCENARIO

As per the report of the Department of Industrial Policy and Promotion, from financial year 2014 (1.2% of GDP [gross domestic product]) to 2018 (1.4% of GDP), approximately 0.2% growth in the expenditure on public health of the total GDP has been found. In spite of that, in India, expenditure on public health is still at the lowest level as compared to many low-income countries like Sri Lanka and Indonesia. So, Government of India is planning to spend 2.5% of GDP on public health by 2025.

As we know the healthcare sector is a fastest growing industry in India and lots of challenges have been found in recent years due to the complex data, such as insufficient domain knowledge, lack of timeliness, and accuracy in diagnosis of diseases (Esteva et al., 2019). Healthcare sector covers many things such as hospitals, medical research, drug discovery, health insurance, telemedicine, and medical equipment. In fact, this sector generates huge revenue and employment and emerging as one of the fastest and largest growing sectors in India. But here one of the major problems is that this also increases the unmanaged biomedical data, which is complex, unstructured, high-dimensional and heterogenous in nature. Thus, to get the fruitful information from the biomedical data, many artificial intelligence (AI) and ML techniques have been applied previously. But due to distinct nature and rapid growth in data, deep learning methods are very much applicable. Deep learning offers analysis of data with speed and precision which is very much required in the healthcare sector and this ability never seen before in another branch of AI (LeCun et al., 2015).

3.2.2   DEEP LEARNING

ML is a subset of AI that helps systems to learn automatically from the environment as well as self-improvement from experience. It makes predictions or decisions without being explicitly programmed. Deep learning is a specialized branch/subclass of ML that applies supervised and unsupervised learning to learn features directly from the data representations. Deep learning performs feature extraction and transformation based on multiple layers of nonlinear processing units. The connection of AI, ML, and deep learning is shown in Figure 3.1.

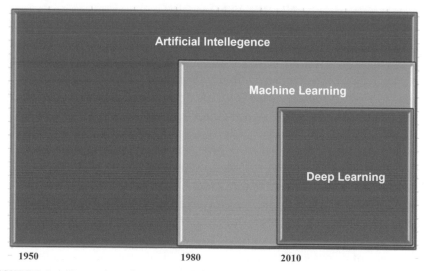

FIGURE 3.1   Connection of AI, ML, and deep learning.

ML applies statistical and data driven rules to convert the given input into the required output. These rules are automatically generated from a large set of examples without use of the explicit human specification. For feature extraction, domain expertise and human engineering are required in a ML system to detect patterns. While, deep learning applies representation learning for pattern recognition. Multiple layers of representation are used in deep learning. These layers are arranged in a sequential manner and contain a large number of nonlinear and primitive operations. A representation of one layer is used as input for the next layer and it continues until optimal representation is obtained.

Deep learning techniques are scalable to large datasets and as an input it can accept multiple data types as shown in Figure 3.2.

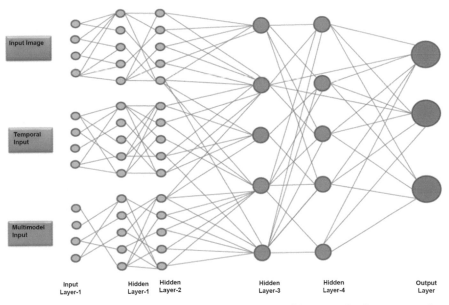

FIGURE 3.2 Representation of deep learning uses a variety of data types for feature extraction.

In deep learning, the network itself capable to perform many tasks that cover filtering and normalization of data that is not possible in the case of the other ML approaches and need human interaction. So, deep learning reduces the preprocessing of data. While, traditional ML approaches are less capable to analyze the natural data in their original form (Esteva et al., 2019). In contrast to ML approaches, deep learning uses automatic representation to perform detection/classification activities. By this way, it reduces the need for supervision and accelerates the process of extracting the action-able insights from the data sets. For example, in healthcare, deep learning applies the multilayered approach to do the classification of data, such as finding noise in clinical data, abnormalities of medical images, formation of clusters based on patient similar characteristics respective to diseases. Due to its architecture, deep learning requires significantly less interaction with programmers to check the accuracy of its result, whereas ML needs more interaction with a human being to check whether the outcome is correct or not.

3.2.2.1   WORKING OF DEEP LEARNING

As traditional artificial neural network (ANN) is the basis of deep learning based on human biological neural networks contains multiple layers and each layer perform required calculations and send the results to the successive layer (Miotto et al., 2017). The number of hidden layers, connection technique and learning capability to extract meaningful information from the given input are the major difference between deep learning and ANN (LeCun et al., 2015).

Deep learning is also known as deep-structured learning or hierarchical learning. Here, deep represents the number of hidden layers in the neural networks. Only two to three hidden layers are available in traditional ANN unlike DNNs have several hidden layers (Rumelhart et al., 1988; Bengio, 2009). So, in deep learning, filtering of data is performed in multiple layers in a cascading mode.

Deep learning uses layered algorithmic architecture for the analysis of data and its accuracy depends on the processing of more and more data. Each successive layer learns from the previous layer and does fine tuning to refine the result. Deep learning trains machine automatically same as the human brain does naturally. It is basically based on the phenomena of connecting biological neurons in the human brain for processing the information. In deep learning no human interaction is required in the learning process like in traditional ML algorithms. Thus, mitigates the overhead on programmer and chances of human error. Deep learning applies representation learning methodologies that contain multiple levels of representation. Here, represen-tation basically holds a set of features which explain the concept individually (LeCun et al., 2015). Another significant feature of deep learning is that during the training session, it can use unlabeled data for feature extraction without the need of human interaction that is very much significant in the case of heterogenous data for learning and acquiring knowledge (Chen and Lin, 2014). The basic architecture of DNNs is shown in Figure 3.3.

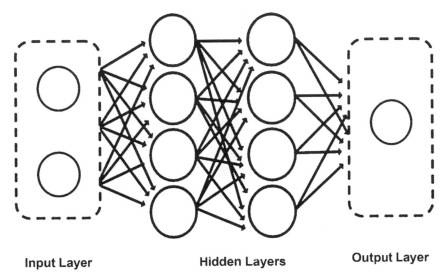

Input Layer   **Hidden Layers**   **Output Layer**

FIGURE 3.3 Deep neural networks with 10 or 100 hidden layers.

Different methods such as DNNs (Le et al., 2011), deep autoencoder, deep belief networks (Hinton et al., 2006), deep Boltzmann machine (DBM), recurrent neural networks (RNNs) (Williams and Zipser, 1989), and CNNs (LeCun et al., 1998, Haykin and Kosko, 2001; Tran et al., 2015) have been designed under deep learning for some specific purposes. Use case of each method depends on the kind of data, type of learning either supervised or unsupervised, and type of activity need to be performed with the data. Thus, the selection of method depends on the said factors that can solve the problem in a better way.

3.2.2.2 DEEP LEARNING IN HEALTHCARE

Deep learning methods help computing to learn directly from data that makes them useful in different applications especially in healthcare. These methods are based on deep architecture and apply hierarchical learning structure that has the ability to integrate heterogeneous data from different datasets. These learning methods allow machines to apply human intelligence to generate high accuracy (Hinton, 2018). In recent years a tremendous growth has been found in the use of ML and AI systems in healthcare (Beam and Kohane, 2018) that relies heavily on human interaction to provide training to machines. But, deep learning methods do not need human interaction for training purposes. They train themselves directly from the data by extracting relevant features using electronic health records (EHRs) and other sources. Deep learning is very much applicable in early detection of diseases, severity of diseases, clinical risk identification, and future probability of hospitalization. In healthcare, deep learning methods help in making clinical decisions specially to detect abnormalities in medical data. Deep learning applies on massive dataset, containing different clinical records of patients and provides a best result using its neural networks. At present, analysis of medical images is a very popular application of deep learning methods. These methods show their performance in automatic detection with high accuracy in skin cancer (Esteva et al., 2017) and diabetic retinopathy (Lee et al., 2019) based on skin images and retinal fundus. Deep learning is helping clinicians to provide better treatment to their patients by extracting hidden patterns and opportunities in the medical data. Medical practitioners are always trying to apply novel approaches to find valid results in healthcare, thus resulting in better medical decisions. Some of the very promising applications of deep learning in healthcarc are as follows.

3.2.2.3 ANALYSIS AND DIAGNOSIS OF MEDICAL IMAGES

CNNs are a type of deep learning methods, especially well-suited for the analysis and diagnosis of medical images (Xu et al., 2016) from different imaging techniques such as CT scans, MRI (Kleesiek et al., 2016), fundus images, X-ray images (Cao et al., 2016; Alcantara et al., 2017). These images are very much suitable for the diagnosis of different critical diseases such as cancer, heart disease, brain hemorrhages, and brain tumor. Researchers from Stanford University claim that CNN is very much efficient to handle big size images.

In a recent survey, CNN has been used in the segmentation of brain pathology (Havaei et al., 2016), computer added detection, shape analysis, and segmentation and shows promising results.

In a study, June 2018, it is found that CNN has identified melanoma with 10% more specificity in the analysis of dermatology images in comparison to medical clinicians. It is also observed that CNN perform better than dermatologist nearly by 7% (Source: https://healthitanalytics.com/features/what-is-deep-learning-and-how-will-it-change-healthcare).

In this context, a DNN has been developed by the team of researchers at the "Mount Sinai Icahn School of Machines" for the diagnosis of neurological problems, such as brain stroke and hemorrhage. The developed deep learning algorithm is found 150 times faster than a radiologist (Source: https://healthitanalytics.com/news/deep-learning-ids-neurological-scans-150-times-faster-than-humans).

In spite of CNN, other deep learning techniques such as use of functional magnetic resonance images in the prediction of Alzheimer's disease (Hu et al., 2016), restricted Boltzmann machine (RBM) for the identification of MRI biomarkers and positron emission tomography (PET) scans with 6% improved classification accuracy as compared to other existing approaches (Li et al., 2015), use of DBM on 3D brain images to get a latent hierarchical feature representation (Kuang and He, 2014), DNN to solve the problem of image labeling (Lerouge et al., 2015), group method of data handling, a multilayered architecture to identify the spleen and liver (Kondo et al., 2014) have also been used for medical imaging and shows outstanding results.

3.2.2.4 PRECISION MEDICINE AND DRUG DISCOVERY

Deep learning helps in precision medicine and the discovery of drugs through identifying the best treatment and prevention techniques to cure diseases. For the analysis purposes, both tasks are used massive volume of genomic, clinical, environmental, person's lifestyle, and other population-specific data. Deep learning provides a platform for the medical researchers and drug stakeholders to explore new patterns in these data sets. Thus, this helps researchers and clinician to understand hidden patterns and other information that is significant to provide better clinical treatment, prevention mechanism, and discovery of genuine medicines for a specific disease. Nowadays, research is going on the use of the effective combination of predictive analysis and molecule-based modeling in deep learning to find the root cause of developing certain types of cancer in people. It is expected that the deep learning will help to analyze the data rapidly and processing time will also be reduced from months/weeks to a few hours.

Many private companies are committed to research in precision medicine. In January 2018, GE Healthcare and Roche Diagnostic announced that they will jointly use deep learning methods for the analysis of critical data sets to develop precision medicines. They will decide to use the combination of data from different sources such as EHR data, in-vivo/in-vitro data, real time data and guidelines for clinical activities to take

effective clinical decisions (Source: https://healthitanalytics.com/features/
what-is-deep-learning-and-how-will-it-change-healthcare). After successful
application of deep learning methods on the combined dataset, in future,
it may be expected that the number of biopsies can be reduced in case
of cancer. In a study, the University of Massachusetts has published its
article in "JMIR Medical Informatics" that deep learning shows much
better than traditional approaches in the identification of "adverse drug
events" with high accuracy (Source: https://healthitanalytics.com/news/
deep-learning-spots-adverse-drug-events-in-unstructured-ehr-data).

3.2.2.5   *PREDICTIVE ANALYSIS AND SUPPORT IN CLINICAL DECISIONS*

Nowadays, healthcare industries and clinicians are showing their lots of
expectation from deep learning for the support in making valid clinical
decisions, predictive analysis of the diseases and showing the possible
outcomes while considering various conditions. In the coming future, it may
be possible that deep learning will be worked as a diagnostic expert in the
inpatient setting and helpful to take decisions in high-risk medical conditions
such as blood disorders, metabolic disorders, and neurological issues.

For example, a project named "ICU Intervene" based on deep learning
has been developed by MIT (CSAIL) researchers, to provide real-time alerts
to clinicians about the patient downturns in the intensive care unit (Source:
https://healthitanalytics.com/news/mit-uses-deep-learning-to-create-icu-
ehr-predictive-analytics).

Google is also working in healthcare to provide a decision support
system for eye diseases. Currently, its subsidiary company "DeepMind"
is working for developing deep learning tool to identify more than 50
different types of eye diseases and appropriate treatment decision for each
one (Source: https://healthitanalytics.com/news/google-backed-deepmind-
creates-deep-learning-cds-for-eye-diseases).

In the same context, an article has been published in *Nature*; it is found
that the proposed deep learning tool maintains accuracy as compared to
clinicians (De Fauw et al., 2018).

According to "DeepMind" scanning through optical coherence tomography is generally used by eye care practitioners to diagnose the eye
condition. This tool presents the detail images of the back of the eye in 3D
form. But, these images are very tough to understand and thus require a
deep analysis system to understand and interpret in the understandable form
when somebody needs urgent treatment. It is possible with deep learning that

can analyze the several scanned images rapidly and could reduce the delay between scan and treatment in a fast forward mode without compromising the quality of treatment.

For taking clinical decisions, EHR is a valid source to collect patient complete medical history, such as treatment and medication activities, test result of different laboratory experiences, clinical diagnosis, and future probability of hospitalization. Such massive volumes of data are required for efficient mining to produce quality results and help in disease management (Andreu-Perez et al., 2015).

Deep learning methods are automatically scaled up to manage massive and distributed data sets. These methods are capable to identify the novel patterns/features from the heterogenous data sets. Thus, deep learning has been adopted in the research of medical informatics to help in clinical decisions and predictive analysis. In a study, CNN has identified the semantic information from the radiology images and respective results (Shin et al., 2016). An effective method for training on large-scale hypertension datasets is proposed by Liang et al. (2014) to perform the effective analysis and produce fruitful information.

In another study, Markers have been identified to predict the human chronological age, from simple blood tests through DNN (Putin et al., 2016). It is already illustrated in literature that DNN has equipped with higher prediction accuracy rather than other traditional approaches. Automatic feature extraction from the EHR database can be achieved by noise reduction in autoencoders without need of additional human interaction (Miotto et al., 2016).

3.2.2.6 SUSTAINABLE PUBLIC HEALTH

Public health is a major issue covers many things in respect to diseases such as identification and prevention measures, healthcare promotion, environmental factors (e.g., air quality), lifestyle, and social behavior. Population plays a vital role in the sustainable public health. Large populations may affect the quality of medication due to large geographical area and unavailability of proper healthcare facility to cover all patients. Many issues such as prediction of disease at the right time, proper medication and drug safety need to be acknowledged and required valid predictive methods to analyze the huge volume of data.

Conventional predictive methods are scalable with the size of data, but they are very much complex, slow in processing, and lack of accuracy required. These methods also require parameterized data that can only be provided by the experts. Also, limited ability to incorporate real-time data is a big issue in monitoring the effect of analysis in disease identification, recommendation of medicine, effect of medicine for the patient, and so on.

In contrast, methods of deep learning are equipped with powerful ability to solve the problem in a generalized way. They do not require human interaction to analyze the data and required information retrieval. Due to these reasons, deep learning methods are recommended as key analysis methods for public health (Huang et al., 2015).

In a report, annual deaths around 60,000 people have been recorded due to poor air quality and it is the major cause of growth of chronic diseases (Ong et al., 2016).

We can see that social media, which is a part of society, can be a rich source of real-time information about the progress track of the various virus infected diseases (influenza, Ebola, and encephalitis). A group of researchers has used the social media services for tracking the continuous health status of the public (Zhao et al., 2015). Exploring the epidemic features can help to understand the cause of progress of diseases and DNN can be very much suitable for this purpose. In a study, twitter posts on antibiotic-related information is categorized into nine different classes using DBN (Kendra et al., 2015). A pretrained RBM-based deep learning method has been used to track the progress of diseases and fine tuning is based on labelled data and back propagation. To identify different types of infections such as norovirus, food poisoning, and campylobacter, deep learning has being used to make a list of keywords (Zou et al., 2016). In literature, it is found that data collected from social media are comparable to the official records about the diseases and shows that it can be used as a good predictor for different diseases. So, by this way of providing medical information in the social media will provide a pathway to do fruitful research and better analysis to strengthen the public health (Horvitz and Mulligan, 2015).

3.3   CHALLENGES AND OPPORTUNITIES

Although deep learning techniques have achieved substantial improvements over ML algorithms in solving healthcare problems and obtained promising results, there remain several challenges need to be recognized and solved by applying appropriate clinical applications of deep learning in the healthcare system. One major challenge is the acceptance of deep learning by physicians due to their doubt on the validity of the results produced by deep learning. Physicians also fear that deep learning is emerging as a substitute of physicians and they will be replaced by deep learning in coming future.

On the contrary, deep learning should be taken at a hand in reducing the work pressure, allowing the physicians to focus on critical portion of the disease, and help them in the diagnosis and treatment activities. In particular, the following issues are considered in the healthcare system.

3.3.1 QUANTITY OF DATA

Construction of the basic brain architecture is an ongoing process that starts from before birth and continues to adulthood. First, learning starts from simple neural connections and basic skills generations among neurons followed by complex circuit and skills. Every second million of new neural connections are formed for some period of time. After that pruning starts which makes brain circuit more efficient.

Deep learning models are somehow based on a human brain architecture that is a group of highly intensive computational models. A multilayer neural network is an example of deep learning, where millions of network parameters are required to be optimized properly to solve any problem. The optimal solution is based on the availability of data on a large scale. Deep learning is very much useful in domains where huge amount of data can be easily available, for example, natural language processing, speech recognition, and computer vision. As a great part of the population has no access to primary healthcare facilities. Consequently, availability of the patient's data for the training of deep learning modules on a particular disease is comparatively very less as required. Deep learning models need tens of millions of sample data when they are applied on heterogenous and complex states of diseases such as chronic heart disease, kidney failure, and cancer to make a reliable and authenticated clinical model for fruitful diagnosis. For example, in the classification of diabetic retinopathy and skin cancer, learning model has been required 128,175 retinal images (Gulshan et al., 2016) and 129,450 skin images (Esteva et al., 2017), respectively. Thus, in many clinical activities, unavailability of huge amount of reliable data is a big issue in healthcare.

3.3.2 QUALITY OF DATA

In the healthcare sector, medical data are highly unstructured, heterogeneous, unorganized, and ambiguous in comparison to other domains. Thus, training deep learning models is a very challenging task in the presence of such huge and scattered data sets. Several issues need to be considered, for example, missing value, data redundancy, less significant data during the training session. EHRs are an example that contain these types of data for a patient. In this context, it is very difficult task for deep learning models to do the pattern recognition from such type of scattered and noisy data (Gianfrancesco et al., 2018).

3.3.3   TEMPORAL ASPECT OF DISEASE

Considering the temporal aspect of disease in the development of deep learning techniques requires temporal data to handle and develop a novel solution. Here, temporal aspect means disease progresses and changes over time that happens in a nondeterministic way (Cheng et al., 2016). Thus, skipping these aspects is a big issue in the proposed techniques so far in healthcare domain (Mehrabi et al., 2015).

3.3.4   COMPLEXITY OF DOMAIN

The healthcare domain is very much complicated in comparison to other domains (e.g., natural language processing, visual recognition, fraud detection, entertainment) due to heterogeneous nature and less knowledge about the cause and progress pattern of diseases (Liang et al., 2014). In fact, it requires a large number of patients for a particular disease to do the clinical analysis, which is practically not feasible most of the time (Pham et al., 2017).

3.3.5   MODEL INTERPRETABILITY

Deep learning models present end to end learning and appear as black-boxes that take data as input and generate output without providing a clear explanation about the basis of prediction. For example, a patient has been diagnosed melanoma with a 0.8 probability, by a deep learning model. In this context, a clear interpretability is required for prediction to convenience the medical practitioners. Deep learning models are viewed with skepticism if they state only the diagnosis. Thus, clear interpretation of the diagnosis of models is a big challenge for the complex clinical practices (Noh et al., 2015).

TABLE 3.1 Result of Research Articles of Deep Learning Techniques in Medical Diagnosis

Author/Reference	Method/Model	Application/Work	Source of Data
de Vos et al. (2016)	CNN	The result shows that the 2D images can be used for 3D localization of anatomical regions	CT
Dou et al. (2017)	CNN	Automated medical image segmentation for liver, heart, and great vessels	MRI
Pan et al. (2015)	CNN	Analysis of multiphase MRI images for grading brain tumor and present grading performance based on sensitivity and specificity. The result shows 18% improvement in the performance on grading using convolutional neural network (CNN)	MRI
Payan and Montana (2015)	CNN	Prediction of Alzheimer disease. The proposed method is far better than existing classifiers. For prediction of the disease status algorithm have used the MRI scan of the brain	MRI
Dubrovina et al. (2018)	CNN	Done classification of breast tissue automatically. Detection of high accuracy on pectoral muscles, that is, 0.83 and lower accuracy on nipple, that is, 0.56	Mammography images
Acharya et al. (2017)	CNN	Automatic detection of a normal and Myocardial Infraction (MI) ECG beats. Average accuracy with noise is 93.53 percent and without noise is 95.22%	ECG
Mehta et al. (2017)	CNN	Automated segmentation of human brain structures	CT
Esteva et al. (2017)	CNN	Successful diagnosis of skin cancer by deep convolutional neural network (CNN). Satisfactory result obtained similar to the diagnosis of 21 board certified dermatologists	Clinical image
Bar et al. (2015)	CNN	Successful detection of chest radiograph data over a dataset of 93 images	X-ray
Kamnitsas et al. (2017)	CNN	Segmentation of brain lesion using multiscale 3D CNN. Mainly three MRI data of the patient has been considered such as traumatic brain injuries, brain tumors, and ischemic stroke	MRI
Mohamed et al. (2018)	CNN	Breast density classifier has been proposed for radiologist to better distinguish two breast density categories, that is, scattered and heterogenous for realistic diagnosis of breast cancer.	Mammography Images

TABLE 3.1   *(Continued)*

Author/Reference	Method/Model	Application/Work	Source of Data
González et al. (2018)	CNN	CNN has been used for staging and prognosis of diseases caused by smoking	CT
Looney et al. (2017)	CNN	Fully automated 3D ultrasound segmentation is used for the placenta to understand the complication of the pregnancy in the first trimester	The 3D ultrasound data
Choi and Jin (2016)	CNN	Striatum segmentation through two serial CNN (global and local). The speed and accuracy of the proposed approach give expected results in the analysis of brain images and other clinical trials	MRI
Bejnordi et al. (2017)	CNN	The better performance of the proposed algorithm in the detection of lymph node metastases in women breast cancer as compared to a panel of pathologists	Images from digital slider
Kleesiek et al. (2016)	CNN	This work presents an algorithm for brain segmentation and shows its usefulness in other clinical activities. The results are very promising and comparable to other existing algorithms	MRI
Rasti et al. (2017)	CNN	Diagnosis of breast cancer has been presented 96.39% accuracy, 97.73% sensitivity, and 94.87% specificity	MRI
Anirudh et al. (2016)	CNN	Detection of lung nodule through 3D CNN is proposed in this article. For training a network, weak label information is used and air tracts in the lungs are excluded by 3D segmentation. Thus, reduces the false positive with a high sensitivity	CT
Roth et al. (2015)	CNN	Presents pancreas segmentation using fully automated bottom-up technique. From 46.6%–68.8% average segmentation accuracy has been maintained by the proposed algorithms	CT
Pratt et al. (2016)	CNN	Diabetic retinopathy diagnosis on 80,000 image data set. Accuracy and sensitivity of the diagnosis are 75% and 95%, respectively	Digital fundus images
Bayramoglu et al. (2016)	CNN	Presents classification of breast cancer histopathology images with two different techniques such as single task CNN and multitask CNN.	Histopathology image
Fu et al. (2016)	CNN	The proposed method improves the performance of retina vessel segmentation by reducing the number of false positive	Fundus images

TABLE 3.1 *(Continued)*

Author/Reference	Method/Model	Application/Work	Source of Data
Akkus et al. (2017)	CNN	Presents the review of deep learning based methods for brain segmentation. Reviews the segmentation of anatomical brain structures and brain lesions through deep learning architecture. Also summarized the features of different deep learning algorithms	MRI
Moeskops et al. (2016)	CNN	Automatic brain segmentation is proposed and the performance of the algorithm is dependent on several key activities.	MRI
Bejnordi et al. (2018)	CNN	Proposal covers the identification and classification of stroma (tumor-associated) from breast biopsy. In this work 2387 digital images have been used for investigating abnormalities among 882 patients. The proposed deep learning algorithm successfully defines the ductal carcinoma (stromal features) in situ grade	Digital images
Li et al. (2018)	CNN	Identification of gastric cancer shows 100% classification accuracy in the result in comparison to other state-of-the-art techniques.	Gastric images
Chmelik et al. (2018)	CNN	The proposed work addresses the lytic and sclerotic metastatic lesions segmentation and classification. The result shows that the proposed algorithm gives better performance in comparison to other algorithms with high accuracy	CT
Causey et al. (2018)	CNN	Lung cancer diagnosis based on lung nodule malignancy prediction. Obtained prediction accuracy was 99%, which is comparable to the accuracy of an experienced radiologist	CT
Prasoon et al. (2013)	CNN	Osteoarthritis risk prediction through automatic segmentation technique on knee cartilage images	MRI
Gulshan et al. (2016)	CNN	Automatic detection of diabetic retinopathy and macular edema in retinal fundus images	Fundus images
Esteva et al. (2017)	CNN	Automatic classification of skin cancer, which is comparable to expert dermatologist	Clinical images

TABLE 3.1 *(Continued)*

Author/Reference	Method/Model	Application/Work	Source of Data
Liu et al. (2015)	CNN	Risk prediction based on an EHR report for heart failure and chronic pulmonary disease	EHR
Nguyen et al. (2012)	CNN	A novel deep learning method has been proposed to automatically identify future risk from the available medical records. Also predict unplanned repetition of disease after discharge	EHR
Zhou and Troyanskaya (2015)	CNN	They have developed an algorithm to predict the effect of chromatin of alteration in DNA sequences	Genomics
Kelley et al. (2016)	CNN	Introduces Basset, an open source package to learn functional activity from DNA sequences	Genomics
Alipanahi et al. (2015)	CNN	Automatic prediction of sequence specificities of DNA and RNA binding proteins	Genomics
Angermueller et al. (2016)	CNN	Prediction of missing methylation states from NDA (single cell) sequences	Genomics
Koh et al. (2017)	CNN	Proposed techniques to map suboptimal to a high-quality dataset in the estimation for several chromatin marks in individuals, species and cell types. The method is helpful in maintaining data quality and cost reduction	Genomics
Ahmed et al. (2016)	DBN-NN	Automatic detection and diagnosis of breast cancer. Overall 99.68% accuracy, 100% sensitivity, and 99.47% specificity have been obtained in the result	Mammography
Cheng et al. (2016)	SADE	Detection and diagnosis of breast lesion and pulmonary nodule: it presents the diagnosis of the benign and malignant nodules. It is found that deep learning techniques can be able to modify/change the CAD system without using explicit design	Breast ultrasound and lung CT
Danaee et al. (2017)	SADE	Works on gene data expression to detect cancer. Results show that the proposed method is very much suitable to manage genes and cancer prediction	Medical images
Youjun et al. (2015)	UGRNN	Prediction of drug-induced liver injury: this model has 86.9% prediction accuracy, 82.5% sensitivity, and 92.9% specificity. The given model provides a significantly better result in comparison to the existing DILI models	Medical datasets

TABLE 3.1 *(Continued)*

Author/Reference	Method/Model	Application/Work	Source of Data
Gao et al. (2015)	CRNN	The proposed method is useful in the clinical management of the cataract, and it can be applied in the diagnosis of other eye diseases	Fundus images
Masood et al. (2015)	SA-SVM	Automatic diagnosis system for skin cancer: the proposed learning model gives promising result in the absence of required labeled data	Dermoscopic images
Han et al. (2017)	CSDCNN	This paper presents multiclassification of breast cancer with accuracy of 93.2% on large scale dataset	Mammography images
Havaei et al. (2017)	DNN	This work is dedicated to brain tumor segmentation and the whole brain has been segmented within 25 s to 3 min.	MRI
Zhang et al. (2016)	RBM	Presents breast tumor classification with 93.4% accuracy, 88.6% sensitivity, and 97.1% specificity in the result	Shear wave elastography
Cha et al. (2016)	DL-CNN	Automatic computerized segmentation system for unary bladder by DL-CNN	CT urography (CTU)
Lsensee et al. (2017)	U-Net	Applies U-Net architecture for the segmentation of brain tumor	MRI
Dalmis et al. (2017)	U-Net	Proposes the segmentation of breast and fibroglandular tissue using U-Net. The average value of DSC for breast and FGT segmentation from 3C U-net (0.933 and 0.850), 2C U-nets (0.944 and 0.811), and atlas-based method (0.863 and 0.671)	MRI
Kumar et al. (2015)	CAD	Classification of lung nodule using deep features of the CAD system with 75.01% accuracy, 83.35% sensitivity, 0.39% false positive	CT
Sun et al. (2016)	CNN, DBN, SADE	Diagnosis of lung cancer using three deep learning algorithms. Accuracy is the result obtained by three algorithms is CNN (0.7976), DBN (0.8119), and SADE (0.7929). DBN has achieved the highest accuracy	CT
Samala et al. (2016)	DL-CNN	The authors have presented detection techniques for micro classification in digital breast tomosynthesis. The best result obtained by operating characteristic curve (AUC) is 0.93	Planar projection image

TABLE 3.1 *(Continued)*

Author/Reference	Method/Model	Application/Work	Source of Data
Wang et al. (2017)	DCNN	Proposes the predictive analysis of prostate cancer through deep learning and "nondeep learning" techniques Accuracy, sensitivity, and specificity of deep learning is 84%, 69.6%, and 83.9%, respectively, while "nondeep learning" technique gives 70%, 49.4%, and 81.7%, respectively, accuracy, sensitivity, and specificity	MRI
Xu et al. (2016)	SSAE	Breast cancer detection through nuclei detection strategy. The proposed SSAE approach can perform better than other state-of-the-art nuclear detection strategies. SSAE shows improvement in F-measure, that is, 84.49% and in AveP, that is, 78.83%	Digital pathology images

SADE: self-adaptive differential evolution, SSAR: stacked sparse autoencoder, UGRNN: update gate recurrent neural network, DILI: drug-induced liver injury, DSC: dice similarity coefficient, CAD: computer-aided diagnosis, SADE: self-adaptive differential evolution, DCNN: deep convolutional neural network, SSAR: sparse stack autoencoder, Class, CSDCNN: structure-based deep convolutional neural network, SA-SVM: simulated annealing-support vector machine, CRNN: convolutional recurrent neural network, DBN-NN: deep belief network-neural network.

3.4 LITERATURE SURVEY

This survey includes systematic review of the practical implementation of deep learning techniques in healthcare system. Different applications of deep learning in medical diagnosis and drug discovery have been considered for this survey. A wide variety of research publications have been taken to ensure the quality of the work. Table 3.1 shows the brief review of research articles of deep learning techniques in medical detection and diagnosis.

3.5 CASE STUDY

Deep learning is a new branch of ML, which based on unsupervised learning and using deep ANNs to study a specific pattern for mapping input to output. Unsupervised learning works just like a newborn baby which does not have any knowledge about his surroundings, but with his instincts, he learned lots of things (Cruz and Wishart, 2006; Cicchetti, 1992).

From its origin, deep learning has been applied to many problems to resolve the challenges of ML algorithms successfully especially in the case of healthcare (Cochran, 1997; Kononenko, 2001; Park et al., 2013; Sun et al., 2006).

In different critical diseases, deep learning is providing promising results as compared to other existing conventional ML algorithms. In this section, case study on three severe diseases such as cancer, diabetes, and Alzheimer has been covered.

3.5.1 CASE STUDY: CANCER

In recent years tremendous growth in cancer patient near to 14 million around the world has been found and they face uncertainty for their life. So, the accurate and real-time information about the cancer is highly recommended to take the necessary action by the clinicians. In some cases, disease identification is fruitful for the medical professionals to provide the right remedy to the patient on time while in most of the cases without correct estimation of the disease may cause of serious illness or death.

Some pathological results have been found more accurate in cancer prediction. But as per the report of Oslo University Hospital, it provides only 60% accuracy in the prognosis of cancer that is a part of the biopsy

(Source: https://towardsdatascience.com/machine-learning-is-the-future-of-cancer-prediction-e4d28e7e6dfa).

Many researchers have been studied on the collected date given by hospitals and applied deep learning for the prediction of esophageal cancer with avoidance of expensive and invasive diagnosis. This type of cancer found in the esophagus. The esophagus is a vacant tube (i.e., food-pipe) that starts from throat to stomach. This helps to swallow the food. Esophageal cancer highly affect the food pipe and further treatment because these diagnosis go through mouth of the person such as various kinds of imaging tests using X-rays (Barium swallow/CT scan), magnetic fields (MRI scan), endoscopy (a camera in a tube, passed down the throat), or even a biopsy (a small piece of tissue removed and examined) (Source: https://researchmatters.in/news/machine-learning-lends-hand-cancer-prediction; Yala et al., 2019; Cruz and Wishart, 2006).

The upcoming new research in cancer prediction focuses on to mitigate all traditional tests and false-negative rate. At the initial stage, it requires various demographic details about the patient such as the use of tobacco, alcohol, smoking, and other medical histories for prediction. The algorithms used for predication are classification algorithms, logistic regression, support vector machine (SVM), random forest, and naive Bayes classifier. By developing serial images of tumors with nonsmall cell lung cancer can predict and provide better cure against clinical diagnosis (Source: https://eurekalert.org/pub_releases/2019–04/aafc-adm041819.php). In a study, it has been found that near about 85% death is caused by lung cancer. In this respect, a neural network-based tool named "ImageNet" is created by researchers at Princeton University and Stanford University to do the correct prediction of lung cancer.

Breast cancer is a kind of cancer that is growing rapidly in women all over the world due to modern lifestyle. In a report, it is found that in the early stage, if cancer is diagnosed successfully with one of the two existing techniques, that is mammography and biopsy then patient survival rate can be enhanced by 80% (World Health Organization, 2014). For the early prediction of breast cancer, a new tool with advanced AI features has been proposed to identify the amount of dense tissue compared to the amount of fatty tissue in a mammogram (Source: https://www.technologynetworks.com/cancer-research/news/using-ai-to-predict-future-risk-of-breast-cancer-319067).

In mammography, breast images are analyzed by the radiologist, while in biopsy a sample of tissue from the affected breast area is examined for recognition and categorization of the tumor through a microscope by a pathologist (Khan et al., 2019). "Benign and Malignant" are the two classifications of tumors in the biopsy. Benign cells are noncancerous and do not invade or spread nearby tissues and other parts of the body respectively. Fibroids and lipomas are examples of the benign tumor (López et al., 2012). Malignant tumors are cancerous and can affect nearby tissues. They start invading from breast tissue to lymph nodes and start spreading other parts of the body such as bones and lever. A biopsy helps to identify the properties of breast cancer tumor (Pöllänen et al., 2014).

In deep learning, CNN is a subclass of DNNs mainly focuses on feature learning that is automatically learned through demonstration of data (LeCun et al., 1998).

In a research work for the correct prediction of the occurrence of spontaneous breast cancer, Listgarten et al. (2004) has used single-nucleotide polymorphism (SNP) profiles of steroid metabolizing enzymes (CYP450s). In all types of breast cancer, spontaneous/nonfamilial breast cancers cover about 90% (Dumitrescu and Cotarla, 2005). This research work is based on a certain permutation of steroid-metabolism gene SNPs that may enhance the improved addition of ecological toxins/hormones in breast tissue, which is the cause of high probability of occurring breast cancer.

Deep learning using the various decision tree models along with a SVM technique to get the maximum accuracy using the SNPs data and prediction power depends upon the model. Validation and accuracy are based on the training methods like cross-validation, bootstrap, and resampling method.

SVM and naïve Bayes techniques have used a set of three SNPs with the highest accuracy while decision tree has used only a set of two SNPs and obtained the highest accuracy in the result. In the case of breast cancer prediction accuracy percentage obtained by SVM, naïve Bayes and decision tree are 69%, 67%, and 68%, respectively.

In recent years, research work in deep learning has been accelerated in cancer prediction that is the most popular disease and images have the dominant role in the analysis (Jiang et al., 2017). Especially cancer research is based on two types of activities such as radiology and pathology. Several recent works on deep learning has included large datasets to train the model and shows comparable results to that of the diagnostic experts across a range of images such as CT scan (Merkow et al., 2017), MRI (Jamaludin et al., 2017), chest X-ray (Rajpurkar et al., 2017), and mammography (Kooi et al., 2017). In research, it is found that CT scan of chest can reduce the mortality rate of lung cancer (Setio et al., 2017).

Lots of work have been done in organ/lesion segmentation including a range of organs and different pathological forms that support deep analysis and present it as an automated system (Litjens et al., 2017). Segmentation tasks may include neuroimaging involves brain tumors, the normal structure of the brain and nonneoplastic lesions (Akkus et al., 2017).

In past, conventional methods have identified numerous types of cancers such as breast cancer (Mazurowski et al., 2014), renal cell cancer (Karlo et al. 2014), and glioblastoma based on the correlation between molecular subtype and prognosis. In contrast, similar work done by deep learning methods has shown promising results based on imaging (Akkus et al., 2017; Korfiatis et al., 2017; Li et al., 2017; Ning et al., 2018; Zhu et al., 2019).

In 2017, a seminal article presents the identification of metastatic breast cancer deposits in lymph nodes (Ehteshami et al., 2017). In this article, 129 WSIs lymph nodes' test set has been used for prediction by 23 teams and has been compared with two benchmarks set by human experts. In comparison to the pathologist, deep learning methods have shown their potential as comparable to pathologist level performance.

In another study, CNN has been applied on 5000 slides for thirteen different types of cancer to map the patterns of "tumor-infiltrating lympho-cytes" and make a correlation with molecular subtypes and survival (Saltz et al., 2018). In the proposed work, a limited number of slides have been used to train the initial model iteratively. Further, pathologists have been used to correct the predictions of this model and feedback for the same has been used as an additional training sample. The whole process has been continued until a satisfactory result found. To ease the morphology-based research, this study provides a way to use the automated image processing in an efficient way that may not be possible if every slide needs a clear annotation by pathologists.

ImageNet is a CNN tool that has been used to solve the Large-Scale Visual Recognition Challenge challenges with error rate close to the Bayes rate in 2012. This tool has combined sensitive parameters based on huge heterogeneous medical data sets of health informatics and predicts accurate and decisional result (Krizhevsky et al., 2012).

Figure 3.4 shows how CNN uses pathological images for cancer prediction. During the training phase, the role of the pathologist is to select the interesting regions on available slide images. These images are then cropped into small slices and used for CNN as for training purposes. Then backpropagation is applied for adjusting the model parameters to generate a prediction on a slice of images. In the testing phase, thresholding has been used to identify the regions of tissue on the slides which are already used by trained CNN. Then prediction on each slice is generated by the model and finally all predictions are aggregated to form a slide level prediction.

Recently, this approach has been used to show the promising result in the identification of invasive ductal breast carcinoma (Cruz-Roa et al., 2014).

In another study, to predict the status of speckle-type POZ protein, deep learning has been used to identify the most abnormal regions on slides for prostate cancer (Schaumberg et al., 2018). In this work, authors have applied a novel technique to identify the problem related to an imbalance in the dataset due to mutations by creating a group of multiple models trained on a dataset having positive and negative numbers of matched slides. In a case of lung cancer, a similar approach has been applied for the prediction of driver mutations in adenocarcinoma and outcomes based on morphological features through deep learning (Coudray et al., 2018; Wang et al., 2018). To understand the clinical behavior of genomic profiling, the deep learning-based model has been providing better support and it further can be used in a combination with image processing to refine the result for better predictions (Chaudhary et al., 2018; Savage and Yuan, 2016).

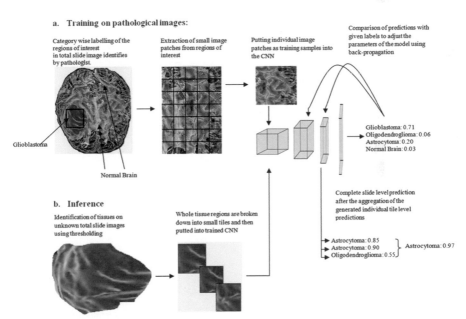

FIGURE 3.4 Role of CNN for image analysis.

Source: Adapted from Levine et al., 2019

A brief overview of deep learning methods has given in Table 3.2 that shows their results on various parameters.

TABLE 3.2 Breast Cancer Identification With Validation Method and Accuracy

Publication	Method	No. of Patients	Type of Data	Accuracy (%)	Validation Method	Important Features
Ayer et al. (2010)	ANN	62, 219	Mammograph, demographic	96	10-fold cross validation	Age, mammography findings
Listgarten et al. (2004)	SVM	174	SNPs	69	20-fold cross validation	snpCY11B2 (+) 4536 T/C snpCYP1B1 (+) 4328 C/G
Kim et al. (2017)	SVM	679	Clinical, pathologic, epidemiologic	89	Hold-out	Local invasion of tumor
Park et al. (2014)	Graph-based SSL algorithm	374	Clinical, pathologic	68	Hold-out	Pathologic_S, Pathologic_T, cell type RT target summary
Eshlaghy et al. (2013)	SVM	547	Clinical, population	95	10-fold cross validation	Age at diagnosis, age at menarche
Park et al. (2013)	Graph-based SSL algorithm	162,500	SEER	71	5-fold cross validation	Tumor size, age at diagnosis, number of nodes
Xu et al. (2012)	SVM	295	Genomic	97	Leave-one-out cross	50-gene signature
Gevaert et al. (2006)	BN	97	Clinical, microarray	AUC = 0.851	Hold-Out	Age, angioinvasion, grade MMP9, HRASLA and RAB27B genes
Delen et al. (2005)	DT	2,000,000	SEER	93	Cross validation	Age at diagnosis, tumor size, number of nodes, histology
Kim and Shin (2013)	SSL Co-training algorithm	162,500	SEER	76	5-fold cross validation	Age at diagnosis, tumor size, number of nodes, extension of tumor

3.5.2   CASE STUDY: ALZHEIMER

Alzheimer is a chronic neurodegenerative disease that occurs due to progressive neurological disorder. This is usually starts with gradual death of brain cells and cause of memory loss and thinking skills (Burns and Iliffe, 2009). It is the main cause of dementia that affects the ability of a person to work independently. It starts with an early sign of forgetting recent activities like conversation, remembering objects (World Health Organization. Dementia—a public health priority 2017, Source: http:// www.who.int/mental_health/neurology/dementia/infographic_dementia/ en/), reasoning/judgment problem, difficulty in learning, and problem with performing routine tasks (World Health Organization. Dementia fact sheet, 2017, Source: http://www.who.int/mediacentre/factsheets/fs362/ en/). As the diseases progresses, different changes may be visualized in a patient behavior such as problem to carry out everyday tasks, rapid change in mood, behavioral changes (e.g., self-injury such as hitting, biting, and scratching to himself), wrong sexual practices (e.g., publicly masturbation/ groping), stealing and throwing objects (Burns and Iliffe, 2009). Till now, there is no effective treatment has been discovered that completely cures this disease. In advanced stages, various complications may occur and result in death.

3.5.2.1   CAUSES OF ALZHEIMER

In a study, researchers have been observed that genetic complications, daily lifestyle and environmental factors are the main causes of Alzheimer (Wilson et al., 2011). Severe genetic changes are one of the main causes of Alzheimer and this is usually onset in the middle age (World Health Organization. Dementia—a public health priority. 2017, Source: http://www. who.int/mental_health/neurology/dementia/infographic_dementia/en/). The main cause of Alzheimer disease (AD) is still a big research issue, but the core problem of this disease is the abnormal functioning of "brain proteins (i.e., plaques and tangles)" that not only even disturb the normal activities of neurons but also releases toxic events. Consequently neurons become dying due to loss of interaction. Region of the brain that controls the memory is firstly affected by the damage. The damaged neurons then spread it and affect the other regions of the brain in a specific pattern. At the late stage of the disease the brain become shrink and in result in death.

3.5.2.2   SYMPTOMS OF ALZHEIMER

The symptoms of AD vary from patient to patient and it emerges gradually over a period of time. The initial symptoms of this disease may be forgetting events/activities, mild confusion, inability to do the activities without any support, problem in recognizing objects, and so on. Changes in Alzheimer symptoms can have three categories, that is, functional, cognitive, and behavioral. Functional changes affect the daily routine work such as managing finance, personal care, and travelling. Finally, patient will be completely dependent on others.

Short-term memory comes under cognitive changes deals with forgetting recent events, inability to recognize the familiar route/faces/objects, loss of learning ability, inability to recognize family and friends, and unable to take decisions.

Behavioral changes occur due to the involvement of patient in socially unacceptable activities such as loss of emotional feeling and change in mood (e.g., anxiety, depression, agitation, lack of interest, and apathy), which is very much difficult for a family to handle and ultimately requires medical care under expert supervision.

In a recent study, deep learning model has been proposed by the researchers of the University of San Francisco for the early prediction of AD by using "fluorine 18 fluorodeoxy glucose PET" of the brain (Ding et al., 2018). This model has an ability to detect the AD up to six years earlier than the existing techniques. In this research work, 2109 prospective ^{18}F-FDG PET brain images from 1002 patients and 40 imaging studies from retrospective independent test set of 40 patients have been collected to perform the clinical diagnosis. Further, the final clinical diagnosis has been recorded. The proposed model has used 90% of the dataset for training purposes and 10% of the remaining dataset for testing purposes. Performance of the proposed model has been compared with the radiologic readers on the basis of different factors such as sensitivity, t-distributed stochastic neighbor embedding, specificity, saliency map, and receiver operating characteristic (ROC). The area achieved by the algorithm under the ROC curve of 0.98 with 82% specificity and 100% sensitivity in the early prediction of final clinical diagnosis of AD. This result has obtained on an average of 75.8 months before the result of final diagnosis.

In other research work, for the prediction of mild cognitive impairment (MCI) and Alzheimer-type dementia (AD-type dementia) on sparse clinical language dataset, a combination of deep language models and DNN named "D2NNLM" has been used (Orimaye et al., 2018). To learn deep learning models researchers have used the higher n-gram vocabulary spaces and experimental work has been performed on the clinical Pitt dataset of the DementiaBank on Alzheimer's disease and related Dementia (Source: https://dementia.talkbank.org/access/English/Pitt.html).

For this dataset, mini-mental state examination and other clinical diagnosis practices have been conducted to collect different types of data such as verbal interviews transcripts, diagnosed MCI data, and different form of AD-type dementia. In the final result, accuracy of the clinical diagnosis is 91.4% for AD-type dementia and gain 98.3% specificity and 98.8% sensitivity.

In a survey of PubMed and Google scholar, deep learning techniques especially CNN and RNN have shown their accuracy such as 96.0% for AD classification and 84.2% for MCI conversion prediction on neuroimaging data (Jo et al., 2019). Improved performance in AD classification has been obtained on the combination of multimodal neuroimaging and fluid biomarkers. Further it has been found that deep learning is still evolving in AD research on different categories of data.

Multimodal RNN, a deep learning approach, has been applied to predict the conversion from MCI to AD (Lee et al., 2019). The researchers have combined "cross sectional neuroimaging biomarkers," "longitudinal cerebrospinal," and "cognitive performance biomarkers at baseline" to develop an integrated framework to improve the prediction accuracy. The proposed prediction model gives 75% conversion accuracy from MCI to AD on single modality of data. After incorporating longitudinal multidomain data the prediction model gives 81% accuracy.

A deep learning-based novel technique is developed for the early diagnosis of MSI and AD (Liu et al., 2014). This technique provides better AD diagnosis as compared to SVM with minimal previous knowledge and treats it as a multiclass classification task. The overall accuracy produced by the deep learning method in binary classification of AD is 87.76%. Also, higher sensitivity values, that is, 88.57% and 74.29% respectively for classification accuracy has been observed. Deep learning method has been shown improvement as 47.42% on overall accuracy and 83.75% on overall specificity as compared to SVM.

3.5.3 CASE STUDY: DIABETES

A common type of chronic disease named diabetes covers a huge population in all over the world. It shows a big threat for human health due to its high growth rate. The cause of diabetes is the presence of higher level of blood glucose than the normal level. This happens due to less secretion of insulin in the pancreas from beta cells or its adverse biological effects or combination of both (Lonappan et al., 2007). Diabetes can be a cause of serious chronic damages and abnormality in various tissues such as eyes, heart, kidneys, nerves, and blood vessels (Krasteva et al., 2011). Diabetes has three categories, type-1 diabetes (T1D), type-2 diabetes (T2D), and gestational diabetes mellitus (GDM).

Patients of T1D come under the age of 30. The symptoms of this category of diabetes are high level of blood glucose, frequent discharge of urine and increased thirst (Iancu et al., 2008). Patients of this category need insulin therapy to maintain blood glucose rather than only oral medications. This is required due of impairments in insulin production. A patient needs multiple daily injections or continuous subcutaneous insulin infusion to maintain the glucose level.

Middle-aged and elderly patients come under T2D mainly suffered from different diseases such as hypertension, obesity, arteriosclerosis, and dyslipidemia (Robertson et al., 2011). Patients under this category suffer from gradual loss of insulin secretion. But, they can opt various remedial options. At the beginning stage of T2D, through medication patients improve their insulin secretion, but at later stage prescribed doses of insulin are required.

Type-3 diabetes or GDM occurs due to interaction of insulin and hormones released from placenta which is a cause of high blood sugar level (Kavakiotis et al., 2017). This occurs during pregnancy and generally disappears after the birth of a baby. Most of the cases there may be chances of occurring diabetes in the newly conceived babies (Han et al., 2014). Beat dietary practices are the best option to reduce the level of diabetes (Kim, 2009). Therapeutic options for GDM are as same as used in T2D.

With immense changes in modern lifestyle and standard of living, patient of diabetes are exponentially increasing. Therefore, quick and accurate diagnosis of diabetes and immediate remedy are the big necessity. Diagnosis of diabetes includes different parameters such as glucose tolerance, blood glucose (fasting), and blood glucose (random) (Iancu et al., 2008; Cox and Edelman, 2009; American Diabetes Association, 2010).

Diabetes can be controlled easily if it diagnosed in the earlier stage. On the basis of patients' medical record, deep learning can be used to predict the diabetes in its preliminary judgement and same can be available for clinicians for further action (Lee et al., 2016; Alghamdi et al., 2017; Kavakiotis et al., 2017).

In a research, for each class of diabetes, some practices are very common to adopt as a routine in daily life by every patient such as timely diagnosis, patient education, medical care on a regular basis, and follow some risk mitigation activities, for example, diabetic foot, retinopathy, nephropathy, and so on.

Earlier, many AI algorithms have been used for the prediction of diabetes, for example, SVM, decision tree logistic regression, and so on (Kavakiotis et al., 2017). By using principal component analysis and neuro-fuzzy inference diabetes patients have been distinguished from normal people (Polat and Güneş, 2007). T2D has been predicted by quantum particle swarm optimization algorithm and weighted least squares support vector machine (Yue et al. 2008). linear discriminant analysis-wavelet support vector machine (LDA-MWSVM) has been proposed to predict the diabetes (Duygu et al., 2011). In this approach, linear discriminant Analysis has been used to reduce the dimension and for feature extraction. In order to predict T2D on high-dimensional datasets, a prediction model using logistic regression has been proposed for distinct onset (Razavian et al., 2015). SVM has been used to predict diabetes as a multivariate regression problem, specially focused on the glucose level (George et al., 2013). In other studies it is found that most of the researchers have improved the accuracy in prediction through ensemble methods (Kavakiotis et al., 2017).

3.6 CONCLUSION

This chapter starts with the motivational significance of deep learning in healthcare. The role of deep learning has been presented incorrect decision making with valid detection and diagnosis of major diseases such as cancer, Alzheimer, and diabetes. Further, the role of the healthcare sector has been discussed in revenue generation and economic growth for the country. As per the report of the Ministry of Health and Family Welfare, India, the healthcare sector may cover up to Rs. 8.6 trillion of the total market capital by 2022 in revenue generation. During the study it has been found that the expenditure on public health is low as compared to low-income countries like Sri Lanka and Indonesia that is an issue of discussion. Government of India is planning to invest 2.5% of the total GDP on public health by 2025. Many things have been covered under the healthcare systems such as hospitals, medical research, drug discovery, health insurance, telemedicine, and medical equipment that generate a huge amount of data. These data are complex and unstructured in nature and getting valid information is a big challenge for the stakeholders involved in the healthcare industry. So, to get the valid information different traditional AI and ML-based techniques have been applied. But due to distinct nature and rapid growth of the data these algorithms are unable to fulfill the need as desired. Deep learning has ability to work with these types of data. It learns directly from data representations and performs feature extraction and transformation through multiple layers of nonlinear processing units. Unlike ML and other traditional techniques, deep learning uses representation learning for pattern recognition and gets the desired output. In recent years, due to a huge amount of heterogeneous data and need of real-time information in healthcare especially for valid clinical decisions, deep learning is playing a vital role in detection and diagnosis of diseases and helping clinicians to provide better treatment to the patients. Different applications of deep learning and challenges have been discussed in the chapter. A research survey on cancer, Alzheimer, heart disease, skin disease, brain tumor, and others has been done using different deep learning methods on various data sources and in each survey deep learning has shown the promising result as required. Three severe diseases cancer, Alzheimer, and diabetes have been taken as a case study to show the performance of deep learning methods for analysis and prediction in a real-time environment. In current time due to high growth rate of cancer patients, valid and accurate prediction of the severity of the disease is highly desirable. As per the report of Oslo University Hospital, approximately 60% accuracy in the prognosis of cancer has been found in pathological results that is an issue of research. In the study, it is found that near about 85% death is caused due to lung cancer. About 90% cases of breast cancer have been found spontaneous/nonfamilial in nature. Alzheimer is another severe disease which occurs due to progressive neurological disorder. This disease gradually kills the brain cells and in result this will be a cause of memory loss and thinking ability. Till now, no effective treatment has been discovered that completely cures this disease. In advanced stages, various complications may occur and result in death. But the right prediction of the disease and better treatment may prolong the life of the patients. Another famous disease is diabetes which comes under the category of the common type of disease that covers a huge population all over the world. This occurs due to the presence of an excess amount of blood glucose rather than the normal level. There are three categories of diabetes such as T1D, T2D, and GDM. Each category of diabetes has specific symptoms and affects the patients based on certain criteria. In the above context, as per the survey and analysis of the deep learning methods on different platforms, it is found that these methods have shown acceptable and promising results as the required and correct prediction of diseases as compared to the existing traditional techniques and pathological results.

KEYWORDS

- **deep learning**
- **healthcare**
- **precision medicine**
- **Alzheimer**
- **diabetes**
- **cancer**

REFERENCES

Abdel-Zaher, A.M. and Eldeib, A.M., 2016. Breast cancer classification using deep belief networks. Expert Systems with Applications, 46, pp. 139–144.

Acharya, U.R., Fujita, H., Oh, S.L., Hagiwara, Y., Tan, J.H., and Adam, M., 2017. Application of deep convolutional neural network for automated detection of myocardial infarction using ECG signals. Information Sciences, 415, pp. 190–198.

Akkus, Z., Ali, I., Sedlář, J., Agrawal, J.P., Parney, I.F., Giannini, C., and Erickson, B.J., 2017. Predicting deletion of chromosomal arms 1p/19q in low-grade gliomas from MR images using machine intelligence. Journal of digital imaging, 30(4), pp. 469–476.

Akkus, Z., Galimzianova, A., Hoogi, A., Rubin, D.L., and Erickson, B.J., 2017. Deep learning for brain MRI segmentation: state of the art and future directions. Journal of Digital Imaging, 30(4), pp. 449–459.

Alcantara, M.F., Cao, Y., Liu, C., Liu, B., Brunette, M., Zhang, N., Sun, T., Zhang, P., Chen, Q., Li, Y., and Albarracin, C.M., 2017. Improving tuberculosis diagnostics using deep learning and mobile health technologies among resource-poor communities in Peru. Smart Health, 1, pp. 66–76.

Alghamdi, M., Al-Mallah, M., Keteyian, S., Brawner, C., Ehrman, J., and Sakr, S., 2017. Predicting diabetes mellitus using SMOTE and ensemble machine learning approach: the Henry Ford ExercIse Testing (FIT) project. PLoS One, 12(7), p. e0179805.

Alipanahi, B., Delong, A., Weirauch, M.T., and Frey, B.J., 2015. Predicting the sequence specificities of DNA-and RNA-binding proteins by deep learning. Nature Biotechnology, 33(8), p. 831.

American Diabetes Association, 2010. Diagnosis and classification of diabetes mellitus. Diabetes Care, 33(Suppl. 1), pp. S62–S69.

Andreu-Perez, J., Poon, C.C., Merrifield, R.D., Wong, S.T., and Yang, G.Z., 2015. Big data for health. IEEE Journal of Biomedical and Health Informatics, 19(4), pp. 1193–1208.

Angermueller, C., Lee, H.J., Reik, W., and Stegle, O., 2016. Accurate prediction of single-cell DNA methylation states using deep learning. bioRxiv, p. 055715.

Anirudh, R., Thiagarajan, J.J., Bremer, T., and Kim, H., 2016, March. Lung nodule detection using 3D convolutional neural networks trained on weakly labeled data. In Medical Imaging 2016: Computer-Aided Diagnosis (Vol. 9785, p. 978532). International Society for Optics and Photonics, Washington, DC.

Ayer, T., Alagoz, O., Chhatwal, J., Shavlik, J.W., Kahn Jr, C.E., and Burnside, E.S., 2010. Breast cancer risk estimation with artificial neural networks revisited: discrimination and calibration. Cancer, 116(14), pp. 3310–3321.

Bar, Y., Diamant, I., Wolf, L., and Greenspan, H., 2015, March. Deep learning with non-medical training used for chest pathology identification. In Medical Imaging 2015: Computer-Aided Diagnosis (Vol. 9414, p. 94140V). International Society for Optics and Photonics, Washington, D.C.

Bayramoglu, N., Kannala, J., and Heikkilä, J., 2016, December. Deep learning for magnification independent breast cancer histopathology image classification. In 2016 23rd International Conference on Pattern Recognition (pp. 2440–2445). IEEE.

Beam, A.L. and Kohane, I.S., 2018. Big data and machine learning in healthcare. JAMA, 319(13), pp. 1317–1318.

Bejnordi, B.E., Mullooly, M., Pfeiffer, R.M., Fan, S., Vacek, P.M., Weaver, D.L., Herschorn, S., Brinton, L.A., van Ginneken, B., Karssemeijer, N., and Beck, A.H., 2018. Using deep convolutional neural networks to identify and classify tumor-associated stroma in diagnostic breast biopsies. Modern Pathology, 31(10), p. 1502.

Bejnordi, B.E., Veta, M., Van Diest, P.J., Van Ginneken, B., Karssemeijer, N., Litjens, G., Van Der Laak, J.A., Hermsen, M., Manson, Q.F., Balkenhol, M., and Geessink, O., 2017. Diagnostic assessment of deep learning algorithms for detection of lymph node metastases in women with breast cancer. JAMA, 318(22), pp. 2199–2210.

Bellazzi, R. and Zupan, B., 2008. Predictive data mining in clinical medicine: current issues and guidelines. International Journal of Medical Informatics, 77(2), pp. 81–97.

Bengio, Y., 2009. Learning deep architectures for AI. Foundations and Trends® in Machine Learning, 2(1), pp. 1–127.

Bengio, Y., Courville, A., and Vincent, P., 2013. Representation learning: a review and new perspectives. IEEE Transactions on Pattern Analysis and Machine Intelligence, 35(8), pp. 1798–1828.

Burns, A. and Iliffe, S., 2009. Alzheimer's disease. British Medical Journal, 338, b158.

Çalişir, D. and Doğantekin, E., 2011. An automatic diabetes diagnosis system based on LDA-Wavelet Support Vector Machine Classifier. Expert Systems with Applications, 38(7), pp. 8311–8315.

Cao, Y., Liu, C., Liu, B., Brunette, M.J., Zhang, N., Sun, T., Zhang, P., Peinado, J., Garavito, E.S., Garcia, L.L., and Curioso, W.H., 2016, June. Improving tuberculosis diagnostics using deep learning and mobile health technologies among resource-poor and marginalized communities. In 2016 IEEE First International Conference on Connected Health: Applications, Systems and Engineering Technologies (CHASE) (pp. 274–281).

Causey, J.L., Zhang, J., Ma, S., Jiang, B., Qualls, J.A., Politte, D.G., Prior, F., Zhang, S., and Huang, X., 2018. Highly accurate model for prediction of lung nodule malignancy with CT scans. Scientific Reports, 8(1), p. 9286.

Cha, K.H., Hadjiiski, L., Samala, R.K., Chan, H.P., Caoili, E.M., and Cohan, R.H., 2016. Urinary bladder segmentation in CT urography using deep-learning convolutional neural network and level sets. Medical Physics, 43(4), pp. 1882–1896.

Chaudhary, K., Poirion, O.B., Lu, L., and Garmire, L.X., 2018. Deep learning-based multi-omics integration robustly predicts survival in liver cancer. Clinical Cancer Research, 24(6), pp. 1248–1259.

Chen, X.W. and Lin, X., 2014. Big data deep learning: challenges and perspectives. IEEE Access, 2, pp. 514–525.

Chen, Y., Li, L., Zhang, G.Q., and Xu, R., 2015. Phenome-driven disease genetics prediction toward drug discovery. Bioinformatics, 31(12), pp. i276–i283.

Cheng, J.Z., Ni, D., Chou, Y.H., Qin, J., Tiu, C.M., Chang, Y.C., Huang, C.S., Shen, D., and Chen, C.M., 2016. Computer-aided diagnosis with deep learning architecture: applications to breast lesions in US images and pulmonary nodules in CT scans. Scientific Reports, 6, p. 24454.

Cheng, Y., Wang, F., Zhang, P., and Hu, J., 2016, June. Risk prediction with electronic health records: a deep learning approach. In Proceedings of the 2016 SIAM International Conference on Data Mining (pp. 432–440). Society for Industrial and Applied Mathematics.

Chmelik, J., Jakubicek, R., Walek, P., Jan, J., Ourednicek, P., Lambert, L., Amadori, E., and Gavelli, G., 2018. Deep convolutional neural network-based segmentation and classification of difficult to define metastatic spinal lesions in 3D CT data. Medical Image Analysis, 49, pp. 76–88.

Choi, H. and Jin, K.H., 2016. Fast and robust segmentation of the striatum using deep convolutional neural networks. Journal of Neuroscience Methods, 274, pp. 146–153.

Cicchetti, D.V., 1992. Neural networks and diagnosis in the clinical laboratory: state of the art. Clinical Chemistry, 38(1), pp. 9–10.

Cireşan, D.C., Giusti, A., Gambardella, L.M., and Schmidhuber, J., 2013, September. Mitosis detection in breast cancer histology images with deep neural networks. In International Conference on Medical Image Computing and Computer-Assisted Intervention (pp. 411–418). Springer, Berlin, Heidelberg.

Cochran, A.J., 1997. Prediction of outcome for patients with cutaneous melanoma. Pigment Cell Research, 10(3), pp. 162–167.

Collins, F.S. and Varmus, H., 2015. A new initiative on precision medicine. New England Journal of Medicine, 372(9), pp. 793–795.

Coudray, N., Ocampo, P.S., Sakellaropoulos, T., Narula, N., Snuderl, M., Fenyö, D., Moreira, A.L., Razavian, N., and Tsirigos, A., 2018. Classification and mutation prediction from non-small cell lung cancer histopathology images using deep learning. Nature Medicine, 24(10), p. 1559.

Cox, M.E. and Edelman, D., 2009. Tests for screening and diagnosis of type 2 diabetes. Clinical Diabetes, 27(4), pp. 132–138.

Cruz, J.A. and Wishart, D.S., 2006. Applications of machine learning in cancer prediction and prognosis. Cancer Informatics, 2, p. 117693510600200030.

Cruz-Roa, A., Basavanhally, A., González, F., Gilmore, H., Feldman, M., Ganesan, S., Shih, N., Tomaszewski, J., and Madabhushi, A., 2014. Automatic detection of invasive ductal carcinoma in whole slide images with convolutional neural networks. In Medical Imaging 2014: Digital Pathology (Vol. 9041, p. 904103). International Society for Optics and Photonics, Washington, D.C.

Dalmış, M.U., Litjens, G., Holland, K., Setio, A., Mann, R., Karssemeijer, N., and Gubern-Mérida, A., 2017. Using deep learning to segment breast and fibroglandular tissue in MRI volumes. Medical Physics, 44(2), pp. 533–546.

Danaee, P., Ghaeini, R., and Hendrix, D.A., 2017. A deep learning approach for cancer detection and relevant gene identification. In Pacific Symposium on Biocomputing (pp. 219–229).

De Fauw, J., Ledsam, J.R., Romera-Paredes, B., Nikolov, S., Tomasev, N., Blackwell, S., Askham, H., Glorot, X., O'Donoghue, B., Visentin, D., and van den Driessche, G., 2018. Clinically applicable deep learning for diagnosis and referral in retinal disease. Nature Medicine, 24(9), p. 1342.

de Vos, B.D., Wolterink, J.M., de Jong, P.A., Viergever, M.A., and Išgum, I., 2016. 2D image classification for 3D anatomy localization: employing deep convolutional neural networks. In Medical Imaging 2016: Image Processing (Vol. 9784, p. 97841Y). International Society for Optics and Photonics, Washington, DC.

Delen, D., Walker, G., and Kadam, A., 2005. Predicting breast cancer survivability: a comparison of three data mining methods. Artificial Intelligence in Medicine, 34(2), pp. 113–127.

Ding, Y., Sohn, J.H., Kawczynski, M.G., Trivedi, H., Harnish, R., Jenkins, N.W., Lituiev, D., Copeland, T.P., Aboian, M.S., Mari Aparici, C., and Behr, S.C., 2018. A deep learning model to predict a diagnosis of Alzheimer disease by using 18F-FDG PET of the brain. Radiology, 290(2), pp. 456–464.

Dou, Q., Yu, L., Chen, H., Jin, Y., Yang, X., Qin, J., and Heng, P.A., 2017. 3D deeply supervised network for automated segmentation of volumetric medical images. Medical Image Analysis, 41, pp. 40–54.

Dubrovina, A., Kisilev, P., Ginsburg, B., Hashoul, S., and Kimmel, R., 2018. Computational mammography using deep neural networks. Computer Methods in Biomechanics and Biomedical Engineering: Imaging & Visualization, 6(3), pp. 243–247.

Dumitrescu, R.G. and Cotarla, I., 2005. Understanding breast cancer risk-where do we stand in 2005?. Journal of Cellular and Molecular Medicine, 9(1), pp. 208–221.

Eshlaghy, A.T., Poorebrahimi, A., Ebrahimi, M., Razavi, A.R., and Ahmad, L.G., 2013. Using three machine learning techniques for predicting breast cancer recurrence. Journal of Health & Medical Informatics, 4(2), p. 124.

Ehteshami Bejnordi, B., Linz, J., Glass, B., Mullooly, M., Gierach, G.L., Sherman, M.E., Karssemeijer, N., van der Laak, J. and Beck, A.H., 2017. Deep learning-based assessment of tumor-associated stroma for diagnosing breast cancer in histopathology images. arXiv, pp. arXiv-1702.

Esteva, A., Kuprel, B., Novoa, R.A., Ko, J., Swetter, S.M., Blau, H.M., and Thrun, S., 2017. Dermatologist-level classification of skin cancer with deep neural networks. Nature, 542(7639), p. 115.

Esteva, A., Robicquet, A., Ramsundar, B., Kuleshov, V., DePristo, M., Chou, K., Cui, C., Corrado, G., Thrun, S., and Dean, J., 2019. A guide to deep learning in healthcare. Nature Medicine, 25(1), p. 24.

Fu, H., Xu, Y., Wong, D.W.K., and Liu, J., 2016, April. Retinal vessel segmentation via deep learning network and fully-connected conditional random fields. In 2016 IEEE 13th international Symposium on Biomedical Imaging (ISBI) (pp. 698–701). IEEE.

Gao, X., Lin, S., and Wong, T.Y., 2015. Automatic feature learning to grade nuclear cataracts based on deep learning. IEEE Transactions on Biomedical Engineering, 62(11), pp. 2693–2701.

Georga, E.I., Protopappas, V.C., Ardigò, D., Marina, M., Zavaroni, I., Polyzos, D., and Fotiadis, D.I., 2012. Multivariate prediction of subcutaneous glucose concentration in type 1 diabetes patients based on support vector regression. IEEE Journal of Biomedical and Health Informatics, 17(1), pp. 71–81.

George, H., Rakesh, P.S., Manjunath Krishna, R.A., Abraham, V.J., George, K. and Prasad, J.H., 2013. Foot care knowledge and practices and the prevalence of peripheral neuropathy among people with diabetes attending a secondary care rural hospital in southern India. Journal of Family Medicine and Primary Care, 2(1), p. 27.

Gevaert, O., Smet, F.D., Timmerman, D., Moreau, Y., and Moor, B.D., 2006. Predicting the prognosis of breast cancer by integrating clinical and microarray data with Bayesian networks. Bioinformatics, 22(14), pp. e184-e190.

Gianfrancesco, M.A., Tamang, S., Yazdany, J., and Schmajuk, G., 2018. Potential biases in machine learning algorithms using electronic health record data. JAMA Internal Medicine, 178(11), pp. 1544–1547.

González, G., Ash, S.Y., Vegas-Sánchez-Ferrero, G., Onieva Onieva, J., Rahaghi, F.N., Ross, J.C., Díaz, A., San José Estépar, R., and Washko, G.R., 2018. Disease staging and prognosis in smokers using deep learning in chest computed tomography. American Journal of Respiratory and Critical Care Medicine, 197(2), pp. 193–203.

Gulshan, V., Peng, L., Coram, M., Stumpe, M.C., Wu, D., Narayanaswamy, A., Venugopalan, S., Widner, K., Madams, T., Cuadros, J., and Kim, R., 2016. Development and validation of a deep learning algorithm for detection of diabetic retinopathy in retinal fundus photographs. JAMA, 316(22), pp. 2402–2410.

Han, L., Luo, S., Yu, J., Pan, L., and Chen, S., 2014. Rule extraction from support vector machines using ensemble learning approach: an application for diagnosis of diabetes. IEEE Journal of Biomedical and Health Informatics, 19(2), pp. 728–734.

Han, Z., Wei, B., Zheng, Y., Yin, Y., Li, K., and Li, S., 2017. Breast cancer multi-classification from histopathological images with structured deep learning model. Scientific Reports, 7(1), p. 4172.

Havaei, M., Davy, A., Warde-Farley, D., Biard, A., Courville, A., Bengio, Y., Pal, C., Jodoin, P.M., and Larochelle, H., 2017. Brain tumor segmentation with deep neural networks. Medical Image Analysis, 35, pp. 18–31.

Havaei, M., Guizard, N., Larochelle, H., and Jodoin, P.M., 2016. Deep learning trends for focal brain pathology segmentation in MRI. In Machine Learning for Health Informatics (pp. 125–148). Springer, Cham.

Haykin, S. and Kosko, B., 2001. Intelligent Signal Processing. Wiley-IEEE Press.

Hinton, G., 2018. Deep learning—a technology with the potential to transform healthcare. JAMA, 320(11), pp. 1101–1102.

Hinton, G., Deng, L., Yu, D., Dahl, G., Mohamed, A.R., Jaitly, N., Senior, A., Vanhoucke, V., Nguyen, P., Kingsbury, B., and Sainath, T., 2012. Deep neural networks for acoustic modeling in speech recognition. IEEE Signal Processing Magazine, 29.

Hinton, G.E., Osindero, S., and Teh, Y.W., 2006. A fast learning algorithm for deep belief nets. Neural Computation, 18(7), pp. 1527–1554.

Hirschberg, J. and Manning, C.D., 2015. Advances in natural language processing. Science, 349(6245), pp. 261–266.

Horvitz, E. and Mulligan, D., 2015. Data, privacy, and the greater good. Science, 349(6245), pp. 253–255.

Hripcsak, G. and Albers, D.J., 2012. Next-generation phenotyping of electronic health records. Journal of the American Medical Informatics Association, 20(1), pp. 117–121.

Hu, X., Wang, T. and Jin, F., 2016. Alzheimer's disease and gut microbiota. Science China Life Sciences, 59(10), pp. 1006–1023.

Huang, T., Lan, L., Fang, X., An, P., Min, J., and Wang, F., 2015. Promises and challenges of big data computing in health sciences. Big Data Research, 2(1), pp. 2–11.

Iancu, I., Mota, M., and Iancu, E., 2008, May. Method for the analysing of blood glucose dynamics in diabetes mellitus patients. In 2008 IEEE International Conference on Automation, Quality and Testing, Robotics (Vol. 3, pp. 60–65). IEEE.

Isensee, F., Kickingereder, P., Bonekamp, D., Bendszus, M., Wick, W., Schlemmer, H.P., and Maier-Hein, K., 2017. Brain tumor segmentation using large receptive field deep convolutional neural networks. In Bildverarbeitung für die Medizin 2017 (pp. 86–91). Springer Vieweg, Berlin, Heidelberg.

Jamaludin, A., Lootus, M., Kadir, T., Zisserman, A., Urban, J., Battié, M.C., Fairbank, J., McCall, I., and Genodisc Consortium, 2017. ISSLS PRIZE IN BIOENGINEERING SCIENCE 2017: Automation of reading of radiological features from magnetic resonance images (MRIs) of the lumbar spine without human intervention is comparable with an expert radiologist. European Spine Journal, 26(5), pp. 1374–1383.

Jensen, P.B., Jensen, L.J., and Brunak, S., 2012. Mining electronic health records: towards better research applications and clinical care. Nature Reviews Genetics, 13(6), p. 395.

Jiang, F., Jiang, Y., Zhi, H., Dong, Y., Li, H., Ma, S., Wang, Y., Dong, Q., Shen, H., and Wang, Y., 2017. Artificial intelligence in healthcare: past, present and future. Stroke and Vascular Neurology, 2(4), pp. 230–243.

Jo, T., Nho, K., and Saykin, A.J., 2019. Deep learning in Alzheimer's disease: diagnostic classification and prognostic prediction using neuroimaging data. arXiv preprint arXiv: 1905.00931.

Kamnitsas, K., Ledig, C., Newcombe, V.F., Simpson, J.P., Kane, A.D., Menon, D.K., Rueckert, D., and Glocker, B., 2017. Efficient multi-scale 3D CNN with fully connected CRF for accurate brain lesion segmentation. Medical Image Analysis, 36, pp. 61–78.

Karlo, C.A., Di Paolo, P.L., Chaim, J., Hakimi, A.A., Ostrovnaya, I., Russo, P., Hricak, H., Motzer, R., Hsieh, J.J., and Akin, O., 2014. Radiogenomics of clear cell renal cell carcinoma: associations between CT imaging features and mutations. Radiology, 270(2), pp. 464–471.

Kavakiotis, I., Tsave, O., Salifoglou, A., Maglaveras, N., Vlahavas, I., and Chouvarda, I., 2017. Machine learning and data mining methods in diabetes research. Computational and Structural Biotechnology Journal, 15, pp. 104–116.

Kelley, D.R., Snoek, J., and Rinn, J.L., 2016. Basset: learning the regulatory code of the accessible genome with deep convolutional neural networks. Genome Research, 26(7), pp. 990–999.

Kendra, R.L., Karki, S., Eickholt, J.L., and Gandy, L., 2015. Characterizing the discussion of antibiotics in the twittersphere: what is the bigger picture? Journal of Medical Internet Research, 17(6), p. e154.

Khan, S., Islam, N., Jan, Z., Din, I.U., and Rodrigues, J.J.C., 2019. A novel deep learning based framework for the detection and classification of breast cancer using transfer learning. Pattern Recognition Letters, 125, pp. 1–6.

Kim, J. and Shin, H., 2013. Breast cancer survivability prediction using labeled, unlabeled, and pseudo-labeled patient data. Journal of the American Medical Informatics Association, 20(4), pp. 613–618.

Kim, J.H., 2009. Estimating classification error rate: Repeated cross-validation, repeated hold-out and bootstrap. Computational Statistics & Data Analysis, 53(11), pp. 3735–3745.

Kleesiek, J., Urban, G., Hubert, A., Schwarz, D., Maier-Hein, K., Bendszus, M., and Biller, A., 2016. Deep MRI brain extraction: a 3D convolutional neural network for skull stripping. NeuroImage, 129, pp. 460–469.

Koh, P.W., Pierson, E., and Kundaje, A., 2017. Denoising genome-wide histone ChIP-seq with convolutional neural networks. Bioinformatics, 33(14), pp. i225–i233.5

Kondo, T., Ueno, J., and Takao, S., 2014, December. Medical image recognition of abdominal multi-organs by hybrid multi-layered GMDH-type neural network using principal component-regression analysis. In 2014 Second International Symposium on Computing and Networking (pp. 157–163).

Kononenko, I., 2001. Machine learning for medical diagnosis: history, state of the art and perspective. Artificial Intelligence in Medicine, 23(1), pp. 89–109.

Kooi, T., Litjens, G., Van Ginneken, B., Gubern-Mérida, A., Sánchez, C.I., Mann, R., den Heeten, A., and Karssemeijer, N., 2017. Large scale deep learning for computer aided detection of mammographic lesions. Medical Image Analysis, 35, pp. 303–312.

Korfiatis, P., Kline, T.L., Lachance, D.H., Parney, I.F., Buckner, J.C., and Erickson, B.J., 2017. Residual deep convolutional neural network predicts MGMT methylation status. Journal of Digital Imaging, 30(5), pp. 622–628.

Krasteva, A., Panov, V., Krasteva, A., Kisselova, A., and Krastev, Z., 2011. Oral cavity and systemic diseases—diabetes mellitus. Biotechnology & Biotechnological Equipment, 25(1), pp. 2183–2186.

Krizhevsky, A., Sutskever, I., and Hinton, G.E., 2012. Imagenet classification with deep convolutional neural networks. In Advances in Neural Information Processing Systems (pp. 1097–1105).

Kuang, D. and He, L., 2014, November. Classification on ADHD with deep learning. In 2014 International Conference on Cloud Computing and Big Data (pp. 27–32). IEEE.

Kumar, D., Wong, A., and Clausi, D.A., 2015, June. Lung nodule classification using deep features in CT images. In 2015 12th Conference on Computer and Robot Vision (pp. 133–138). IEEE.

Le, Q.V., Ngiam, J., Coates, A., Lahiri, A., Prochnow, B., and Ng, A.Y., 2011. On optimization methods for deep learning. In Proceedings of the 28th International Conference on International Conference on Machine Learning (pp. 265–272). Omnipress.

LeCun, Y., Bottou, L., Bengio, Y., and Haffner, P., 1998. Gradient-based learning applied to document recognition. Proceedings of the IEEE, 86(11), pp. 2278–2324.

LeCun, Y., Bengio, Y. and Hinton, G., 2015. Deep learning. Nature, 521(7553), pp. 436–444.

Lee, B.J. and Kim, J.Y., 2015. Identification of type 2 diabetes risk factors using phenotypes consisting of anthropometry and triglycerides based on machine learning. IEEE Journal of Biomedical and Health Informatics, 20(1), pp. 39–46.

Lee, G., Nho, K., Kang, B., Sohn, K.A., and Kim, D., 2019. Predicting Alzheimer's disease progression using multi-modal deep learning approach. Scientific Reports, 9(1), p. 1952.

Lerouge, J., Herault, R., Chatelain, C., Jardin, F., and Modzelewski, R., 2015. IODA: an input/output deep architecture for image labeling. Pattern Recognition, 48(9), pp. 2847–2858.

Levine, A.B., Schlosser, C., Grewal, J., Coope, R., Jones, S.J., and Yip, S., 2019. Rise of the machines: advances in deep learning for cancer diagnosis. Trends in Cancer, 5, pp. 157–169.

Li, F., Tran, L., Thung, K.H., Ji, S., Shen, D., and Li, J., 2015. A robust deep model for improved classification of AD/MCI patients. IEEE Journal of Biomedical and Health Informatics, 19(5), pp. 1610–1616.

Li, Y., Li, X., Xie, X., and Shen, L., 2018, April. Deep learning based gastric cancer identification. In 2018 IEEE 15th International Symposium on Biomedical Imaging (ISBI 2018) (pp. 182–185). IEEE.

Li, Z., He, Y., Keel, S., Meng, W., Chang, R.T., and He, M., 2018. Efficacy of a deep learning system for detecting glaucomatous optic neuropathy based on color fundus photographs. Ophthalmology, 125(8), pp. 1199–1206.

Li, Z., Wang, Y., Yu, J., Guo, Y. and Cao, W., 2017. Deep Learning based Radiomics (DLR) and its usage in noninvasive IDH1 prediction for low grade glioma. Scientific Reports, 7(1), p. 5467.

Liang, Z., Zhang, G., Huang, J.X., and Hu, Q.V., 2014. Deep learning for healthcare decision making with EMRs. In 2014 IEEE International Conference on Bioinformatics and Biomedicine (BIBM) (pp. 556–559). IEEE.

Listgarten, J., Damaraju, S., Poulin, B., Cook, L., Dufour, J., Driga, A., Mackey, J., Wishart, D., Greiner, R., and Zanke, B., 2004. Predictive models for breast cancer susceptibility from multiple single nucleotide polymorphisms. Clinical Cancer Research, 10(8), pp. 2725–2737.

Litjens, G., Kooi, T., Bejnordi, B.E., Setio, A.A.A., Ciompi, F., Ghafoorian, M., Van Der Laak, J.A., Van Ginneken, B., and Sánchez, C.I., 2017. A survey on deep learning in medical image analysis. Medical Image Analysis, 42, pp. 60–88.

Liu, S., Liu, S., Cai, W., Pujol, S., Kikinis, R., and Feng, D., 2014, April. Early diagnosis of Alzheimer's disease with deep learning. In 2014 IEEE 11th International Symposium on Biomedical Imaging (ISBI) (pp. 1015–1018). IEEE.

Lonappan, A., Bindu, G., Thomas, V., Jacob, J., Rajasekaran, C., and Mathew, K.T., 2007. Diagnosis of diabetes mellitus using microwaves. Journal of Electromagnetic Waves and Applications, 21(10), pp. 1393–1401.

Looney, P., Stevenson, G.N., Nicolaides, K.H., Plasencia, W., Molloholli, M., Natsis, S., and Collins, S.L., 2017. Automatic 3D ultrasound segmentation of the first trimester placenta using deep learning. In 2017 IEEE 14th International Symposium on Biomedical Imaging (ISBI 2017) (pp. 279–282). IEEE.

López, C., Lejeune, M., Bosch, R., Korzynska, A., García-Rojo, M., Salvadó, M.T., Álvaro, T., Callau, C., Roso, A., and Jaén, J., 2012. Digital image analysis in breast cancer: an example of an automated methodology and the effects of image compression. Studies in Health Technology and Informatics, 179, pp. 155–171.

Mamoshina, P., Vieira, A., Putin, E., and Zhavoronkov, A., 2016. Applications of deep learning in biomedicine. Molecular Pharmaceutics, 13(5), pp. 1445–1454.

Masood, A., Al-Jumaily, A., and Anam, K., 2015. Self-supervised learning model for skin cancer diagnosis. In 2015 7th International IEEE/EMBS Conference on Neural Engineering (NER) (pp. 1012–1015). IEEE.

Mazurowski, M.A., Zhang, J., Grimm, L.J., Yoon, S.C., and Silber, J.I., 2014. Radiogenomic analysis of breast cancer: luminal B molecular subtype is associated with enhancement dynamics at MR imaging. Radiology, 273(2), pp. 365–372.

McGuire, S., 2016. World cancer report 2014. Geneva, Switzerland: World Health Organization, International Agency for Research on Cancer, WHO Press, 2015.

Mehrabi, S., Sohn, S., Li, D., Pankratz, J.J., Therneau, T., Sauver, J.L.S., Liu, H., and Palakal, M., 2015, October. Temporal pattern and association discovery of diagnosis codes using deep learning. In 2015 International Conference on Healthcare Informatics (pp. 408–416). IEEE.

Mehta, R., Majumdar, A., and Sivaswamy, J., 2017. BrainSegNet: a convolutional neural network architecture for automated segmentation of human brain structures. Journal of Medical Imaging, 4(2), p. 024003.

Merkow, J., Lufkin, R., Nguyen, K., Soatto, S., Tu, Z., and Vedaldi, A., 2017. DeepRadiologyNet: radiologist level pathology detection in CT head images. arXiv preprint arXiv:1711.09313.

Miotto, R., Li, L., Kidd, B.A., and Dudley, J.T., 2016. Deep patient: an unsupervised representation to predict the future of patients from the electronic health records. Scientific Reports, 6, p. 26094.

Miotto, R., Wang, F., Wang, S., Jiang, X., and Dudley, J.T., 2017. Deep learning for healthcare: review, opportunities and challenges. Briefings in Bioinformatics, 19(6), pp. 1236–1246.

Moeskops, P., Viergever, M.A., Mendrik, A.M., de Vries, L.S., Benders, M.J., and Išgum, I., 2016. Automatic segmentation of MR brain images with a convolutional neural network. IEEE Transactions on Medical Imaging, 35(5), pp. 1252–1261.

Mohamed, A.A., Berg, W.A., Peng, H., Luo, Y., Jankowitz, R.C., and Wu, S., 2018. A deep learning method for classifying mammographic breast density categories. Medical Physics, 45(1), pp. 314–321.

Mohan, A., Blough, D.M., Kurc, T., Post, A., and Saltz, J., 2011, November. Detection of conflicts and inconsistencies in taxonomy-based authorization policies. In 2011 IEEE International Conference on Bioinformatics and Biomedicine (pp. 590–594). IEEE.

Ning, Z., Luo, J., Li, Y., Han, S., Feng, Q., Xu, Y., Chen, W., Chen, T., and Zhang, Y., 2018. Pattern classification for gastrointestinal stromal tumors by integration of radiomics and deep convolutional features. IEEE Journal of Biomedical and Health Informatics, 23(3), pp. 1181–1191.

Noh, H., Hong, S., and Han, B., 2015. Learning deconvolution network for semantic segmentation. In Proceedings of the IEEE International Conference on Computer Vision (pp. 1520–1528).

Ong, B.T., Sugiura, K., and Zettsu, K., 2016. Dynamically pre-trained deep recurrent neural networks using environmental monitoring data for predicting PM 2.5. Neural Computing and Applications, 27(6), pp. 1553–1566.

Orimaye, S.O., Wong, J.S.M., and Wong, C.P., 2018. Deep language space neural network for classifying mild cognitive impairment and Alzheimer-type dementia. PLoS One, 13(11), p.e0205636.

Pan, Y., Huang, W., Lin, Z., Zhu, W., Zhou, J., Wong, J., and Ding, Z., 2015, August. Brain tumor grading based on neural networks and convolutional neural networks. In 2015 37th Annual International Conference of the IEEE Engineering in Medicine and Biology Society (EMBC) (pp. 699–702). IEEE.

Park, C., Ahn, J., Kim, H., and Park, S., 2014. Integrative gene network construction to analyze cancer recurrence using semi-supervised learning. PLoS One, 9(1), p.e86309.

Park, K., Ali, A., Kim, D., An, Y., Kim, M., and Shin, H., 2013. Robust predictive model for evaluating breast cancer survivability. Engineering Applications of Artificial Intelligence, 26(9), pp. 2194–2205.

Payan, A. and Montana, G., 2015. Predicting Alzheimer's disease: a neuroimaging study with 3D convolutional neural networks. arXiv preprint arXiv:1502.02506.

Pham, T., Tran, T., Phung, D., and Venkatesh, S., 2017. Predicting healthcare trajectories from medical records: a deep learning approach. Journal of Biomedical Informatics, 69, pp. 218–229.

Polat, K. and Güneş, S., 2007. An expert system approach based on principal component analysis and adaptive neuro-fuzzy inference system to diagnosis of diabetes disease. Digital Signal Processing, 17(4), pp. 702–710.

Pöllänen, I., Braithwaite, B., Ikonen, T., Niska, H., Haataja, K., Toivanen, P., and Tolonen, T., 2014, October. Computer-aided breast cancer histopathological diagnosis: comparative analysis of three DTOCS-based features: SW-DTOCS, SW-WDTOCS and SW-3-4-DTOCS. In 2014 4th International Conference on Image Processing Theory, Tools and Applications (IPTA) (pp. 1–6). IEEE.

Prasoon, A., Petersen, K., Igel, C., Lauze, F., Dam, E., and Nielsen, M., 2013, September. Deep feature learning for knee cartilage segmentation using a triplanar convolutional neural network. In International Conference on Medical Image Computing and Computer-Assisted Intervention (pp. 246–253). Springer, Berlin, Heidelberg.

Pratt, H., Coenen, F., Broadbent, D.M., Harding, S.P., and Zheng, Y., 2016. Convolutional neural networks for diabetic retinopathy. Procedia Computer Science, 90, pp. 200–205. Clinical Diagnosis and Management of Alzheimer's Disease. CRC Press, Boca Raton, FL.

Putin, E., Mamoshina, P., Aliper, A., Korzinkin, M., Moskalev, A., Kolosov, A., Ostrovskiy, A., Cantor, C., Vijg, J., and Zhavoronkov, A., 2016. Deep biomarkers of human aging: application of deep neural networks to biomarker development. Aging, 8(5), p. 1021.

Pyakillya, B., Kazachenko, N., and Mikhailovsky, N., 2017, October. Deep learning for ECG classification. Journal of Physics: Conference Series (Vol. 913, No. 1, p. 012004). IOP Publishing.

Rajpurkar, P., Irvin, J., Zhu, K., Yang, B., Mehta, H., Duan, T., Ding, D., Bagul, A., Langlotz, C., Shpanskaya, K., and Lungren, M.P., 2017. Chexnet: radiologist-level pneumonia detection on chest x-rays with deep learning. arXiv preprint arXiv:1711.05225.

Rasti, R., Teshnehlab, M., and Phung, S.L., 2017. Breast cancer diagnosis in DCE-MRI using mixture ensemble of convolutional neural networks. Pattern Recognition, 72, pp. 381–390.

Razavian, N., Blecker, S., Schmidt, A.M., Smith-McLallen, A., Nigam, S., and Sontag, D., 2015. Population-level prediction of type 2 diabetes from claims data and analysis of risk factors. Big Data, 3(4), pp. 277–287.

Robertson, G., Lehmann, E.D., Sandham, W., and Hamilton, D., 2011. Blood glucose prediction using artificial neural networks trained with the AIDA diabetes simulator: a proof-of-concept pilot study. Journal of Electrical and Computer Engineering, 2011, p. 2.

Roth, H.R., Farag, A., Lu, L., Turkbey, E.B., and Summers, R.M., 2015, March. Deep convolutional networks for pancreas segmentation in CT imaging. In Medical Imaging 2015: Image Processing (Vol. 9413, p. 94131G). International Society for Optics and Photonics, Washington, DC.

Rumelhart, D.E., Hinton, G.E., and Williams, R.J., 1988. Learning representations by back-propagating errors. Cognitive Modeling, 5(3), p. 1.

Russakovsky, O., Deng, J., Su, H., Krause, J., Satheesh, S., Ma, S., Huang, Z., Karpathy, A., Khosla, A., Bernstein, M., and Berg, A.C., 2015. Imagenet large scale visual recognition challenge. International Journal of Computer Vision, 115(3), pp. 211–252.

Saltz, J., Gupta, R., Hou, L., Kurc, T., Singh, P., Nguyen, V., Samaras, D., Shroyer, K.R., Zhao, T., Batiste, R., and Van Arnam, J., 2018. Spatial organization and molecular correlation of tumor-infiltrating lymphocytes using deep learning on pathology images. Cell Reports, 23(1), pp. 181–193.

Samala, R.K., Chan, H.P., Hadjiiski, L.M., Cha, K., and Helvie, M.A., 2016, March. Deep-learning convolution neural network for computer-aided detection of microcalcifications in digital breast tomosynthesis. In Medical Imaging 2016: Computer-Aided Diagnosis (Vol. 9785, p. 97850Y). International Society for Optics and Photonics, Washington, DC.

Savage, R.S. and Yuan, Y., 2016. Predicting chemoinsensitivity in breast cancer with'omics/ digital pathology data fusion. Royal Society Open Science, 3(2), p. 140501.

Schaumberg, A.J., Rubin, M.A., and Fuchs, T.J., 2018. H&E-stained whole slide image deep learning predicts SPOP mutation state in prostate cancer. bioRxiv, p. 064279.

Setio, A.A.A., Traverso, A., De Bel, T., Berens, M.S., van den Bogaard, C., Cerello, P., Chen, H., Dou, Q., Fantacci, M.E., Geurts, B., and van der Gugten, R., 2017. Validation, comparison, and combination of algorithms for automatic detection of pulmonary nodules in computed tomography images: the LUNA16 challenge. Medical Image Analysis, 42, pp. 1–13.

Shin, H.C., Lu, L., Kim, L., Seff, A., Yao, J., and Summers, R.M., 2016. Interleaved text/ image deep mining on a large-scale radiology database for automated image interpretation. Journal of Machine Learning Research, 17(1–31), p. 2.

Stojadinovic, A., Nissan, A., Eberhardt, J., Chua, T.C., Pelz, J.O., and Esquivel, J., 2011. Development of a Bayesian belief network model for personalized prognostic risk assessment in colon carcinomatosis. American Surgeon, 77(2), pp. 221–230.

Sun, W., Zheng, B., and Qian, W., 2016, March. Computer aided lung cancer diagnosis with deep learning algorithms. In Medical Imaging 2016: Computer-Aided Diagnosis (Vol. 9785, p. 97850Z). International Society for Optics and Photonics, Washington, DC.

Sun, Y., Goodison, S., Li, J., Liu, L., and Farmerie, W., 2006. Improved breast cancer prognosis through the combination of clinical and genetic markers. Bioinformatics, 23(1), pp. 30–37.

Tran, T., Nguyen, T.D., Phung, D., and Venkatesh, S., 2015. Learning vector representation of medical objects via EMR-driven nonnegative restricted Boltzmann machines (eNRBM). Journal of Biomedical Informatics, 54, pp. 96–105.

Wang, B., Mezlini, A.M., Demir, F., Fiume, M., Tu, Z., Brudno, M., Haibe-Kains, B., and Goldenberg, A., 2014. Similarity network fusion for aggregating data types on a genomic scale. Nature Methods, 11(3), p. 333.

Wang, S., Chen, A., Yang, L., Cai, L., Xie, Y., Fujimoto, J., Gazdar, A., and Xiao, G., 2018. Comprehensive analysis of lung cancer pathology images to discover tumor shape and boundary features that predict survival outcome. Scientific Reports, 8(1), p. 10393.

Wang, X., Yang, W., Weinreb, J., Han, J., Li, Q., Kong, X., Yan, Y., Ke, Z., Luo, B., Liu, T., and Wang, L., 2017. Searching for prostate cancer by fully automated magnetic resonance imaging classification: deep learning versus non-deep learning. Scientific Reports, 7(1), p. 15415.

Wei, J., He, J., Chen, K., Zhou, Y., and Tang, Z., 2017. Collaborative filtering and deep learning based recommendation system for cold start items. Expert Systems with Applications, 69, pp. 29–39.

Wickramasinghe, N., 2017. A convolutional net for medical records. Engineering in Medicine and Biology Society.

Williams, R.J. and Zipscr, D., 1989. A learning algorithm for continually running fully recurrent neural networks. Neural Computation, 1(2), pp. 270–280.

Wilson, R.S., Barral, S., Lee, J.H., Leurgans, S.E., Foroud, T.M., Sweet, R.A., Graff-Radford, N., Bird, T.D., Mayeux, R., and Bennett, D.A., 2011. Heritability of different forms of memory in the Late Onset Alzheimer's Disease Family Study. Journal of Alzheimer's Disease, 23(2), pp. 249–255.

Xu, J., Xiang, L., Liu, Q., Gilmore, H., Wu, J., Tang, J., and Madabhushi, A., 2015. Stacked sparse autoencoder (SSAE) for nuclei detection on breast cancer histopathology images. IEEE Transactions on Medical Imaging, 35(1), pp. 119–130.

Xu, R., Li, L., and Wang, Q., 2014. dRiskKB: a large-scale disease-disease risk relationship knowledge base constructed from biomedical text. BMC Bioinformatics, 15(1), p. 105.

Xu, T., Zhang, H., Huang, X., Zhang, S., and Metaxas, D.N., 2016, October. Multimodal deep learning for cervical dysplasia diagnosis. In International Conference on Medical Image Computing and Computer-Assisted Intervention (pp. 115–123). Springer, Cham.

Xu, X., Zhang, Y., Zou, L., Wang, M., and Li, A., 2012, October. A gene signature for breast cancer prognosis using support vector machine. In 2012 5th International Conference on BioMedical Engineering and Informatics (pp. 928–931). IEEE.

Xu, Y., Dai, Z., Chen, F., Gao, S., Pei, J., and Lai, L., 2015. Deep learning for drug-induced liver injury. Journal of Chemical Information and Modeling, 55(10), pp. 2085–2093.

Yala, A., Lehman, C., Schuster, T., Portnoi, T. and Barzilay, R., 2019. A deep learning mammography-based model for improved breast cancer risk prediction. Radiology, 292(1), pp. 60–66.

Yue, C., Xin, L., Kewen, X., and Chang, S., 2008, December. An intelligent diagnosis to type 2 diabetes based on QPSO algorithm and WLS-SVM. In 2008 International Symposium on Intelligent Information Technology Application Workshops (pp. 117–121). IEEE.

Zhang, Q., Xiao, Y., Dai, W., Suo, J., Wang, C., Shi, J., and Zheng, H., 2016. Deep learning based classification of breast tumors with shear-wave elastography. Ultrasonics, 72, pp. 150–157.

Zhao, L., Chen, J., Chen, F., Wang, W., Lu, C.T., and Ramakrishnan, N., 2015, November. Simnest: Social media nested epidemic simulation via online semi-supervised deep learning. In 2015 IEEE International Conference on Data Mining (pp. 639–648). IEEE.

Zhou, J. and Troyanskaya, O.G., 2015. Predicting effects of noncoding variants with deep learning-based sequence model. Nature Methods, 12(10), p. 931.

Zhu, Z., Albadawy, E., Saha, A., Zhang, J., Harowicz, M.R., and Mazurowski, M.A., 2019. Deep Learning for identifying radiogenomic associations in breast cancer. Computers in Biology and Medicine, 109, pp. 85–90.

Zou, B., Lampos, V., Gorton, R., and Cox, I.J., 2016, April. On infectious intestinal disease surveillance using social media content. In Proceedings of the 6th International Conference on Digital Health Conference (pp. 157–161). ACM.

CHAPTER 4

Assistive Devices and IoT in Healthcare Functions

ABHINEET ANAND[1*], SAI PRASAD MISHRA[2], and SUBRATA SAHANA[2]

[1]Chitkara University Institute of Engineering and Technology, Chhitkara University, Punjab, India

[2]SCSE, Galgotias University, Greater Noida

*Corresponding author. E-mail: Abhineet.mnnit@gmail.com

ABSTRACT

Assistance to humans in the form of hardware for people with difficulties (or disabilities) is no new thing rather it has been part of human experience since ancient times. Internet of Things products for people who are not capable of any particular things are readily available to assist them in their daily life activities. In this literature, a study of different devices and their comparative study have been performed. Different categories of devices and their study in structured way have been carried out to learn and list the things happening in this domain. Also it is also going to help how the future products are supposed to be designed so that it may help mankind to live a better life.

4.1 INTRODUCTION

A healthy nation they say is a wealthy nation. People get ill, accidents happen, and emergencies arise, that is why healthcare is important. Healthcare can be defined as the diagnosis, treatment, prevention and management of injuries, diseases, illnesses, which helps in preserving physical and mental well-being of humans. Healthcare is divided into various areas to meet health needs of everyone in a nation and worldwide. It comprises of hospitals, clinics, medical devices, health insurance, medical tourism, and assistive technologies. Healthcare industry will continue to thrive as long as humans exist and hence forms a major part of any nation's economy. The Indian healthcare sector is growing at a quick pace as it is providing public healthcare coverage and accessibility to various healthcare tools.

Technology is a major part of the modern-day healthcare system. Latest technology provides us with many benefits to lead a healthy life. People depend on innovations in technology to lead stress-free life. Many companies have been focusing on developing healthcare technologies and building IT solutions for them. Patients now have access to best diagnostic tools and new cutting-edge treatments. The year 2016 is considered as the biggest year of healthcare technology innovations. There were many innovations including medical devices and gadgets. The year 2017 witnessed innovations and healthcare solutions in the fields of healthcare technology infrastructure, care models, and disease management applications. The year 2020 will see a great increase in the health data across cloud and mobility solutions that is estimated to reach US $83 million and thus the data collected from healthcare sector to reach US $280 billion.

Modern technologies such as cloud and big data have transformed the information and technology in healthcare. There is a huge amount of data collected from different resources in the field of healthcare. Big data helps in analyzing, making predictions about, and preventing huge risks every day, whereas cloud helps in reducing the wastage and improving efficiency in research and development. It also helps in facilitating efficient health exchange information.

However, still, to reach such a large population of society, including the elderly and people who are prone to chronic diseases, is difficult. While technology cannot stop aging or eradicate chronic diseases, it can help to make it easier in terms of accessibility. Internet of Things (IoT) has enlarged the ambit of care delivery in healthcare, and IoT-based medical devices have become channels of pervasive healthcare to reach patients at the right time (Domingo, 2012). With the real-time monitoring of health condition connected to a smartphone, it has become easier for doctors or authorized persons to keep a track of the health condition of patients regardless of the place, time, and situation. The IoT devices collect and transfer health data such as blood pressure, oxygen and blood sugar levels, weight, ECGs, as discussed and shown in Figure 4.1.

There are many applications of IoT such as cancer treatment, continuous glucose monitor and insulin pens, automated insulin delivery, connected inhalers, and promotion of hygiene hospitals.

FIGURE 4.1   Healthcare using IoT.

4.1.1   IoT AND ASSISTIVE TECHNOLOGY

Before IoT technology, many disabled people bounded themselves or were depended on other people for doing things for them. However, today, due to advancement in cutting-edge technology with devices and software systems, it has become easier for the disabled person to cope up with difficulties and they can face almost any challenge of daily life easily. IoT technology truly brought the era of assistance to a new start and challenged the big industries including healthcare, education, and rehabilitation centers to integrate IoT with the assistive technology (AT), as AT devices are proficient for individuals with disabilities. IoT assistance has improved the way the services were provided to visually impaired, deaf, and hearing-impaired people and also people with different health conditions to track as well as improve their condition. With IoT leading the blind, the latter can better understand and perceive its surroundings to react fast.

4.2   ASSISTIVE TECHNOLOGY

AT are products and systems that enhance the daily life of persons. It is any item or piece of equipment or software program that is used to maintain or increase the capabilities of disable or sick people.

AT can be communication boards made of cardboard or special-purpose computers, software and hardware, specialized learning material, curriculum aids, and many more. AT devices aid people having difficulty in walking, talking, hearing, standing, balancing, remembering, aiming, and speaking and help them live a normal life.

AT devices are built on hardware and software to assist the disabled. Nowadays, many AT devices are built using artificial intelligence (AI) technologies, including real-time speech-to-text transcription and various recognition tools. In 2018, Microsoft introduced the AI for accessibility program to improve the process of creating devices to benefit people with disabilities or tackle health-related issues (Delgado, 2017).

Eye-graze tracking helps people with physical impairments to move a mouse pointer on the computer screen with the help of a communication board. Hearing aids can help people with greater hearing loss. This is done by creating an electrical channel of medium replacing the anatomical structures. Speech-generating devices help people with communication difficulties to communicate with people better and easily. Robotic exoskeletons help paralyzed individuals to move around better. AT devices have given people the ability to interact with the outside world. They have become their new ears, eyes, and voice to work and lead independent individual lives or to communicate with others.

4.2.1   HISTORY

The foundation period was somewhat in 1900s because there was no particular moment that can be considered as discovery of AT. Signed in 1988, the Tech Act provided funds to assist each state in developing consumer-responsive systems that access assistive services and information. It was the first to provide the definition of AT and a process for evaluating the current needs of individuals with disabilities.

The Soldier Act Rehabilitation of 1918 was implemented as a concept in disability support for soldiers with not just money but also training and preparing them for new jobs. This traced back its roots to World War I. It provided job placement, training, and AT devices such as prosthesis to soldiers with disabilities. They were trained so as to match their new jobs with their "new" abilities. In 1951, the Braille typewriter was introduced, which had keys with each key corresponding to the six dots in the Braille code. This allowed people to type in Braille. In 2008, a lighter and quieter AT version was introduced that is still in use today. The Rehabilitation Act

(1973) was followed by the Disability Act (1997) and the Technology-Related Assistance for People with Disabilities Act (1988) that saw a continuous development of AT devices. The information age backed its progress and increased focus on computer-related AT.

4.2.2 ATIA

The Assistive Technology Industry Association (ATIA) is a nonprofit member-ship organization of manufacturers, sellers, and providers of technology-based assistive devices and services. ATIA members actively participate in providing a gamut for disabilities such as blindness and low vision, computer access problems, deafness and hard of hearing, communication disorders, learning disabilities, cognitive disabilities, mobility impairment, augmenta-tive and alternative communication devices (AACs), etc.

ATIA members are exceptional and skilled with a storehouse of experience and knowledge valuable that helps better understand how to build an AT that would meet the unique needs of different individuals. They have experience with AT devices or products adapting to individual situations and find one-of-a-kind solutions for different consumers with different disabilities. The ATIA conference is held annually since 1999 that showcases products and services for the AT community that comprises of users, educators, and industry and government professionals. In addition to this, ATIA sponsors working groups and also finds ways to promote their work to the professionals and the general public (Lawson, 1962).

The ATIA and its members also organize online webinars that teach practitioners and people interested in AT and AT devices.

4.2.3 ASSISTIVE TECHNOLOGY IN HEALTHCARE

AT has always been an integral part of the healthcare industry (Figure 4.2) (Scherer and Glueckauf, 2005). It enables people to live a productive, inde-pendent, and self-dignified life. AT assists people to have a normal healthy life and provides support services, long-term care, and improved health conditions to people with disabilities. Without assistance to people, they feel excluded, isolated, dependent, and usually get locked into poverty; thus increasing the impact of the disease and effect of incapability on their family, friends, and society. AT helps the elderly population to be able to live an independent life. The most commonly used AT devices are walking sticks, spectacles, wheelchairs, hearing aids, and walkers. Figure 4.3 is showing the symbol used to show the differently enabled people reserved speciality.

FIGURE 4.2   Assistive technology.

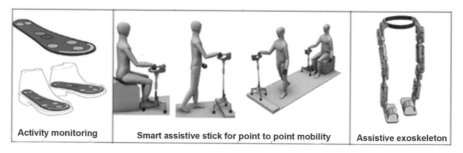

FIGURE 4.3   Activity monitoring using sensor.

For elderly, the development in AT and robotics can make a real difference, to make them able to do their own work at such an age. RoboCoach Xian is an assistive robot trainer that imitates human movements and teaches exercises to senior citizens. Enhanced with sensor technology like motion sensors, it personalizes exercises that are gentle to help senior citizens to stay active. It also provides physical, mental, and cognitive therapy to elderly who suffered from disorders. There are similar robotic technologies that help in improving mobility of patients as they rest. Automated bathing machines can interact and monitor patient's progress. As shown in Figure 4.4, how we can monitor the activity of old person or differentially enabled person with the help of sensor.

AT can also be used to track the health conditions (Mukhopadhyay, 2014) of normal people during daily activities and exercises such as heart rate, sleep tracking, and many other things. It also helps doctors to keep a track of the health condition of their patients and create a report on the basis of analysis performed, irrespective of their physical presence near the patient.

There is also a wide variety of technologies offering virtual assistance to anyone who has access to Internet. A database developed by the National Institute on Disability and Rehabilitation Research includes information about more than 21,000 assistive devices currently in use. Out of these, 6000 devices were listed in the early 1980s. With elderly people constituting 8.5% of global population and a rise in noncommunicable diseases, it is estimated that more than 2 billion people will need at least one assistive product by 2030 and two or more for elderly people. Today, more than one billion people need one or more assistive devices (or products) globally. In a review of data from surveys in 2005, it was estimated that 14%–18% of people aged 65 and over used AT solutions and only 20%–30% have access to such a variety of AT due to a lack of awareness, availability, and in some cases finance. The Pew Research Centre report says just 18% of this group owned smartphones in 2013, compared to 42% today. This greater interaction with technology has substantially increased the number of AT users. People aged below 45 were more likely to complain about the unmet needs for AT than the elderly group. Figure 4.4 shows different health enabling technologies for pervasive healthcare.

Different types of assistive technology fields have shown in Figure 4.5. Assistance to humans in the form hardware for people with difficulties (or disabilities) is not a new thing, rather it has been a part of human experience since ancient times, such as the eyeglasses were invented in Italy at around 1268–1289 and wheelchair was first used in the 5th century in China. As discussed earlier, AT solutions range from low to high tech, depending on the purpose and use. AT may be bought such as a hearing device, modified such as a wheelchair to perform multiple other functions, and custom made such as creating a prosthetic hand with the help of a 3D printer (Figure 4.5). A particular AT device may fit into one or many categories depending upon the individual's use and requirement. We can broadly classify the AT solutions into 10 categories (Figure 4.6).

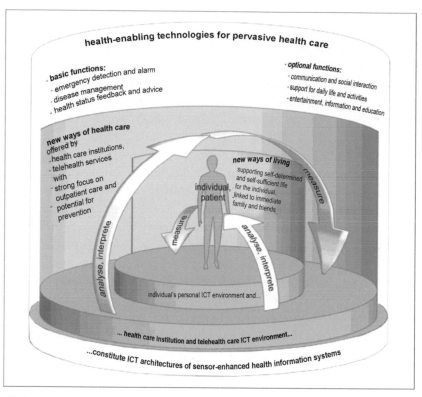

FIGURE 4.4   Health-enabling technologies for pervasive healthcare.

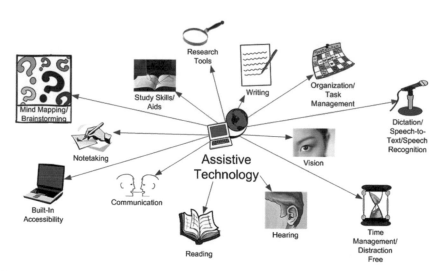

FIGURE 4.5   Types of assistive technology.

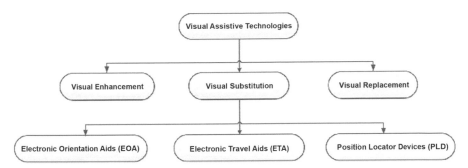

FIGURE 4.6 Types of visual technology.

4.2.3.1.1   Vision

AT products for people who are blind (or visually impaired) assist them in their daily life activities including reading, accessing computers, walking on roads, and other needs as shown in the chart in Figure 4.6. Some examples are magnifiers that include physical or software application to enlarge the images or text for a clear view, talking devices like a talking thermostat, Braille display that is an electromechanical device for displaying Braille characters for people who cannot use a computer keyboard, and screen reading software called optical character recognition (OCR) that is text-to-speech recognition software.

4.2.3.1.2   Hearing

AT products for people who have hearing difficulties such as deaf people assist them in their daily life activities including communication and other needs. Some examples are personal sound amplification products (PSAPs) that offer many hearing-aid benefits, simple vibrating alarm clocks, doorbells with flash lights, face-to-face dual keyboard communication systems, and amplified communication devices. People with hearing disabilities depend more on textual content and similarly on text-based assistive devices.

4.2.3.1.3   Hearing Loop

Also known as induction loop, it is a system that uses electromagnetic energy to transmit sound. It consists of four parts: a sound source such as a public address system or a microphone or a telephone, an amplifier, a thin loop of wire that goes around the room, and a receiver worn in the ears as a headset (Figure 4.7).

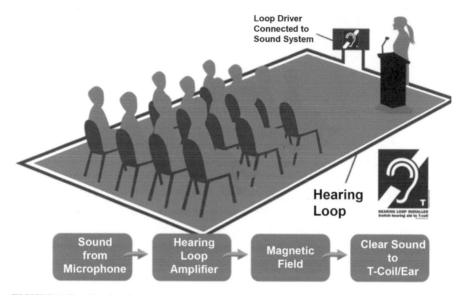

FIGURE 4.7   Hearing loop.

4.2.3.1.4   Working of a Hearing Loop

A miniature wireless receiver, a hearing loop receiver directly built into hearing aids, picks up the amplified sound that travels through the loop and create an electromagnetic field. To pick up the signal, a listener must be wearing the receiver and must be within range of the loop. As the sound is picked up directly by the listener, the sound is much clearer, with less background noise from the nearby environment (Coutinho et al., 2011).

Amplified sound (American Speech-Language-Hearing Association, 2002) can also be transmitted through radio signals used by FM systems. They can transmit signals up to 300 ft and can also be used in public. Usually, these devices are used in classrooms or halls, where the instructor wears a small microphone connected to a transmitter and the listener wears the receiver. People wear a wire around the neck called a neckloop with a telecoil inside their hearing aid to convert the incoming signal into magnetic signals. As these signals can transmit through walls, the listeners should be tune to a different signal than those outside the room.

Infrared systems use infrared light to transmit sound signals (Figure 4.8). The transmitter converts sound signals into light signals and beams it to a receiver that is worn by a listener where they are then decoded back to sound. As with FM systems, people whose hearing aids have a telecoil may also wear a neckloop to convert the infrared signal into a magnetic signal (Fransen and others, 2006). Unlike induction loops or FM systems, the infrared signal cannot pass through walls, making it particularly useful in courtrooms where often confidential information is being discussed. Infrared systems cannot be used in areas with too many light sources (Izsó, 2015).

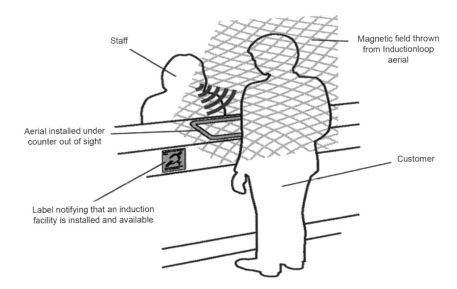

FIGURE 4.8 Loop system.

Loop systems are portable, about the size of a mobile phone; thus making it possible for people with hearing loss to execute their daily activities effectively (Figure 4.8). Personal amplifiers are useful in places like while watching TV or traveling in a car.

4.2.3.1.5 Telecoil

A telecoil, also called a t-coil, is a coil of wire that acts as a miniature wireless receiver, which is installed inside many hearing aids and cochlear implants. Its primary purpose is to provide clear and crisp sound to a listener over a telephone. It is also used with a variety of assistive devices for disabilities, such as FM systems, infrared systems, and personal amplifiers.

The telecoil works by receiving an electromagnetic signal from the hearing loop and then turning it back into sound within the hearing aid or cochlear implant, eliminating much of the distracting background noise to deliver sound customized for one's own need. For people who have trouble hearing, who do not have a hearing aid, loop receivers with headsets can provide similar benefits that matches one's need.

4.2.3.1.6 Speech Communication

AT products for people who have speech disabilities assist them in face-to-face communication while speaking to other individuals. Some examples are voice amplification systems used for people who cannot speak loudly enough to be heard in a noisy place or who have such medical conditions that they speak softly, artificial larynx, electrolarynx, or throat back that is an assistive medical device of size as small as an electric razor, communication boards, speech output software, and speech generating devices to translate words into speech.

4.2.3.1.7 Learning and Cognition Development

AT products support people who have problems related to learning, memory, focus, and organization. Some examples are memory aids, which are gadgets or systems that help in improving memory and recall, text-to-speech software systems to support learning, notetaking systems for helping people with low memory power to remember things, mobile applications specialized for increasing the cognitive and learning abilities, audio books for those who have reading problems, and voice recorders to record a person's own voice messages.

FORBRAIN: It is an auditory processing product produced by a start-up company called Sound For Life Ltd. It is a revolutionary patented device to aid people with speech and auditory disabilities by using auditory feedback. FORBRAIN is like a wireless headset with ground-breaking technologies to enhance the specific patterns of voice by creating an enhanced audio-vocal loop delivering voice directly via bone structure. This audio-vocal loop device is a natural process that can significantly increase attention and concentration improving one's verbal working memory and short-term memory. Using FORBRAIN is as simple as reading text out loud for a few minutes or speaking to another person (Calabrese et al., 2007).

4.2.3.2   FORBRAIN

4.2.3.2.1   Bone Conduction

The sound travels faster than air. As an experiment, plug your ears with your fingers and say something, you will hear how your voice resonates clearly in your head, despite your muted ears (Figures 4.9 and 4.10).

FIGURE 4.9   Learning and Cognition Development 1.

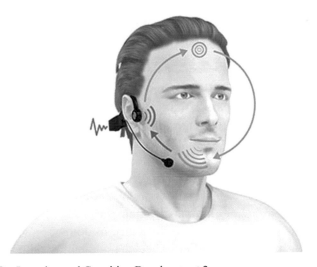

FIGURE 4.10   Learning and Cognition Development 2.

4.2.3.2.2   Dynamic Filter

It enhances specific frequencies of speech to increase memory, attention, and sensory processing.

4.2.3.2.3   Auditory Feedback Loop

This is a natural audio-vocal loop that draws on the ability of auditory discrimination, awareness, and integration of rhythm that each person can activate effortlessly (Mandell et al., 2007).

4.2.3.3   MOBILITY AND POSITIONING

AT products for people who need assistance while moving around, seating, or positioning help disabled and elderly people a lot to move independently without anyone's support. Some examples are wheelchairs for people with leg-related or posture-related problems, walkers for senior citizens to assist them while walking as generally at such an age ligaments tend to tear or weakness causes pain, power chairs equipped with additional products to provide postural and pressure management, canes or crutches also act as a mobility and seating aid to increase their balance and stability, and electric or hand-wheel scooters for the disabled so that they can travel freely outside.

4.2.3.4   DAILY LIVING

AT products for older people with functional limitations due to aging and also for disabled people increase independence when performing daily-life activities such as bathing, personal hygiene, dressing, eating, and other basic home activities including shopping, cleaning, money management, etc. (Katz, 1983). Some examples include toothbrush aid, which is a simple, easy to use and one of a type assistive device to aid in oral hygiene, dressing aids like button hooks and zipper pulls, long handle shoe horn to easily put on shoes while standing with less effort and less or no bending required and from any angle, Reacher is a device that usually helps a disabled or elderly person who cannot reach to things or face difficulty in doing so, adapted kitchen tools and eating utensils, modified wheelchairs such as with a cup holder or buttons to perform specific tasks, assistive robots like vacuum cleaners, automatic soap cleansers, book stands, switch-adapted products like adaptive toys for children and teens with special needs and switch-adapted plush toys, and many more (Figure 4.11).

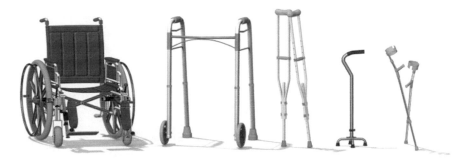

FIGURE 4.11   Mobility and positioning.

4.2.3.5   ENVIRONMENTAL ADAPTIONS

Well-designed AT products that help disabled people to easily move around a building such as in a house, office, hospital, or other buildings enable them to access various equipment independently in their surroundings. These include systems based on IoT such as automatic open/close doors; controlling lights, temperature, and curtains with a remote; and many other environmental needs. Some examples are door openers, lifts, elevators, remote-control appliances, voice-control security check and other switches, and voice or other activation devices. Various types of controllers can be used to control particular equipment like playing a video. Environmental control is a general term for these types of devices, commonly abbreviated as EC.

4.2.3.6   VEHICLE MODIFICATION AND TRANSPORTATION

AT products that are designed for the safe transportation of people increase independence through vehicle adaptations (Figures 4.12 and 4.13). In recent years, a variety of options have been made available to the disabled people in terms of personal and public transport. Mobility Works and National Highway Traffic Safety Administration contained detailed information about rehabilitation programs and modified vehicles. Some examples are safety locks to lock down and tie wheelchairs to car floor or any moving vehicle, ambulatory rider seater options, ramps and lifts to easily move in and out of a vehicle, raised roofs, adaptive seat belts to provide better positioning and help children to better interact with the surroundings, and senior living transport vehicles for senior citizens for safe and reliable transport.

FIGURE 4.12   Vehicle modification and transportation 1.

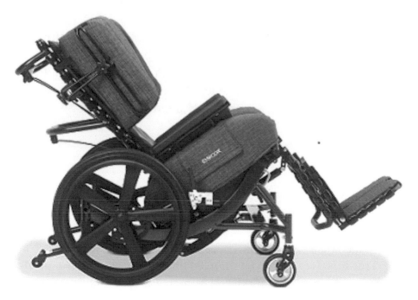

FIGURE 4.13   Vehicle modification and transportation 2

4.2.3.7 COMPUTER AND COMPUTER-RELATED PERIPHERALS

These are AT devices that help people with disabilities to use computers. A peripheral device connects to a computer externally and adds functionality to it. Despite high-resolution color displays and better graphical user interface (GUI), for visually impaired person, it is difficult to read and understand what is written on the screen. Some examples of computer-related assistive devices to help the disabled are a screen magnifier (Figure 4.14), which is a specialized software that magnifies the computer screen and enlarges text or any virtual content for people with low or blurred vision, alternate keyboards, input devices like voice recognition software, which takes speech as an input from the user, rate enhancement applications, and output devices such as screen reading accessibility that speaks out the output to the user (Beaver and Mann, 1995).

FIGURE 4.14 Screen magnifiers.

4.2.3.8 RECREATION AND LEISURE

AT solutions also make people able to play sports and perform recreational and leisure activities (Figure 4.15). The quality of life is decided by a person's social interaction and his/her activities. These are essential for human growth and development. Young teens and children who are disabled cannot participate in sports, and these hindrances decrease their self-esteem and self-belief. Some assistive solutions are switch-adapted toys, adapting equipment for sports like modified wheelchairs, electronically or mechanically adapted equipment, online or virtual recreational activities like virtual reality, electronic aids like timers and remote controls, computer or computer-facilitated activities like touch screens and interactive white boards, and many more (King et al., 2003).

FIGURE 4.15   Recreation and leisure.

4.2.3.9   MEDICAL INDUSTRY

There are many assistive devices that are used in medical healthcare centers (Figure 4.16). These AT devices for public provision are provided by therapists, orthopedic practitioners, and physicians. To compensate for the disability and make people participate in social and daily activities, various assistive solutions are provided after proper examination for need of devices and human support. Some of the examples are bath chairs, cane, and crutches.

Prosthetics involves the use of artificial limbs or prostheses to improve the condition of a person suffering from limb loss and is developed by a unique combination of appropriate materials and design that fits the individual's need, such as lower limbs or prosthetic parts (for the lower limbs) for stability in standing and walking, upper limbs or prosthetic parts (for the upper limbs) for reaching out and grasping, and especially designed shoes, walking frame, and wheelchairs (Figure 4.17) (Jarcho, 1981).

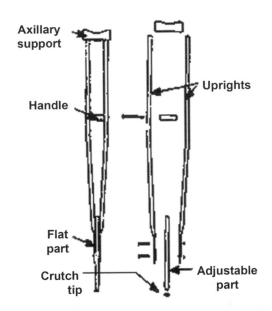

FIGURE 4.16 Medical industry.

Prosthetics

FIGURE 4.17 Lower limbs or prosthetic parts.

4.2.3.10 WORKING OF PROSTHETIC DEVICES

All prosthetic limbs are not created the same. Their design depends on the following few factors:

- body type,
- type of amputation,
- upper extremity,

- below elbow,
- lower extremity above the knee,
- below the knee,
- size,
- shape,
- strength of the residual limb, and
- lifestyle

Generally speaking, prosthetic legs and prosthetic arms have the same function. They may just have different ways to deliver that function.

The various components of your prosthetic device are as follows:

Socket: The most important component of a prosthetic arm or prosthetic leg is actually the one that is not visible from the outside. The socket is important because prosthetic devices have to be worn because of a lot of pressure on that residual limb, and if the socket does not fit right, it will cause a lot of pain and discomfort to the user (Figure 4.18). To ensure a perfect fit for the socket and greater durability, the prosthetics are precisely made using methods such as melding, robotic carving, which is the most accurate fabrication process, and the 3D laser scanning technique.

FIGURE 4.18   Example of Sockets.

An above-the-knee amputation will have two joints: the knee and the ankle. The knee joint will be designed to allow the leg to naturally swing forward. Knee and ankle joints as well as elbow joints can be computerized so that a computer can remotely control the swing of the device as well as the shock absorption when in use.

Finally, it may have a foot or hand attachment that can range from very basic to fully functional.

Research is currently being done to expand the capabilities of modern-day prosthetic devices to deliver functionality as close as the biological capability of a person.

Orthotics are products that involves precision and creativity in design and fabrication of orthoses (external braces) that acts to control weakened parts of the body. Orthotics are commonly used at the cervical region, the lower limbs, the pelvic and lower limbs, the pelvic region, the thoracic and back region, and the upper limbs. Government hospitals and various campaigns provide the above to the public free of cost.

4.2.3.11   SAFETY/SECURITY

AT devices that help provide safety to a disabled or an elderly person. These devices help people with disabilities to keep up themselves and their family safe. Some examples are: bed rail with easy adjustment attached to any side of bed, specialized locks like Wireless Remote-Controlled Doors and Accessible Combination Locks which are best for people who are blind or have low vision, and AT Alarms. There are many software-based applications that keep live track. InstaCare application notifies the family members or authorized doctor in case of an emergency or call for help on a touch of a button. This electronic button is paired with a smart device like a smart phone. InstaCare has a built-in motion sensor to keep a continuous track on the activities and serves as a panic button.

4.2.4   CHOOSING THE RIGHT ASSISTIVE TECHNOLOGY

There are hundreds of AT devices in the market today, and it is very important to pick the right one with the best fit according to the person's requirement, setting, and comfort (Figure 4.19). It is a multiple-step process that takes understanding and time (Galitz, 2007). The steps below define the process of choosing and obtaining the right assistive device or solution.

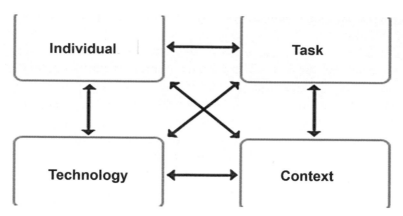

FIGURE 4.19   Choosing the right assistive technology.

1. **State the main goal:** What is the purpose of using the assistive device? What you want to do with the AT device? Will technology help the user to do what he/she cannot do right now or limited in doing?
2. **Access the situation:** In this step, input is taken from the user, user's family members, school, and medical professionals. Sometimes, this list extends to co-workers, caretakers, and related neighbors, that is, anyone who has experience with user or knowledge of AT or offers expertise. This depends on the limitations and requirement of the user. Also, the time up to which the particular device is useful to the user as well as AT is determined.
3. **Choosing a device/system:** Is the device simple to use? Does it accomplish the required task? Is this the most efficient way? Can it adapt to changing situations? Is it a cost-effective method? These are some important questions needed to be asked. Augmented reality fairs are also a good chance to check out options.
4. **Expert recommendation:** Before buying any of the AT devices, find the right term "experts" to help get the right device for the user. These "experts" may include doctors, physicians, therapists, and educators. Suggestions from people who have had similar experience can also help a lot. There are also many AT experts all around the country, in each state.
5. **Selecting a vendor/dealer:** An important thought in buying equipment is the dealer's responsiveness. The dealer should be able to provide technical support and service. Dealer's should also be technically sound with proper training.

6. **Pursue funding:** The cost of assistance technology solutions can be high and so funding can be a lot of help and saves a lot of time and effort. Some of the potential resources from where you can get funding are health insurance plans such as a family health insurance plans, ICICI health plans, etc., in which the amount that is to be insured must be paid out-of-pocket before the health insurer pays its share like on monthly basis, public plan programs, charitable groups for public healthcare, or loans. Manufacturers or retailers or wholesalers may offer discounted rates such as on a used or refurbished item. There should proper documentation and papers for appealing for loan or from a charitable group. Initial requests may not be accepted but appeals can be successful.

7. **Identify training needs:** Disabled people with AT devices should get proper training and instructions. This is the responsibility of the dealer, a representative of the manufacturer, a staff person (educational institution), or hospital nurses (medical institution).

8. **Regular check-ups:** There should be a conduct of follow-ups with a particular interval of time. Short-term follow-up should be in a couple of months or weeks and long-term re-evaluation should be done on a regular basis, like once a year or two.

9. **Some important points to note**
   • Test the AT device before buying it. Do not follow the advertisement or "AT device for month" articles.
   • Do not force buy the AT device. Be sure of its objective and purpose.
   • Before purchasing the AT device, please make sure to know about how to use it and make sure item is a good fit.
   • There are various types of assistive technologies. High-tech and low-tech devices do make some difference in the lives of individuals with disabilities. Some low-tech devices with lower cost do more effective job than a high-tech system. Low-tech devices are mostly easy to use, easy to use, and are easy to fix. High-tech devices are usually specialized engineering or technology and because of that they have usually a high cost of repair or replace.

4.2.5 ASSISTIVE TECHNOLOGY AND MOBILE APPLICATIONS

In this era of advancing technologies, there are a number of IT companies that are focusing a lot on assistive technologies and contributing to this.

Today, there are numerous mobile applications that are providing AT and its solutions. Each application has a specific purpose with an easy to use interface with great intuitiveness and accessibility. The application is kept updated with the latest features. In fact, such applications are very easy and fun to use by people with disabilities. Various categories of applications are as follows:

- **Hearing:** These types of software applications provide "visualized sound" to offer a new experience for the disabled or elderly people who have lost their hearing power or those whose hearing is weak. Once the users' hearing aid is worn off, they can enjoy various features like flash notifications, mono audio, adapt sound, hearing-aid compatibility, creating vibration sensation with different patterns for different purposes such as check on the incoming application notification or an incoming call or an alarm (Warick et al., 1997).

- **Vision:** Innovative features can also help people with blurred vision to be able to read with great ease and get the most out of today's mobile technology. Some applications for this purpose are as follows:
    - *Screen magnifier:* This application helps to magnify the screen size or with resolution so that each digital content on the mobile becomes enlarge and is easy to view for the user. This can be done simply by zoom in and zoom out by tapping on the screen.
    - *Color adjustment:* This can be used to change the screen colors to increase the screen readability for the color-blinded people.
    - *Negative colors:* One can select the optimal display for their eyes.
      Font size: This feature can change the textual size on the mobile for an enlarged view.
    - *Dexterity:* If there are several gestures to use and it is difficult for you to use your device, then in this case control it with an intuitive interface. The settings can be accessed conveniently for better user experience. Some of the features include assistant menu, which provides shortcuts or direct access, touch and hold delay feature, which lets the user to set the recognition time for tapping and holding the screen. This provides the user to perform some extra action on your screen and easy touch mode.
    - *Touch control:* Often, user makes unintentional touches on screen. This application allows us to control the touch response, making the response more accurate. It provides user with more functionalities to do with the device with a single touch.

There are many more features that make applications so wonderful, such as easy answering and calling with the help of the hardware buttons like the volume and power buttons. Some manufactures provide software applications to work with movement of the phone or with its location like it locks the screen when the phone is in a pocket or a purse and shaking phone for flashlight.

4.2.6 REPAIR AND MAINTENANCE

Assistive devices should be well built and maintained properly to keep it working of a longer period of time (Inge and Shepherd, 1995). If the AT device breaks down easily in a very short time, then it is not a viable option. AT devices should also be easily repaired or replaced. Choosing an assistive solution is a very important part as of the Equalization of Opportunities for Persons with Disabilities for disabled people.

There are certain plans for students with disabilities to help them access the facilities and not worrying of their maintenance as a student. When an AT device is a part of student's individualized education plan (IEP), the school has the responsibility of making certain that the individual is getting access to the AT device for the purposes of implementation. In most cases, schools are responsible for the maintenance, repair, and replacement of the device. Under the Individuals with Disabilities Education Act (IDEA Act), a school district is responsible for providing AT devices that are part of special education, including all the related services like supplementary aids and repair services. The device is to be provided at no cost to parents.

Repair means improving the poor condition or no working condition of the AT devices by means of some modifications, while maintenance refers to modifications or replacement of parts to prevent possible failures while the device is in the working condition. Cost and ease of the repair depend on the design of devices, knowledge of the repairer, and availability of infrastructure near users. Cost often deters many disabled people from getting their devices getting repaired or maintained. Poor people find it extremely hard to buy new parts or new devices. The same is the case for rural areas. If the repairing shop is far away from home or in another city, then costs of transportation and lodging become a barrier.

CBR: CBR stands for community-based rehabilitation (Lane, 1997), which aims to help people with disabilities by establishing a community-based medical integration, equalization of opportunities, and physiotherapy (Figure 4.20). It provides people with disabilities to have access to AT devices and ensure their good quality by ensuring maintenance to help them participate in their day-to-day activities. The main strength of the CBR acts is that it can be made available in the rural areas with limited infrastructure and is not restricted to only professionals (Chatterjee et al., 2003).

FIGURE 4.20   Community-based rehabilitation.

Some outcomes of the CBR are as follows:

- CBR personnel have knowledge about the AT, assistive devices, and mechanisms for specialized devices for different types of disabilities.
- People with disabilities and their families are provided with training on how to properly make use of the device and follow-up to ensure the proper use and care for their assistive devices.
- Local people are able to get access of assistance devices and simple repairs and maintenance are provided to them.
- Barriers providing access to devices or inadequate information should be reduced with proper financial and service support.
- These devices should be made available across all the regions of the country irrespective of their geological location.

4.3   CONCLUSION

This chapter presents an overall view from the chapter-specific findings on what are AT and AT devices, how they work, and the various healthcare-assistive devices that help the disabled and elderly people. Healthcare technology has come a long way in providing services that uplift the disabled person to live a rather normal life. Inclusion and performance are essential parts of a human dignity and human right. Technology has empowered the healthcare industry to provide services that benefited many individuals with their disabilities. While AT devices have fulfilled the desire of most of the individuals, they still are not accessible by everyone. Medical and social care are inaccessible because of their comparatively high cost, geographical location, and average after sales services. Government agencies and many NGOs are working together to provide free AT services in rural and distinct areas throughout the country. There should be regular security checks before delivery of software and hardware devices to disabled people and customer care should be installed at various locations to provide better services, longevity of products, and avoid further injuries. There are many medical conditions that are hidden and AT solutions can provide services for certain diseases and certain stages during medical condition. Ultimately, software and mobile applications have provided environment that provide better analysis of needs of consumers' need and provide devices accordingly. Proper training should be provided to consumers on how to use their devices, maintain them and monitor their own progress. Finding the right service provider for buying assistive devices for the disabled or elderly person is a very important step and one should consider many things before buying them such as selecting, designing, and maximizing the output of devices. Assistive devices hold promise for partial or permanent effects of impairment of an individual and enhancing their capabilities with proper products (hardware and/or software) and proper follow-up when there are societal and environmental limitations. Not only the evolution of AT solutions has benefited the disabled, elderly, students, healthcare industry, but they also created new areas of employment for the youth and the disabled.

KEYWORDS

- **healthcare**
- **IoT**
- **assistive devices**
- **heath-enable technologies**
- **assistive technology**

REFERENCES

American Speech-Language-Hearing Association, *Guidelines for Fitting and Monitoring FM Systems*. American Speech-Language-Hearing Association, 2002.

Beaver K. A. and Mann, W. C. "Overview of technology for low vision," *Am. J. Occup. Ther.*, vol. 49, no. 9, pp. 913–921, 1995.

Calabrese, C., *et al.*, "A perivascular niche for brain tumor stem cells," *Cancer Cell*, vol. 11, no. 1, pp. 69–82, 2007.

Chatterjee, S., Patel, V., Chatterjee, A. and Weiss, H. A. "Evaluation of a community-based rehabilitation model for chronic schizophrenia in rural India," *Br. J. Psychiatry*, vol. 182, no. 1, pp. 57–62, 2003.

Coutinho, R. S., Dauk, M. A., and Mu, C. "Wireless audio distribution system with range based slow muting." Google Patents, 2011.

Delgado, A. D. *Exoskeleton Technology: Applications as both an Inpatient Locomotor Training Device and Exercise Device*. Icahn School of Medicine at Mount Sinai, 2017.

Domingo, M. C. "An overview of the Internet of Things for people with disabilities," *J. Netw. Comput. Appl.*, vol. 35, no. 2, pp. 584–596, 2012.

Fransen, A. et al., "Integrated telecoil amplifier with signal processing." Google Patents, 2006.

Galitz, W. O. *The Essential Guide to User Interface Design: An Introduction to GUI Design Principles and Techniques*. John Wiley & Sons, 2007.

Inge K. J. and Shepherd, J. "Assistive technology applications and strategies for school system personnel," in *Assistive Technology: A Resource for School, Work, and Community*, pp. 133–166, 1995.

Izsó, L. "The significance of cognitive infocommunications in developing assistive technologies for people with non-standard cognitive characteristics: CogInfoCom for people with non-standard cognitive characteristics," in *Proceedings of the 2015 6th IEEE International Conference on Cognitive Infocommunications (CogInfoCom)*, 2015, pp. 77–82.

Jarcho, M. "Calcium phosphate ceramics as hard tissue prosthetics," *Clin. Orthop. Relat. Res.*, vol. 157, pp. 259–278, 1981.

Katz, S. "Assessing self-maintenance: activities of daily living, mobility, and instrumental activities of daily living," *J. Am. Geriatr. Soc.*, vol. 31, no. 12, pp. 721–727, 1983.

King, G., Lawm, M., King, S., Rosenbaum, P., Kertoy, M. K., and Young, N. L. "A conceptual model of the factors affecting the recreation and leisure participation of children with disabilities," *Phys. Occup. Ther. Pediatr.*, vol. 23, no. 1, pp. 63–90, 2003.

Lane, J. P. "Development, evaluation and marketing of assistive devices," *Technol. Disabil.*, vol. 6, no. 1–2, pp. 105–125, 1997.

Lawson, B. E. A. "Apparatus for fabricating a socket mount." Google Patents, 1962.

Mandell, J., Schulze, K., and Schlaug, G. "Congenital amusia: an auditory-motor feedback disorder?," *Restor. Neurol. Neurosci.*, vol. 25, no. 3–4, pp. 323–334, 2007.

Mukhopadhyay, S. C. "Wearable sensors for human activity monitoring: A review," *IEEE Sens. J.*, vol. 15, no. 3, pp. 1321–1330, 2014.

Scherer, M. J. and Glueckauf, R. "Assessing the benefits of assistive technologies for activities and participation," *Rehabil. Psychol.*, vol. 50, no. 2, p. 132, 2005.

Warick, R., Clark, C., Dancer, J. and Sinclair, S. "Assistive Listening Devices: A Report of the National Task Force on Quality of Services in the Postsecondary Education of Deaf and Hard of Hearing Students," 1997.

CHAPTER 5

Impact of IoT on Healthcare-Assistive Devices

R. INDRAKUMARI[1*], RISHABH KUMAR SRIVASTAVA[1], SUBBA[2], and MANAVALAN[3]

[1]SCSE, Galgotias University, Greater Noida, India

[2]Sri Manakula Vinayagar Engineering College, Control Organization, Puducherry

[3]Central Drugs Standard, D.G.H.S, Ministry of Health & Family Welfare, New Delhi

*Corresponding author. E-mail: indramurugesh25@gmail.com

ABSTRACT

The Internet has grown which let human being to access and utilize the services on a universal scale using traditional hosts, mobile devices such as smart phones across the globe. By linking the objects and devices, the Internet of Things (IoT) will fully utilize the network potential and facilitate the application of innovative services to a large set of scenarios, such as home and building automation, smart cities, healthcare, etc. Wearable devices can continuously capture several times a second for days, weeks, or months which negatively impact in the storage volume and battery capabilities thus making the wearable devices too bulky that is impractical to wear. Wearable technology prevents an unknown from gaining access the devices without authentication. The wearable technology built a solution which can sense the wearer of the wearable device with the help of bioelectrical impedance signal. Analyst and developer predict that wearable technology will impact the cultural and technological landscapes soon and it may change the nature of hand-held devices, mobile phones entirely. Some of the wearable devices include glasses, watches, e-textiles and smart fabrics, contact lenses, caps and beanies, jewellery such as bracelets and rings. This chapter begins with the introduction of wearable Internet of things, its attributes, and footprint of wearable technology in pharmaceuticals by considering the ethical issues and safety measures.

5.1   INTRODUCTION

Latest developments use the potential of remote communication technology using wireless systems to incorporate and synchronize information from various medical devices with the aid of Internet of things (IoT). IoT makes intelligent and smart devices that are recognized as the current technological revolution. As its archetypal case, IoT-based assistive devices are becoming popular to mitigate the issues associated with various devices (Fan et al., 2014). Ubiquitous wireless sensor network (WSN) technologies evaluate, infer, and recognize the indications from assistive devices, thus changing the techniques of healthcare systems with the help of IoT. The actuators and sensors unify impeccably and the collected information is shared across platforms to build a common operating picture (Gubbi et al., 2013). The IoT-based assistive devices capture the health data of patients and send them to respective clinical assistance. Many hospitals use IoT to locate patients and personnel and medical devices.

Assistive technology (AT) is a broad term that covers assistive, adaptive, and rehabilitative devices for people with some disabilities or elderly populations (Wilkie, 2010). People with any kind of disability face problems in performing the activities of daily life (ADLs) independently. ADLs include self-care activities such as mobility, bathing, eating, grooming, etc. AT is a powerful tool through which these people can perform the ADLs independently or without any assistance (Hoenig et al., 2003). For example, a wheelchair provides a disabled person with mobility. According to a survey done by the World Health Organization (WHO), around 15% of the world population suffers from a certain kind of disability (Krahn, 2011). Due to the advancement in the world, sedentary work has increased, which has led to more work and no exercise, which has significantly raised the problem of diabetes (majorly type II). According to the WHO survey in 2014, around 422 million people were suffering from diabetes. WHO has claimed that around 7.2 million deaths are due to the increased blood pressure in the world (WHO, 2019). Due to AT, people with disabilities and other problems have an opportunity of more positive and easygoing lifestyle, with an increase in social participation, security, and control and reduced costs on the problems.

The WHO's Global Collaboration on Assistive Technology (GATE) program is working actively to provide access to assistive technology to all. AT is an interface between persons and the lives they would like to lead. In this chapter, there are discussions on various AT devices and its applications in healthcare.

5.2 TYPES OF SENSORS FOR ASSISTIVE DEVICES

Sensors play an important role in the design and development of assistive devices as they collect the accurate data for monitoring health. The technologies like micromechanics and microelectronics have paved the way for the invention of various sensors to monitor human activities with low power consumption. Based on the working mode, the sensors are classified into invasive sensors and noninvasive sensors.

5.2.1 INVASIVE SENSORS

In invasive sensors, the body fluids are used to collect the health-related data. Blood plays a vital role in collecting the crucial parameters from various organs. Apart from blood, living cells are also used to gather the status of living organs. The samples are collected from humans through natural cavities. An example of invasive sensor is an ex vivo sensor that monitors blood gases and pH during cardiopulmonary bypass. This sensor is suitable for continuous parameter monitoring system (Islam and Mukhopadhayay, 2017).

5.2.2 NONINVASIVE WEARABLE SENSORS

Noninvasive wearable sensors do not need the body fluid, and hence, it is not necessary to penetrate the body using incision or injection; thus, these are painless and more attractive (Table 5.1). The body fluids used in this sensor may be sweat, skin interstitial fluids, saliva, and tears (Bandodkar and Wang, 2014).

5.3 WORKING PRINCIPLES OF ASSISTIVE DEVICE SENSORS

The working principles of sensors are based on different techniques like optical, electrical, and piezoelectric effects and electrochemical sensing.

TABLE 5.1   Invasive and Noninvasive Sensors

Invasive/Implantable Sensor	Noninvasive/Wearable Sensor
Pulse oximeter	Electronic pill for drug delivery
Glucose sensor	Retina implants
Temperature	Deep brain simulator
Electromyography	Pacemaker
Electroencephalogram	Wireless capsule endoscope
Blood pressure	Implantable defibrillators
pH value	Cochlear implants

5.3.1   *ELECTROCHEMICAL SENSORS AND IMPEDANCE SENSORS*

Impedance sensors and electrochemical sensors are the important classes of wearable sensors for monitoring physiological parameter measurements. Electrochemical sensors are further classified into aerometric, potentiometric, and conductive sensors that use capacitive and resistive methodology to fabricate different sensors. Capacitors are the building blocks of the electronic world. The ability of a capacitor to store an electrical charge is called as capacitance. Touch is the vital human sensory channel, and the technology used to respond to the physical touch is often called as capacitive sensing. A capacitive sensor provides low temperature dependence, high sensitivity, and low power consumption, with the capacity of sensing various chemical and physical parameters. Different types of capacitive sensors are co-axial cylindrical, parallel-plate, fringing field, and cylindrical cross-capacitor sensors (Rowland et al., 2011). Capacitive sensors are suitable for both invasive and noninvasive parameter measurements. The fringing field of the capacitor has the ability to sense the texture, location, and strength of the samples (Dean et al., 2012). Electrochemical sensors are highly portable, highly sensitive, low cost, and useful in many hand-held analyzers that are based on electrolytes and metabolites.

The working of the sensors starts with gathering input from targeted devices, and the inputs are classified into three different categories: the target input that is the actual input measured by the sensor, interfering input that refers to the sensitive input, and the modifying input that causes a change in the input–output relation of the sensor to the target and the interfering inputs. Based upon the characteristics, the wearable sensors are classified into static (e.g., body temperature) and dynamic sensors. The static sensors hold the characteristics of accuracy, sensitivity, threshold, resolution, tolerance, span, linearity, short-term and long-term drift, hysteresis, response time, interchangeability, cross-sensitivity, recovery time, and yield ratio (Rucco et al., 2018). Dynamic characteristics handle the performance characteristics of the sensor inputs such as ramp, step sinusoidal, and ramp. The output response for the step input is transient, which reaches a steady state and then return to the initial value during recovery. The ramp input signal produces linear output response. The nth-order polynomial mathematical equation relates the electrical output of a sensor to the input parameter. The electrical output may be current, voltage, and phase; the order of the equation may change according to the complexity of the sensor.

5.3.2   ASSISTIVE DEVICES' COMMUNICATION PROTOCOLS

A communication system for assistive devices is a novel technology that connects the human and machine (Kim et al., 2015). Wireless communication is vital for assistive devices to transmit data to neighboring devices, which creates several issues in transmission (Jiang et al., 2015). The wireless communication system aims at short-range communication like body area network (BAN) and personal area network (PAN) as a transmission conduit. Assistive devices use wireless communication to set up BAN to transmit data to proximate devices. In early days, the radio transmission technique is used in BAN, which is susceptible to wiretapping. Assistive devices transfer most sensitive data that should be preserve securely (Jeong et al., 2012). Moreover, intrabody communication is wireless and the electric-field distribution of assistive devices uses the human body as a conducting wire using the finite difference time domain method (Zimmerman, 1996), and hence, radio transmission is not applicable. Zimmerman has introduced the intrabody communication system (Sasamori et al., 2009).

The hardware design for an intrabody wireless communication system for an assistive device is explained in Figure 5.1, which depicts the information transmission of an intrabody network to proximate devices. It accommodates a serial interface unit, which acts as an on-chip communication system, a serializer/deserializer, and a modem. The entire communication module is managed by a processor through serial interface that increases the efficiency of the system by using first-in-first-out (FIFO) methodology and transforms the data into serial form. The serial transformed data is converted into a transmission signal with a specified frequency using a modulator. The deserializer transfers the data to the serial interface unit and the main processor.

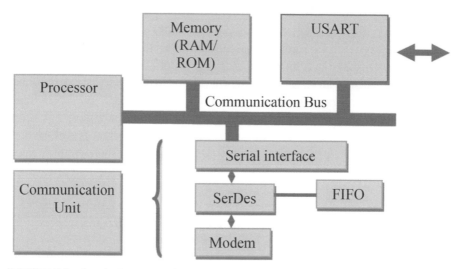

FIGURE 5.1   Intrabody communication system—hardware architecture.

5.4   SPEECH RECOGNITION IN HEALTHCARE

Assistive devices in healthcare are emerging successfully to solve many issues. Language technologies have the capacity to help people to understand and access the information easily (Pearson et al., 2010). Especially, speech recognition provides dominant applications in the eHealth system. Speech recognition system consists of microphones, sound cards, and speech engine software (Al-Aynati and Chorneyko, 2003). In radiology, the implementation of speech recognition reduces the turnaround time from 15.7 to 4.7 h (Callaway et al., 2002). As radiologists are dealing with huge volume of data, typing the report by hand takes more time (Warfel and Chang, 2004). A telephone-based dictation interface speech recognition system is available to record the details dictated by the radiologist, which speeds up the report-generating process. This method is often referred as back-end speech recognition. Improvement in the reporting of surgical pathology is analyzed, and cases signed out in 1 day improved from 22% to 37% (Singh and Pal, 2011). Front-end speech recognition software is also in practice for physicians to generate the reports with the help of personal computers. Speech recognition software is providing benefits to people with disabilities. Cerebral palsy and motor neuron disease patients are getting benefited by speech recognition software. Many companies are recruiting persons with disabilities by making voice recognition software available for computer control and data input. Communication software is also available in markets to assist visually impaired to operate computers by converting text to word.

5.5 VENTRICULAR ASSISTIVE DEVICE

A ventricular assistive device is an electromechanical device used to assist people with heart failure. The ventricular assistive device contains a balloon that is wrapped around the delicate portion of the heart to promote the blood flow. Based on patient's health condition, the ventricular assistive devices are designed as left ventricular assist device, right ventricular assist device or biventricular assist device (Sen et al., 2016). Traditionally, the ventricular assistive devices contain a pump to circulate blood, a controller to control the activities of the device, a power supply to operate the device, and a drive line to connect the right atrium with the pulmonary artery and the left atrium with aorta.

Nowadays, heart transplantation is considered as the most successful long-term surgical treatment for heart failure. However, receiving the organs for transplantation is a tedious process. In this situation, a ventricular assistive device is considered as the treatment modality as it acts as a bridge to transplantation. This device supports the patient until the donor is available. In some cases, when the patient's health condition does not support for cardiac transplantation, the ventricular assistive device acts as destination therapy.

5.6 BLOOD PRESSURE MONITORING

Blood pressure is a very important factor along with the heart rate, the body temperature, oxygen saturation, etc. The measurement of the blood pressure is expressed in terms of the maximum heart beat (systolic pressure) over minimum heart beat (diastolic pressure; Siddiqui, 2011). Generally, the blood pressure is measured in the units of millimeter of mercury (mmHg). The blood pressure is written in two figures:

1. *Systolic pressure*: This is the pressure when the heart pushes the blood out of the heart.
2. *Diastolic pressure*: This is the pressure when your heart rests in between the beats.

According to the WHO, the global estimation of people suffering from blood pressure in 2008 was around 40% of the total world population. Blood pressure is majorly of two types: (1) low blood pressure and (2) high blood pressure.

High blood pressure, also known as "hypertension," occurs when the blood pressure reading of an individual is "140 over 90 mmHg" or higher. If any individual suffers from high blood pressure, it means that there is lot of extra strain on his heart and blood vessels, which can later on increase the rate of heart attack or stroke.

Low blood pressure, also known as "hypotension," occurs when the blood pressure reading of any individual is lower than "90 over 60 mmHg." The causes of low blood pressure can vary from dehydration to any surgical disorders or serious medical issues. Having a low blood pressure is not a great deal of concern, but at a very low blood pressure, the body can feel dizziness or faintness, which can be a serious health issue.

Thus, there is a serious need for finding out such devices that can help people to know about their blood pressure without going to doctors every time and reducing their hospital bills. There is always need for assistive devices by the help of which the population can help themselves to keep a check on their diseases without the involvement of their doctor's every time.

There is always a need for such devices that can help people, and they should be user friendly so that people can use them on their own and does not require any kind of help from the doctors and other people. There are many such devices made for the people suffering from hypertension and there is also new development done on improved devices.

IoT-based blood pressure monitoring machines are available nowadays. The major function of these machines is to measure the systolic and diastolic pressure, which is basically used to measure the pressure in the arteries (Pickering, 2002). The oscillometric technique is used to measure the systolic and diastolic pressure in this machine. The data recorded by the machine are then stored to a connected database, through a connected Wi-Fi, which can be accessed remotely by anyone (Babbs, 2012). Thus, by using this device, a patient can measure his/her blood pressure by themselves without requiring any kind of involvement of the doctors that can save a lot of manpower.

The oscillometry technique is very common these days in the automatic blood pressure measuring devices. In order to measure the blood pressure using the oscillometry technique, a cuff is placed on the upper arm of the patient and inflated to a pressure above the patient's systolic pressure that causes the flow in the arteries to stop. After this, the pressure in the cuff is decreased slowly below the systolic pressure of the patient that causes the flow of the blood into the arteries walls and a variation is recorded. The pressure in the cuff is reduced below the patient's diastolic pressure that allows the blood to flow normally in the blood arteries. Variations can occur at any time, when the cuff is inflated above the systolic pressure of the patient. The pressure in the blood vessels is transferred to the air, present in the cuff, which in turns sends the variations to a pressure transducer that converts the measurements into analog signals, through which the systolic and diastolic pressure of a patient can be detected. By using this oscillometric technique, there is a possibility to design an assistive device that can be connected to the database through a Wi-Fi, the data from which can accessed remotely. The block diagram is shown in Figure 5.2.

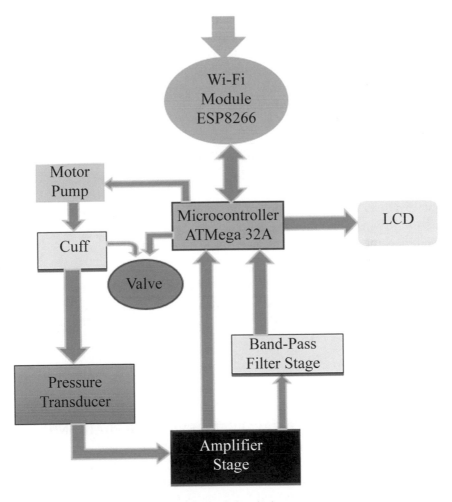

FIGURE 5.2 Blood pressure monitoring assistive device.

Pressure transducer and microcontroller: The work of the transducer is to convert the vibrations received in the cuff into analog electric signals. Later on, these signals are filtered and amplified to get the required pulse waveform. The microcontroller that is used is of 8 bit based on the reduced instruction set computer architecture, ATmega 32A.

Amplifiers and filters: The output received from the pressure transducer is in millivolts, which should be amplified. Thus, an amplifier is used with a gain of 220. Since the frequency of the human pulse wave is in the range of 0.6–6.4 Hz, there is a need for a band pass filter. These band pass filters try to reduce the noise in the waveform and extract the frequencies only in this range.

ESP8266: This is a low-cost development board that contains the important general purpose input/output, universal asynchronous receiver–transmitter, and Wi-Fi. The Wi-Fi module is connected to the microcontroller, and the recorded blood pressure data is send to the database. There is an IoT-based platform by the name Thing Speak that helps to collect and store the recorded blood pressure to cloud.

5.6.1 COMPARISON OF THE IoT AND COMMERCIAL BLOOD PRESSURE MONITORING DEVICES

Table 5.2 lists the comparison of the commercial blood pressure machine with the IoT-based blood pressure machine. This result shows this new IoT-based machine is accurate and can be used by the public.

TABLE 5.2 Comparison of IoT and Commercial Blood Pressure Monitoring Devices

Number of Trails Done	Commercial Digital Blood Pressure Monitoring Devices	IoT-based Blood Pressure Monitoring Devices
1	125/85	132/91
2	132/86	135/94
3	1110/72	114/75

5.7 IoT-BASED ASSISTIVE WALKER DEVICE FOR FRAIL AND VISUALLY IMPAIRED PEOPLE

More than 285 million people in the world are visually challenged and are facing reduced mobility and falls issues (Lacey et al., 2006). Elderly people are also suffering from the same issues, and more than one-tenth of the falls causes serious injuries (Tinetti et al., 1988). Apparently, these people need an extra support for stable walk and balance, which cannot be provided by conventional walkers and canes that do not have modern technology. Hence, a smart device is important to ensure the safety of the visually impaired and elderly person. IoT is considered as the base for the smart assistive devices. The IoT-based assistive walker for frail and visually impaired people consists of both hardware and software. The electrical part is considered as the hardware, which accommodates a sensor unit, a control unit, and the output. The software holds maps to assist and apps to find the exact location of the victims. The sensor gathers the information regarding the location and the surroundings of the system. If any obstacles are found in the path of the walker, the sensor senses the position of the object and transfers the details to the controller via IoT, which alerts the user through output devices and thus avoids falling or fatality.

The IoT-based walker architecture is divided into three layers, namely,

- a perception layer,
- a network layer, and
- an application layer.

The perception layer sometimes called as the recognition layer (Suo et al., 2012) is the lowest layer of the IoT architecture, responsible for collecting information like direction, position of the object from the environment and thing, and conversion of the data into the digital form. This layer uniquely identifies the address by utilizing communication technologies such as Bluetooth, RFID, 6LoWPAN, and Near-Field communication (Silva et al., 2017). The network layer is considered as the brain of the architecture, and it is responsible for secure data transmission between perception and application layers (Suo et al., 2012). This layer is the convergence of communication networks and the internet. The application layer is the topmost layer of the traditional IoT architecture that provides personalized-based services based on the users need thus reduces the gap between the user and the applications.

Figure 5.3 shows the architecture of the IoT-enabled assistive walker. The user makes a request to go to park through his/her Internet-connected mobile phone. The request is transmitted to the network layer, which process the request and transfer the data to the application layer. This layer guides the user to do necessary steps to reach the park safely.

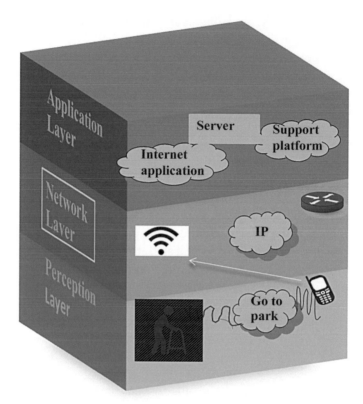

FIGURE 5.3   IoT applications to assist an elderly/physically challenged person.

5.8   GLUCOSE LEVEL MONITORING

Diabetes mellitus is a chronic disease that affects many people around the world. Due to an increase in the sedentary work around the globe and advancement in the technology, according to WHO, nearly 422–500 million people suffer from diabetes) (WHO, 2018). Over the past few decades, this disease has almost grown like roots in human society. There is someone or the other in today's world who is suffering from this chronic disease. Diabetes is a disease where the blood glucose (aka blood sugar) of an individual is very high. In the human body, blood glucose is the major source of energy that provides the cells with the power to work, and it comes from the food that an individual take. Insulin is a hormone in the human body that is produced by the pancreas, which helps the glucose reach the cells of the body for energy. Sometimes, the body is not able to produce enough insulin (or no insulin) or does not use insulin well, which results in the glucose to remain in the blood, as a result of which the glucose circulates in the blood and does not reach the cells, raising in turn the glucose level of the blood and causing this disease. Diabetes is of two kinds: type I and type II. If a person suffers from the type I diabetes, then the body of the person is not able to produce insulin. The immune system destroys the cells that produce insulin. As a result, the person has to take insulin in order to stay alive (Marker et al., 2018). If the person suffers from type II diabetes, then the body does not make insulin or use it well. This is the most common type of diabetes.

Due to this increasing problem of diabetes, there is always a need for innovative technology that can help the people to keep track of their disease on their own. Many such pharmaceutical companies are working every day to bring such devices to everyone. With the help of these devices, people will be able to freely and independently track the status of their sugar level. A study that was conducted by Polisena et al. (2015) at the Canadian Agency for Drugs and Technology in Health in 2009 found that storing and sharing self-monitored blood glucose using home telehealth tools (such as PDAs or fax machines), supported with physician feedback, showed improved glycemic levels and reduced hospitalizations. There are various glucose-monitoring devices available in the market that are manufactured and marketed by some famous pharmaceutical companies and helping people to keep a track of the blood glucose level independently. These glucometer kits come along with a device that tells the reading of the glucose level, with the help of test strips. In order to use this glucometer, the person pricks the skin (commonly his finger) and applies the blood sample onto the test strip, which is inserted into a meter. The glucose of the blood reacts with the chemicals in the test strips, and then, an electric current passes through determining the level of glucose in the blood sample and provides numerical results on the meter. Thus, by using these glucometer kits, an individual can get his/her glucose level in seconds.

Wearable technology is the new trend in the glucose level monitoring industry that brings a new trend in testing glucose (Gonzales et al., 2019). These wearable devices comprise of gadgets that can be worn and equipped with various sensors and wireless connectivity to assist the glucose level monitoring, personalizing treatments, connecting with health-care providers, and even deliver medication to the body when needed. Some wearable includes skin patches, contact lenses, and footwear.

Skin patches: These are small patches that enclose some sensors that measure the blood sugar level in sweat and automatically release a dose of insulin to check the glucose level in the blood. The patch can be attached to an individual body, and in the case of low blood glucose level, it will send a message automatically to the smartphone that reminds the individual to eat. Some patch systems require a wire to transmit the data, but some pharmaceutical companies are working on the patches to send the data wirelessly. A pharmaceutical company has developed a FreeStyle Libre Flash glucose monitoring system. It is a kind of patch placed at the back of the arm and is made up of a small and round sensor with microfilaments that measure glucose levels in beneath-the-skin fluids per minute. There is an external device that reads the sensor through the clothes scans. The same is already in use in certain parts of Europe.

Contact lens: Brian Otis and Babak Parviz are exploring smart contact lenses that could monitor blood glucose levels through human tears for Google X (Parviz, 2014). A leading pharmaceutical company has agreed to license and commercialize this product once it is available. They are also trying to make lenses that could help in compensating the poor eyesight, which is a common problem with people suffering from diabetes. Google in 2015 was granted a patent for this type of contact lens that can measure the blood glucose level of the humans through his/her tears.

Footwear: The developments in technology are not only restricted to self monitoring. The technological developments are also prevalent in preventing some common diabetes complications such as diabetic neuropathy, which results in limb amputation. Currently, some scientists are working on prototype socks and shoes that are embedded with thermal and pressure sensors, which can point out specific areas on the feet of human beings that have an insufficient blood supply (Park, 2005). A mobile application will be connected to this footwear that will alert the wearer if one area of the foot is not getting blood supply. It can also inspect some kinds of cuts or soft tissue damage, in which an infection is most likely to develop. Such technology will reduce the cases of amputations. Researchers working at the Fraunhofer Institute in Germany are working and testing a sock that is equipped with 40 tiny sensors. These sensors are spread across the sole, heel, top of the foot, and ankle to get a 3D reading. When a person stands on one foot for too long and the pressure starts to build up, the sensors send a signal to a wireless device that communicates with a smartphone, which in turn alerts the person to shift his/her weight to the other foot. Work is being held on making this sock washable. The Southern Arizona Limb Salvage Alliance (SALSA) of the Department of Surgery at the University of Arizona is researching on Smart Sox, which is a kind of stocking made up of fiber optics and some sensors that monitor pressure, temperature, and joint angles. This helps in the avoidance of development of foot ulcers. Still, some testing is going on for this Smart Sox.

5.9   ELECTROCARDIOGRAM MONITORING

Heat rate is a very important and critical parameter in the human body. Doctors use medical devices and apparatus to measure the parameters in/of the human body. For heart rate measurement, doctors use a heart rate monitor. In this section, there is an introduction to the ECG monitoring system based on IoT. This innovative device measures the heart rate of an individual and sends the recorded heart rate in bpm (beats per minutes) to a connected database on cloud. With the help of this device, the doctors can examine the parameters in real time. Also, they can analyze the health of their patients who are currently not admitted to the hospital. One more main advantage of this device is that it can be installed in the ambulance, and all the parameters including the heart rate of the patient can be measured and uploaded on a cloud. This data can be send to the doctor beforehand the patient arrives in the hospital so that the doctor can start preparing for the treatment of the patient. In this section, we will also talk about a smart device by the name SanketLife marketed by Agatsa (Tangri, 2017).

5.9.1   IoT IN ECG

The Registrar General of India has reported that the death caused by cardiovascular diseases led to 17% of total deaths and 26% of adult deaths in 2001–2003. It increased to 23% of total and 32% of adult deaths in 2010–2013. Currently, in India, only the deaths due to the cardiovascular diseases are increased to 40% since 2015 (Gupta et al., 2016). The government in every financial year allots a huge amount of money for the health sector to perform various test and operations at very subsidized rates. With the help of this ECG machine, the doctors can track the various health parameters of the patients who are at remote locations using the cloud platform. This will also help the patients to know about their health parameters.

There are very good and advanced ECG monitors available in the market, but no one has the feature of saving the parameters to a cloud server. In this section, we will discuss how the sensor can work and help to avoid the deaths due to cardiovascular disease.

5.9.2 WORKING OF THE ECG SENSORS

This ECG monitor will consist of majorly two parts:

i) patient monitoring and
ii) signal monitoring.

This ECG sensor (AD8232) can be used with a wrist band that can be tied on the wrist. AD8232 is a very cheap sensor; apart from being a cheap chip, it has very good impedance and gain properties. AD8232 will provide the ECG signal to a controller chip that is based on an ARM 7 controller. The microprocessors will receive the ECG signals and the processing will be done. These signals will be recorded in bpm. This will be divided into various segments of the time domain. After this, the device will be transferring the data through a mobile app to a database server. Then, the database server will upload the results on the cloud server (Satija et al., 2017).

The doctors with the help of the cloud platform can read these signal parameters, and the records will be shown with respect to all the time domains along with the information of the patient such as name, age, and gender. The major advantages of this device are that it can give a probability to a greater extent. The device is portable and user friendly. This device can be used anywhere, and the results can be accessed by the doctor from anywhere across the globe. Since all the data is stored in the cloud server, it can be accessed from anywhere and anytime. Another such device is SanketLife, which is marketed by Agatsa and made in India. SanketLife is of the size of a credit card, and it is based on a mobile-based leadless ECG machine. The device works by placing both the thumbs on the slots provided in the machine, and the reading is comparable to a single leaded device with an accuracy of 98%. SanketLife allows measuring the electrical activity of the heart through sensors, and the reading is transferred to a mobile phone by the usage of a low-energy Bluetooth technology. The device is provided with three sensors that are used to take complete 12-lead electrocardiograms by contact with the skin. After the signal is processed, the data is displayed in the mobile as s PDF report is generated. This PDF report can be shared with the doctor. This device can be synced with any smartphone, and the reports can be seen anywhere and anytime. The present feature of this device includes the display of the ECG reports and evaluating the stress levels. However, the next iteration of the technology will enable this device to send the reports to a panel of doctors for a quick review. There are also attempts made to make this compatible to detect other various diseases through the ECG reports (Figure 5.4).

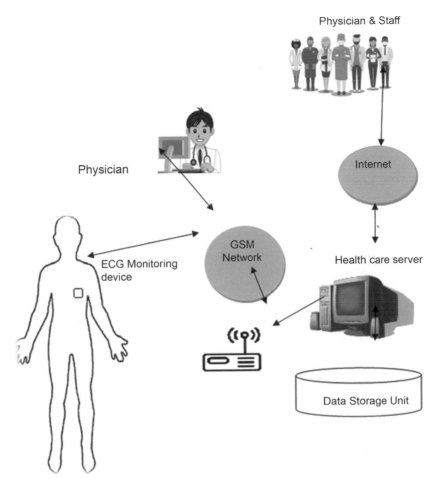

Physician & Staff

Physician

Internet

GSM
Network

ECG Monitoring
device

Health care server

Data Storage Unit

FIGURE 5.4 Wearable mobile electrocardiogram architecture.

5.10 BODY TEMPERATURE MONITORING

Body temperature is one of the most important factors in maintaining the health of our body, especially in infants. Due to the sudden increase in chronic diseases in the world, there is an important need for keeping a track of the body temperature. Any kind of increment or decrement in the body temperature can point to any kind of serious health issue. Talking about the infants, there is always a need for keeping a check on their body temperature, as any kind of small change in their body temperature can cause them to feel uneasy and they need to feel comfortable at all times. The same is the situation with the elderly people; they can also feel uncomfortable if there is something wrong with their body temperature. Due to the rapid development in the field of wearable devices, there arises a need for making a device that can measure the temperature of the human body.

In this 21st century, we want everything to be listed with the IoT; thus, it has played an important role in the field of healthcare. There are new devices that are made or improved every day. The IoT and the mobile services have made the manufacturing of these devices possible and have helped people to share their health conditions to the hospital staff such as doctors, nurses, etc.

Regular high or low body temperature at a particular time or any event can hinder the functions or the body and can affect the daily routines of a person. It can cause serious health issues, and visiting the doctors every time can result in a change in medication and loss of good health and money. For example, if the body is affected by any kind of bacterial or virus infection, the body temperature will suddenly increase, which in turn can create health issues and affect the regular routine of the individual. According to "Healthline," which is a health blog, the average temperature for babies is 97.9–99°F and for adults, it is 97–99°F. In Malaysia, devices that could measure the body temperature of the babies are available, and still, there are many devices yet to come.

5.10.1   IoT IN BODY TEMPERATURE MONITORING SYSTEMS

MosChip has designed an IoT-based hardware and software system that can track down various health conditions of the patients (Moschip, 2018). These devices are connected to a real-time system that can share the information with the doctors of the patients. Table 5.3 lists the temperature trends in the body and their effect on the body (Satija et al., 2017).

The devices can be connected to Bluetooth. Bluetooth is a low-power technology that can connect any device to the mobile systems. Thus, Bluetooth is the solution of the connectivity to the device to mobile phones. The device is compact, handy, and works on 3.3 V battery. The device has a wireless media that has interfacing to the temperature sensors.

5.10.2   WORKING PRINCIPLE OF BODY TEMPERATURE MONITORING SYSTEMS

The device or the temperature patch can be connected to the human body where it can measure the accurate temperature. The location of the device on the body may differ from person to person. The device will collect the data from the body within a particular time interval. This data will be shared with smartphones with the facility of Bluetooth. The application that is designed for the iOS and Andriod platform will collect the data, segregate the data, and, in turn, send the real-time data to the cloud application and services through the help of Wi-Fi (refer to Figure 5.5) (Satija et al., 2017).

TABLE 5.3 Temperature Trends in the Body and Their Effect on the Body

Low Body Temperature (Regular Trend)	High-Body Temperature (Regular Trend)
Addison's disease	Sweating
Diabetes	Chills and shivering
Drug/alcohol abuse	Headache
Hypothyroidism	Muscle aches
Infection	Loss of appetite
Kidney failure	Irritability
Liver failure	Dehydration
Sepsis	General weakness
Side effects of medications	Unusual skin rash, especially if the rash rapidly worsens
Shock	Unusual sensitivity to bright light
Fast breathing/asthma	Stiff neck and pain when you bend your head forward
Cancer	Mental confusion
Stress	Persistent vomiting
Insomnia	Difficulty in breathing or chest pain

With the help of this device, the doctors can keep a close look at his/her patient reports and can suggest medication immediately. This device includes an alarm for high or low temperatures, medication alerts, and a reminder for the doctor to visit the patient.

These devices can be used for measuring the body temperature of infants. Infants need special attention and care, and this device can help the parents. This system can be connected through the smartphones of the baby's parents, through a wireless network, such as Wi-Fi, and can be provided with an alert alarm that can notify the parents if the body temperature of their baby is higher or lower than the normal temperature (Zakaria et al., 2018).

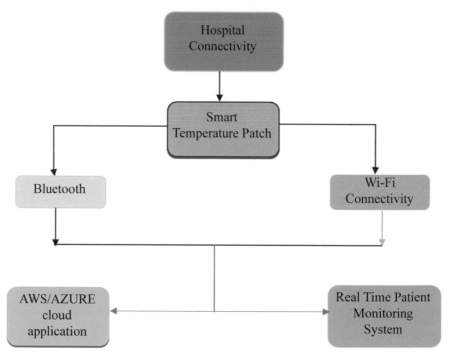

FIGURE 5.5   Working principle of a body temperature monitoring device.

5.10.3 *WEARABLE IoT-BASED BODY TEMPERATURE MONITORING SYSTEMS*

There must be a question arising, why cannot we make a band that can measure all the critical parameters of the human body? The solution is a wearable band that will be having various sensors to measure the different body parameters. The band can be manufactured by collaborating various sensors that have the capability of measuring the ECG, blood glucose, body temperature, blood pressure, heart rate, sweat sensing, etc. Due to a lack of computation capability of the sensing devices, these data can be sent to a smartphone or tablet, which in turn processes the raw data and produces the output for the user. However, there is another problem: keeping the track of all such parameters will require an operation on a 24/7 basis, where the smartphones or tablets will lack (Zakaria et al., 2018).

However, after the advancement is done in the field of cloud computing, the data that the sensors collect can be sent to the cloud servers (Ferreira et al., 2015) with the help of the Wi-Fi facility. Any authorized user can easily access all these data with the help of internet connectivity anytime and from anywhere (Xiong et al., 2012). Then, all these data can be accessed by the doctors and the hospital facility in order to improve the health or increase/ decrease the medication of the patient. These data can also be accessed by the patient themselves and even the family members on their mobile phones or tablets through an application and an internet connection. A diagram for overall healthcare IoT embedded framework is given in Figure 5.6 (Alahi and Mukhopadhyay, 2019).

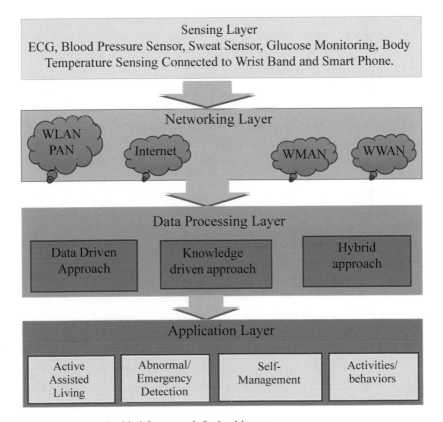

FIGURE 5.6   IoT-embedded framework for healthcare.

5.11   SECURITY THREATS OF ASSISTIVE DEVICES

The basic requirements for security and privacy in assistive devices are almost same as other wireless devices. This section addresses the various security threats of the assistive devices and their solutions. Physical attack is the attack on communication link or physical components of the assistive devices. Jamming is a process that blocks the wireless communication between the sources to destination with the help of a specialized device. Tampering of assistive devices is intended to access the sensitive information, and interfacing attack introduces unwanted signal and noise into the legitimate user's radio frequency communication among assistive devices. Malicious node injection is intentionally adding malicious node into the edge of the IoT with the aim of altering the vital data. Physical damage is destroying the components of assistive device either partially or completely. Malicious code injection alters the controlling software and functional components of software framework of assistive devices. Sleep-deprived attack exhausts the battery power of the assistive devices. Network attack is to exploit the networking capability of assistive devices in a communication network. Traffic analysis attack is to sniff the traffic flow of data in and out of the assistive devices by injecting vulnerability into the traffic. Denial of service floods the traffic network of the assistive devices in the network, and hence, the beneficiaries are not able to participate in the network communication. Message replying attack manipulates the user commands and executes the same to create malfunctioning of the devices. In Sybil attack, the authentication of the user is hacked and the sensitive data are misused.

5.12   CONCLUSION

AT includes the system and services regarding the delivery of assistive services and products. AT is a valuable therapeutic instrument for people who need special care. This chapter demonstrates the need of assistive devices and the corresponding services related to their provision. Assistive health technologies help the people to live longer irrespective of their health conditions. People with disabilities are experiencing various obstacles which isolate them from participating in social and community activities. Assistive devices improve the lifestyle and functioning of people with disabilities. For elderly people, assistive devices provide greater control over their own lives.

KEYWORDS

- **Internet of things (IoT)**
- **assistive technology (AT)**
- **noninvasive sensors**
- **impedance sensors**
- **electrochemical sensors**

REFERENCES

Alahi, M. E. E., & Mukhopadhyay, S. C. (2019). IoT enabled smart sensing system. In *Smart Sensors, Measurement and Instrumentation Smart Nitrate Sensor*, Springer, Cham, 115–130. https://doi.org/10.1007/978-3-030-20095-4_2

Al-Aynati, M. M., & Chorneyko, K. A. (2003, June). Comparison of voice-automated transcription and human transcription in generating pathology reports. Retrieved from https://www.ncbi.nlm.nih.gov/pubmed/12741898

Babbs, C. F. (2012). Oscillometric measurement of systolic and diastolic blood pressures validated in a physiologic mathematical model. *Biomedical Engineering Online, 11*(1), 56.

Bandodkar, A., & Wang, J. (2014). Non-invasive wearable electrochemical sensors: a review. *Trends in Biotechnology, 32*(7), 363–371.

Callaway, E. C., Sweet, C. F., Siegel, E., Reiser, J. M., & Beall, D. P. (2002). Speech recognition interface to a hospital information system using a self-designed visual basic program: Initial experience. *Journal of Digital Imaging, 15*(1), 43–53.

Dean, R., Rane, A., Baginski, M., Richard, J., Hartzog, Z., & Elton, D. (2012). A capacitive fringing field sensor design for moisture measurement based on printed circuit board technology. *IEEE Transactions on Instrumentation and Measurement, 61*(4), 1105–1112.

Fan, Y. J., Yin, Y. H., Xu, L. D., Zeng, Y., & Wu, F. (2014). IoT-based smart rehabilitation system. *IEEE Transactions on Industrial Informatics, 10*(2), 1568–1577.

Ferreira, B., Rodrigues, J., Leitao, J., & Domingos, H. (2015). Privacy-preserving content-based image retrieval in the cloud. *Proceedings of the IEEE 34th Symposium on Reliable Distributed Systems (SRDS)*.

Gonzales, W. V., Mobashsher, A., & Abbosh, A. (2019). The progress of glucose monitoring—A review of invasive to minimally and non-invasive techniques, devices and sensors. *Sensors, 19*(4), 800.

Gubbi, J., Buyya, R., Marusic, S., & Palaniswami, M. (2013). Internet of Things (IoT): A vision, architectural elements, and future directions. *Future Generation Computer Systems, 29*(7), 1645–1660.

Gupta, R., Mohan, I., & Narula, J. (2016). Trends in coronary heart disease epidemiology in India. *Annals of Global Health, 82*(2), 307.

Hoenig, H., Taylor, D., & Sloan, F. (2003). Does assistive technology substitute for personal assistance among the disabled elderly? *American Journal of Public Health, 93*(2), 330–337.

Islam, T., & Mukhopadhayay, S. (2017). Wearable sensors for physiological parameters measurement: physics, characteristics, design and applications. In S. Mukhopadhyay & T. Islam, *Wearable Sensors Applications, Design and Implementation*. IOP Science, pp. 1–31.

Jeong, Y., Son, S., Choi, H., & Lee, S. (2012). Ambulatory remedial clinic system for ubiquitous healthcare. In *Proceedings of the Conference on Advances in Computing, Control, and Telecommunication Technologies*. Elseiver, pp. 37–38.

Jiang, H., Chen, X., Zhang, S., Zhang, X., Kong, W., & Zhang, T. (2015). Software for wearable devices and opportunities. In *Proceedings of the* IEEE 39th Annual Computer Software and Applications Conference (COMPSAC).

Kim, S. D., Lee, S. M., & Lee, S. E. (2015). Secure communication system for wearable devices wireless intra body communication. In *Proceedings of the IEEE International Conference on Consumer Electronics (ICCE)*, p. 408.

Krahn, G. L. (2011). WHO world report on disability: A review. *Disability and Health Journal, 4*(3), 141–142.

Lacey, G., Namara, S. M., & Dawson-Howe, K. M. (1998). Personal adaptive mobility aid for the infirm and elderly blind. In: Mittal V.O., Yanco H.A., Aronis J., Simpson R. (eds). *Assistive Technology and Artificial Intelligence*, Lecture Notes in Computer Science, vol 1458, pp. 211–220, Springer, Berlin, Heidelberg. https://doi.org/10.1007/BFb0055980

Marker, D. A., Mardon, R., Jenkins, F., Campione, J., Nooney, J., Li, J., … Rolka, D. (2018, November 30). State-level estimation of diabetes and prediabetes prevalence: Combining national and local survey data and clinical data. Retrieved from https://www.ncbi.nlm.nih.gov/pubmed/29931829

MosChip. (2018, January 23). IoT based smart tracking of body temperature – IoT blog. Retrieved from https://moschip.com/blog/iot/IoT-based-smart-tracking-of-body-temperature

Park, S. (2005). Plantar foot pressure analysis during golf swing motion using plantar foot pressure measurement system. *Korean Journal of Sport Biomechanics, 15*(1), 75–89.

Parviz, B. (2014). The visionary behind the glass. Retrieved from https://www.eecs.umich.edu/eecs/about/articles/2014/Babak_Parviz_the_visionary_behind_google_glass.html

Pearson, J. F., Brownstein, C. A., & Brownstein, J. S. (2010). Potential for electronic health records and online social networking to redefine medical research. *Clinical Chemistry, 57*(2), 196–204.

Pickering, T. G. (2002). Principles and techniques of blood pressure measurement. *Cardiology Clinics, 20*(2), 207–223.

Polisena, J., Lavis, J. N., Juzwishin, D., McLean-Veysey, P., Graham, I. D., Harstall, C., & Martin, J. (2015, May). Supporting the use of health technology assessments by decision-makers. Retrieved from https://www.ncbi.nlm.nih.gov/pmc/articles/PMC4748346/

Rowland, R., Pachepsky, Y., & Guber, A. (2011). Sensitivity of a capacitance sensor to artificial macropores. *Soil Science, 176*(1), 9–14.

Rucco, R., Sorriso, A., Liparoti, M., Ferraioli, G., Sorrentino, P., Ambrosanio, M., & Baselice, F. (2018). Correction: Rucco, R., et al. Type and location of wearable sensors for monitoring falls during static and dynamic tasks in healthy elderly: A review. Sensors 2018, 18, 1613. *Sensors, 18*(8), 2462.

Sasamori, T., Takahashi, M., & Uno, T. (2009). Transmission mechanism of wearable device for on-body wireless communications. *IEEE Transactions on Antennas and Propagation, 57*(4), 936–942.

Satija, U., Ramkumar, B., & Manikandan, M. S. (2017). Real-time signal quality-aware ECG telemetry system for iot-based healthcare monitoring. *IEEE Internet of Things Journal*, *4*(3), 815–823.

Sen, A., Larson, J. S., Kashani, K. B., Libricz, S. L., Patel, B. M., Guru, P. K., … Farmer, J. C. (2016). Mechanical circulatory assist devices: a primer for critical care and emergency physicians. *Critical Care*, *20*(1).

Siddiqui, A. (2011). Effects of vasodilation and arterial resistance on cardiac output. *Journal of Clinical & Experimental Cardiology*, *2*(11).

Silva, B. N., Khan, M., & Han, K. (2017). Internet of Things: A comprehensive review of enabling technologies, architecture, and challenges. *IETE Technical Review*, *35*(2), 205–220.

Singh, M., & Pal, T. R. (2011). Voice recognition technology implementation in surgical pathology: Advantages and limitations. *Archives of Pathology & Laboratory Medicine, 135* (11), 1476–1481.

Suo, H., Wan, J., Zou, C., & Liu, J. (2012). Security in the Internet of Things: A review. In *Proceedings of the International Conference on Computer Science and Electronics Engineering*.

Tangri, R. (2017, July 6). Innovation India: Agatsa's SanketLife device takes ecg monitoring to the next level. Retrieved from https://decisionresourcesgroup.com/blog/innovation-india-agatsas-sanketlife-device-takes-ecg-monitoring-next-level/

Tinetti, M. E., Speechley, M., & Ginter, S. F. (1988). Risk Factors for falls among elderly persons living in the community. *New England Journal of Medicine, 319*(26), 1701–1707.

Warfel, T. E., & Chang, P. J. (2004). Integrating dictation with PACS to eliminate paper. *Journal of Digital Imaging, 17*(1), 37–44.

WHO (2019). Raised blood pressure. Retrieved from https://www.who.int/gho/ncd/risk_factors/blood_pressure_prevalence_text/en/

Wilkie, J. (2010). Using assistive technology and telecare to provide people with learning disabilities with improved opportunities to achieve greater independence. *Journal of Assistive Technologies, 4*(3), 50–53.

Xiong, N., Vandenberg, A., & Han, W. (2012). Green cloud computing schemes based on networks: a survey. *IET Communications, 6*(18), 3294–3300.

Zakaria, N. A., Saleh, F. N. B. M., & Razak, M. A. A. (2018). IoT (Internet of Things) based infant body temperature monitoring. In *Proceedings of the 2nd International Conference on BioSignal Analysis, Processing and Systems (ICBAPS)*.

Zimmerman, T. (1996). Personal area networks: Near-field intrabody communication. *IBM Systems Journal, 35*(3/4), 609–617.

CHAPTER 6

Smart Fall Detection Systems for Elderly Care

PRATIK BHATTACHARJEE[1*] and SUPARNA BISWAS[2]

[1]Department of Computer Science & Engineering, Brainware University, Barasat, West Bengal, India

[2]Department of Computer Science &Engineering, Maulana Abul Kalam Azad University of Technology, West Bengal, India

*Corresponding author. E-mail: bukaida@gmail.com

ABSTRACT

Fall is considered to be one of the major health problems for senior adults. According to a report published by World Health Organization, early fall detection is an active problem in the old age group people. The report showed that the falling problem affects 28%–35% of people around 65 years of age and 32%–45% for those over 70 years. So this domain has attracted the attention of researchers to search for an affordable and easy to use solution. This remained an open challenge as no uniformly acceptable solution could be provided so far. The scientists have proposed multiple solutions based on different approaches in providing a successful patient care system (PCS).

In this chapter, we have tried to discuss the different state of the art methodologies proposed by the researchers in recent time. This chapter is aimed to provide a brief idea about this research domain starting with very basic concepts. A prototype fall detection system developed by the authors are discussed in the latter part of the chapter that is useful to show one practical implementation of such a system. This prototype, on the testbed, showed an accuracy of 94.45%.

6.1 INTRODUCTION

The expectancy of human life has been increased greatly in the 21st century due to the revolution in medical science and medicine. People in their eighties and nineties are not so uncommon today in many families. Some of them can perform their daily activities of their own and some are dependent on caregivers. According to a statistic by NCOA, USA, one in four Americans aged 65+ falls each year. Every 11 s, an older adult is treated in the emergency room for a fall; every 19 min, an older adult dies due to a fall. Falls are identified as the primary cause of lethal injury and the utmost common reason of nonlethal shock-related hospitalizations in senior citizens (Lim et al., 2014).

As the joint families across the world are splitting, the working couples sometimes have no options but to let their parents taken care by the caregivers. It is not always possible for the caregivers to accompany the aged persons, especially if they can move by themselves. So, a real-time fall monitoring system (Bai et al., 2012) is required to monitor their movement. As the age-old people are generally reluctant as well as forgetful about the wearable sensors, so the monitoring should be done by a device that they will love to carry (El-Bendary et al., 2013). In the age of smartphone and social media, the lonely seniors often spend most of their time with this device and usually tend to carry them anywhere they move. So, a smartphone is chosen as a monitoring device to detect sudden fall that may occur, during their solo morning/evening walk (Hegde et al., 2013). This is the social direction of choice of smartphone as the monitoring device (Igual et al., 2013). The technical reason behind is that the smartphone is now considered as a sensor hub consisting of an accelerometer; a gyroscope; a global positioning system (GPS); a magnetometer; gravity, proximity, and light sensors; and many more (Li et al., 2009).

After the introduction of high-speed Internet in the beginning of 21st century, the definition of computing has changed rapidly. The concept of Internet of Things (IOT) has changed the definition of traditional client–server computing environment by integrating smart objects, sensors, computers, and computing components to extend the range and computing capacity beyond the local hardware limitations (Perera et al., 2013). Devices equipped with smart sensors and network connectivity (such as smartphones) now can be used in conjugation with IOT for effective fall detection over a wide movement area (Hegde et al., 2013).

6.1.1   IoT BASICS AND IMPORTANCE

The classical definition of IoT is "A system consisting of interconnected computing devices, power-driven and digital technologies, objects, creatures or people which are provided some unique identifiers and the capacity of transferring data in a network without the need of communication between humans or interaction between human and computer."

Now, the basic aspect of IoT is the connectivity to each and everything possible automatically. In a very simple way, it is a network that connects everything with every other thing using some communication medium. This aspect makes every node that are taking part in IoT to become a "smart" node or device. Essentially, the IoT architecture requires the following three aspects:

- A sending device that can send information to the system, e.g., a sensor
- A receiving device that is receiving and processing that information automatically, for example, a processing server.
- A device that can do both, for example, our cellular phones.

The intelligent devices can communicate among themselves and can also take decisions of their own using some machine learning (ML) techniques and applying artificial intelligence (AI) (Perera et al., 2013).

The Internet has opened an information superhighway to extend the connectivity across the world. The IoT devices are using this infrastructure to connect among themselves. So, IoT is basically an extension of the control of Internet starting from computers and smartphones to a wide range of other things, processes, and environments. IoT offers businesses and people a better understanding and control over the objects and surroundings that spread beyond the range of the Internet. Also, by applying so, IoT permits businesses and people to be more linked with the circumstances and to achieve more efficient and greater work.

A look of a typical IoT architecture is shown in Figure 6.1.

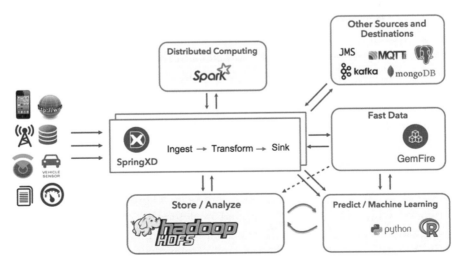

FIGURE 6.1 IoT architecture (photo courtesy: Maheshwar Ligade).

6.1.2 NONCONVENTIONAL I/O DEVICES

The IoT-based devices are usually spread across a wide geographical region and follow a heterogeneous architecture. This demands a system that can handle nonconventional input devices such as sensors and both online and offline data. These kinds of I/O devices are often referred to as "distributed I/O." The main properties that are observed in a distributed I/O system are devices having a small area and a greater variety of I/O options like digital and analogue stations, temperature calculations, and counter inputs. These linked devices provide a flexibility that old-style devices are unable to achieve. A significant advantage of this distributed method is a short cable for signal measuring as the devices are positioned near to the sensors. Direct link between the sensors do not need signal training during giving the usual signal inputs for those rare and specific sensors.

By using dependable and traditional communication buses like Ethernet and RS485 with protocols like Modbus/TCP, Modbus/RTU, Profibus, and even ASIC, modules can be combined into current systems that require a lesser cost and an elastic architecture.

6.1.3 ROLE OF IoT IN HEALTHCARE

There has been a rapid change in medical science and healthcare after the introduction of sensor-based automatic monitoring systems using wireless body area network (WBAN).

A body area network (BAN) is also known as WBAN or body sensor network (Arya and Bilandi, 2014). It is a wireless connection between various wearable sensors in body. These sensors may be implemented inside of human body or outside such as human can bring in various positions, in pockets, in hand or in bags. The development of WBAN started around in 1995 around the idea of using wireless personal area network (WPAN) to make a communication between different parts or around the human body (Filipe et al., 2015). After nearly 6 years, the term "BAN" used to denote systems in which communication is totally within, on, and in the instantaneous immediacy of a human body.

The swift progress of biological sensors, less power combined circuits, and wireless communication has empowered a novel group of wireless sensor networks, which is now being applied in determining vehicles, harvests, organization, and well-being. The sensors that are integrated in the human body face different physical changes and display the patient's health condition irrespective of their position. The data will be communicated wirelessly to an external processing component (Song et al., 2007). The device is able to immediately spread all the data in actual time to the clinicians all over the world. If any emergency is noticed, the doctors will instantly notify the patient by providing suitable messages or alarms.

Primary BANs are applied in the health-care field, where constant monitoring and sorting of important parameters of people suffering from long-lasting diseases like diabetes, breathing problem, and cardiac attacks are considered. A BAN that is placed on a patient is able to notify the clinicians, even before having a cardiac attack, by monitoring changes in their important symptoms. A BAN on a diabetic patient whenever required vaccinates insulin automatically through a pump. Further, this technology is applied in sports, military, or security domain. Covering the skill to various fields also supports interaction by continuous exchanges of data between humans or between humans and machines.

6.1.4 WBAN ARCHITECTURE

The ICT-based health-care monitoring structure may be classified into three layers, viz., tier-I, tier-II, and tier-III, as shown in Figure 6.2.

Tier-I: It is the first layer of communication in which data communication takes place among the sensors mounted in the human body. The sensors reads the physiological data from the subject and send it to the "Sink," which is a personal server.

Tier-II: This is the next layer of WBAN in which the Sink and the access point (AP) communicates with each other.

Tier-III: This is the outermost layer in which the AP communicates with a medical server in cloud via Internet. This server requires authorization.

6.1.4.1 APPLICATIONS OF WBAN

WBAN finds applications in

- telemedicine and remote patient monitoring,
- lifestyle and sports, and
- military.

6.1.4.2 ADVANTAGES OF WBAN

The advantages of WBAN are as follows:

- It is used for the detection of critical diseases.
- It is used for monitoring real-time health data and providing advice.

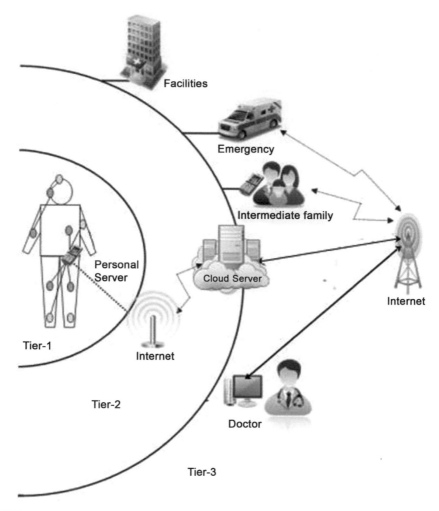

FIGURE 6.2   WBAN communication layers.

- It is used in military applications for security purposes.
- It is helpful in sports and daily lifestyle.

6.1.4.3   DISADVANTAGES OF WBAN

The disadvantages of WBAN are as follows:

- It is less secured.
- Implementation of the security technique in sensor nodes is difficult.
- It needs energy-efficient sensor nodes.

Most of the modern hospitals and health-care centers are now using WBAN-based equipment for patient monitoring. However, it is still to be implemented in the rural areas where qualified medical persons are not available in sufficient numbers for the continuous manual monitoring.

6.2 INTRODUCTION TO MODERN SMARTPHONE

A smartphone, by definition, would have a sophisticated multitasking operating system, for example, iOS, Android, etc. high-profile web accessibility, a full-featured desktop web browser (e.g., Safari etc), a full-featured music player and video player, display photos, a wide rray of sensors, 3G/4G and wireless LAN (Wi-Fi) connections, TV out, etc. A smartphone should be able to download and install applications and may have a virtual or physical QWERTY standard keyboard.

6.2.1 SMARTPHONE AS A SENSOR HUB

6.2.1.1 EMBEDDED/INTERNAL MOBILE PHONE SENSORS

Most of today's smartphones are open, programmable, and come with several embedded sensors. The number and types of sensors in mobile phones vary depending on the underlying mobile phones platforms and usability. Some of the state-of-the-art embedded mobile phones sensors are listed as follows.

Accelerometer: Acceleration may be defined as the rate of change of velocity over time. An accelerometer is usually an electromechanical instrument that is used to quantify acceleration values. Such accelerations can be static (acceleration due to gravity) or dynamic for sensing the movement or vibrations of a mobile device.

The environment of an element can be understand in a better manner using the accelerometer. Different types of movements may be determined by this tiny device such as the subject is moving uphill, the maximum tilt it can survive before falling down, or if it is flying horizontally or angling downward. The smartphones rotate their display automatically (portrait/landscape) based on the tilt of the phone.

Traditional accelerometers contain multiple axes: the two-dimensional movements are determined by the two axes, while the third is used to determine the position. The smartphones use these three axes, while it is sufficient for a car to use two axes to determine the impact moments. These devices are highly sensitive as they are supposed to read even a tiny change in acceleration. The degree of accuracy is highly dependent on the sensitivity.

Gyroscope: The angular rate sensors or angular velocity sensors popularly known as gyroscope sensors are the devices that can measure angular velocity. The angular velocity may be defined as the change in rotational angle/time. The unit of angular velocity is degrees/second or rotation/second (RPS). Gyro devices can measure or uphold rotational motion. An example of a small and cheap gyroscope is a microelectromechanical system (MEMS) that can determine angular velocity. The rotational speed is determined by the angular velocity.

Magnetometer: A magnetometer measures the magnetic fields and so can point toward north by changing the voltage output to the phone.

It determines the way by which an Apple Maps or Google Maps is to be shown when a compass application is triggered. It also supports the stand-alone compass applications.

Magnetometers can detect magnetic metals, so they are also used in metal detectors, and this is how the metal detector applications are supported in smartphones.

Nevertheless, this sensor works in conjugation with the accelerometer and GPS unit of the smartphone to determine the exact location of the subject and also the way the device is pointing in the navigation routes.

GPS: GPS technology communicates with the satellite in space to determine the location of the subject via latitude and longitude. It does no require any data connection and can perform perfectly without mobile signal (however, the map will look blurry as they cannot be downloaded fully).

The GPS contacts with multiple satellites to determine the location depending on the angles of intersection. However, it may find difficulties in locking if the device is used at indoor or the sky is cloudy due to the inability to contact with the satellites.

The GPS is an extremely power-hungry device and can drain up the battery very fast. The battery saving guides of every phone suggests turning GPS off while not in use. Tiny gadgets like smartwatches avoid including GPS module in their systems.

The cell phone towers are also an alternative way to find the location of the device. Modern GPS units essentially associate GPS signals with other data, such as signal strength of the cell, to determine further accurate location data.

Barometer: A barometer is used to determine air pressure. This data can be used in identifying changes in weather and measuring the altitude.

Camera: Every smartphone nowadays is equipped with a camera that can be used to capture still images/videos, which can be used later for various purposes. Advanced smartphone technology nowadays uses more than one sensor for better result in image capturing.

Air humidity sensor: Samsung released its Galaxy S4 model in 2013 that was the first smartphone to accommodate an air humidity sensor. The optimum temperature and humidity can be determined based on the measurement of humidity in the air by this sensor. However, these sensors are available in the premium segment smartphones only.

Heart rate sensor: The heart sensor uses an LED and optical sensors to measure the heartbeat. The LED produces light in the direction of the skin, and this sensor measures the reflected light wave.

The pulse causes a difference in the light intensity. The heartbeat is determined by counting the intensity changes between the tiny pulsations of the blood vessels. It is used by many health and fitness applications.

Barcode/QR code sensors: Barcode sensors use the reflected light from the code to determine the readings. It creates an analog signal with changing voltage that characterizes the barcode. This analog signal is then transformed into a digital form and decrypted to divulge the data in it. Barcode sensors are used for scanning the barcoded materials or QR codes.

Pedometer: A fitness tracker applications use this sensor to count the steps that a subject takes. Pedometers internally make use of the data generated by the accelerometer that can be used to observe the movements such as walking or running.

Touchscreen sensors: The touchscreen has an electrical current continuously flowing through it, and a touch on the display causes a change in the signals. The device takes this change as input. Earlier smartphone models tend to use resistive touchscreens until Apple first introduced a capacitive touchscreen. However, now all the smartphones use capacitive touchscreens only.

Proximity sensor: A proximity sensor measures the closeness of an object by using an infrared (IR) LED and IR light detector. This sensor automatically turns off the touchscreen functionality during a call reception by detecting the proximity of the face to avoid unintentional input via skin. The IR sensor releases a beam of light, invisible to human that is reflected back.

Ambient light sensor: This sensor detects the environmental lights and adjusts the screen brightness accordingly. It is termed as Auto Brightness Leveler that can increase or decrease the brightness of the screen to keep away the eye from soaring.

Biometrics: Biometric sensors can identify the various classification characteristics of the human individuals and can be used to provide an additional layer of security for the devices. This may include fingerprint recognition, iris recognition, and complete facial recognition.

Biometric sensors are heavily used to unlock the phones and authenticate payment during purchases.

Moreover, biometric sensors can also be applied to collect heart rate and SpO_2 (the estimate of arterial oxygen saturation) of a person to be used for any health-related application.

Microphone: A microphone is just a simple sensor that can detect and measure the loudness of sound. Although microphone sensors are available in different sizes and with different sensitivities, smartphones mostly use micron-sized electret microphones.

Microphones are also used for voice-based search and voice commands for digital assistants like Google Assistant, Siri, Alexa, Cortana, etc. in addition to making regular voice calls.

Thermometer: Every smartphone is equipped with an inbuilt thermometer that monitors the fluctuation of temperature inside the device and battery. If there is any overheating, the device automatically shuts down to prevent any type of damage to itself or the user.

Nevertheless, some high-end mobile phones do come with supplementary thermometers for measuring ambient temperature. One such model is Samsung Galaxy S4 that comes with a thermometer that can measure external temperature. These thermometer sensors can be utilized by different applications to sense the room temperature.

The commonly available mobile phone-based sensors are summarized in Table 6.1.

6.2.2 HEALTH MONITORING SENSORS IN A SMARTPHONE

The health monitoring sensors, also known as biosensors, are self-contained analytical devices that include a biologically active substance in close contact with a suitable transduction component to detect (reversibly and selectively) the density or movement of chemical substances in a sample. The common mobile phone sensors that can be used for health monitoring are listed below.

TABLE 6.1 Some Supported Sensors in a Smartphone

Category	Name	E_m/E_x	PC/EC	A/P
Tactile	Proximity	E_m/E_x	EC	A/P
Acceleration	Gyroscope	E_m	PC	P
	Accelerometer	E_x	PC	P
Thermal	Temperature	E_x	EC	P/A
Image	CMOS camera	E_m	EC	P/A
	Camcorder	E_x	EC	A

TABLE 6.1 Some Supported Sensors in a Smartphone

Category	Name	E_m/E_x	PC/EC	A/P
Light	Ambient light	E_m/E_x	EC	A
	Back illuminated	E_x	EC	P
Location	Digital compass	E_m	EC	A
	GPS	E_m	EC	P
Height	*Altimeter*	–	*EC*	*P*
Hydro	*Moisture*	E_m	*EC*	*P*
	Humidity	E_x	*EC*	*P*
Medical	Barometer	E_m	EC	P
	Heart rate monitor	–	EC	P
	Biosensors	–	EC	P
Acoustic	*Microphone*	E_m	*EC*	*P*
Radio	RFID	–	EC	A
	Bluetooth	E_m	EC	A

E_m: embedded, E_x: external, PC: proprioceptive, EC: exteroceptive, A: active, and P: passive

Microphone sensor: The feel of the patient may be assessed using a microphone sensor, for example, patients having the myotonic syndrome. Myotonia is a type of disorder categorized by sluggish relaxation of muscles after contraction, which can result in a trouble in movement. The patients need to inform their heath data by calling the data collection centre within 8 weeks of consultation. An automated voice response scheme characterized symptoms into four categories: muscle stiffness, weakness, pain, and tiredness.

Camera sensor: The telemedicine and remote doctor consultation uses a mobile phone camera sensor to obtain useful statistics about images and videos of a patient through a proper application. One such application is in the field of the tele-dermatology, in which the skin images of the patient are utilized by the doctor for diagnosis. The domain of mobile device camera may be further extended by attaching special components with the phone. As an example, a light microscope may be designed based on the mobile phone camera. The zoomed-in image from the optical attachment is passed to the phone camera. Studies observed that camera resolution is sufficient to detect blood cell and microorganism morphology that may lead to an automatic local analysis. The detection of tuberculosis has been done already as a case study, using such a system. The device is inexpensive and easily transportable, which can be greatly useful for various reasons.

Accelerometer sensor and geolocation facilities: The accelerometers can be used to find the physical activity level of a person. The importance lies in reducing the danger of having several chronic diseases. Numerous special devices are available based on an accelerometer that can be used to calculate the activity level depending on step count. These devices are known as pedometers. The step pattern is recognized by capturing the accelerometer readings. A few pedometers are also capable of calculating approximate amount of burned calories. In general, built-in mobile phone accelerometers can provide the equivalent functionalities similar to a pedometer. This removes the need for having an additional wearable device.

Different popular mobile platforms support different pedometer applications. Even though pedometer-like systems are very convenient for physical movement monitoring, their primary application area is only on step counting without considering other daily activities, like walking or running. For a truly accurate physical activity tracking, a system must be able to identify various types of activities, such as walking, running, bicycle riding, car driving, etc. An interesting and useful application of the smartphone accelerometer can be observed in project *mPhysio* that offers rehabilitation service. The user of the system (usually the patient herself) does not require to come physically to the rehabilitation centre numerous times but is able to do the rehabilitation exercises at their own places. The training is remotely monitored using the mobile phone accelerometer.

However, more sophisticated sensors like heart rate monitor and other biometric sensors are being made available in modern high-end mobile phones. So, we will soon see a total revolution in real-time patient monitoring systems that will be fully automatic and portable.

6.3 FALL OF SENIORS AND THEIR POSSIBLE IMPACTS

The fall of the elderly adults is a serious problem for the family and the people who live with the elderly persons (Mubashir et al., 2013). Falls are primary problems in the seniors as these may cause substantial injury and even death. This is because of the difficulties arising from falls that result in a substantial reduction in functional status, grave injuries, and an increase in the utilization of medical services. The fall may occur at the indoor (bathroom, bedroom, living room, kitchen, etc.), on a staircase, or at outdoor. While it is easier for a caregiver to identify the fall at indoor, the situation is not the same for outdoor fall. Often unkonwn people are hesitant as well as reluctant in the case a stranger been fallen down (Igual et al., 2013). So, an alarming system for the external fall and an urgent notification to the relatives and caregivers must reach in time to save the life.

The frailty index (Lee et al., 2014) is often used to classify the physical condition of the seniors. The phenotype of frailty classifies elder adults as frail when they persist three or more among five criteria and being at risk of frailty if they have one or two criteria: *slow walking speed*, *weak grip strength*, *exhaustion*, *low physical activity level*, and *unintentional weight loss*. The quality of life is one of the governing factors for increasing the risk of frailty.

6.3.1 AVAILABLE MONITORING AND ASSISTING DEVICES

The advancement in the field of IoT, robotics, and AI has opened a lot of opportunities in developing intelligent and automated devices using cameras, sensors, and other nonconventional I/O devices. A lot of work has already been done on the various types of automated fall detection and activities of daily living (ADL) monitoring devices and techniques (Hijaz et al., 2010). These fall detection systems (FDS) are divided into two categories—context aware (visual monitoring) and context free (sensor-based monitoring), as shown in Figure 6.3.

Many experimental and commercial devices are available nowadays to track ADL and fall depending on the situation. The wearable sensors, especially smartwatches and smartbands (e.g., Apple Smart Watch, MI Band, etc.), are now commercially available for use and can be monitored both locally and remotely (Figure 6.4). The inexpensive ones use the threshold-based algorithms, while the expensive ones use ML-based algorithms for greater accuracies. They may or may not use live data streaming.

6.3.2 NEED OF REAL-TIME DETECTION BASED ON LIVE DATA

A fall is a challenge to balance or strength that results in the inability to stay upright. This may happen due to stumble or illness for young adults and a disease and decay of physical ability for aged persons (El-Bendary et al., 2013). Neurological disorder, Parkinson's disease, etc. may cause fall irrespective of any age.

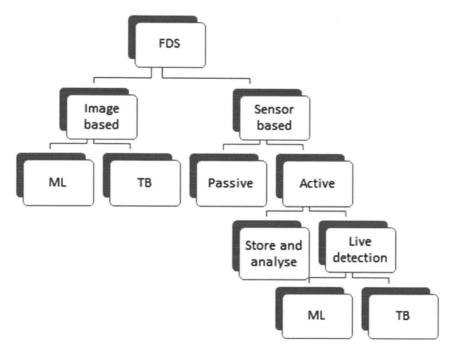

ML= Machine Learning based, TB= Threshold based

FIGURE 6.3   Classifications of FDS.

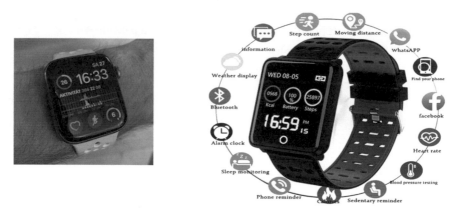

FIGURE 6.4   Some of the wearable smart watches [picture courtesy Amazon.com].

While it is very difficult to prevent the fall, timely detection and treatment can save life of many persons. Often the time between the fall and treatment becomes crucial for preventing any damage or unfortunate events. So, the reliable and timely detection of fall is of great importance (Wang et al., 2008). The store and analyze approach used in most of the state-of-the-art fall detection mechanisms using ML approaches may consume crucial time for generating a warning. On the other hand, a threshold-based approach provides good fall detection accuracy based on live data stream and can generate a quicker warning compared to ML-based approach (Huang et al., 2008). In real life, timely warning is more important than avoiding a few false warnings, so the threshold-based approach is mostly followed for detection (Buzin Junior and Adami, 2018). However, fine-grained fall like before and after fall postures are difficult to be detected in this way. The ML-based approaches may be used for this purpose (Ruan et al., 2015).

6.4 DIFFERENT FALL MONITORING APPROACHES

The methods of monitoring the fall may be divided into three types such as (1) a nonambulatory sensor-based method, (2) a wearable sensor-based method, and (3) a computer image-based method.

In the auditory fall recognition method, identification of fall procedures depends on the quivering of frequency of the subject. However, wearable sensor-based methods depend on kinematic sensors like the gyroscope and accelerometer to identify falls from ADL. The computer image-based method performs a real-time monitoring of the subject through the camera, and the postures are identified by any computer-based algorithm. It is more accurate than the other two methods. The caregiver has to give minimum effort for such a monitoring system. However, this method is still in its nascent stage. The conventional methods still need a lot of improvement through further research.

6.4.1 NONAMBULATORY SENSOR-BASED METHOD

These systems are based on microphones and IR sensors. The technique is analogous to the camera-based techniques. The design of such systems is usually simple and cheap. It involves an acoustic or ambient sensor along with a computer. The collected data found from the sensors are then passed for analysis to a PC (Lee et al., 2014). The investigation is done depending on some predefined conditions and cut-off thresholds for fall detection (Figure 6.5).

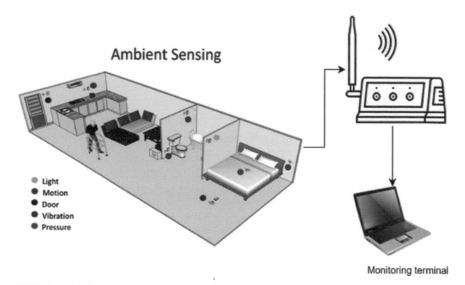

FIGURE 6.5   Architecture of the nonambulatory sensor-based monitoring system.

Source: Reprinted with permission from Patel et al., 2012. © 2021 BioMed Central Ltd. https://creativecommons.org/licenses/by/4.0/

Perceptions: This method removes the privacy issues that are usually associated with image-based techniques. The design is simple and cheap. However, such sensors are usually very subtle to noise. So, they are not very useful in external environments (Ruan et al., 2015). Although it is possible to monitor more than one subject at a time, it requires a substantial amount of further research. Overall, it is very useful for indoor applications (Nasution and Emmanuel, 2007).

6.4.2   WEARABLE SENSOR-BASED METHOD

This method has several advantages over the nonambulatory method (Perry et al., 2009). The system uses either an accelerometer or gyroscope or both to distinguish falls from daily activities (Buzin Junior and Adami, 2018). The sensors usually send the data to a dedicated microcontroller or a PC. The wearable sensors are capable of working independently. So, it is possible to monitor the activities of an elderly subject (Dinh et al., 2009) continuously.

Most commercial cellular phone companies are now manufacturing wearable sensor-based smartbands and smartwatches. Although the accuracy of such devices is still in their nascent stages, they are rapidly becoming popular among the common people (Figure 6.6).

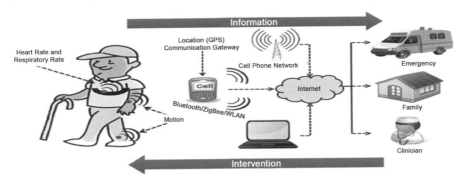

FIGURE 6.6   Architecture of the wearable sensor-based monitoring system.

Source: Reprinted with permission from Patel et al., 2012. © 2021 BioMed Central Ltd. https://creativecommons.org/licenses/by/4.0/

Perceptions: The wearable sensors are cheap and immune to external noise. So, they can be used for both indoor and outdoor monitoring. They have many advantages over the nonambulatory methods.

No special infrastructure is required except for remote monitoring. Hence, pre-establishment of a communication network is not required like the other methods. However, the poor battery life and reluctancy of the seniors to use it are its main disadvantages. The weight of the device may pose another problem for the person wearing it.

6.4.3   COMPUTER IMAGE-BASED METHODS

The image-based systems capture raw images and extracts useful information form them for further analysis (Juang et al., 2008). The perspective views from multiple cameras and video sources may be used to generate data. This enables the system to see the subject for analysis (Miaou et al., 2006). The computer vision is the procedure in which a machine, such as a digital computer, usually unsupervised, analyzes an image and tells the information in that image (Cucchiara et al., 2004). The image-based technique comprises of three portions like the identification of features, pattern classification founded on those features, and finally pattern recognition (Figure 6.7).

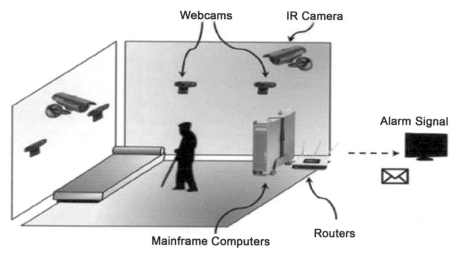

FIGURE 6.7   Computer image-based monitoring system.

Source: Reprinted with permission from Patel et al., 2012. © 2021 BioMed Central Ltd.
https://creativecommons.org/licenses/by/4.0/

Perceptions: Image-based techniques can monitor multiple persons simultaneously. One major drawback of the wearable sensor-based methods is that it requires the senior subject to wear the device frequently and the on device alarm is ineffective if the fallen person becomes senseless. These devices are mostly battery-driven and require frequent recharge due to high power consumption by multiple active sensors. These difficulties can be addressed by the computer image-based methods. It delivers greater accurateness compared to other two methods. The system can use a GSM to alert the caregiver in case of a fall. However, due to the fixed locations of the cameras, the system is range-bound. Extending the range requires fixation of a larger number of cameras. A full-fledged communication infrastructure is necessary for successful communications, whereby several cameras are linked to a solitary server that upholds the databases. Inevitably, such an infrastructure upsurges the setup price and is also not very effective in an outdoor scenario.

6.5   FALL DETECTION METHODOLOGIES

The fall detection methodologies are implemented using any of the three methods discussed above. It involves two things: *detection of fall* and *analysis of fall*. While several state-of-the-art methods were proposed for the detection techniques that use both online and offline data, the threshold-based methods are quite popular. However, these methods are not very efficient to analyze the fine-grained falls. The fall-posture analysis can be efficiently done by using some ML techniques like *K*-nearest neighbor (KNN), support vector machine (SVM) (Foroughi et al., 2008), random forest, decision tree, etc. These types of methods are slower than the threshold-based approaches but provide more detail analysis of fall that may be used for future treatment of the subject.

The following sections will give a brief idea of each method along with their advantages and disadvantages.

6.5.1 THRESHOLD-BASED METHODS

The threshold-based methods are fast, light weight, and most popular methods for the detection of fall (Huang et al., 2009). T. The system usually takes the raw acceleration data from the three-axis accelerometer and combines them using either signal vector magnitude (SVM) method or a Euclidean distance-based method. As any fall event causes a huge acceleration change, a predefined cut-off threshold value is compared against it (Tsinganos and Skodras, 2017). If the present acceleration exceeds the threshold, then the event is detected as fall and an appropriate warning is generated. The mathematical expression used to combine the acceleration data is given as follows:

$$\text{SVM} = \sqrt{(Ax)^2 + (Ay)^2 + (Az)^2},$$ where Ax, Ay, Az are acceleration components along the *x*-, *y*-, and *z*-axis, respectively.

The Euclidean distance can be calculated by subtracting the previous reading from the current reading and then combing them:

If $Ex = Ax_{(i+1)} - Ax_i$, $Ey = Ay_{(i+1)} - Ay_i$, and $Ez = Az_{(i+1)} - Az_i$ be the Euclidean distances along the *x*-, *y*-, and *z*-axis, respectively, then

$$\text{EuDi} = \sqrt{(Ex)^2 + (Ey)^2 + (Ez)^2}$$

Now, if $\text{SVM}_{acc} > \text{SVM}_{acc}$ (threshold) or $\text{EuDi} > \text{ED}$ (threshold), then the event is recorded as fall.

Although this method is good for detection, it may generate a number of false alarms for fall-alike events such as stumble, fast sitting, or sudden increase in speed due to any nonfall event.

Some researchers tried to extract the posture information by calculating the *pitch, roll*, or *yaw* values that are nothing but a change in the angle of the body along the x-, y-, and z-axis from accelerometer or gyroscope readings. However, they are nowhere near the accuracy of a ML-based approach that analyzes the data against a trained system.

6.5.2 MACHINE-LEARNING-BASED METHODS

The ML-based methods depend on a trained machine for the analysis of data. The machine is first trained against the known data set such that it can analyze the outcome (classification) for similar unknown data. The fall here is detected usually by posture analysis where the *laying posture* of the subject for a certain amount of time, from any other nonlaying posture is denoted as fall. The popular classifiers used for this purpose are *decision tree* (Sarkar et al., 2019) *KNN, random forest*, and *SVM*. Some researchers also used nonconventional models such as *hidden Markov model* (Thome et al., 2008)), *logistic regression*, etc. with good accuracy.

The ML-based systems can precisely identify prefall, fall, and postfall postures. They can also distinguish between a true fall and fall-alike events. Different fine grain falls like fall left/right/face-up/face-down, etc. and postures like fall from sit/stand/walk/climbing up staircase/climbing down staircase, etc. can also be identified with good accuracy.

However, it is difficult for a ML-based model to work on live data as they are based on the store and analyze principle. This can be overcome by storing the live data and analyzing it within a very short interval of time (say 10 s), periodically. This will help to refresh the result and also can store the previous results for future analysis. By carefully choosing the refreshing frequency, the nominal delay will hardly have any effect on generating fall warning. However, the classification time greatly depends on the hardware support of the analyzing system, and hence, a good modern server is preferred in such cases.

6.5.3 HYBRID OR COMBINATIONAL APPROACHES

Most modern approaches combine the benefits of both the above methods by keeping one part of the model as threshold-based and the rest based on ML. Generally, the fall detection part is based on the threshold-based approach and an early warning is generated for the possible detection of fall. This minimizes the delay in detection by testing the live data stream from the device. The data stream is simultaneously fed into the ML module for fine grain analysis. If after analysis the ML module finds the earlier warning as a false alarm, then it sends a secondary message to nullify the earlier information; otherwise, it starts analyzing the pre- and postfall information to detect the posture before and after the fall. If the ML module is appropriately trained, then it can also estimate the possible damage by analyzing the intensity of fall. It can also predict if the person has become immobile by analyzing the fall and can send appropriate emergency messages to multiple destinations for immediate attention.

6.6 PROTOTYPE FALL DETECTION AND CLASSIFICATION SYSTEM

We have developed a prototype fall detection and prefall analysis system using the hybrid approach. In the present prototype, we have considered the FDS and ADL as a common unit for detection and analysis of the fall (both indoor and outdoor). While the FDS module is a threshold-based approach on a live data stream, the analysis module is based on ML classifications using the KNN classifier. If a fall is detected, the system sends warning, specifying the last posture of the subject before fall, along with the location (outdoor) and date and time. All the data are stored in a file for future references.

There are different smart home devices available (both commercial and experimental) that are capable of detecting a fall. However, most of them do not tell any additional information except that a fall has been detected along with time of fall. As the head injury is the most common and severe after fall incident for seniors, so the amount of injury greatly varies depending on initial body posture (sitting/laying/standing/walking). The tendency of losing balance on a particular posture may provide additional information about the phenotype of the subject that may help in future treatment.

6.6.1 ARCHITECTURE AND DESIGN

Since the time period is crucial for the fallen person, a threshold-based warning system detects the fall from live data and generates warning (if fall is detected). The data is further fine-grained based on the type of fall using supervised machine learning algorithms such as KNN, SVM (Foroughi et al., 2008) random forest, etc. It further examines whether it was a true fall or false alarm (due to fall-alike events) in the initial warning and rectifies it if necessary. If it was a true fall as per the classifier, then a second layer of information is provided, indicating the type of fall. However, this will be usually based on the store and analyze methodology, and hence, a nominal delay may be expected in processing the information.

A common android mobile phone is chosen as the data acquisition device for the senior subjects due to the reasons stated earlier. The architecture consists of two main modules—a threshold-based module that detects the fall, based on live acceleration data, and an ML module that detects the posture of the subject in every 20 s. We have used the SVM_{acc} method for the detection of fall. The ML module is based on KNN with K = 3, for the detection of prefall posture. If a fall is detected, then the GPS sensor sends the coordinate (latitude and longitude) to the Google server, which in turn returns the address of the fallen subject. The ML module returns the prefall posture, which is then combined with the address and fall information to produce the complete warning message with date and time.

The architecture that is used is displayed in Figure 6.8.

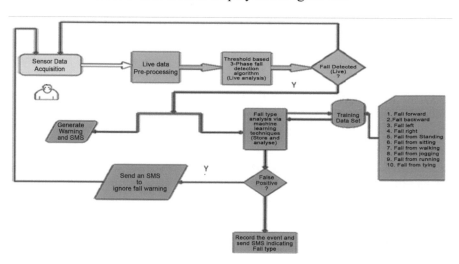

FIGURE 6.8   A simple hybrid fall detection and analysis model.

6.6.2 ALGORITHM

The algorithm is divided into three components: data acquisition, data processing, and output integration. The acceleration and gyroscope data are captured by the data acquisition server and sent to the appropriate modules for processing. The outputs are then combined to produce final output.

Algorithm 6.1: The three-phase fall detection process

1. Initialize the server and mobile [Receiver and Sender]
2. Read the 3 axis accelerometer data from the smart phone.
3. If the data is not received for more than 10 seconds then

    3.1 Generate visual fall alert with audible warning at the server.
    3.2 Send SMS to relative of the subject

4. Convert the data into SVM$_{acc}$ using the formula

$$SVMacc = \sqrt{\left(Ax\right)^2 + \left(Ay\right)^2 + \left(Az\right)^2}$$

5. [*Check if SVM$_{acc}$ is below and above the threshold values (g< and >2g, g=9.8m/sec^2) Phase 1*]

    if SVM$_{min}$ <g and SVM$_{max}$ >2g then

    if Timestamp(SVM$_{max}$) - Timestamp(SVM$_{min}$) < 2 seconds

    goto step 6

    else

    goto step 2

6. [Check the number of records. *Phase 2*]
    if (record_count>150)

    [*Subject fell*]

    record timestamp and goto step 7

    else

    goto step 2

7. [Check if SVM$_{acc}$ is below the *g* value for more than 20 seconds –*Phase-3*]

    Initialize SVM$_{acc}$=SVM$_{min}$ and IniTime=timestamp(SVM$_{acc}$)
    while (SVM$_{acc}$ < g)

begin loop:

    current_time= timestamp(SVM$_{acc}$)
    if(current_time-IniTime)>20 seconds [*Subject fell and could not self-recover*]

    Generate visual fall alert with audible warning at the server.

    Send SMS to relative of the subject.

    Halt server operation and display warning continuously.

    endif

end loop

6.6.3 IMPLEMENTATION

The system is implemented using a common Android mobile phone (Redmi 6A) running on Android 8.1 (Oreo), using Wi-Fi connectivity with a desktop server running on Windows 10. The code is implemented using Python 3.7. The ML module is developed using the KNN classifier with $K = 3$. The data capturing module receives the accelerometer and gyroscope data at a rate of 40 data per second. We have used an overlapping window of 2 s for synchronization. The fall detection module receives only the live acceleration data that is analyzed using a threshold-based approach. The posture identification module receives both the live acceleration and gyroscope data and identifies the posture from four possible alternatives: laying, sitting, standing, and walking through an already trained ML module. We have trained the module from six thousand local data collected from five volunteers of both the genders and a wide range of age groups from 10–15, 20–30, 35–45, 50–60, and 60–70 years. The localized data set is used to obtain a better result on the unknown subjects who are also the local users.

The implementation architecture is shown in Figure 6.9.

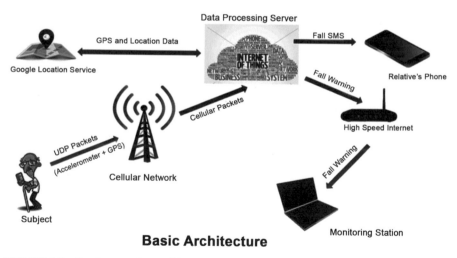

FIGURE 6.9   Implementation architecture.

6.7 RESULT ANALYSIS

The data is collected @ 40 Hz for three scenarios, namely, normal walking (no-fall), fall but recovered (no-warning but the event recorded), and fall and not recovered (audio–visual warning). The below output (Figure 6.10) shows a case where (a) the subject fell but recovered, (b) the subject fell and not recovered, and (c) the subject in his normal motion.

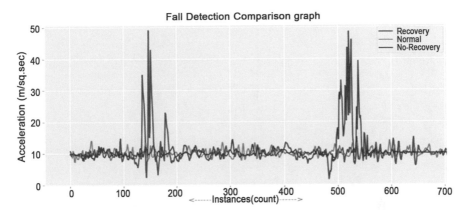

FIGURE 6.10 Comparison graph.

In the above graph, it can be observed that the fall accelerations are similar in both the recovery and no-recovery cases. However, the normal portions of all the three cases are similar before the fall occurs (up to record 100). After the fall between record 100 and 200, the subject recovered and the SVM_{acc} values are again at par with each other. However, when the "fall with no recovery" case occurred between record 490 and 550 (approx.), the after-fall graph is quite different. As the subject did not recover and there is no movement, the SVM_{acc} value, as a result, almost remains stationary.

6.7.1 FALSE ALARM

In Figure 6.11, we have evaluated the cases of "stomping" and "fast sitting," which may generate the similar acceleration values as fall. We have analyzed the cases one by one, as follows:

i) *Stomping*: Even though we got the threshold values that are higher than the highest value of fall, the duration is well below the minimum threshold time that is required to record it as a fall. So, no warning was generated.

ii) *Fast sitting*: The fast sitting generated the acceleration values whose peak differences are (max–min) well below the required threshold value; hence, this case was also not recorded as a fall, which is the correct interpretation.

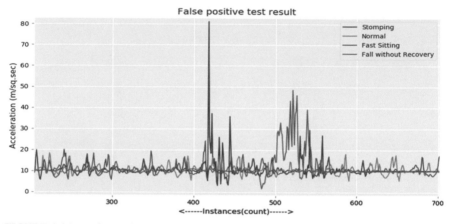

FIGURE 6.11   False positive cases.

6.7.2   *CORRECT PREDICTION*

Figure 6.12 shows the warning at the monitoring terminal when a fall without self-recovery is detected and an immediate SMS is sent to the mobile phone/s of relative/s specifying the posture, location, and date and time along with the regular fall waring message. The system time, warning time, and SMS time are almost the same, considering all possible delays.

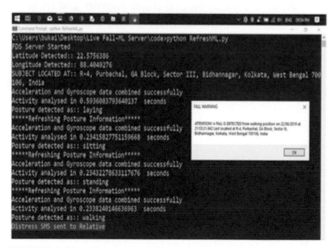

FIGURE 6.12   Warning and SMS.

6.7.3 COMPARISON AND ACCURACY TABLE

The multiple trials and the fall detection accuracies are shown in Table 6.2. The overall accuracy as observed is *94.45%.*

TABLE 6.2 Results of a Few Trials on Different Cases

Type of Activity	Number of Trials	Correct Interpretation	Accuracy (%)
Activity of daily living (normal, no warning)	150	40	100
Fell but recovered (no warning)	150	138	92
Fell and not recovered (warning + SMS)	150	139	92.67
Stumble (false positive)	150	135	90
Fast sitting (false positive)	150	138	92
Device stopped sending data suddenly (warning + SMS)	50	50	100

Overall 94.45% accuracy

The accuracy in detecting the posture is tested using the KNN classifier on a test data size of 1350 stored randomly, and the result is listed in Table 6.3.

TABLE 6.3 Calculated Accuracy Parameters

Activity	Precision	Recall	f1-score	support
STANDING	1.00	0.97	0.99	329
SITTING	1.00	0.99	1.0	372
WALKING	0.97	1.00	0.98	327
LAYING	1.00	1.00	1.0	322

The different average accuracies are shown in Table 6.4

TABLE 6.4 Average Accuracies

micro avg	0.99	0.99	0.99	1350
macro avg	0.99	0.99	0.99	1350
weighted avg	0.99	0.99	0.99	1350

The confusion matrix using KNN (K=3) is displayed in Figure 6.13.

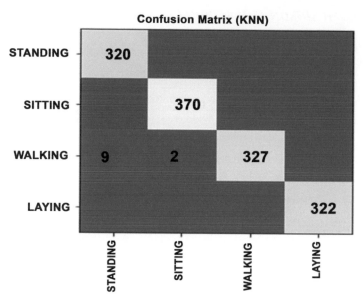

FIGURE 6.13   Confusion matrix.

6.8   FUTURE RESEARCH DIRECTIONS IN AI-BASED HEALTH ASSISTIVE SYSTEMS

Assistive healthcare is having a healthy growth being developed with support of AI wings besides other enabling technologies. This emerging research domain is attracting budding researchers with many of its interesting and yet unexplored challenges some of which are discussed here.

1. **Security issues of sensitive patients' health record:** Sensory health data saved as electronic health record (EHR) needs to be accessed by multiple stakeholders like doctors, patients' relatives, pathologists, pharmacists, Insurers, etc. for their specific interests. So, access control to ensure privacy and security must be defined in terms of confidentiality, integrity, and availability of sensitive patients' disease-related data.

2. **Challenges of handling unlabeled, unstructured, missing, erroneous, redundant data in HER:** Another issue is selection of ML, deep learning (DL) or AI techniques depending on the quality of data in EHR as it is always not labeled, correct, structured, and complete. On structured data set, ML techniques such as supervised (labeled data), unsupervised (unlabeled data), semisupervised (mixed data)

are applied. SVM, decision trees, random forest, KNN, etc. are popular supervised ML techniques for classification of labeled data. On unstructured data, DL techniques such as CNN, DNN, DBN, and RNN are being popularly applied. So, preprocessing and analysis of huge sensory data for knowledge extraction based on which expert systems will function is a real challenge.

3. **Energy efficiency and network lifetime:** Heterogeneous devices and communication links having varying constrained resources are involved in data sensing, transmission, and processing from the local end to the remote end. Among resources, energy source is the limited battery power that must be efficiently used to keep health assistive application undisruptive with enhanced network lifetime. So, applications and services must be energy efficient.

6.8.1 HUMAN MONITORING OR MACHINE-BASED MONITORING?

Though IoT-based and ML-enabled smart intelligent health-care systems are in high demand, it often comes as a dilemma when point of real acceptance by general people is the goal. The confusion about such automated supports is that is this technology system going to replace the traditional human monitoring system? Or would machine-based monitoring be equally compatible, reliable, and available at service like human monitoring? This technology-enabled smart health-care monitoring is often mistakenly considered as replacement of existing traditional human monitoring systems for people in need, specifically elderly people suffering from age-related ailments that may be chronic or critical. To afford expert human monitoring, nowadays both in urban and rural areas, is becoming expensive and sometimes not feasible due to unavailability. Also, the prerequisite of manual monitoring involving human is confinement of both the persons (the person who monitors and the person being monitored) at indoor within a specified area either at the home or at hospital due to the requirement of being in proximity of monitoring devices, such as to measure blood pressure, body temperature, glucose level, pulse rate, ECG signal, etc. to ensure seamless monitoring, which is making this system unpopular. The same service if can be extended with the same or improved quality irrespective of mobility of persons involved does not hamper daily activities of general people who needs to be outdoor due to routine works like morning or evening walk, shopping, etc. and enhances the quality and standard of living. Advanced technology support comes as a saviour at this point to assure location aware monitoring in both normal and emergency conditions. So, in smart health monitoring systems, human monitoring and machine-based monitoring compliment each other to make the whole system complete, accurate, timely, efficient, intelligent, cost-effective, and user-friendly. Continuous routing monitoring is done by biological sensors and processed remotely at cloud servers to notify caregivers who provide advice as and when necessary. In the case of any emergency condition, like sudden deterioration in health condition or fall or accident identified as abnormal condition by analyzing abrupt changes in sensed vital parameters, the person involved in human monitoring gets an alert message in his/her smartphone along with date, time, and location of the person in distress so that he can reach to the location to provide initial aid or to transfer him to a nearby hospital or doctor without delay.

6.8.2 *FALL PREDICTION, IS IT POSSIBLE?*

Intelligent systems using sensors, smartphone, cloud, IoT, AI, ML, etc. for FDS are already in place. Though these systems are getting immensely popularized, the accuracy of such systems is always doubtful in common people due to either false fall detection or not detecting actual fall events. In the first case, a false alert may wrongly direct relatives or caregivers causing harassment in terms of time and anxiety, which in turn may cause another unwanted event like accident or fall due to rushing to the location of the subject in distress. In the second case, it may cause havoc to patients' life. So, 100% accuracy of FDS may be questionable, but with support enabling intelligent technologies, performance may be a nearby satisfactory level. To avoid false alarms, smartphone-based FDS using ML outperforms threshold-based FDS because the earlier one can combine multiple inputs such as vital health parameters with accelerometer and gyroscope sensory data to draw an inference that the fall has actually happened or not with enhanced accuracy in comparison with threshold-based FDS in which only accelerometer and gyroscope data are compared with a predefined threshold. For example, if an actual fall event happens, then with an abrupt increase in accelerometer sensor signal, heart rate or pulse will also increase along with body temperature. So, a rule can be set to define fall and no fall combining all these inputs. To greatly refine results, persons' demography can also be an input. Besides, ML-based systems can identify simple or composite human postures/activities along with a combination of fall and posture to accurately identify fall. The appropriate scenario for this could be as follows: if the smartphone itself falls (not the person carrying/using it), then an abrupt change in accelerometer data may generate false alarm detecting it as a fall of the corresponding person. This can be avoided if the accelerometer data stream may be analyzed over some time window (a few milliseconds) followed by immediate preceding and succeeding postures of the subject in concern (which will be the same here), and it would be correctly identified as no-fall.

6.8.3 *DISEASE PREDICTION AND MEDICAL ASSISTANCE*

Another aspect of machine-based monitoring is that it may help in early disease prediction to provide this knowledge to the doctor or caregiver for giving him a direction toward proper timely diagnosis to assure primary care that will help in avoiding secondary and tertiary care. Now, if an intelligent fall detection system can identifies fall along with immediate previous posture every time then it may find a pattern or relation among several factors such as repeated fall from a specific posture (e.g., walking, sleeping, etc.). Frequent falls from walk posture in comparison to others on the same pathway may lead to prediction of an imbalance problem, which may be caused by fluctuation in blood pressure abruptly or neurological disorders. Fall from sleeping posture of elderly people mostly happens at night time when seamless monitoring by human intervention may always not be possible, but technology-enabled, sensor-based smart monitoring would continue to alert the human monitor toward avoidance of any fatal impact.

6.9 CONCLUSION

This chapter includes smartphone-based fall detection systems enabled by advanced technologies such as IoT, ML, etc. to extend timely monitoring, primarily by a machine and exert support by humans alerted by an intelligent system to ensure smart healthcare with user mobility support. Societal drive, technological advancements, change in demography of population in today's world, urge for improved quality of living, etc. are the driving factors behind this emerging wing of research. Functional frameworks of such smart FDSs, different techniques for efficient fall detection, proposed three-phase FDS for accurate detection illustrated by a detailed flowchart and algorithm along with some representative results showing accuracy as well as false alarms generated by wrong detection of fall, etc. are given. This implementation-based approach followed by future research directions would invite interests of researchers in this domain of research.

KEYWORDS

- **fall detection system (FDS)**
- **patient care service (PCS)**
- **smartphone sensors**
- **location-based service (LBS)**
- **human activity monitoring**

REFERENCES

Arya, Bilandi N. A review: Wireless body area networks for healthcare. *International Journal of Innovative Research in Computer and Communication Engineering*, vol. 2, no. 4, 2014.

Bai Y.-W., Wu S.-C., Tsai C.-L. Design and implementation of a fall monitor system by using a 3-axis accelerometer in a smart phone. In *Proceedings of the 16th IEEE International Symposium on Consumer Electronics*, Harrisburg, PA, USA, June 4–6, 2012, pp. 1–6.

Buzin C. L. Junior and Adami A. G. SDQI—Fall detection system for elderly. *IEEE Latin America Transactions*, vol. 16, no. 4, pp. 1084–1090, Apr. 2018.

Cucchiara R., Prati A., Vezzani R. An intelligent surveillance system for dangerous situation detection in home environments. *Intelligenza Artificiale*, vol. 1, no. 1, pp. 11–15, 2004.

Dinh A., Teng D., Chen L., Shi Y., McCrosky C., Basran J., et al. (Eds.). Implementation of a physical activity monitoring system for the elderly people with built-in vital sign and fall detection. Presented at the *6th International Conference on Information Technology: New Generations*, Las Vegas, NV. IEEE, April 27–29, 2009.

El-Bendary N., Tan Q., Pivot F.C., Lam, A. Fall detection and prevention for the elderly: A review of trends and challenges. *International Journal on Smart Sensing and Intelligent Systems*, vol. 6, pp. 1230–1266, 2013.

Filipe L., Fdez-Riverola F., Costa N., Pereira A., Wireless body area networks for healthcare applications: Protocol stack review. *International Journal of Distributed Sensor Networks*, vol. 2015, pp. 1–23, 2015.

Foroughi H., Rezvanian A., Paziraee A. (Eds.). Robust fall detection using human shape and multi-class support vector machine. Presented at *6th Indian Conference on Computer Vision, Graphics and Image Processing*, Bhubaneswar, India. IEEE, December 16–19, 2008.

Hegde R., Sudarshan B.G., Kumar S.C.P., Hariprasad S.A., Satyanarayana B.S. Technical advances in fall detection system—A review. *International Journal of Computer Science and Mobile Computing*, vol. 2, pp. 152–160, 2013.

Hijaz F., Afzal N., Ahmad T., Hasan, O. Survey of fall detection and daily activity monitoring techniques. In *Proceedings of the International Conference on Information and Emerging Technologies*, Karachi, Pakistan, June 14–16, 2010, pp. 1–6.

Huang B., Tian G., Li X. A method for fast fall detection. Presented at *7th World Congress on Intelligent Control and Automation*; Chongquing, China. IEEE; June 25–27, 2008.

Huang C.-N., Chiang C.-Y., Chang J.-S., Chou Y.-C., Hong Y.-X., Hsu S. J., et al. Location-aware fall detection system for medical care quality improvement. Presented at the *3rd*

International Conference on Multimedia and Ubiquitous Engineering, Qingdao, China. IEEE, June 4–6, 2009.

Igual R., Medrano C., Plaza I. Challenges, issues and trends in fall detection systems. *BiomedEng Online*, vol. 12, 2013.

Juang C., Chang C., Wu J., Lee D. Computer vision-based human body segmentation and posture estimation. *IEEE Transactions on Systems, Man, and Cybernetics—Part A: Systems and Humans*, vol. 39, no. 1, pp. 119–133, Jan. 2009.

Lee J., Robinovitch S., Park E., Inertial sensing-based pre-impact detection of falls involving near-fall scenarios. *IEEE Transactions on Neural Systems and Rehabilitation Engineering*, vol. 23, no. 2, p. 266, Mar. 2015.

Li Q., Stankovic J. A., Hanson M. A., Barth A. T., Lach J., Zhou G. Accurate, fast fall detection using gyroscopes and accelerometer-derived posture information. In *Proceedings of the 6th International Workshop on Wearable and Implantable Body Sensor Networks*, Berkeley, CA, pp. 138–143, 2009, doi: 10.1109/BSN.2009.46

Lim K. H., Jasvindar K., Normala I., Hoo B. K., Yau W. K., Mohmad S., Lai W. Y., Sherina M. S. Risk factors of home injury among Asian. *Journal of Gerontology & Geriatrics*, vol. 8, no. 2, p. 5, 2013.

Miaou S.-G., Sung P.-H., Huang C.-Y. A customized human fall detection system using omnicamera images and personal information. Presented at the *1st Transdisciplinary Conference on Distributed Diagnosis and Home Healthcare (D2H2)*, Arlington, VA.IEEE, April 2–4, 2006.

Mubashir M., Shao L., Seed L. A survey on fall detection: Principles and approaches. *Neurocomputing*, vol. 100, pp. 144–152, 2013.

Nasution A. H., Emmanuel S. (Eds.). Intelligent video surveillance for monitoring elderly in home environments. Presented at the *IEEE 9th Workshop on Multimedia Signal Processing*, Crete, Greece. IEEE, October 1–3, 2007.

National Council on Aging, Falls Prevention Facts. Retrieved from https://www.ncoa.org/news/resources-for-reporters/get-the-facts/falls-prevention-facts/ (Last accessed July 15, 2019).

Patel, S., Park, H., Bonato, P. et al. A review of wearable sensors and systems with application in rehabilitation. J NeuroEngineering Rehabil 9, 21 (2012). https://doi.org/10.1186/1743-0003-9-21

Perera C., Jayaraman P., Zaslavsky A., Christen P., Georgakopoulos D., Dynamic configuration of sensors using mobile sensor hub in internet of things paradigm. In *Proceedings of the IEEE 8th International Conference on Intelligent Sensors, Sensor Networks and Information Processing*, Melbourne, VIC, 2013, pp. 473–478.

Perry J. T., Kellog S., Vaidya S. M., Jong-Hoon Y., Ali H., Sharif H. Survey and evaluation of real-time fall detection approaches. In *Proceedings of the 6th International Symposium on High-Capacity Optical Networks and Enabling Technologies*, Alexandria, Arab Republic of Egypt, pp. 158–164, December 28–30, 2009.

Ruan W., Yao L., Sheng Q., Falkner N., Li X., Gu T. TagFall: Towards un-obstructive fine-grained fall detection based on UHF passive RFID tags. 2015, doi: 10.4108/eai.22–7-2015.2260072

Sarkar S., Raj R., Vinay S., Maiti J., Pratihar D. K. An optimization-based decision tree approach for predicting slip-trip-fall accidents at work. *Safety Science*, vol. 118, pp. 57–69, 2019.

Song S., Cho N., Yoo H., A 0.2-mW 2-Mb/s digital transceiver based on wideband signaling for human body communications. *IEEE Journal of Solid-State Circuits*, vol. 42, no. 9, pp. 2021–2033, 2007.

Thome N., Miguet S., Ambellouis S. A real-time, multiview fall detection system: A LHMM-based approach. *IEEE Transactions on Circuits and Systems for Video Technology*, vol. 18, no. 11, 1522–1532, 2008.

Tsinganos P., Skodras A. A smartphone-based fall detection system for the elderly, 2017, doi: 10.1109/ISPA.2017.8073568

Wang C.-C., Chiang C.-Y., Lin P.-Y., Chou Y.-C., Kuo I.-T., Huang C.-N., et al. Development of a fall detecting system for the elderly residents. Presented at the *2nd International Conference on Bioinformatics and Biomedical Engineering*, Shanghai, China, May 16–18, 2008.

Yoo H., Wireless Body Area Network and its Healthcare Applications, 2013.

Yu B. Wireless Body Area Networks for Healthcare: A Feasibility Study, 2009.

Yu X. Approaches and principles of fall detection for elderly and patient. In *Proceedings of the 10th IEEE International Conference on e-Health Networking, Applications and Services*, Singapore; pp. 42–47, July 7–9, 2008.

CHAPTER 7

Smart Sensors Transform Healthcare System

AMRITA RAI,[1*] SHYLAJA VINAYKUMAR KARATANGI,[1]
RESHU AGARWAL,[2] and OM PRAKASH[3]

[1]Electronics and Communication Eng., G.L. Bajaj Institute of Technology and Management, Greater Noida, Uttar Pradesh, India

[2]Amity Institute of Information and Technology, Amity University Noida, Uttar Pradesh, India

[3]Electronics and Communication Eng., St. Marry College of Engineering, Hyderabad, Telangana, India

*Corresponding author. E-mail:amritaskrai@gmail.com

ABSTRACT

Over the past few decades, life expectation has increased significantly. Due to mobility difficulties or other health problems, elderly people who live on their own often need support. In such cases, an independent supporting system may be helpful. One of the most exciting trends and innovations in the recent history of technological advancement is Internet of Things (IoT). In recent years, it has garnered much attention to lighten the anxiety on healthcare systems caused by the aging population and a rise in chronic illnesses. The current development and growth in the arena of IoT is providing great potential in the route of the innovative era of healthcare. The vision of the healthcare is expansively preferred, as it advances the excellence of life and health of humans, involving several health regulations. The continuous increase of multifaceted IoT devices in health is broadly tested by challenges such as powering the IoT terminal nodes used for health monitoring, real-time data processing, and smart decision and event management. Sensors can collect the patient data dynamically to stimulate preventive care, diagnostics, etc. and to measure treatment results. This chapter focuses on sensors that are nonintrusive and noninvasive and exclude sensors that are implantable and on the motivation of the basic concept of smart sensors that are used in healthcare and monitoring systems for helping elderly peoples and are proven useful in medical and home environments. This chapter briefs about different smart sensors and their impact on human life, which will help in future research. Also, it proposes a standard model for application in future IoT healthcare systems.

7.1   INTRODUCTION

This chapter addresses the main issues of healthcare access, handling chronic diseases, ignored healthcare services, and the ability of the healthcare delivery systems to enhance the cultural proficiency, worth, workforce, funding, information technology, and emergency alertness of the inhabitants based on smart sensors. Furthermore, this chapter elaborates the accountability of the healthcare system that plays a vital role in recognition in the public health sector and collaborates with the governmental health agencies. The healthcare system is not the only or even the robust element of health, but it is very important. Having health insurance either through a private plan or through a publicly financed program is a minimum requirement for routine access to healthcare for most people across the world. Health insurance coverage is associated with better health outcomes for adults as well as elderly people from chronic diseases.

Today, in the most countries, the quality of life has been improving a lot due to significant transformation in medical equipment, which reflects improve public healthcare. There are many smart and wearable medical equipment of various categories that have been demonstrated in medicinal and home environments for enhancing the life of senior people. The modern improvements in microelectronics and VLSI allow the improvement of cheaper devices that are generally used by several individuals as health monitoring and observing tools. Automatic healthcare monitoring and intensive care unit are based on small mountable sensors, actuators, and smart improved wireless transmitter and receiver technologies that provided powerful and accurate solutions, which make people to monitor and observe anyone's health from anywhere, being somehow secure (Angelov et al., 2019). Nowadays, the medical device market needs various things to add the value of devices and data; it requires real-time analytics for improving decision and transforming health information exchange to take fast actions.

These devices are also portable for both communication and monitoring. As a result, while implementing any portable healthcare device, some key features are taken into account for facilitating portability among medical devices and monitoring systems required by hospitals. Some of the key features are standardization, availability of structure, expertise of resources, regulatory and compliance issues, data life cycle management, and cyber security management. We look forward to such devices because they are transportable, stress-free to use, and compact in size and lightweight. A classic example of a complete healthcare system (CHS) with smart sensors that commonly uses a smart microcontroller and various smart sensors for sensing and monitoring various diseases and sending information through electronics media to a doctor's mobile phone or any family member who will be responsible for emergency assistance is shown in Figure 7.1. The key purpose of such systems is based on smart sensors that are carried by persons anywhere and can continuously monitor the health in real time and generate alarm for any abnormal health condition. The CHS is very useful for elderly people for monitoring the heart rate, blood pressure, and body temperature and caring in the hospital or at home. All the information can be handled by different smart sensors and microcontroller-based systems.

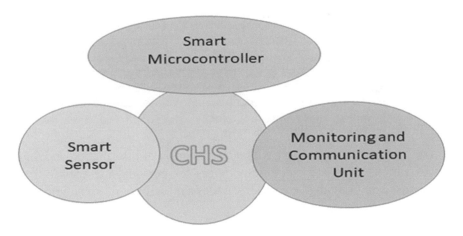

FIGURE 7.1   Basic diagram of a CHS with sensors.

In the modernization era, all digital devices are becoming smart and making use of personalised data, which brings innovation to all fields based on their applications. In such cases, one of the revolutions is in healthcare technology. While there are numerous troubles and obstructions to their appropriation, these reasons can never again prevent us from grasping advancements that could have positive effect on human lives. As the healthcare system run by the government has protocols like waiting time and a lack of equipment and some specialized doctors, and the system in private hospitals has everything is expensive, people are looking forward to electronics-based healthcare systems (Figure 7.2).

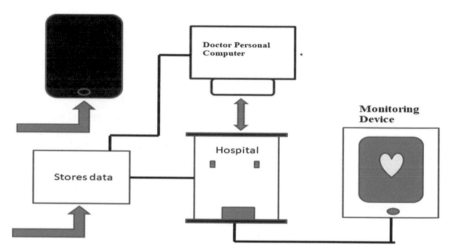

FIGURE 7.2   Role of sensors in a complete healthcare system in hospitals.

In today's daily life, electronics-based devices play a big role in various areas such as entertainment, communication, education, sports, and security systems. It is the right time for medical innovation, and utilizing current digital developments may cause upheaval in the social insurance industry as well.

The progress in technology with a combination of information and function of various on-board electronic devices for personal therapeutic treatments, based on individual conditions, opens a massive door for an improved and available healthcare system.

Advancements in health data innovation (health IT) present a chance to expand medicine adherence rates, measure drug adherence, improve care, improve general populace health, and decrease human services costs. Fruitful treatment of illnesses with physician recommended drugs requires reliable utilization of the prescriptions as endorsed. However, research demonstrates that meds normally are not utilized as coordinated (Tzanoukosa et al., 2016).

7.2 SENSING TECHNOLOGY IN THE HEALTHCARE SYSTEM

At present, due to advancement in semiconductor VSLI technologies, low-power processors, sensors, and Big Data analytics are coupled with intelligent wireless networks. All of these are an essential part of Internet of Things (IoT), and it is the root cause for the improvements and innovations in sensing technologies.

In the past decade, sensors and sensor systems have been extensively utilized to sense our encompassing environment and to facilitate our daily lives. Nowadays, sensing technology shows rapid development in different areas, like healthcare, monitoring, tracking, etc. Actually sensors do not have intelligence capabilities, so they alone do not provide intelligence, but we can build intelligence by integrating and analyzing data from different sensors and sensor networks platforms, for various applications such as, e-health systems, surveillance systems, tracking systems, monitoring systems, disaster management systems, manufacturing systems, vehicular systems, etc.

For most part for locally established medicinal services, the course of action incorporates correspondences, imaging, detecting, and human–supercomputer interface innovations under attack by conclusion, healing patients without bothering their lifestyle. It is likely to be believable for the improvement of a minimal effort for medicinal detecting, correspondence and examination gadget that is continuous checking web permitted physical conditions of patients. The IoT framework gives dynamic as well as progressing course of action of patients, crisis facilities, supervisor and doctors segregated as of checked data correspondence from starting spot to objective with extreme goal of distant seeing.

All data from smart sensors are controlled through the application-specific integrated circuit (ASIC). The other elements of the CHS system are a D/A converter, an A/D converter, an oscillator circuit, a digital signal processing (DSP) circuit that are associated with the ASIC consisting of simple signal conditioning. The circuit is fueled by two silver oxide (Ag_2O) batteries having 35 h of working limit with a supply voltage of about 3.1 V and a pore utilization of 15.5 mV. All information is collected by ASIC through a transmitter that transmits to the base station for the specialist to recognize the issue. This innovation is expected to be more modified and aimed for explicit ailment medications. Using smart sensors in CHS has many benefits:

- easy design,

- high reliability,
- system flexibility,
- minimum cables' interconnection,
- high performance, and
- small rugged packing.

Disadvantages of Smart Sensors

- When we upgrade smart sensors and when we have to mix old devices with new sensors, extra care needs to be taken since they may not be compatible.
- If a bus wire fails, all framework is down, which is not the situation with discrete wiring. However, with discrete wiring, in the event that one sensor fails, it might be important to close the framework down. By using of a redundant backup bus, this problem of bus wire failure can be alleviated.

The applications of smart sensors include scientific, civil, e-health, military, and home applications.

7.2.1 GAS SENSORS

Gar sensors are one of the most popular sensors for healthcare system and come under the classification of chemical sensors, which are used to determine the concentratiom of gas in their surroundings. It is a good sensing system for environment monitoring applications such as air quality monitoring, gas leakage detection in hospitals or any places, breathe test for alcoholic persons, and electronics noise in medical science (Bogue, 2014; Lin et al., 2015). Optical, capacitive, surface acoustic wave, catalytic, electrochemical, and semiconductor gas sensors are the different types of gas sensors. Gas sensors can be divided into two categories based on their sensing properties (Liu et al., 2012; Yamazoe and Shimanoe, 2002; Lee et al., 1996): first, on the basis of variations in electrical properties like MOS-based sensors, polymer-based sensors, carbon nanotube sensors (Thai, 2011), etc., and second, on the basis of variations in other properties (for example, optical sensors, calorimetric sensors, gas chromatographs, ultrasonic-based acoustic sensors, etc.) (Petculescu et al., 2006).

7.2.2 BIOCHEMICAL SENSORS

The chemical or biological amount is converted into an electrical signal by using biochemical sensors. A biosensor incorporates a chemically sensitive layer, a transducer, a receptor (biocomponent), and an electronic signal processor (De la Guardia, 1995). The types of biochemical sensors are as follows:

- oxygen sensor,
- carbon dioxide sensor,
- surface reaction measurement sensor,
- flow sensor,
- glucose detector,
- concentration sensor,
- pH sensor,
- acidity sensor, and
- scattering measurement sensor.

Basic Characteristics of Biosensors

- Linearity—To determine high substrate concentrations, sensors should be highly linear.
- Sensitivity—It represents the electrode response value with respect to the substrate concentration.
- Selectivity—There must be minimum chemical interference for obtaining correct results.
- Response time—It is the time required to achieve 95% of the response.

Applications of Biosensors

Biosensors are applied for the

- analysis of food,
- analysis of biomolecules,
- development of drug,
- detection of crimes,
- diagnosis in the medical field,
- monitoring of the environment,
- biological warfare as detection systems,

- replacement of organs, and
- manufacturing of pharmaceuticals.

7.2.3 WIRELESS SENSOR NETWORKS

A wireless sensor network is a self-configuring network of small sensor nodes that use radio signals to communicate among themselves and is deployed in quantity to understand, monitor, and sense the physical world. The key attributes of any remote sensor network include:

- power consumption constraints for nodes using batteries or energy harvesting,
- possibility to cope with node failures,
- node's mobility
- nodes that are heterogeneous in nature,
- scalability to large-scale deployment,
- capability to operate in inverse environmental conditions,
- simple to use, and
- cross-layer design.

The advantages of wireless sensor networks are as follows:

- No fixed infrastructure is required for network setups.
- These are useful for nonreachable places such as rural areas, mountains, deep forests, etc.
- There are flexible as if there is random situation where an additional workstation is needed.
- The implementation price is low.
- Very less wiring is required.
- New devices can be accommodated at any stage.
- These have flexibility when undergoing any physical partitions.
- A centralized monitoring system is used for its access.

The disadvantages of wireless sensor networks can be summarized as follows:

- It is less secure with respect to the wired network.
- It has low speed with respect to the wired network.
- It has complex configuration with respect to the wired network.
- It is easily influenced by noise.
- The communication speed is low with respect to the wired network.
- The cost is still high.

In terms of health applications, these are used in remote monitoring of physiological data, tracking and monitoring patients and doctors inside a hospital, drug administration, etc.

7.2.4 RFID: THE BEDROCK OF SMART HEALTHCARE

A smart healthcare system is one in which data is collated at all important points, stored precisely, and retrieved whenever needed. This exercise shifts the attention for medical equipment and device management to patient care. This leads to healthier care services and improves the brand of the hospital. Another area of interest where radio-frequency identification (RFID) plays a vital role in healthcare system in hospitals is during surgical procedures (Jackson, 2008).

Three main components are involved in any RFID-based system: (1) an application host, which is used to interfacing of ID data read from a data reader using encoding and decoding into a personal computer or any server mainframe, (2) an RFID tag for storing the identification information or code, and (3) a tag reader or tag integrator for sending polling signals to an RFID transmitter responder to the tag identifier (Karmakar et al., 2008).

7.3 SMART HEALTHCARE: SERVICES AND APPLICATIONS

The smart sensors with IoT applications in the fields of medicine and healthcare will benefit patients to utilize the best therapeutic help, briefest treatment time, low restorative expenses, and most attractive administration. Monitoring health is imperative to be checked normally so as to ensure that our body continually keep fit and remains in a phenomenal condition. Mostly, the crucial parameters watched for health monitoring are heartbeat rate (HBR), weight, temperature, blood pressure, and glucose level (Sundaravadivel et al., 2018). These parameters will translate some significant data with respect to body health; for instance, high temperature indicated fever, while an unsteady pulse is a sign of heart issue. One of the techniques to perform health checking is to utilize remote patient monitoring. This technique uses a remotely controlled smart sensor, monitors by collecting data and images, and sends information to a base station for display, illumination, and storage of patient history. Such "home telehealth" applications may incorporate utilizing telemetry gadgets to catch a particularly essential sign. Such administrations can be used to enhance the utilization of visiting attendants or to get therapeutic counsel from a specialist in a period where a medical clinic blunder is the sixth driving reason for preventable demise; having sensors imbedded in hardware could serve as a line of defence and reliability. With the assortment of remote checking administrations now accessible, devices can cooperate to make a complete data organizer. For instance, the medical setup associated with sensors like blood pressure, HBR, ultrasound, or other devices that could naturally transfers all collected data to healthcare experts. Consequently to fabricate equipment progressively this is suitable by allowing consistent checking of patient wellbeing (Sidheeque et al., 2017). Various applications and services of smart sensors are discussed below.

7.3.1   e-TABLET

An e-tablet, which consists of a multichannel sensor, is used for remote biomedical computations in the body. After researching for long time, researchers found that with the help of some sensors, they can detect diseases through IOT. This proposed work composed of a small or a general pill-sized e-tablet that contains multichannel sensors, an antenna, a wireless transmitter, an edible battery, and a microcontroller. These components are combined so as to preserve its tiny size, solid assembly, and a security profile fit for restorative use. Figure 7.3 explains the structure of an e-tablet.

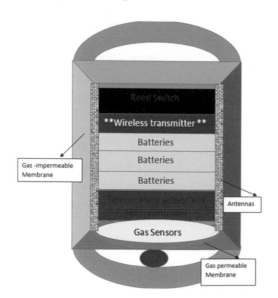

FIGURE 7.3   Structure of an e-tablet.

Therefore, it is composed in a small pill size that can be swallowed and get into through the gastrointestinal tract. Once swallowed, it starts connecting to the system to detect the abnormalities in the body. An e-tablet is customized with components and the outer coating of the e-tablet is made of chemical-resistant polyether ether ketone. The use of an e-tablet will free clients from intrusive techniques, for example, catheters, endoscopic instruments, or radioisotopes that gather data for the stomach-related tract.

Drug conveyance utilizing an electronic pill will likewise be controlled with on-board gadgets, empowering exact and versatile conveyance designs, which are not yet conceivable by different methods. With the aid of the e-tablet, we can analyze the health from top to bottom and point-by-point examination of diseases. In addition to that, its uses extend from medication conveyance to exploring explicit areas of the human body to target various sorts of cancer, pH level of solutions, human body temperature, damaged tissues, gastric problems, biomarkers measurement, and HBR. The evaluation of HBR is used to reduce the heart attack, which is a major disease in today's world. All these functions will be carried out by an edible battery outfitted with fitting sensors. The significance of an edible battery is that it is not toxic to the human body. An e-tablet also contains a tiny camera that captures all informative pictures and sends them to the system; with the help of these data, doctor can analyze the further report of the patient and can also detect alterations in the initial stage of major diseases.

The working of an e-tablet is shown in Figure 7.4. This device setup can transmit the basic data such as acidity, pressure, and temperature levels or also send the images of esophagus problems and intestines to the system, which in turn can analyze the following diseases like cancer, heart burn, esophagitis, and eosinophilia diseases. An e-tablet is further used to measure the muscle constriction, simplicity of entry, and different elements of the body to uncover data that was inaccessible before. In 1972, some doctors researched and made developments with the help of an electronic pill. It is called as a medicinal monitoring system, which process parameters like temperature, pH, conductivity, and dissolved oxygen.

An e-tablet with multichannel sensors detects the diseases or abnormalities of the human body. First, it is comprised of a silicon diode joined to the substrate, and manufactured on two silicon chips situated next to the face end of the container. It is utilized to distinguish the body temperature and weight. The utilization of silicon IC makes these sensors helpful, and it comes effortlessly. A second sensor is used to determine the pH of the solutions. A third sensor is used to determine the damage tissues, body water content (which shows the kidney, lung, and liver condition), salt absorption, the breakdown of natural mixes into charge colloids, and bile emission. A fourth sensor is used to ascertain the rate of dissolved oxygen and identify the activity of aerobic bacteria in the small and large intestines. The last fifth sensor is used to measure the HBR through the blood flow and also with the assistance of cameras captures the images of blockage of the blood flow to the heart and abnormal blood and valve circulation (Susarla et al., 2018; Ashrafuzzaman et al., 2013).

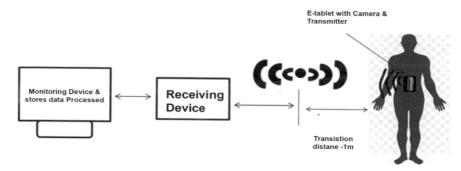

FIGURE 7.4   Working of an e-tablet with smart sensors and an IoT device.

With an e-tablet, there many advantages to consider for which the proposed chapter will be more reliable: tiny size and an effective accessible well-being framework are of great importance. It is kept medication movement, which is with minimum side effects of the drugs and their helpful valve boosting. The impact of medications is expected to happen quicker. Its instant response as an e-tablet gives real-time analysis of the body to easily identify the diseases and also the drug reaction to the body.

7.3.2   SMARTWATCH

Today, technology and sensors portability makes smartwatches as most popular wearable devices. Some people adopt smartwatches not only for fitness purpose but also to reflect their social psychological behavior. Experimental results reveal that the smartwatch usefulness and visibility are important factors that are based on a combination of fashion and technology. Smartwatches, among numerous wearable devices, have turned into a significant beginning stage for the wide spread of wearable gadgets

(Figure 7.5). Likewise, working and perceivability of a conventional watch can position it as extravagance, decent, and classy (Carlson, 2015). The expanded enthusiasm for the new innovation is similarly reflected by the enormous measure of applications offered by smartwatches, for example, more than 10,000 applications for the "Apple Watch", and more than 4000 applications for the "Android Wear" (Curry, 2015). Such type of watches has the potential to provide and monitor health in daily life by empowering self-checking of individual action; getting feedback depending on action measures; taking into consideration of patterns of behaviors; and supporting bidirectional correspondence with human services suppliers and relatives. Be that as it may, keen watches are a rising innovation and research on these gadgets is at an early stage. The watch is intended to install various types of sensors empowering a few functionalities: the acknowledgment of labeled features by methods for RFID innovation; the acknowledgment of signals of the lower arm by utilizing inertial sensors; and the acknowledgment of fingers' motion, hand motions, and handles by detecting the power applied by ligaments in the wrist. Studies show that the initial heart rate (HR) after birth of a new born baby is the core of commencement and assessment of neonatal revival. Be that as it may, clinical evaluation by auscultation of heart sound or palpation of the umbilical cord to get the HR was observed to be both questionable and inaccurate, so electronic smartwatches are used for monitoring HR of an extremely preterm baby.

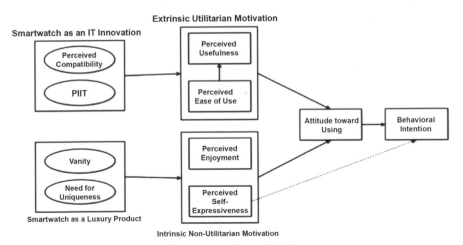

FIGURE 7.5   Smartwatch use as luxury as well as technology.

Source: Reprinted with permission from Choi and Kim, 2016. © Elsevier.

7.4 IoT IN SMART HEALTHCARE

The IoT is a network of physical components (similarly as a "smart device") and various other things, which are associated with instruments like sensors, actuators, and programming. The structure forms collect information from various points of an environment and transfers that data through Internet. Global standards initiative on IoT in 2013 pictures IoT as "the structure of the data society." The IoT not only transfers the collected data but also controls the environment remotely over the existing system, which gives entryways for a progressive direct blend to PC-based systems from the physical world and realizing improved adequacy, accuracy, and monetary bit of leeway.

IoT is extended with actuators and sensors, and advancements lead to include a wider class of modernized physical frameworks, for instance, smarthomes, grids, smartcities, intelligent health, and excellent transportation (Figure 7.6). Everything is inquisitively prominent through embedding its processing framework within the present Internet foundation (Sidheeque et al., 2017).

FIGURE 7.6   Overview of IoT.

Source: Reprinted from https://www.sensorsexpo.com/iot-ecosystem

7.4.1   APPLICATIONS OF IoT

The fundamental idea of using IoT is for patients hospitalized in a hospital whose physiological condition needs to be monitored continuously irrespective of the presence of doctors or others in the hospital. Health sensors are utilized to collect far-reaching physiological data and utilization entries, the cloud to investigate and store the data, and a brief timeframe that later forwards the isolated information remotely to parental insights to support further examination and audit, as shown in Figure 2 of Chamberlin (2016). Thus, it replaces a way toward having a fitness expert dropped through by standard intervals headed for verifying the patient's key signs; adequately a consistent modernized development of data. Along these lines, it meanwhile improves by thoroughly considering unsurprising idea and chops down the expense of idea by cutting down the expense of standard procedures in favor of ideas notwithstanding information about social affair and examination (Ahmed et al., 2016).

Various citizens in the different parts of the world encounter terrible physical conditions since they do not have the right to convincing health check-up and can exist as essential situation patients. Though remote plans related to IoT, it will provide the experience of service as similar to face to face consultation (Figure 7.7). The game plans can be used to securely discover an understanding of health-related information by an assortment of sensors, data can be important for most of calculations toward look at the statistics as well as after that offer it during remote system by means of restorative specialists can be able to build fitting fitness proposition (Zworykin, 1957). IoT is changing remote patient monitoring, customizing treatment, improving results, and bringing down human service costs. For example, wearable ultrasound-based sensors empower senior citizens to live autonomously longer by checking their exercises and recognizing falls. The IoT is a stage that empowers the continuous capture of data, encourages gathering and investigation of this data, and furnishes the capacity to impart it to different partners to make an associated domain. This genuinely necessary problematic advancement will help settle the present difficulties in businesses and will definitely improve health results at a lower cost of consideration.

As per another report from MarketResearch.com, people are forcing IoT market segment to strike $117 billion by 2020. Research office Gartner predicts that more than 40% of the organizations anticipate that IoT should have a transformational impact on their activities throughout the following three years.

7.4.2   DOES THE IoT HELP?

The information-fueled medicinal services division can profit fundamentally by the utilization of IoT. IoT-driven advancements can encourage information-empowered customized investigation of patient's health, improved clinical results, and successful patient monitoring. Clinics are utilizing IoT to alter human services and its powerful future prospects in the social insurance vertical. A portion of the usages of IoT are as follows.

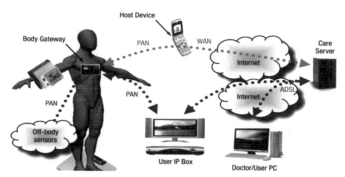

FIGURE 7.7   Working and applications of smart sensors in healthcare.
Source: Reprinted.

7.4.3 PERSISTENT DISEASE ADMINISTRATION

IoT overcomes any issues with the assistance of gadgets that screen a patient's physiological condition (for instance, blood glucose level, blood pressure for hypertensive patients, weight for diabetic patients, and so forth). The intermittent data sent in by these contraptions could be used to perform particular examinations.

7.4.4 DISTANT SCIENTIFIC MONITORING AND CONVALESCENT HOSPITAL

This dimension of motorization empowers providers to move the endeavors of routine checking and field association to remotely observing work power and in this manner sparing cost. Besides, remote checking has successfully shown results, for instance, lessened set off rates and extended staff gainfulness.

7.4.5 WELLNESS AND PREVENTATIVE CARE

The presentation of IoT, in a general sense, as a wearable advancement has made health supervision beneficial. Such tireless openness of data empowers the customer to explore and relate various parameters.

IoT clearly offers a certification of changing human administrations with the usage of advancement. Convincing consolidation of IoT with standard courses of action can be a power multiplier to change medicinal services with hardware. Likewise, they are moreover looking in effective inpatient care, postrelease care, and all-around preventive well-being and health. Our Indian health structures are irrefutably tried on the physical organizations that can be offered, and India as a nation has a deficiency of the health organizations which is open on the Internet. In this situation, using practical tiresome advance pairs with customary courses of action can unbelievably empower us to develop the extent of human administrations to all of the people who need it. This is an accomplishment win situation for the IT game plan industry, the healthcare providers, the patients, and the system with everything taken into account. The economy supporting these is plainly going to bit of leeway, and it can make an incredibly sound business condition and besides enlarging the passage to first-class healthcare.

7.5 SMART HEALTHCARE: CHALLENGES, VULNERABILITIES, AND OPPORTUNITIES

Smart sensors will have considerable effect on the healthcare system in the years to come, but they have some challenges, vulnerabilities, and opportunities. This implementation of information and communication technology (ICT) within the smart healthcare engineering offered to the e-health, which is designed to report organizational problems, challenges, and the management of healthcare records, also released the option to telemedicine and remote relationship between medical professionals and patients. A graphical summary of the challenges and opportunities that have been identified and classified is shown in Figure 7.8.

7.5.1 IDENTIFICATION OF THE CHALLENGES TO BE FACED IN THE PHASE OF GATHERING DATA

A big challenge in smart healthcare system is to collect data from the sensor network and use all data in different resources by the user and hospital. Besides its superficial simplicity, transmitting data in different heavily sensorized environments, where users/patients stored and used their own data, despite important problems and radio planning, is a must, and a simple cloud network and IoT cannot work sufficiently to manage it, so it has a separate and new platform to gather all of the data and monitors it through another platform, namely, the Internet of Medical Things (IoMT). The main challenge in smart sensor healthcare system is to transform smart sensor into a wearable device, which is suitable for medical equipment to collect data. Also, planning for a radio environment for the collection of transmitted data and another cloud platform for storing that data is required.

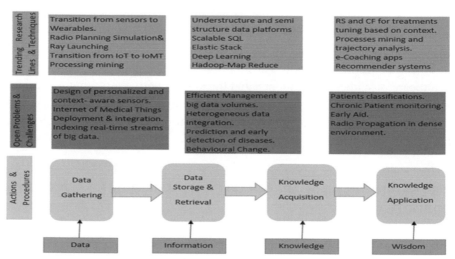

FIGURE 7.8   Summary of the challenges and opportunities of the healthcare system.

Source: Redrawn from Solanas et al., 2017.

This appropriation of data and correspondence advances (ICT) in the social insurance industry brought forth the alleged electronic well-being (e-wellbeing).

UbiPILL was proposed by Ilkko et al. (2009). This device is focused on individuals having issues in remembering to take their medicine on time. Having older individuals at the top of the priority list, a consistent interoperation among UbiPILL and UbiHOMESERVER has been intended to dependably screen the medication box exercises by a Web program of any customer device.

Further, a versatile mindful methodology for arranged medicinal gadgets in portability mindful e-health situations was proposed by Kliem et al. (2012). This methodology is a cost-effective and area self-sufficient observing framework. Basic circumstances require fly system coordination and data transmission running from spaces like patient's home, restorative practices, ambulances, and crisis facilities, where each region may identify with a substitute master. Therefore, the sensible and checked restorative information should be able to trade among dissimilar gadgets by thought of safety, in addition, to assurance matter.

An in-house drug administration framework dependent on RFID innovation was proposed by Parida et al. (2012). This framework is required to assume a critical job in the healthcare industry by following the medication, for example, normal just as the crisis prescription by the clients with or without the RFID tag. The framework is outfitted with a camera and an electronic framework to follow the clients. The primary advantage of this framework is that it very well may be utilized by a wide range of clients including senior-level or less taught people.

Further, a framework that joins the records of electronic patients by means of high-rate procurement of physiological patient information was proposed by Clifton et al. (2013). They clarified that AI advances introduced inside medicinal service data frameworks can give a clinically preferred position with the likelihood to improve patient outcomes.

Another system monitoring the individuals for sleep disorders like insomnia was proposed by Hamida et al. (2013). This system helps in the analysis of sleep data and provides secure transmission of the stored results. The biggest advantages of this system are its safety measures and no operating cost.

IoT hub remotely observing the patients for soundness of more established individual groups in the home was proposed by Ray (2014). This framework is practically portable, financially savvy, and postpone-tolerant. In any case, this framework needs in help for crisis medicinal services for basic old individuals.

Additionally, a smart pill box was proposed by Huang et al. (2014). This framework remembers the issues of elderly individuals to give full drug security. The method of reminding about medicine to the patient is a tablet box that plans proper medication so that mishandling could be avoided. Regardless of effortlessness, the early frameworks were bulky because of enormous electronic parts and batteries utilized and are focusing only on the pH, temperature, and weight (Zworykin, 1957; Mackay, 1959). A gadget must be profoundly set inside the body, which makes the remote correspondence intriguing because of its encompassing standard; the ongoing efforts by electronic medicine have additionally be restricted to low-frequency transmissions (Chen et al., 2009; Johannessen et al., 2006; Valdastri et al., 2004; Wang et al., 2008; Thone et al., 2009; Park et al., 2002; Kfouri et al., 2008). Existing strategies for electronic healthcare frameworks experience the ill effects of various disadvantages (Cramer et al., 1989; Grosset et al., 2006; Olivieri et al., 1991; Shalansky et al., 2004).

The proposed work has built up a basic electronic tablet gadget dependent on a standard multichannel sensor that defeats a portion of these constraints. The basic diagram of the structure of this framework is trailed by an assessment of its utilization in observing different sorts of growth, harmed tissues, measuring biomarkers, and HBR.

7.6 CONCLUSIONS AND FUTURE ASPECTS

Smart sensors will convey a higher level of interaction and more technological developments in smart healthcare systems. The integration of smart sensors with healthcare systems provides a benefit to control and monitor the hospitals as well as home elderly care systems. An important step for the implementation of a smart sensor in the healthcare system is the adoption of sensing technologies, implementation of techniques, and IOT-based approaches for a wide range of applications.

Its instant response as an e-tablet, which is composed of an antenna, an edible battery, microprocessors, and other elements, gives real-time analysis of the body to easily identify the diseases and also the drug reaction to the body.

7.7 FUTURE RESEARCH ASPECTS

Advancement in digital gadgets utilizing customized information will draw out a transformation in social insurance technology. While there are numerous challenges and boundaries to their function, these reasons can never again prevent us from grasping advancements that could positively affect our lives.

The creation of the transistor has prompted radiometry cases with test circuits for the location of ailments and variations from the norm by inner investigation of the gastrointestinal tract even in confined regions where utilization of conventional endoscopy was not allowed. Be that as it may, these containers could not be utilized successfully, as these transmit just from a single channel, have enormous segments, and experience the ill effects of poor dependability, low affectability, and short lifetimes. These were later tried by utilizing research laboratory-type sensors, for example, glass pH terminals, resistance thermometers, etc.

In the following couple of years, we can expect working models of these thoughts accessible with the utilization of novel materials for batteries. As of now, lithium is being utilized; yet, scientists visualize a change to sodium.

This is to furnish humankind with effectively open, sheltered, solid, and low-cost medicinal services.

KEYWORDS

- IoT
- healthcare
- technology
- wearable sensors
- e-Tablet
- multichannel sensor
- e-Health

REFERENCES

Ahmed M. U., Björkman M., Čaussević A., Fotouhi H., Lindén M., An overview on the Internet of Things for health monitoring systems, Social Informatics and Telecommunications Engineering, 169, 2016, pp. 429–436.

Ali B., Awad A. I., Cyber and physical security vulnerability assessment for IoT-based smart homes, Sensors, 18, 2018, pp. 1–17. doi:10.3390/s18030817 www.mdpi.com/journal/sensors.

Angelov G. V., Nikolakov D. P., Ruskova I. N., Gieva E. E., Spasova M. L., Healthcare sensing and monitoring. In: Ganchev I., Garcia N., Dobre C., Mavromoustakis C., Goleva R. (Eds). Enhanced Living Environments. Lecture Notes in Computer Science, vol. 11369, 2019. Springer, Cham.

Ashrafuzzaman M., Mazaharul H. M., Chakraborty C., Rafi M. M. K., Tabassum, T. Rashedul, H., Heart attack detection using smart phone, International Journal of Technology Enhancements and Emerging Engineering Research, 1(3), 2013, 23–27.

Bhattacharyya D., Kim T.-H., and Pal S., A comparative study of wireless sensor networks and their routing protocols, Sensors, 10, 2010, 10506–10523, doi:10.3390/s101210506 www.mdpi.com/journal/sensors.

Bogue, R., Towards the trillion sensors market, Sensor Review, 34, 2014, 137–142.

Bowen M., Smith G., Considerations for the design of smart sensors, Sensors and Actuators, A, 46–47, 1995, 516–520.

Carlson, J., Apple Watch becomes a study on attention. The Seattle Times, 2015. http://www.seattletimes.com/business/apple-watch-becomes-a-study-onattention.

Chamberlin B., Healthcare Internet of Things: 18 Trends to Watch in 2016. IBM Center for Applied Insights, 2106. https://ibmcai.com/2016/03/01/healthcare-internet-of-things-18-trends-to-watch-in-2016

Chen X., Zhang X., Zhange L., Li X., Qi N., Jiang H., Wang Z., A wireless capsule endoscope system with low-power controlling and processing ASIC, IEEE Transactions on Biomedical Circuits and Systems, 3(1), 2009, 11–22.

Chuah S. H.-W., Rauschnabel P. A., Krey N., Nguyen B., Thurasamy R., Lade, S., Wearable technologies: The role of usefulness and visibility in smartwatch adoption, Computers in Human Behavior, 65, 2016, pp. 276–284. www.elsevier.com/locate/comphumbe.

Choi J., Kim S., Is the smartwatch an IT product or a fashion product? A study on factors affecting the intention to use smartwatches, Computers in Human Behavior, 63, 2016, pp. 777–786. www.elsevier.com/locate/comphumbe.

Clifton D. A., Wong D., Clifton L., Wilson S., Way R., Pullinger R., Tarassenko L., A large-scale clinical validation of an integrated monitoring system in the emergency department, Journal of Biomedical and Health Informatics, 2013, 17(4), 835–842, doi: 10.1109/JBHI.2012.2234130.

Cramer J. A., Mattson R. H., Prevey M. L., Scheyer R. D., Ouellette V. L., How often is medication taken as prescribed? A novel assessment technique, Journal of the American Medical Association, 261(22), 1989, 3273–3277.

Curry, D., Apple Watch hits 10,000 apps: How do Android wear, Pebble, and Samsung compare? Digital Trends, 2015. http://www.digitaltrends.com/wearables/apple-watch-apps-comparison.

Cui, Y., Wei, Q., Park, H., Lieber, C.M., Nanowire nanosensors for highly sensitive and selective detection of biological and chemical species, Science, 293, 2001, 1289–1292.

De la Guardia, M., Biochemical sensors: The state of the art, Microchimica Acta, 120, 1995, 243–255.

Din S., Paul A., Smart health monitoring and management system: Toward autonomous wearable sensing for Internet of Things using big data analytics, Future Generation Computer Systems, 91, Feb. 2019, 611–619.

Eastman P., IOM report: Minorities receive unequal medical treatment even when access is similar, Oncology Times, 24(5), May 2002, 31–32.

Grosset K. A., Bone I., Reid J. L., Grosset D., Measuring therapy adherence in Parkinson's disease: A comparison of methods, Journal of Neurol Neurosurg Psychiatry, 77(2), 2006, 249–251.

Hamida S. T.-B., Ben Hamida E., Ahmed B., Abu-Dayy A., Towards efficient and secure in-home wearable insomnia monitoring and diagnosis system. In: Proceedings of the13th IEEE International Conference on Bioinformatics and Bioengineering, Chania, Greece, 2013, pp. 1–6.

Hong N., Li D., Yu Y., Xiu Q., Liu H., Jiang G., A computational framework for converting textual clinical diagnostic criteria into the quality data model, Journal of Biomedical Informatics, 63, 2016, pp. 11–21.

Huang S., Chang H., Jhu Y., Chen G., The intelligent pill box – Design and implementation. In: Proceedings of the IEEE International Conference on Consumer Electronics, Taipei, Taiwan, 2014, pp. 235–236.

Ilkko L., Karppinen J., UbiPILL: A medicine dose controller of ubiquitous home environment. In: Proceedings of the 3rd International Conference on Mobile Ubiquitous Computing Systems, Services, and Technologies, Sliema, Malta, 2009, pp. 329–333.

Institute of Medicine, The Future of the Public's Health in the 21st Century. The National Academy Press, Washington, D.C., 2013.

Jackson, J., Ready, aim, record: army's prototype system uses RFID tags to track weapons use. GCN Government Computer News, 2008.

Johannessen E. A., Wang L., Wyse C., Cumming D. R. S., Cooper J. M., Biocompatibility of a lab on a pill sensor in artificial gastrointestinal environments, IEEE Transactions on Biomedical Engineering, 53(11), 2006, 2333–2340.

Karmakar N. C., Roy S. M., Ikram M. S., Development of a low cost compact low profile phase array antenna for RFID applications. In: Mukhopadhyay S. C., Gupta G. S. (Eds.). Smart Sensors and Sensing Technology. Springer, Berlin, 2008, pp. 333–342. https://doi.org/10.1007/978-3-540-79590-2_22

Kfouri M., Marinov O., Quevedo P., Faramarzpour N., Shirani S., Liu L.W.C., Fang Q., Deen M. J., Toward a miniaturised wireless fluorescence-based diagnostic imaging system, IEEE Journal of Selected Topics in Quantum Electronics, 14(1), 2008, 226–234.

Kliem A., Hovestadt M., Kao O., Security and communication architecture for networked medical devices in mobility-aware eHealth environments. In: Proceeding of the IEEE 1st International Conference on Mobile Services, HI, USA, 2012, pp. 112–114.

Lee D. D., Chung W. Y., Choi M. S., Baek J. M., Low-power micro gas sensor, Sensors and Actuators B, 33, 1996, 147–150.

Lin Y.-L., Kyung C.-M., Yasuura H., Liu Y., Smart Sensors and Systems. Springer, Cham, 2015. https://doi.org/10.1007/978-3-319-14711-6

Lin Y.-C., Wei K.-C., An electronic smart watch monitors heart rate of an extremely preterm baby, Aug. 2017, pp. 214–2115. http://www.pediatr-neonatol.co.

Liu X., Cheng S., Liu H., Hu S., Zhang D., Liu H. N., A survey on gas sensing technology, Sensors, 12(7), 2012, 9635–9665.

Mackay R. S., Radio telemetering from within the human body, IRE Transactions on Medical Electronics, 6(2), 1959, 100–105.

Morgantia E., Angelinib L., Adamia A., Lalannec D., Lorenzellia L., Mugellinib E., A smart watch with embedded sensors to recognize objects, grasps and forearm gestures. In: Proceedings of the International Symposium on Robotics and Intelligent Sensors (IRIS 2012), 2012.

Olivieri N. F., Matsui D., Hermann C., Koren G., Compliance assessed by the medication event monitoring system, Archives of Disease in Childhood, 66(12), 1991, 1399–1402.

Parida M., Yang H.-C., Jheng, S.-W., Kuo C.-J., Application of RFID Technology for in-house drug management system. In: Proceedings of 15th International Conference on Network-Based Information Systems, Melbourne, Australia, 2012, pp. 577–581.

Park Y. J., Ahn J., Lim J., Kim S. H., "C-chip" platform for electrical biomolecular sensors. In: Lin Y. L., Kyung C. M., Yasuura H., Liu Y. (Eds.) Smart Sensors and Systems. Springer, Cham, 2015, pp. 3–24. https://doi.org/10.1007/978-3-319-14711-6_1.

Park H. J., Nam H. W., Song B. S., Choi J. L., Choi H. C., Park J. C., Kim M. N., Lee J. T., Cho J. H., Design of bi-directional and multi-channel miniaturized telemetry module for wireless endoscopy. In: Proceeding of the 2nd International IEEE-EMBS Special Topic Conference on Microtechnologies in Medicine and Biology, Madison, USA, 2002, pp. 273–276.

Petculescu, A., Hall, B., Fraenzle, R., Phillips, S., Lueptow, R.M.: A prototype acoustic gas sensor based on attenuation, Journal of the Acoustical Society of America, 120, 2006, 1779–1782.

Ray P. P., Home Health Hub Internet of Things (H3 IoT): An architectural framework for monitoring health of elderly people. In: Proceedings of the International Conference on Science Engineering and Management Research, Chennai, India, 2014, pp. 3–5.

Shalansky S. J., Levy A. R., Ignaszewski A. P., Self-reported Morisky score for identifying nonadherence with cardiovascular medications, Annals of Pharmacotherapy, 38(9), 2004, 1363–1368.

Sidheeque A., Kumar A., Balamurugan R., Deepak K.C., Sathish K., Heartbeat sensing and heart attack detection using Internet of Things: IoT, International Journal of Engineering Science and Computing, 7(4), 2017, 6662–6666.

Solanas A., Casino F., Batista E., Rallo R., Trends and challenges in smart healthcare research: A journey from data to wisdom. In: Proceedings of the IEEE 3rd International Forum on Research and Technologies for Society and Industry (RTSI), Modena, 2017, pp. 1–6., doi: 10.1109/RTSI.2017.8065986

Sundaravadivel P., Kougianos E., Mohanty S. P., Ganapathiraju M. K., Everything you wanted to know about smart healthcare: Evaluating the different technologies and components of the Internet of Things for better health, IEEE Consumer Electronics Magazine, 7(1), 2018, 18–28.

Susarla M., Akhil C., Reddy A., Hema, D. D., Heartbeat detection and monitoring using IOT, Journal of Network Communications and Emerging Technologies, 8(5), 2018, 18–20.

Thai T. T., Yang Y., DeJean G. R., Tentzeris M. M., Nanotechnology enables wireless gas sensing, IEEE Microwave Magazine, 12, 2011, 84 –95.

Thone J., Radiom S., Turgis D., Carta R., Gielen G., Puers R., Design of a 2 Mbps FSK near-field transmitter for wireless capsule endoscopy, Sensors and Actuators A: Physical, 156(1), 2009, 43–48.

Tzanoukosa G., Athanasiadisb E., Gaitanisc A, Georgakopoulosd A., Chatziioannoue A., Chatziioannoud S., Spyroub G., SPNsim: A database of simulated solitary pulmonary nodule PET/CT images facilitating computer aided diagnosis, Journal of Biomedical Informatics, 63, Oct. 2016, 357–365.

Valdastri P., Menciassi A., Arena A., Caccamo C., Dario P., An implantable telemetry platform system for in vivo monitoring of physiological parameters, IEEE Transactions on Information Technology in Biomedicine, 8(3), 2004, 271–278.

Wang K., Yan G., Jiang P., Ye D., A wireless robotic endoscope for Gastrointestine, IEEE Transactions on Robotics, 24(1), 2008, 206–210.

Yamazoe N., Shimanoe K., Theory of power laws for semiconductor gas sensors, Sensors and Actuators B, 128, 2002, 566–573.

Zeinab, K. A. M., & Elmustafa, S. A. A. (2017). Internet of things applications, challenges and related future technologies. *World Scientific News*, 2(67), 126–148.

Zworykin V. K., Radio pill, Nature, 179(4566), 1957, 898.

## CHAPTER 8

Healthcare Applications of the Internet of Things (IoT)

RITAM DUTTA[1*], SUBHADIP CHOWDHURY[2], and AHMED A ELNGAR[3]

[1]*Surendra Institute of Engineering and Management, MAKAUT, West Bengal, India*

[2]*DSMS Group of Institutions, West Bengal University of Health Sciences, West Bengal, India*

[3]*Faculty of Computers & Artificial Intelligence, Beni-Suef University, Beni Suef City, Egypt*

Corresponding author. E-mail: ritamdutta1986@gmail.com

ABSTRACT

In modern days, the Internet of Things (IoT) has been recognized as one of the most significant areas of future technology for academic and industry applications. The Internet of Everything is an uprising technology envisaged as a global network of machines and devices, capable of interacting with each other. This chapter presents recent trends of IoT technologies for the successful deployment of IoT-based products with real-time applications. In this review, various IoT real-time applications are thoroughly discussed which is related with healthcare applications. In healthcare paradigm, IoT-based technology enhances the quality of care, ease the end users with real-time functions, cost-effective approach toward health-care service providing, efficient telemedicine to cover remote areas, uses of IoT-based applications in pharmaceuticals, robotics, health economics, health insurances, effective policy making, and others. IoT-based healthcare services are the future of healthcare, which will assist the machine learning and artificial intelligence-based healthcare models. Finally, several possible technical and managerial challenges are studied with recent literature survey.

8.1 INTRODUCTION OF THE INTERNET OF THINGS

An IoT, which is also known as the Internet of Everything technology, is forecasted that it will reach 25 to 27 billion units by 2020–2021 (Gartner, 2014). From production line and warehousing to retail delivery and store shelving, the IoT is transforming business processes by providing more accurate and real-time visibility into the flow of materials and products. Firms will invest in the IoT to redesign factory workflows, improve tracking of materials, and optimize distribution costs. For example, both John Deere and UPS are already using IoT-enabled fleet tracking technologies to cut costs and improve supply efficiency. In many hospitals, doctors use iOS enabled watch to EMR and track patient visits with the help of technology. Aware point introduces sensor-based tracking system for equipment and patients using IoT-based technology in real time. Many techno-companies introduce live environmental stressor receptors to monitor the mental health of the patient or consumers.

8.2 INTERNET OF THINGS TECHNOLOGIES FOR EVERYDAY USES

There are few essential IoT technologies widely used for the deployment of successful IoT-based products and services: Wireless sensor networks (WSN), radio-frequency identification (RFID) and cloud computing.

8.2.1 WIRELESS SENSOR NETWORKS

The WSN having spatially distributed sensors can cooperate with RFID systems to monitor any systems and also provide better status report about their temperature and locations (Atzori et al., 2010; Gubbi et al., 2013). Earlier WSN were used in cold chain logistics for thermal and chilled packaging to transport temperature-sensitive products (White and Cheong, 2012). In healthcare, this system is in use with multiple tracker and tracers of patient identification, remote monitoring of medications, saline and fluid administration, remote monitoring of patient's health statistics, and others. WSN are also used for maintenance and tracking systems.

8.2.2 RADIO-FREQUENCY IDENTIFICATION

RFID uses electromagnetic fields to automatic identification and can easily track the tags attached to any object. Passive RFID tags rely on radio-frequency energy transferred from the reader to the tag to control the tag without any electric supply. Electronic tolls, any product level tracking, are few examples of passive RFID. Active RFID tags have self-electric supply and can initiate communication with a reader. External sensors are equipped with active RFID to monitor pressure, temperature, and so on. Semi-passive RFID tags use batteries to power the integrated circuits for communication. In healthcare, the tag is usually use for identification purpose of the patient. For an error-free therapeutic environment, RFID technology can be used. Moreover, it will look after the security of the patients to track the movements, will track the traffic system if a patient need to transfer from one department to another for diagnosis or other procedures (Amendola et al., 2014), will track sterile container from sterile supply department, track biomedical waste for identification, segregation, transportation, treatment, and others.

8.2.3   CLOUD COMPUTING

The major requirements of many IoT applications are having substantial data storage, ultrafast processing speed to enable real-time decision making, and high-speed broadband networks to rivulet data, audio, or video (Gubbi et al., 2013). Cloud computing provides easy access to handle huge data sets and process them for the exceptional number of IoT devices in real time.

In healthcare, this cloud computing system will help to trace the remote sensors data, build database for preventive, primitive, therapeutic services to patients, in medical record management, telemedicine (Kim et al., 2010), countrywide database for availability of bloods in blood bank with group and Rh factors, derive data from traffic control system to make green corridor for organ donations, and so on.

8.3   VARIOUS INTERNET OF THINGS REAL-TIME APPLICATIONS

Real-time IoT applications on devices and systems need to ensure the reception of data or messages and timely response. The inbuilt intelligence of IoT applications on devices can identify the problems with ease, observe the test-environment, communicate with each other, and potentially resolve problems without the need for human intervention. The IoT facilitates the development of myriad industry based and user-specific IoT applications. Whereas devices and networks provide physical connectivity, IoT applications enable device-to-device and human-to-device interactions in reliable manner. Quality control, monitoring of several facilities like derive patient health status data, medication status, medical bill for patient, insurance related data, live tracking system of various IoT-based monitoring system in therapeutic treatment, and so on.

8.4   VARIOUS LIMITATIONS IN IOT SYSTEM DEVELOPMENT

Based on the IoT ground report survey, this section discusses limitations in IoT development by enterprises. It has also been observed that data centers face challenges in security, the enterprise, consumer privacy, data storage management, server technologies, and data center networking (Bradley et al., 2013). Several technical and managerial challenges, viz. privacy, data mining, and security, are discussed in this section.

8.4.1   PRIVACY CHALLENGE

An IoT is likely to improve the quality of people's lifestyle (Fichman et al., 2005). While it continues to gain momentum through smart home systems and wearable devices, confidence in and acceptance of the IoT will depend on the protection of users' privacy. Health-related data of a hospital or healthcare centers are always under privilege communication and professional secrecy. Thus the medical record is the property of the hospital but hospital cannot share the information without the permission of the patient. To use the cloud computing and database management system with the IoT in various healthcare applications, where the prescription or the treatment procedures are online like telemedicine and doctors and patients will connect each other in online platform. So, the breach of data is one of the privacy challenges to implement IoT in healthcare.

8.4.2   CHALLENGES IN DATA MINING

Artificial intelligence (AI) required huge data to be implanted in neural hub and healthcare data are most sensitive data where a patient's life is in stake. Thus, this data mining to successfully program health related model is a real challenge for health workers and IoT support providers.

8.4.3 SECURITY THREATS

Irrespective of having many advantages of the IoT systems, it also faces security threat from hackers and other cyber criminals. A recent study by Hewlett Packard (Hewlett Packard, 2014) revealed that 70% of the most commonly used IoT devices contain serious vulnerabilities. Lack of security and privacy will create resistance to adoption of the IoT by firms and individuals (Sundmaeker et al., 2010; Li and Johnson, 2002; Manyika et al., 2011). These major issues can only be resolved by training developers to integrate security solutions, like firewalls, into products and make sure that the users utilize IoT security features without any threat.

Since the IoT technology is such a recent area of research, so there is still a lack of studies on the social, behavioral, economic, and managerial aspects of the IoT. Now the applications of this IoT in recent healthcare models are discussed below, based on the recent studies of healthcare applications. Basically, IoT are used in everyday life and will be used in each and every aspects of our life. Like in a smart home, all the home appliances like televisions, air-conditioning systems, water heater, gas in kitchen, level of water in water tank, switches of electric supply to various goods, timekeeping devices, and others will communicate among themselves to provide secure, smart, low power absorption, remotely controllable environment. Even it will control the burglary alarm and remote monitoring system, door lock system, voice recognizers for more safety. In healthcare, these smart homes can assist elderly people, younger offspring, pets, terminally ill patients, disable persons, and others. Even the system can call the doctor or emergency services with live health status, alarm for fire or other hazards. Today's' smart technology like android-based apps and other facilities will reduce the running and implementation cost of the IoT-based smart systems and making it a low-cost system for all. It will form a smart city with smart administration where the hospitals also become smart hospital.

8.5 IoT IN HEALTHCARE

IoT and healthcare have a long-term relationship. Firstly, computer-based monitoring system was formed and turned into an electronic medical record system (EMRS). Where all the departments are interconnected through intranet and accessed by authorized persons only. In healthcare system, the hospitals are using this technology to access all the patient-related data like identity of the patient, all prescription written by doctors, all diagnostic reports, medical and nonmedical items billing, pharmaceutical indents, stationary indents, and many more. Nowadays, big hospitals are using these medical records as case study to the medical students, as medical record is the property of the hospital (Mogli, 2016).

8.5.1 SEVERAL APPLICATIONS OF IoT IN HEALTHCARE

IoT has several applications in healthcare, like data mining, smart medications, smart diagnostic systems, wireless sensors to observe a patient remotely, in telemedicine and much more. There are few examples of IoT in healthcare services till date: ambient-assisted living (AAL), the internet of m-health thing (m-IoT), adverse drug reaction (ADR), community healthcare (CH), children health information (CHI), wearable device access (WDA), semantic medical access (SMA), indirect emergency healthcare (EMH), embedded gateway configuration (EGC), embedded context prediction (ECP), and others (Islam et al., 2015); beside it healthcare applications like: different monitoring tools for diagnosis a patient's vital statistics and objective statistics like body temperature, glucose level, pulse-oximeter, ECG, and others. Moreover, management tools for emergency communication, transportation facility like ambulance controlling, smart emergency transportation system for accidents where the IoT-based technology will locate the accident place and automatic send signals to nearest rescue center and report the damage, smart mobile-based telemedicine applications, blood bank connectivity for availability etc.

AAL is a tool for elderly adults which assist them to live better life. A large number of population (around 20%) will become 60 or more aged within 2050 (UN, 2001). The old-aged populations are mainly facing several problems like chronic diseases, ortho-related diseases, Alzheimer's disease, disability, and others. Thus, they require special healthcare and AAL will support their needs. AAL will assist to track the activities of the aged people in the smart home, it can detect any fall or other accidents, can set reminder for medications, camera can assist tracking devices, can call ambulance and near one for emergency, and can do so many things like this (Rashidi and Mihailidis, 2013). It will use cameras with motion detectors, smart tiles, PIR, active infrared, RFID, magnetic switches, and others connected with an IoT topology.

m-IoT is generally a mobile-based sensor, communicating and computing technology. Basically several android or windows or iOS-based applications for healthcare are included in this IoT topology. Several hospitalization, pharmacy-based apps are primarily included with several IoT-based applications like mobile-based sensors, tracers, trackers connected to cloud-based system to live feed of the patient's health statistics like body temperature, glucose level, allergy level, inhaler for COPD patients, tracking aged patient's activities, and others. This computing system uses smartphone with the help of IoT and sensors efficiently to provide healthcare services. Doctor–patient interface can also be possible with this communication system in telemedicine.

ADR can be monitored through IoT system with the help of near field communication system, or IRDA, or a similar technology. It can monitor all the allergic reactions, renal functions, liver functions, or the affect on pregnant woman or infants of the medications through intelligent system. This will help the patients with minimum reactions and minimize the chance of side-effects.

CH and CHI also use a unique combination of IoT connectivity to introduce the ICT (information and communications technology) approach for healthcare promotion. ICT will help to retain the medical record in online platform to communicate with remote area's patients to tertiary hospital. The success of different error free diagnostics, medical advices, vaccination programs depend on ICT, and ICT will be connecting through the help of various IoT platforms.

Apart from this, various devices like clinically grade wearables can send live data to the receptor that send it to cloud-based database to monitor the patient's condition in live streaming to the physicians. It can manage the patient's data to monitor the vital data, diagnosis, treatment, and so on. Various models like semantic medical access platform, or various embedded gateways, or prediction models help the physicians with the help of IoT's to identify and treat the diseases more accurately. It can track the medication and patient's healthcare status live from anywhere and send emergency care if needed. It also helps the disable and differently-able persons to adhere the normal lifestyle like any other persons enjoy.

8.6 FUTURE OF THE IoT IN HEALTHCARE

The current versions of IoT that applied in healthcare system are discussed everywhere. Let's talk about the futuristic scenario of IoT in healthcare field. As we know, IoT can work in a vast field which will be multidimensional in nature. As for example, smart homes that can call ambulance for any medical emergency with suggestion about low-traffic area, and wireless connectivity with GPS enabled footstep counting wrist watches or smartphone that can predict possible cases of hypoglycemia of a diabetic patient. Thus our own personal stuffs can save our life.

In a true sense, if a well-connected ideal healthcare system one wants to be formed in future, they have to think about IoT. Without the network and connectivity of various heterogeneous everyday stuffs, AI cannot work properly. An AI-based healthcare system requires huge data mining and well connectivity with various monitoring devices. It requires energy efficient, huge storage, and different bioinformatics devices that can connect a human body with the IoT topology. For this various methods and applications have to work together. Let us discuss some futuristic IoT-enabled healthcare processes that save human life with affordable cost and more efficiently than today it is.

8.6.1 FUTURE OF IoT IN MEDICAL PROCESSES

With the help of IoT and AI, the diagnosis and therapeutic services will become more efficient and accurate. In diagnosis, one can use smart nano-technology to diagnose a disease more accurately.

8.6.1.1 SMART DUST

Here, the use of "Smart dust" will become common. Today we use huge source of radiations, like X-rays, CT scan, MRI, which have an ability to penetrate our body and facilitate the doctors with real-time pictures or video of internal organs. By using this scanning mechanism doctors can make 3D pictures of the affected limb and viscera. But during the diagnosis procedures, patient have to consume large amount of radiations repeatedly due to poor skill of the practitioner or poor maintenance of equipment. This is a problem associated with under-developed and developing countries like India.

As per Atomic Energy Regulatory Board, Government of India, the permissible limit of radiation exposure is 1 mSV/year for public and 20 mSV/year for occupational exposure (aerb.gov.in, 2017). But due to frequent treatment for cancer with radiotherapy, emergency X-ray, or repeatedly scan, orthopedic emergencies may expose the patient to more than permissible limit of exposure.

Smart dust is a collection of tiny wireless microelectromechanical sensors that can detect the small changes in environment like vibration, light, temperature, and so on. With the help of smart capsule, this tiny dust may be injected or orally feed to the patient and the dust may collect all the data, dye the path with harmless connectivity, and make a 3D picture of the affected area without the exposure of radiation. This will change the scenario of the therapeutic processes. Here, the physician not only get the picture but also the changes of the affected limb in microlevel, more accurate, and live streaming detected by smart dust. This will help the physician to detect the whole problem at once. Even the smart dust will detect the microorganisms inside the human body and identify the bacteria or virus and avoid the unnecessary blood tests.

In near future, patients need to take a capsule loaded with smart dust, which can detect any changes in the body and send the signal to the doctors or the patient himself/herself well in advance.

If the smart dust can identify the microorganisms and work in cell level, then this is obvious that the incurable cancer cells or the curse of HIV can be easily identified well in advance and even the smart dust can use to destroy the affected cells or microorganisms that an antibiotic may be failed to treat. Nanoparticle oncology already provides the preliminary path for this breakthrough technique (Egusquiaguirre et al., 2012).

8.6.1.2 AUTOMATED MEDICATION SYSTEMS

IoT can not only facilitate the invaluable data on health statistics but also help to administrate smart medication systems. With the monitoring systems, the required medicine injector also attached with the target area, may be as an injector, or already implanted system. Recent administration of closed-loop insulin delivery system (Dana Lewis and Scott Leibrand, 2015) is an important example. Here the automated insulin will restore the function of the body from hypo- or hyperglycemic position with the help of continuous glucose monitoring system.

Here, the patient need to take a medication that releases medicine (like sustain release medicine) time-to-time with the help of microsensors that send the signal to the smart medicine capsule as per required.

Nowadays, IoT system is used to make medicine with digital tracker. This will help to identify the patients that they take their medicine timely. Proteus and Otsuka Pharmaceutical Co. was the first company who introduces FDA-approved drug with digital tracking system (proteus.com/press-releases, November 14, 2017).

8.6.1.3 DISABILITY AND MORBIDITY REDUCTION

Prosthetic implant is one of the ancient surgery treatments for removing disability. From the ocean of Vikings to the medieval war, the history is evident of the artificial unusable eyes, artificial hand with attached swords, and so on. artificial hand or foot is normal in surgery. But, nowadays, the use of AI with several different prosthesis techniques gives eyesight to a blind very easily. Artificial foot or limbs will be connected with neurological substances is the future, where the patient with artificial hand can easily take a cup of coffee and sip on it. Already connected contact lenses, artificial eyesight, and intelligent exoskeleton system for disable persons are in vogue. The digital era and use of IoT can do miracle, as an example the great scientist Stephen Hawking was diagnosed with a motor neuron disease ALS (amyotrophic lateral sclerosis). He uses thought-controlled wheel chair, where with the movement of his cheek, the IR sensor attached with his glasses catches the word he tries to mention and predictive words are appeared on his 12″ computer screen. Then he chooses the appropriate word and speech synthesizer allows him to deliver the speech effectively (How It Works Daily, 2016).

Thus, IoT will be the solution of motor neuron diseases and disability to interact within the machine and the disable part and brain functions. A disable person can lead a complete life in near future with the help of IoT and machine learning technology. Using different modules like home automation system Xbee module, LED monitors, RF signals will use to create communication between aged and technology. For disable and old persons, ZigBee-based voice recognition platform can connect them with the IoT that take voice command and help them accordingly (Gagan, 2016).

For differently able persons like blind or deaf can be easily be helped through use of IoT in large scale. Mowat sensors, Nottingham Obstacle Detectors (NOD), and so on will be used for obstacle detection for persons with eye-sight disability. Vive ring will be used for hearing disable persons to take care about the talking or sound like alarm or horn and show it in a display. Hand Talk also recognizes the sound and voices and makes it in a display and sound box of deaf and dumb persons (Varghese, 2016).

Automated assistive wheelchairs, hearing aids, or goggles can be implemented with the help of IoT technology and implanted sensors and chips in musculoskeletal system to make an automated topology that will help the physical disable persons to move on.

8.6.1.4   ROBOTIC SURGERY

In near future, the robotic surgery will be error free and completely based on AI, where a patient can program the OT Suit for his/her own surgery.

Especially for astronauts, these systems are in initial stage. But in future, the OT Suit will be able to examine the patient, detect the need of OT, and operate the patient with full efficiency. Thus it will reduce the gap between doctor–patient ratios and lower the postoperative infection rate.

Different defense organizations now want to build intelligent dresses that have their own monitoring system. This monitoring system can easily detect any health-related issues and dress itself can do some initial first aid treatment. Same system in near future will develop for high-risk jobs and even for personal protection, where if any accident happens, the smart dress automatic address some vital injuries before the ambulance come will or treatment commenced.

The application of robotics in healthcare is divided in different sectors like smart medical capsules, surgical robotics, prosthetics using surgical robots, motor coordination analysis and treatment, robot assisted mental and social therapy, robotized patient monitoring (TNO, 2008). The robots are used to correlate with computer integrated system for surgical and therapeutic purposes. But the limitations to take decisions, robotics required human operators. Thus, the recent IoT-enabled environment gives the opportunity to control multiple nanobots or minimal invasive surgery (Scutti, 2015), even remote surgery via internet-based IoT platform and robots. Even android-based platform can be used to operate the robotic equipment remotely using Raspberry Pi (Ishak and Kit, 2017). This will minimize the human interface with the sterile equipment and patient. Thus prevented the postoperative hospital acquired infections. Microbots can be taken with capsules or injected by syringe and it will take care of the affected area or limb without surface cut and minimize the length of stay of the patients as well as saving the time of the surgery (Gaskell, 2017). In nursing care, the robot may assist the nurse as per the response of the patient. Like robot Cody, created by Georgia tech in 2009, is a robotic nurse who assists the nurses. Nurses can operate it to use direct physical interface (DPI) and it will behave as per the respond of the patient. In physiotherapy robot is using the entire globe as assistive exoskeletal system, or assist in motor coordination therapy, or sustaining muscle therapy (McNickle, 2012).

8.7 FUTURE OF IoT IN HEALTHCARE MANAGEMENT SYSTEM AND DECISION-MAKING

IoT not only help healthcare system's efficiency to provide healthcare for patients, but it also help to reduce the cost of treatment.

In modern times, the quality treatment requires out-of-pocket cost. In developing countries like India, the transparencies of healthcare providers are under the questions. Patients and their relatives often complain about the costly treatment and over charges for unnecessary procedures. Below are some issues that need to be addressed and how IoT can help in this:

8.7.1 TRANSPARENT HOSPITALIZATION AND TREATMENT PROCEDURES

Many unhappy patients and the relatives of patients are questioning about the treatment processes. In today's world, patients are well informed about the hospital, its costs, rating in different health related websites, about the diseases and medicines, and so on. When a patient admitted to a hospital, the information about the patient is not sufficient for anxious patient relatives. As per professional secrecy and privilege communication, doctors cannot told the whole treatment processes to the relatives. The only medium to bridge the gap is counseling. The mutual trust of the patient and hospitals are also at stake.

To remove this weakness, IoT can hold an important position. All the patients or relatives may have smartphones, where they can store the app related to the hospital. Here, with secure connection and OTP-based security checkup, the patient can get approval, patient's relative can log in, and the app deliver the live update about diagnosis procedures prescribed by the doctor, the diagnosis that is already done, the medications and the indent from pharmacy, the status of the patient, the current bill, and so on.

Figure 8.1 is an idea that how would be the app changes the scenario of patient–doctor relationship.

8.8 ERROR-FREE TREATMENT

Several errors occur due to negligence or emergency or human err. Many cases are reported in media like operations misplaced error to identify the right limb which would be operated or removed. As per Dr. Girdhar J. Gyani (Economic Times report, August 2, 2016) reported to the media, 5.2 million medical errors are notified in India annually.

With the help of tracers, sensors, and digital marketers the hospital can easily remove the medical mistake. Wrong limb for operation, wrong medication, multiple same diagnosis, and identification of the patient reduced significantly with the help of tracers and markers. If the technology is used to mark the patient and IoT associated with the machinery of the operative area, then the chance of human error is minimal.

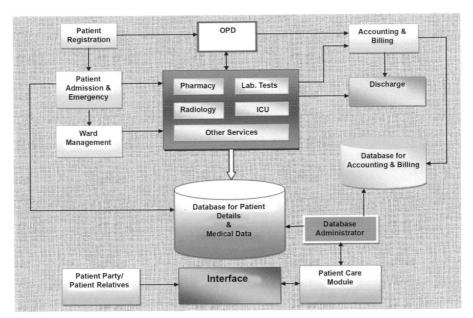

FIGURE 8.1   Flowchart of smart IoT-based healthcare management system.

Source: Reprinted from Layek and Chowdhury, 2018. Open access.

8.8.1 TELEMEDICINE

In India, major changes will be impact the rural healthcare. The telemedicine system is now not only serve the hospital to hospital scenario, but it can connect a remote healthcare center with doctors through wireless mobile computing, sensor networking, and cloud computing. Some projects are already running successful.

In West Bengal, Rural Health Kiosk in Barrha, Birbhum; Siuri, Birbhum; and Bally, Sundarban was introduced by ITRA Media Lab Asia (itra. medialabasia.in, 2016) with the help of several universities like Jadavpur, Calcutta University, NIT Durgapur, and others. In the kiosk, the e-health sensor kit is provided and an android-based application is developed. Cloud-based database is developed and sensor-cloud infrastructure is implemented. When patients come to kiosk, they firstly give their measure to the health service provider of the kiosk. Some sensor-based e-health kit is attached with them and they sit in front of a screen where the assigned doctor assists them with the help of video calling. The android-based system sends the patient data live to the system of the doctor. Then the doctor sends the prescription through online and kiosk takes the printout of the prescriptions with the digital signature. The problem of doctors in the remote areas for outpatient-based care can be introduced and thus health for all can be reached to the most remote part of India.

The success story of cloud computing and android-based outpatient healthcare delivery system or modern telemedicine gives idea to support smart healthcare goals for health for all themes based on IoT.

8.8.2 DATABASE AND MEDICAL RECORDS

IoT system enables the electronic medical record more efficient. Doctors may reach to the patient file easily an on go, and all the vital statistics of the patient live streaming also reached to the doctors. Database is one of the first achievements of this century, this century started with data-driven technologies which eventually turned up as AI-based century where IoT has biggest role. In medical record, an idea about one smart system for the whole country can be implemented through IoT and big data uses. The medical record can be stored in a web-based platform where all the patient data like reports and prescriptions are kept and can be accessible by the doctors at the time of visit (Chhatlani et al., 2016).

8.9 SMART HEALTHCARE SYSTEM FOR THE WHOLE COUNTRY— AN IDEA THAT CAN CHANGE THE INDIAN SUBCONTINENT

The idea about unification of all citizens' data with biometric application is already implemented in India in the name of Aadhar Card by the Unique Identification Authority of India. Here, the enrolment number till date is more than 120 crore (Aadhar act, 2016). This Aadhar is not only identification for citizens, but the biometric databases also help them in various ways.

Like the Aadhar card, one unified database system for patients of India can be introduced. Here, the basic connectivity for all the citizens can be traced trough Aadhar card for cost-effective measurements. India already has sufficient citizens who hold an Aadhar card. This card can be linked with the healthcare database of India. This model is a smart healthcare provider model in large scale which can connect all the hospitals and healthcare centers under one umbrella of IoT-based cloud-computing services. The basic model is dependent on the following points:

8.9.1 UNIFIED MEDICAL RECORD FOR ALL CITIZENS

The medical record services are provided by the hospitals and health centers through intranet, where the accesses of the record are only subject to patient's authorization or judicial. Otherwise the record is the property of the hospital and they can use it for medical audit or as a case study.

Using of Aadhar card number, government can implement IoT-based e-medical record for all the citizens, where the requirement for unique identification for a single patient in multiple hospitals are not required.

8.9.2 WHY IS THIS REQUIRED?

Generally, patients have to carry multiple diagnostic reports and prescriptions if they go to a hospital for treatment. Due to modern age competition of private hospitals and access to government facilities, the patient usually have to carry a large number of reports for medical record history. For a long run, a hospital has the capacity to take care of the medical record for a certain time. OPD records are not available to the patients as well as hospital's outdoor due to heavy flow of patients. Only inpatient records can be accessed. Now, if a patient wants to go to another hospital, they need to carry the physical report. And due to unawareness, the patient may misplace the reports. There are many other disadvantages:

1. Patient may misplaced the physical records and have to do several repetitive unnecessary diagnosis.
2. One hospital does not see another hospital's report easily, if patients misplaced it.
3. Medical history cannot be feasible to the doctors for prompt treatment.
4. Repetitive out-of-pocket cost is associated with the nonretention of medical record.
5. Government or authority cannot measures the standard of treatment thus poor clinical auditing.
6. Poor implementation of quality measurements.
7. Time and cost of the treatment will become high, thus mortality and morbidity cases may arise for a serious patient.

Now, if the unified medical record for a patient can be implemented, then many advantages will appear as follows:

1. Only one medical record number will appear for a single patient.
2. No need to carry the huge physical medical records. Only the Aadhar number required to input the medical record and doctors can accesses the medical records of the patient easily in one singular platform.
3. All patient health-related data are updated into the medical record countrywide and any public or private hospital can access the record if the patient wants to take services from the provider.
4. Clinical audit for public and private hospitals will be easier and can be standardized.
5. New research data for an effective and efficient treatment can be highlighted to study the patient medical record for homogeneous disease.
6. Time, cost, procedures for a same diseases in different hospitals can be measured.
7. Standardizations of treatment and diagnosis can be implemented to the whole country.
8. It helps to set the healthcare policy to the government.

8.9.3 IMPLEMENTATION

This implementation part is easy as the big database handling is already present there in India. Just need to connect the cloud-based patient care database with Aadhar database. Here, all the test reports, prescriptions, and all the data related to patient treatment are attached with the patient care database. The database stored each medical record like they are stored in the hospital's own medical record. Each hospital can access the patient care database of their own and if the patient comes for service, and then all the history of treatment.

The patient will carry their identity card to the hospital. The hospital will log the identity card and patient will receive the permission page for authorization. When patient will be authorized, the hospital will be able to access all the data base of the patient but cannot edit it. Thus, the medical history of the patient can be reached.

1. Here, the Aadhar card number will be connected to the patient medical record database.
2. Patient's medical database can be accessed by the patient and the hospitals after hospital getting authorization from the patient.

3. The hospital can access their part of medical record of the patients any time but not the whole history without permission. Thus if hospital want, they can abolish to take medical records of their own. Cause the medical record of the hospital can be separately accessed in the system. This will reduce the maintenance and retention cost of the records drastically.

4. Medical audit of all hospitals and healthcare providers are easier if appropriate authority like medical council of India has access to the database.

5. Policy makers have access to this database.

6. Clinical and medical audits are super easy with this system. Even screening of the treatment procedures and standards of different hospitals and healthcare providers are easier.

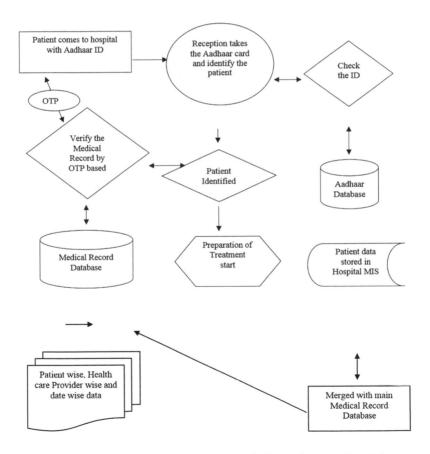

FIGURE 8.2   Simple flowchart of Aadhar-based medical record system for whole country.

For this simplified processes, the whole nation can join in a common network of healthcare practices. Different approaches toward a common homogeneous problem (like dengue) are minimizing through this procedure. From multiple theories of therapeutic procedures, drugs can be easily measurable. Through this, the best practice can be recognized.

Through this system, antibiotic drug resistance also minimized, because the physician has the access to the previous health records. Pharmaceuticals also can be accessed through this portal so that self-medication with the help of harmful drugs can be reduced.

Moreover, the insurance coverage for the patients can be linked with this database. From this, the requirements of the health insurance, the coverage of the health insurance, and the access to the third party administrators can be monitored, implemented. Hospital need not take any health insurance related cards, single UID will cover the whole things.

All the hospitals and health sectors are under unified scanner, so the work measurements and standardization of preventive, therapeutic, and primitive care can be implemented. The monitoring of the medication issues, different predictions of epidemics, uses of drugs, patient allergic history, cost of care for a particular diseases, morbidity and disability rates, monitoring of the different policies like polio vaccinations, antivenom usage, blood bank usage, incidence and prevalence of diseases can be easily measured and monitored. The performance of the providers can be measured through this platform.

8.10   SMART HEALTHCARE AND HOSPITAL SERVICES

IoT has a tremendous application in healthcare sector. With the help of this technology, not only smart cities and homes will be emerged, but smart healthcare facilities will also be emerged, never-before-seen. Here, the ideas of smart healthcare facilities are based on several smart city projects and telemedicine systems for remote areas.

The inpatient healthcare procedures are generally organized in secondary or tertiary care multi or super specialty hospitals. Let's see the use of IoT in hospital's day-to-day procedures for better healthcare. The majority of the patient satisfaction and dissatisfaction lays with the time management and ambience. So, the prompt proactive responses toward the patient and patient relatives are primal to the healthcare industry. Unlike hospitality industry, here anxious relatives and sufferer patients are entertained for healing purposes. Attitude toward ailing people are different than who comes for a leisure tour. Outside ambience, luxury rooms and facility can help to retain patient for a certain level. But now, IoT plays a big role in a modern hospital.

8.10.1 RECEPTION

The IoT facility is first observed in the reception area. Patient may get a number for queue and wait in the waiting hall unless his or her turn comes. Smart queue management is the key to satisfy the patient in this window of hospital. Patient may use smart card, provided by the hospital to retrieve the patient data easily, apart from patient ID and hospital information system. The smart card may be tagged using RFID or other technology to track the patient inside the hospital to help him or her for correct sequence of OPD, diagnosis, and other tests. The online prescription provided by the doctor may directly indicate in the pharmacy so that they can prepare the medication before the patient arrived to them.

8.10.2 INPATIENT AREA

When a patient takes admission, the tagging of the patient with bar code or other tracers will be done. It will help to trace the patient for security purpose, and for identification of the patient to remove the error chance of treatment. This will prevent the duplicity of diagnosis, decrease the time of the transportation of the patient in between departments. Diagnostic center can retrieve the emergency patient's file first and arrange the queue depending on it. The queue systems automatically rearranged and displayed the emergency patient's entry into the test area, so the other waiting patients cannot be confused and claim to find the reason.

8.10.3 HOSPITAL INFORMATION SYSTEM

This intelligent system will track all the department associated with hospital like inpatient area, pharmacy, billing, finance, HR, maintenance, doctors, nurses records, store, and so on. All the patients' medical records and prescription will be uploaded to the system. So that all the reports of diagnosis, doctors' prescription and suggestion, nurses works, pharmacy indents, bill of the patients, vital statistics of the patients can be traced live. Doctor can monitor the condition of the patient and can update about any medication.

Patient relatives can track the medications and bill of the patient live and transparently. Doctors can send the prescription with digital signature, all the reports of diagnosis can be uploaded to the facility. This will reduce the time for every department. The needs for walking to all the departments can be reduced through this smart process. It will reduce the time for reports, prescription, procedures, and queue for diagnostic procedures, discharge summary, and timing.

8.10.4   OPERATION THEATER

The OT through this IoT can be equipped with several sensors, which can detect any changes in environment. This smart system can reduce the contamination from dirty zone to clean and sterile zone of the OT. Effective zoning with smart IoT sensors reduces the hospital acquired infection (nosocomial infection).

8.10.5   CENTRAL STERILE SUPPLY DEPARTMENT

After doing the sterilization of the used equipment, effective tracers and sensors can look after any misuse or signal of the expiry of nearby unused sterile items. Thus the hospital infection can be reduced from equipment.

8.10.6   MEDICAL WASTE MANAGEMENT

The huge medical wastes can be reducing to implement the smart IoT-based system. This can also detect leakage or spill of medical waste. The tracers can indicate the collection, segregation of waste. After the segregation, smart indicators report the treatment processes to avoid any mistake. It can reduce the medical waste with smart indent of medication and equipment. The intelligence tag may reduce the error of segregation and treatment procedures of misfit container or misguided waste removal, wrong treatment procedures.

8.10.7   ENERGY SAVING

Effective IoT-based sensors and lighting system can save energy. It can make sure to turn the unused machinery in sleeping mode and use only the equipment required. Smart lighting system can reduce the electricity bill for finance department.

8.10.8   LAUNDRY AND LINEN SERVICES

Effective IoT-based linen and laundry services save time and remove stain and germs from the used linen. Hospital can easily identified the dirty and clean linen easily and the store can easily identified the unused clean linen which may cross the expiry date.

8.10.9   BED MANAGEMENT

Smart IoT can calculate the occupancy rate of the hospital, thus send signals to the admission and emergency department to hold or release the patient for wards/ICU, or others. Smart bed can reduce the mobile monitors and directly send the vital signals of patient to the doctors or nurses, alarm them for any emergency situation.

8.10.10   CONTROLLING OF INFLOW OF GUESTS AND GERMS

The smart IoT system can detect the environmental changes very easily, thus can be used to detect unwanted access to security areas, control the guests for admitted patient and accompany, can wend reminders for using handwash and hand sanitizer after treating a patient or any other thing. It can be implemented with HVAC system of the hospital to control the weather inside the patient area.

8.10.11   NURSING CARE

IoT can calculate the medication procedures. Thus it sends reminder if any medication time arises, helps the nurses for taking care to a terminally-ill patient who cannot use the nursing calling system manually. Smart monitors also send signals for nature's call like urination for very ill patients automatically so the nurses can take care of the patient. Any sudden changes in the monitors, the inflow of fluid to the patients like saline or sustained release injections can be send reminders to the appropriate authority prior the empty the bag.

8.10.12   DIAGNOSIS

Smart diagnosis can reduce the exposure of the patient to a radiation hazard area, analyze more accurately the affected area, and suggest treatment to the doctors. It can help to produces 3D modeling system.

8.11   FRAMEWORK OF SMART HEALTHCARE SYSTEM

A smart hospital uses biosensors, wireless technology for connecting and tracking several monitors and machine in one cloud-based database topology like Bluetooth, RFID, and others to maintain a patient information system. This information system is containing all the departments like patient personal data, medical history, registration and admission, any past prescription, billing department, pharmacy indents, doctor's portal, medical records, surgery, and others.

Basically the patient identification and patient data through biosensors or smart tags are connected to the cloud-based database of the hospital or chain of hospitals. The management information system of the hospital are connected to this cloud-based database, and the doctors or nurses have an access to the portal to remotely visit the patient's livestreaming information using IoT technology. Even they can control the machinery remotely using the IoT-based services that can be support a PC or smart phone-based applications.

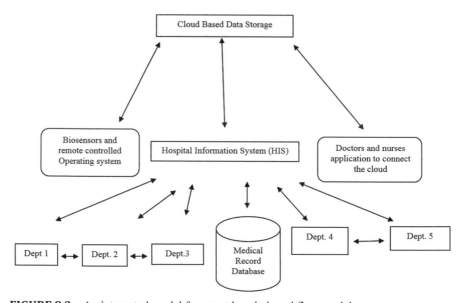

FIGURE 8.3   An integrated model for smart hospital workflow model.

The basic model for a smart hospital, we can find some from the literature study, as for example:

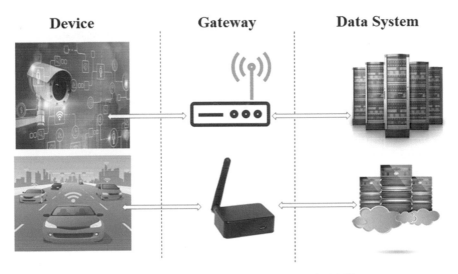

FIGURE 8.4   Architecture of smart hospital (redrawn) (Yu et al., 2012).

This model is a hypothetical model based on Yu et al. (2012) and divided in perception layer, network layer, and application layer. Modern IoT-based smart hospitals are using several tools like embedded technology, sensor network, wireless communication, RFID, and others. The cloud-computing technology will be used to setup such centers where the smart hub of the hospital can be connected through heterogeneous platforms like smartphone-based android or iOS, windows PC platform, several devices like Bluetooth, Zigbee, and others. The biosensor interface will make connectivity with the computing system and cloud-based database system, where the doctors can directly monitor the whole health status of the patients. The alarm should be send to the doctors by pager or SMS or any other means and promptly. The main limitations are use of IP-based IoT platforms, where the separate IP bases for different devices may be not applicable in long run. For that, another unified systems may be applied, where there will be no need to change the IP address but portable addresses are formed and in action. The architecture of the smart hospital-based on several inputs has to be stored and monitored by one cloud-computing system to take all the output in systematic processes. Through a database management system the healthcare procedures are livestreaming to the respective authorities and required constant monitoring of the processes by sensors for any fault. Here, one leakage or fault can send wrong inputs to the system. Low-power consumption and low-energy consumption of the machinery is essential to host such big IoT topology. The IoT sensors will help to maintain the machinery in optimum condition so that unnecessary consumption of power can be stopped (Shah et al., 2018). Audit of several managerial and clinical data is essential to run the system smoothly. Open source software may be used in this sector so one can modify and implement new systems or subsystems when required. Open source software is more cost effective and modification freedom is there. A hospital information system should be established in cloud-based database system so that the tracking becomes easy and robust in nature.

8.12   CONCLUSIONS

The IoT has immense opportunity for the healthcare sector. Smart hospitals and healthcare sectors are the future of the healthcare providers. With the help of AI and IoT, the ICT can be implemented more accurately. It will reduce the medical cost, increase the quality of the treatment and care, and make a secure future with zero defects.

As per the WHO, health is a state of complete physical, mental, and social wellbeing and not merely any absence of disease or infirmity. So, the application of the health is also multidimensional in nature. Not only the physical condition of the patient but also the social environment and the mental state of the patient are applicable in healthcare delivery system. In service sector, the SERVQUAL model is use to identify the service gap to reinforced the quality control over the service. Services are mostly intangible in nature, thus health also cannot be measured easily. The service gap in a healthcare delivery mostly creates for gap between expected and actual timing of the delivery of services. The delay in the processes may consider harmful for the patient's health as well as managerial inefficiency. The hospital's brand depends on several factors, and real-time prompt service is one of the most important aspects of it. The IoT can be used for queue management, where the patient can get timely services without delay in the queue. The online procedures of paper works, reports, and prescriptions can reduce the total walking time from department to department. Thus, this service gaps can be minimized by using IoT technology. Another issue is service error in terms of medical error. This is also minimized by live tracking and sensors of IoT. Various managerial apps, biosensors, and others jointly coordinate the total treatment of a patient that reduces the valuable time and enhances the patient–doctor correlations.

National Accreditation Board for Hospitals and Healthcare Providers has total 10 modules and required many paper works. Through IoT, all the required modules can meet to establish a feedback report system from various departments and can assimilated in one cloud-based computing to see the compliances of the clauses. Quality can be implemented if the monitoring system is good and the sensors can deliver the changes promptly and corrective measures can be managed to introduce automated system.

Smart HVAC and disaster control system can prevent any fire or similar disaster automatically by sending signals for any fictitious events and take corrective action primarily. Through IoT-based system, the disaster committee can easily identified the area of fault and take corrective measures to control the situation.

Through biosensors and other robotics based and AI-based modern healthcare interface can treat a patient more efficiently. That will reduce the errors, time, and length of stay of the patients. The incidence of a disease can be predicted by the IoT and data analysis through cloud computing. The prevalence of a disease can be well monitored and surveillance of the same is possible to introduce the IoT-based devices. The equipment can be controlled remotely, like telemedicine. In near future, the automated healthcare center will require only some trained staffs that will take care of the automated equipment attached with wireless cloud-based computing system. Patients only have to approach to the center and the telemedicine portal will check the patient remotely, diagnose the patient remotely using DPI technology and even operate the patient without reaching them directly. It will reduce the variables in result of the treatment so reduce the risk factor for patient's life.

IoT also has an impact in rehabilitative care too. The prosthesis, physio-therapy assistant and nursing assistant robots and sensors do miracle. It can take care of the aged persons and people with disability. In big data and cloud computing the IoT maximizes its present in healthcare sector.

Thus, the IoT has immense effectiveness in the harness of technology in healthcare industry and will use in futuristic platforms.

KEYWORDS

- **Internet of Things (IoT)**
- **client value**
- **managerial challenge**
- **healthcare**
- **sensors and cloud computing**
- **therapeutic services**

REFERENCES

Amendola, S., Lodato, R., Manzari, S., Occhiuzzi, C., and Marrocco, G., (2014). RFID technology for IoT-based personal healthcare in smart spaces, *IEEE Internet of Things Journal*, 1(2), 144–152.

Atomic Energy Regulation Board, Govt. of India, Published on 15/05/2015, https://aerb.gov.in/english/radiation-protection-principle [Accessed on August 1, 2019].

Atzori, L., Iera, A., and Morabito, G. (2010). The Internet of Things: a survey. *Computer Networks*, 54(1), 52787–52805.

Bradley, J., Barbier, J., and Handler, D. (2013). Embracing the Internet of Everything to capture your share of $14.4 trillion. *Cisco White Paper*. Retrieved from http://www.cisco.com/web/about/ac79/docs/innov/IoE_Economy.pdf [Accessed on July 22, 2019].

Chhatlani, A., Dadlani, A., Gidwani, M., Keswani, M., Kanade, P. (2016). Portable medical record using Internet of Things for medical devices, *IEEE, e-ISSN: 2472–7555, IEEE Explorer* October 26, 2017, DOI: https://doi.org/10.1109/CICN.2016.93 [Accessed on August 5, 2019 online].

Economic Times (2016). https://health.economictimes.indiatimes.com/news/industry/5–2-million-medical-errors-are- happening-in-india-annually-dr-girdhar-j-gyani/53497049, August 2, 2016, Economic Times, [Accessed on August 2, 2019].

econsultancy.com, https://econsultancy.com/internet-of-things-healthcare/ [web Accessed on July 27, 2019].

https://medium.com/neodotlife/dana-lewis-open-aps-hack-artificial-pancreas-af6ef23a997f [web Accessed on Aug 10, 2018]. April 07 2015, Neo.Life Article.

Egusquiaguirre, S.P., Igartua, M., Hernandez, R.M., Pedraz, J.L. (2012). systems for cancer therapy: advances in clinical and preclinical research, *Clinical and Translational Oncology*, ISSN online: 1699-3055, 2012, 14: 83-93, DOI 10.1007/s12094-012-0766-6.

Fichman, R., Keil, M., and Tiwana, A. (2005). Beyond valuation: "Options Thinking" in IT project management. *California Management Review,* 47(2), 74–96.

Gagan, (2016), IOT based system for person with physical disability, *IJIREEICE*, 4(Special issue 2), 158–160, DOI: 10.17148/IJIREEICE/NCAEE.2016.31

Gartner (2014). Gartner says the Internet of Things will transform the data center, Retrieved from http://www. gartner.com/newsroom/id/2684616 [Accessed on July 21, 2019].

Gaskell, A. (2017), The future of robotic surgery, Article published in IoT Zone of DZone, https://dzone.com/articles/the-future-of-robotic-surgery [Accessed on August 5, 2019].

Gubbi, J., Buyya, R., Marusic, S., and Palaniswami, M. (2013). Internet of Things (IoT): a vision, architectural elements, and future directions. *Future Generation Computer Systems*, 29(7), 1645–1660.

Hewlett Packard. (2014). HP study reveals 70 percent of Internet of Things devices vulnerable to attack. Retrieved from http://www8.hp.com/us/en/hp-news/press-release. html?id=1744676#.VOTykPnF-ok, [Accessed on July 25, 2019].

Howitworksdaily.com, 2016, https://www.howitworksdaily.com/how-stephen-hawkings-wheelchair-works/, published on January 8, 2016 [Accessed on August 2, 2019].

Il Kon Kim, Pervez Z., Khattak A.M., Lee S., Chord based identity management for e-healthcare cloud applications. *Applications and the Internet (SAINT), 2010 10th IEEE/IPSJ International Symposium on*, vol., no., pp. 391–394, July 19–23, 2010.

Ishak, M.H., Kit, N.M., 2017, Design and implementation of robot assisted surgery based on Internet of Things (IoT), *IEEE*, DOI: 10.1109/ACOMP.2017.20 (IEEE Xplore: Accessed on August 5, 2019).

Islam, S.M.R., Kwak, D., Kabir, M.H., Hossain, M., Kwak, K., The Internet of Things for healthcare: a comprehensive survey, Published on 2015, *IEEE Access*, DOI: 10.1109/ Access.2015.2437951

Layek, K., Chowdhury, S. (2018). Integrated hospital management system to reduce patient disputes & grievances, *IOSR-JBM*, 2, 34–37.

Li, X., and Johnson, J. (2002). Evaluate IT investment opportunities using real options theory. *Information Resources Management Journal*, 15(3), 32–47.

Manyika, J., Chui, M., Brown, B., Bughin, J., Dobbs, R., Roxburgh, C., et al. (2011). *Big Data: The Next Frontier for Innovation, Competition, and Productivity*. McKinsey & Company. Retrieved from http://www.mckinsey.com/insights/business_technology/big_data_the_next_ frontier_ for_innovation.

McNickle, M. (2012). 10 Medical Robots that could change Healthcare, Information Week, Published on June 12, 2012, https://www.informationweek.com/mobile/10-medical-robots-that-could-change-healthcare/d/d-id/1107696 [Accessed on August 3, 2019].

Media Lab Asia, 2016, https://itra.medialabasia.in [Accessed on August 3, 2019].

Mogli, G.D. (2016). Medical Records Organization and Management', second edition, *Jaypee Brothers Medical Publishers*. Proteus Digital Health (2017).

https://www.proteus.com/press-releases/otsuka-and-proteus-announce-the-first-us-fda-approval-of-a-digital-medicine-system-abilify-mycite/, press release November 14, 2017 [Accessed on August 1, 2019].

Rashidi, P., Mihailidis, A. (2013). A survey on ambient-assisted living tools for older adults. *IEEE Journal of Biomedical and Health Informatics,* 17(3), 579–581.

Scutti, S. (2015). Medical robots are not just the future of healthcare, but part of the present, Medical Daily, published on January 22, 2015, https://www.medicaldaily.com/medical-robots-are-not-just-future-health-care-part-present-318898 [Accessed on August 1, 2019].

Shah, J., Soni, S., Darji, F., Chandak, s., Shetty, A. (2018). Smart hospital using IoT, *IOSR-JEN*, e-ISSN: 2250–3021, 9, 26–32.

Sundmaeker H., Guillemin, P., Friess, P., and Woelffle´, S. (2010). Vision and challenges for realising the Internet of Things. *CERP-IoT*, March 2010, available at https://perso.esiee. fr/~bercherj/Documents/data/KK3110323ENC_002.pdf [Accessed on July 20, 2019].

TNO 2008, reporting, Robotics for healthcare, *TNO Quality of life.*

UIDAI, Govt. of India, 2016, https://uidai.gov.in/about-uidai/unique-identification-authority-of-india/about.html [Accessed on August 3, 2019].

UN, Report (2001). World population ageing: 1950–2050, pp. 11–13.

Varghese S. (2016). Application of IoT to improve the life style of differently abled people, *IOSR-JCE*, e-ISSN: 2278–0661, pp. 29–34.

White, C. C., III, and Cheong, T. (2012). In-transit perishable product inspection. *Transportation Research Part E: Logistics and Transportation Review*, 48(1), 310–330.

Yu, L., Lu, Y., Zhu, X. (2012). Smart hospital based on Internet of Things. *Journal of Network*, 7(10), 1013–1021.

CHAPTER 9

Mobile-App-Enabled System for Healthcare

VIKRAM SANDHU* and HARLEEN KAUR

Guru Nanak Dev University, Amritsar, Punjab, India

Corresponding author. E-mail: Sandhu.vikram@yahoo.com

ABSTRACT

This chapter examines the state of the art in mobile clinical and health-related apps. We discuss the concept of "apps as a medical device" and the relevant regulatory controls. World is experiencing an extraordinary phenomena in the field of interpersonal communication. This enables people to communicate across vast geographical distances, until now inaccessible, especially in developing countries. Mobile phones because of their high levels of penetration hold tremendous potential as they provide opportunities, never imagined before. China leads as the country with maximum number of mobile phone users; India has the third largest number of mobile phone users in the world, nearly 56% among them have access to Internet in their devices for average of 3–4 h/day. In USA, 83% have mobile phones and 60% have access to broadband services. Findings suggest that rural India has seen significant increase in "penetration" and "teledensity" compared to urban India. Smartphone applications recently introduced in mobile phones will further enable the m-health industry to successfully reach out to 500 m of a total 1.4 bn. Smartphone users in 2015 research conducted by Pew internet and American life project found 17% of adults and 25% of young adults using cell phones for seeking overall health information.

9.1   A HEALTHCARE PROFESSIONAL'S DILEMMA

In Asian countries, especially in India, you'll find maximum population in the rural areas who can't afford to travel to such long distance and bear the cost of treatment. The Fortis Escorts hospital uses healthcare application for booking appointment and providing basic treatment to ease the treatment process. Thanks to such applications, patients no longer have to wait for long hours in queue and these apps operate in regional language too. Since implementing the applications, the mHealth usage has increased by 45% than the previous years. And it has become more efficient as well profits of hospitals are expected to jump by 30%. Now, the time has been reduced for treatment through this technology to one minute. Suppose all this happening at your end!

   WHAT WOULD YOU DO? WILL YOU PROMOTE IT?

9.2   BACKGROUND

Who has not watched the biggest movie of the decade Terminator and they use "Skynet" in it? What is "Skynet"? It is the notion of Internet of things (IoT). Appeal of this concept is infinite, with amazing promises to improve our lives. The world is entering an era of computing technology that many are calling IoT in which things refer to an entity or physical object that has a unique identifier, an embedded system and the ability to transfer data over a network (Alexia Mourtou1, internet of things an article, 2015). Internet of things is playing major role in healthcare industry to increase the accuracy, reliability, and productivity of electronic devices (Journal of Communications, April 2017). According to Gartner inclusion (a technology research and advisory corporation), there will be nearly 28 billion devices on the IoT by 2020. IoT can change the scenario of rural area by monitoring remote health and emerging notification systems. One of the concepts in the IoT is the mobile health or as commonly known as m-health. mHealth offers an elegant answer to a problem commonly faced in the medical field; how to access the right information when and where needed in highly dynamic and distributed healthcare organizations. The coming age group may well observe an upheaval in the cure and deciphering of diseases. Bruce E. Johnson, president of ASCO, stated that the emerging side effects can be deciphered and cured at a faster pace because of the present day technology which has boomed simply the care for both patients and their doctors to ease the lumber of disease free environment (ASCO meeting, June 2018). Mobile apps cover the whole healthcare chains, that is, information collection, deterrence, identification, management, and observation. However medical professionals and patients are presently being teeming with health apps, eventually they will have obscurity in deciding the right application without understanding its usefulness. Applications especially those related to health are multifarious as observed from the above ideas depicting clearly which way the wind is blowing.

9.3 DEFINING mHEALTH

1. *eHealth:* Information and communication technology consisting of Computers, mobile phones, and satellite communication will utilize information electronically for healthcare services.
2. *mHealth:* Mobile information usage—such as PDAs and mobile phones—for assisting healthcare services and applications.

mHealth and eHealth are tangled together—both are utilized to enhance health conditions and their technologies functioning in combination. For example, various eHealth projects engage digitalizing patient files and fabrication of an electronic "vogue" that preferably will regulate right to utilize patient data within a national scheme (United Nations Foundation Report, 2009).

Mobile devices provide new scenario for healthcare communication research. mHealth or mobile health is described as the practice of "exchange of important information and use of network in mobile devices for healthcare sector," which is a buoyant innovation that makes important communication possible among consumers and deliverers and help in providing preventive techniques for different potential diseases by utilizing features and ubiquitous presence of mobile phones all over the globe (Dutta et al., 2016). Still, no standardized definition of mHealth has been documented. The training provided with help of mobile devices like smartphones and various network related devices refers to mHealth according to Global Observatory for eHealth. It is made of many things but mainly depends on utilization and grubstaking of a smartphone's basic use of voice and text message service, even its multifaceted functionalities and applications (WHO, 2011a, b). mHealth is described as the utilization of smart devices with the competence to shape, amass, recuperate, and communicate statistics in potential time to the consumers for the reason of enhancing patient protection and value of care in its broad nous.

9.4   WHY mHEALTH?

At this instant it feels like the whole world—including telecommunications companies, service contributors, nongovernmental organizations, more so the critics—is keen to place a little "m" as a prefix for most of the services that perhaps be conveyed on the smart platforms, the utmost being mBanking. The aforementioned bandwagon will surpass, but the little "m" is critical to observe segment dependent commune and lawmakers on what to do to bind the impending network techniques and other services. Informal utilization of smart technology for availing treatment service poses a problem to understand its benefits. Developing countries are tremendously getting an answer of "YES" when asked about mHealth usage. mHealth has its use beyond the horizon from as small as data recording to as huge as emergency services support. Mobile phone's simplified and understandable function makes it easy for usage by any age or income group in turn making it a superior platform for the health servers to have a magnanimous reach. The choice of language feature in mobile phone is making illiterate communicate an convey information too. Not only this, its low cost and flexible payment plans like EMI has made it available to common public. As soon as users share their smart devices amongst themselves, the widen benefits provided to them relating to health and emergency and even further (Mechael, 2006). Facilities like short messaging services and of late prerecorded message help in fast deliverance of messages for example alerts to have their daily dose or book an appointment. Decentralized health system can be made centralized by advancement of wellbeing-related software applications, because of which real-time feedback, preprogrammed automated services, and many more services are provided (Lacal, 2003).

Progress and cure of chronic diseases occur in daily life outside of traditional clinical surroundings. To decide and regulate treatment for these diseases, doctors depend greatly on patient records of warning signs, side effects, and purposeful status. Characteristically, patient's record at clinic visits which are months apart, and evoke correctness can be extremely changeable. mHealth creates feasibility for patients to gather and divide pertinent data at any time, not only when they come about to visit a clinic, permitting more rapid convergence to best treatment. For example, an epileptic patient is able to self-report on medicine and dose taken and the quantum and extent of seizures and its reaction. The application conveys this data in real time to the doctor, who then looks for motif of response and direct the patient to quantify his medications accordingly.

Thus, enthused by remarkable development and outcomes of mHealth the global wellbeing plan-makers and supplier are reinforcing this segment as a novel warhead to brawl adjacent to global wellbeing issues. The sort of vocalization, video and recordings provide considerably increased access to commune and offer right time explanation relating to a person's wellbeing hence showing that mHealth is a well-established podium which has the aptitude for the same. Undeniably, real, and right time services could be provided to the customers by authorizing providers with enhanced diagnosis. Thus, with a fine planned and vigorous infrastructure it is thought to alter healthcare by producing assets accessible to healthcare professionals and consumers (Mechael, 2009).

9.5   MHEALTH AND ITS APPLICATIONS AROUND THE WORLD!

Twelve common mHealth applications (redrawn) (Labrique et al., 2013).

9.5.1 PATIENT EDUCATION

The aforementioned application of mHealth approach centres basically on the consumer, formulating a new way to communicate information for the purpose to enhance consumers' intellect, differ their approach hence shaping their conduct.

> For example, Toothflix 2.0, it includes videos in both English and Spanish, arranged accordingly for quick access. An important patient information exchange instrument for wellbeing services awareness, case study reception, informed approval or entertainment is possible with this application. ADA's criterions for clinical brilliance are reflected with the help of up-to-date content. 3D animations of dental matter and management, plus affected-curer scenes to put real-life patients at ease are shown in each video.

9.5.2 POINT-OF-CARE INVESTIGATIONS

Relating innate collective control of smart devices or linking smart devices to an integrated, autonomous, peripheral gadget which can assist remote scrutinizing of patients, hence expanding coverage of wellbeing services for the commune and even patients' home.

> For example, EyeQue Insight app allows you to test your visual acuity. Its patented technology screens distance vision from 20/20 to 20/400 in less than 3 min; so that patients can stay informed on his and his family's vision needs. Not more than 6 persons can utilize this app with family sharing enabled. It uses English as the main language and children above the age of 4 years can use it.

9.5.3 VITAL SIGNS RACKING

Smart phone-based registration facilities help in the recognition and listing of appropriate customers mainly for explicit facilities, in bid to enhance liability of schemes for developing absolute and apt care plus to recognize and trounce discrepancies in disease results. Tracking essential events facilitates in upholding of population records and fortitude of major development indicators, such as maternal and neonatal natality.

For Example, Prizma-G Medical Innovations—it is the companion app of G-Medical's Prizma device—your personal health tracker; with this app you will have a comprehensive overview of your health measuring: ECG, heart rate, SpO_2, temperature, stress level assessment. In addition, tracking of blood pressure, weight and Glucose level, manually adding results taken with other third-party devices is also available. The option to schedule reminders to never forget taking your measurements ever again is also available.

9.5.4 DATA COMPILATION AND REPORTING

One of the initial changes in global mHealth practices was that it permitted forefront personnel's and healthcare system to move from paper-supported systems to the near-immediate recording of reports or patient data, that is, e-records. Compilation of records initiates from the server to decipher health system or disease statistics, based on time, location, or personnel involved.

For example, Advanced MobileDoc is completely integrated with Advanced EHR and anything we create or change is done within the secure cloud and immediately available to your staff. It helps in scheduling and managing appointments. It creates, transmits, print and electronically renew prescriptions and create patient notes using any template from Advanced EHR. It has the feature to view and sign lab results and view patient history, insurance and responsible party. Many more such features are included too.

9.5.5 e-RECORDS

Electronic health records were available to only those who were concerned with the same patients, allowing medical professionals the right to utilize patient records on restricted computers. mHealth gave it the boost it deserved by allowing it to break these walls and make record available unanimously. Now, doctors can electronically record the treatment they provide and record patient test results throughout mHealth system to obtain patient account from the records.

> For example, GenexEHR is a simple App to take control of the health information, ftreeing us from the confines of a paper world. This gives doctors, nurses and us the flexibility to access and share our health information securely when and where it is needed. It has features like is captures and maintain paper investigations, prescriptions, X-rays, etc. in medical documents. It allows us to maintain and share your glucometer, blood pressure, and weight reading and view prescriptions and get reminders for individual medicines etc.

9.5.6   e-SUPPORTS

It includes knowledge, procedures, rules, and registry. Make certain of medical personnel's adherence to rules is the chief amenity in implementing multifaceted care strategy. Basically, changing tasks, like screening tests responsibility, from doctors to nurse's often necessitate adjusting to processes intended for experimental employees to correlate with restricted formal guidance. Mobile health proposals that integrate real-time care maintaining instruments with mechanized sorting and depending on principles training helps guarantying value of treatment for these task-changing situations by making health personnel to follow defined rules timely.

> For example, eASYapp electronic Antimicrobial Decision- A collection of all real time services, decisions, sustainable and correction instrument which supports antibiotic governance related tasks. This application promotes real time care solution finding for doctors, pharmaceutical companies and other paramedical staff with examination advice on correct and apt antibiotic choice based on recommendations, even supports antibiotic creatinine clearance test for all ages based on dosing and standardised antibiotic deliverance manners. Correction instruments support profits recognition including observing managerial even personal antibiotic regulation systems presentation with the help of downloadable AMS team involvement record compilation forms and even standardised plus downloadable recommended routine study and de-escalation studies.

9.5.7 DOCTOR'S GROUP

One of the main features of telemedicine technology is that it helps in doctor-to-doctor information sharing with the help of smartphone which is useful in correlating treatment with assistance in specialist guidance for health professionals, at the right time and place. Furthermore, sharing information involves video, records, and voice; but, smart devices permit interlinking of all these forms.

For example, Curofy—a reclusive health application mainly for health professionals which supports them to keep updated especially in the segment of new advances in medicine including changes in medical journals even the practical case consultations between doctors in order to provide their paramount in their practice. Health professionals can converse various medical specialities, resolute studies with other health professionals. Each day not less than 300 cases are discussed on this app. Even the most recent medical guiding principles and declarations from IMA are provided on this app helping doctors to stay conversant about the newest IMA events and CMEs. This app helps in providing information about most recent medical jobs and help in applying with a single click and many more such services.

9.5.8 APPOINTMENT BOOKING

Work appointments and setting up tools help frontline workers by keeping them conversant by sending on the go alerts of approaching or tardy services, in turn enhancing responsibility by making doctors revisit a priority. Developing country settings often have a limitation of doctors, creating it to be a problem to grant regular patient revisits utilizing old age paper-based techniques.

For example, Asian Connect- it lets a person connect to the Asian Hospitals Chain of Blue Sapphire Healthcare Private Limited. It provides helpful tools to manage your health with convenience of a smart phone. We can search doctors and specialities. Make and manage appointments, manage medical history, access lab reports, provide service feedback. A person can easily schedule appointments, access medical reports and get exclusive discounts.

9.5.9 CONTINUED MEDICAL KNOWLEDGE

Continuing medical education is the major foundation of treatment in developed countries. Smartphone is utilized to impart regular guidance to professionals who have to deal with distanced and remote doctors, through right to use to instructive videography, educational texts including synergistic trainings which will strengthen skills given at the time of practice session.

For example, CNL: clinical nurse leader Q&A—it helps nurses to prepare for their ACCN clinical nurse leader certification with self-assurance. It includes more than 360 unsolved questions with thorough descriptions and its imagery and is formulated by experts. There are more than 220 hard inter-rogatory questions, more than 250 descriptive electronic book matters; and more than 160 must-know vocabulary provisions; hundreds of preparatory strategies and suggestions; boundless admittance to ALL groups of patient evaluation, healthcare strategy, parallel management, proof- based training, case studies and many more services: and helps in thorough result trailing, making all the petite jiffy's adding up to something gigantic.

9.5.10 TRAINING STAFF

Health professionals frequently work between rural populations, with only infrequent contact with managerial professionals. Electronic control panel allow administrators to trail the routine of community health professionals on their own or at the dissimilar levels with the help of communicating the quantum of electronic output or even by potential-time GPRS following by professionals as they bear out their ground conduct.

For Example, Touch Surgery: it has surgical Videos which prepare for different surgical examinations and help to study novel practices and examine information with touch surgery no matter when or where, it's a multiaward claiming surgical practice podium for health professionals and surgeons researched by world's most important establishments. Over 100 residency US programs include its usage and is authorized by the AO foundation, American Association for Surgery of the Hand. A descriptive imitation of surgical actions is provided and prepares for procedure no matter when or where. It helps in mastering new techniques from top physicians.

9.5.11 MANAGEMENT OF FLOW OF GOODS AND SERVICES

Mobile health applications direct and handle stocks and amenities of necessary merchandise so they received noteworthy worldwide consideration. Somewhat easy applications that permit remote centers or medical stores to record and convey regular stock levels of medicines and other amenities or to order extra supplies electronically have been enforced in various countries.

For example, Syft synergy software 4.0.1.02—Supply chain management application. It is a comprehensive platform for enterprise-wide visibility and control of inventory and cost. Managing supply-related activities in silos does not help. Syft Synergy—a platform solution- helps to bridge the gaps, providing total visibility and control of the supply chain. It includes features like master data management, inventory services, warehouse, perioperative point-of-use, procedural point-of-use, and distribution.

9.5.12 COST EFFECTIVENESS

Mobile health and mobile investments are interlinking swiftly the field of financial operations and medicine resulting in disbursement for medical care, amenities, or medicines. It creates demand and supply enticement strategies simpler to organize and measure. These schemes center on reducing financial gaps to heed for patients, and they are trying new ways of influencing doctors to stay on rules and/or afford advanced quality care.

For example, star health insurance—the largest health insurance company in India launched the first of its kind mobile app for customers providing instant policy renewal, track the updated status of your claim, find nearby star network hospital, locate branch offices in your locality, one touch to customer care and medical advice toll-free numbers and get quote for various products and purchase them hassle free without any documentation are few of the features of this health applications.

9.6 PRESENT MOBILE APPLICATIONS

In current decade, there has been amplified study on network related telemedicine utilizing present smart device information providing services, mainly in developed countries, for conformist citizen and armed forces utilization. But, the ever rising equipment cost and the restricted bandwidth of the present bracket of smart devices telecommunication services have limited the broader utilization of the services inside the general potential sectors of the healthcare organizations. However, in the past few years some budding 3G and 4G-based mHealth applications with medical wireless techniques have been mentioned in the creative writing (Kotz, 2011).

9.6.1 *LIMITATIONS OF PRESENT WIRELESS TECHNIQUES FOR MHEALTH*

1. The need of a lithe and interlinked telemedical technique of the various mobile telecommunication alternatives is lacking. This lack of connection subsists due to the complexity of accomplishing functioning capability among telecommunication practices and present smart device usage guidelines.
2. Limitation among worldwide smart devices and satellites is caused due to elevated price of information connections.
3. Refrained accessibility of smartphone Internet linkage and communication admittance is present because of bandwidth margins.
4. A composite segment such as healthcare is tricky to alter. The major alterations are the managerial alterations that are frequently necessary for this sector to help form telemedicine platform. These necessary managerial alterations mainly have an effect on how medical professionals and other hospital staff drops or increases power as a consequence of these alterations.
5. Petite and extended financial prices and operational circumstances for medical professionals and medical care sector are not yet wholly explicit.
6. Means of expense mainly for smart telemedicine techniques need improvement and guidance.
7. Shortage of enticement for demanding experts to exercise smartphone telemedicine because it is perceived as a further burden for which they are not rewarded is observed.

9.7 CHARACTERISTIC CLASSIFICATIONS OF MHEALTH

Based on the mHealth definitions it can be classified pertaining to the characteristics of the cause and purpose of the medical information surge:

1. Patient to administrator
2. Patient to doctor
3. Doctor to doctor
4. Physician to specialist system
5. Patient to medical patient relationship management system.

Based on the case group, mHealth systems can be categorized as follows:

1. mHealth for patients (curative mHealth)
2. mHealth for fit people (preventive mHealth)
3. mHealth for the chronically ill or susceptible patients

Categorization derived from the technology utilized in mHealth system is given in Table 9.1.

9.7.1 VARIOUS SORTS OF RISKS OCCURRING DUE TO USE OF HEALTH APPLICATIONS

-   Issues (Tables 9.2 and 9.3) (Whittaker R, 2012).
-   Opportunities (Table 9.4) (Thomas Martin, August 2012).

TABLE 9.1   Broadcast Rate Per App

mHealth-Technology	Broadcast Rate Per Mobile App			
Quantum of apps utilized by mobile-device	Confined: Bluetooth	Confined to intermediate range: WLAN 802.11a/b	High range: GSM/GPRS, CDMA	High range: UMTS
One app	<1 MBd	2–54 MBd	10–115 kBd	0.144–2 MBd
Multitudinous apps	<1 MBd	1–27 MBd	< 10 kBd (of guaranteed transmission capacity)	<1 MBd

Note: Bd, baud.

To draw the concentration of consultants and officials on the thriving mHealth mission there is also need to give confirmation of sustainability in provision to totality of possibility and the aptitude for measurement. In periods of possibility, the utilization of mobile phones in healthcare services can be abridged at two points: the first, as a designed course of applied involvement utilizing smart phones for a variety of reasons in the health organization, and the second, as a crude development of impulsive

TABLE 9.2   Various Sorts of Risks Occurring Due to Use of Health Applications

Various risks in rising order of rigorousness	Major stockholders affected	Example of situations where this menace could take place	Remedies to manage this menace
Trouncing of repute	Doctors/associations	Applications exhibits responsive data about medical personnel's or services provided	Improved security
Trouncing of confidentiality	Consumers (in this case patients)	Meagre security of consumer records Misplace consumer data due to mishandling of device	Encoding Avoid mishandling of consumer data storage devices
Low quality consumer data	Consumer (aka patients)/medical staff/hospitals (e.g., operational records)	Applications permit inappropriate data to be entered into consumer reports or allow retrieval when handled by someone else	Data justification on admission and retrieval from genuine apps
Underprivileged lifestyle or clinical choice	Consumer/medical staff	Wrong consumer report utilized in discrepancy measurement details Inappropriate information or exploration tools Inadequate recommendation or statistics Unsafe communication	Ensure appropriate data is retrieved Confirm statistics appropriately encoded Usage of behavior methods that are proven for showing health changes
Improper but changeable medical action	Consumer/medical staff	Inadequate medication suggestion	Advice based on the test conducted on sample data Respond to the patients facility of feedback
Inappropriate and unchangeable medical action	Consumer (aka patients)/medical staff/hospitals (accountability experience)	Inappropriate statics controlling various activities of an application	Accept protected and significant software design and inventive techniques Methodically ensure design and test coding and user interface

TABLE 9.3   Issues Facing the Implementation of mHealth

Sector	Concerns
Rules and Authorization	• Seclusion and record security
	• FDAs guidelines of mHealth proposals as medical services
	• Medical services among the countries and with admiration to medical custom jobs (e.g., diagnosis directives)
	• Information measure or range accessibility
Mobile systems	• Agreement among various networks
	• Agreement among various policies and proprietary schemes
	• Charge to the people or consumer
	• Reporting in distant areas
Health organization	• Inappropriate examples of sustainable industry designs
	• Inadequate compensation
	• Inappropriate indulgent of assessment of mHealth
	• Medical roles responsibility and incorporation into medical system
	• assimilation into e-records and health communication schemes
	• Contraindicating health communication techniques precedence broader prospective price
Mobile health practice	• Need of means for the requirement of information in a better way
	• Incorrect focus on the applications or on privileged population
	• Authority in mHealth
	• Freely accessible applications not otherwise appraised and without source in presumption or confirmation
	• Unconnected or isolated projects due to presenting platform or proprietary schemes
Exploring	• Require expert guided research
	• Necessitate demonstration of usefulness and cost efficacy
	• Disparity in rapidity and suppleness among research and expertise progress
	• Quantum of reach or right to use for the underserved

TABLE 9.4   Opportunities to Address Problems in mHealth Functioning

Sectors	Opportunities
Rules and authorization	• Union-level control
	• Synchronization of electronic commerce and health service
Mobile systems	• Mutual values for cooperating
	• Contemplation of open-assessed architecture or uniform edges
	• Services cooperation and association for mHealth
Health organization	• Utilization of chances of present health restructuring savings (e.g., revelation projects; antagonism in electronic health reporting services; encouragement of area projects and estimation)
Mobile health practice	• Association with consumers to extend explanation to their dilemmas
	• Establishment of theory and confirmation of what is effective
	• Cooperations and mutual education for duplication and development, incorporation of population record, and assimilation of health services
	• Contemplation of open-based services and other means to diminish obstacles to further complete integrated proposals
Exploring	• Deliberation of substitute research processes to elevate pace and maintain obstinacy, including careful reflection of analogies
	• Addition of evaluation of amplified admittance
	• Printing of influential research & measuring of active intrusions

Sustainability issues: Scope and scale (Arul Chib, 2013).

utilization and acceptance by entities. Most of the researches integrated in the cited literature reviews scrutinize the earlier occurrence namely, pilot studies without expanded execution.

9.8   POTENTIAL OF SMART PHONES TO ENHANCE HEALTH IN THE DEVELOPING WORLD

Similarly essential to the cost-efficiency and extensibility of mHealth is its aptitude to provide a useful means for dealing with promising health requirement. Health professionals note that in the upcoming few years, officials and health servers in the developing country will be strained to twirl their hub to hindrances and early recognition rather than untimely cure of noncommunicable diseases, such as cancer, as well as the health requirement of aging residents. These alterations are caused by vogues such as movement from rural to urban sectors, financial development, and altering dietary practices. As developing countries attempt and create important developments in the spread of communicable diseases, standard revenue stages amplify along with typical life anticipation. Even a trivial elevation in revenue results in altering dietary behavior, and expenditure of meat produced and processed foods is correlated to the reduction of cancer. Late recognition of these diseases directs to reduced endurance rates and abridged life anticipation, and has pessimistic effects for societal and fiscal improvement. Developing world is being tackled with a twofold encumber of managing and include the spread of communicable diseases while fighting a wide variety of strange health disputes.

9.8.1 OUTLOOK HEALTH REQUIREMENTS IN DEVELOPING NATIONS

Mobile health is better placed to deal with these disputes utilizing equipments presently obtainable. For instance, just as short messaging system vigilance is helpful in increasing public health alertness of communicable diseases, this same sort of awareness can be utilized to guarantee patient observance with management of persistent diseases such as cancer. Short messaging system alerts can be remitted to deal with persistent diseases and psychological health problems in metropolitan cities such as smoking termination and sustenance mementos. Various middle-revenue nations in the developing world (i.e., India, Russia, etc.,) are previously observing a change from transmissible diseases toward persistent diseases (such as cancer). In these nations, there is already proof that mobile health applications are tested by tackling broader choice of persistent noncommunicable diseases, with main focus on preventive treatment technology.

9.9 IMPACT OF THESE MOBILE HEALTH SYSTEMS

Recognized studies and initial project evaluations—in both the developed and developing nations—express that mobile applications enhances the competence of healthcare deliverance and eventually makes healthcare services to be further effectual. The future goal, and anticipation, is that mobile health systems will have a provable and noteworthy constructive effect on medical results such as decreased infant death rate, longer life extent, and reduced retrenchment of disease. Much of the enthusiasm over the impact of mobile health systems on the developing nations is that where mobile health facilities were placed since the untimely part of the decade is now enhancing appropriate data that specifies that most of the anticipated profits are happening. These researches are balanced by those carried out in the developed nations where smart phones attain a soaring level of diffusion than a decade ago which have commenced to create a noteworthy confirmation pointing to the health products and competent gains that can be formulated from the considerable plan and execution of mobile health programs and projects (United Nations Foundation, 2009).

9.9.1   ENHANCED PATIENT WELLBEING

Cited medical researches of mobile health systems show an increasing strong report for extended mobile health execution. Patient health has been enhanced in many ways. Better conformity with treatment administrations: a 2010 Thai research proposed that diabetes patients who got daily SMS of medication reminders increased to over 90% observance. An application known as SIMpill that utilizes mobile techniques to observe and express medication observance also shows assurance.

9.9.2   ENHANCED HEALTH APPLICATIONS RESULTS

Effectiveness enables better quality of care. With competence, heightened results can be achieved and levied upon broader populace, and service systems can be reinforced. Illustrations of recognized effectiveness include the following:

1. Developed nations face diverse financial and edifying situations from those established there, the effects of the research works may be in the form of pertinent programs, mainly because developed nations diseases become highly rampant in the developing nations.
2. The World Diabetes Foundation proposed that by 2050, 90% of all emerging diabetes patient will be found in developing nations, which will necessitate innovative advances for handling diabetes and even other persistent diseases.
3. Research works carried out in the developed nations may also grant helpful results in observation and measurement, as well as study formulation. There lingers a requirement for more proof of mobile

health efficiency, as observed by continuing, repeatable enhanced results in either health or financial terms.

4. Such research works would be mainly important in developing nations, and guarantors should keep on evaluating growth in order to ascertain pertinent evidence of perception and reinforce the research for measuring projects all over the world.

9.10 INDUCEMENTS FOR MULTIPLE STAKEHOLDERS: MOBILE HEALTH VALUE CHAIN

One of the vital characteristics for thriving and justifiable mobile health projects is to counterfeit strong enterprises, predominantly athwart systems be it for profit or nonprofit sector. A congealed apprehension of the requirements and heeds of these various stakeholders is necessary in bid to assemble their vigor and sources. One way to recognize these advantages is through value chain investigation, or an appraisal of the association between all institutes and actions in the profit-oriented or liberation method of a product or service. Various players—straddling from the consumers to the tools trader—in the mobile health value chain are given below in the following table (United Nations Foundation, 2009):

Consumers or resident (Mobile user)	Enhanced health conclusions
Healthcare supplier	Further proficiency and useful relief from health provisions
Non-governmental organizations	Progressing organizational aims and goals, attract endowment
Establishments	Proficient organizational goals
Administration or law-makers	Highly competent healthcare terms and efficient management
Equipment supplier	Device income creation, enhanced brand awareness
Service supplier	Earnings from service costs, enhanced subscriber support
Application related remedies deliverer	Earnings from added applications authorization costs
Substance management	Improved quantum of readership or earnings
Opportunity provider	Earning from sales

9.11   MAJOR ACHIEVEMENTS FOR MOBILE HEALTH

Factors depend on combination of mobile health literatures and observations of present-day service opportunities, according to which the following factors were given which are vital to ensure the expandability and sustainability of mobile health systems across the nations (Akter and Ray, 2010).

9.11.1   PATIENT CENTRIC RESULTS

Patient centered (not healthcare organization dependent) healthcare is now gaining momentum as one of the main issues, because sustainability of the opportunity provided and entitlement of the patients are highly linked. As said by Haux, "Research, is nothing but a focus on the consumer healthcare needs in the early stage." Hence centering on patient needs, following categorization has been identified which is vital to ensure organizational growth.

Affordability: One of the major problems that were identified for mobile health programs were to make certain that services are within patients means. There is a need to consider various ways to decrease fee of providing healthcare services to a quantum of population by utilizing wireless network communications. This is the result of the major expansion of the mobile health which is delivered through its ability of providing price efficient services.

Accessibility: Data dispensation setting and extensibility of the mobile health networks are affected mainly due to network problems. Developing nations face a major issue of network coverage which in turn affects the delivery of mobile health applications. For example, health management in rural India commenced primary health call offices to receive calls in various states; but, 70% of the calls each day are disrupted because of weak smartphone network exposure.

Responsiveness: There is 40% of population that is not aware about mobile health services. So it is important to make them alert about these applications and their availability with the help of rigorous communication services utilizing all types of mass media (e.g., TV, radio, etc.). This will enable mobile health services to create elevated need for its utilization. Restricted awareness is observed as one of the hurdles that healthcare deliverers are facing in commencing, achieving, and sustaining mobile apps for health.

Suitability: Easiest and verified wireless-based applications have a proposed advantage to expand beyond the walls. In this scenario, smartphones are in a beneficial position to advance mobile health platform because the bases is in place with an enormous acceptance of about 5 billion habitants of the total population in the world. Even, smartphone-based simple apps (e.g., curefit or, Alert txt89 platform) have extensive user acceptance, because they offer easy, cost efficient, and practical solutions.

9.11.2 SERVICE VALUE

Value should be at the center of all mobile health applications to promise a bigger level of concern for patients. Right to quality has always been one of the main considerations in healthcare, even if the deliverance of the service is done by different modes like communication technologies. Reduced value service forms the major issue in challenges to be faced by healthcare organizations and leads to additional cost and care on the part of medical professionals and their staff. Lack of dependability and competence by the service paradigms is becoming a major challenge to be faced by mobile health practicing organizations and especially on the information and efficiency of the healthcare deliverers, seclusion and safety of information and moreover their consequence on fulfilment, future use purpose and value of healthy life. Different categories have been formulated below to necessitate immediate actions.

Information and reliability of the provider: Only some medical professionals have the education, direction, or instance to get used to hand-held equipment with their multifarious contributions, tricky and undependable applications, and dreading information loss. In fact to levy valuable fitness facilities, there is necessity to acquire additional information and ability to use smart and different other applications securely and efficiently. Adequate preparation shall allow experts to offer the utmost managerial decision.

Quantum of access and examining devices: There are shortcomings in mobile devices that are used to provide healthcare services that should be understood by the healthcare providers and acted upon. There are many limitations a few them are listed below:

1. Screen size—larger the screen size better for the user.
2. Processor power—more the processor power better for the user.
3. Memory—higher the memory more the information which can be stored.

4. Bandwidth—better the bandwidth better the extensibility of the devices.

5. Battery lives—higher the battery life more time availability to enhance knowledge of the user, even at the time of emergency battery life come in handy.

These limitations often confine their ability to use smart applications.

This is observed as in case of confined display size and reduced image enhancement mobile devices often confine the mobile applications, such as blood glucose indicator.

Effective compatibility: Complexity in mobile health application often needs an included use of wireless paradigm, Internet, and various networks in an utmost flawless way. Therefore, effective similarity across various paradigms characterizes a huge problem for mobile health solutions. High speed communication systems are still not accessible in various developing nation settings. This lack might delay the action of some complicated mobile health applications that need congregated improved value of voice, visualization, and records.

Facts exchangeability: For any nation the ability of the communication arrangements to exchange information is a pivotal point in enhancing an incorporated wellbeing communication scheme. But, alternatively this is ignored because of inability of various communication systems; this in turn prohibits access to vital information exchanged over these systems. Like, in Bangladesh, the patient record base and e-wellbeing reports that smart healthcare application paradigms sustain on users have not been obtainable to the local healthcare industry; therefore, no knowledge exchanging is admissible between the systems in bid to enhance consumer care.

9.11.3   ASSOCIATION AND CORPORATION

Mobile health sector is now in a sturdy state to move ahead by exchanging technology and applications with smartphone users, public health associations, and autonomous health service deliverers. Original associations are main point in fetching capable mobile schemes to extent. The participation of varied stakeholder (For example, patients, deliverers, organizations and regulators) paves the way for flourishing mobile health functioning. Upon such participation mobile health associations can gain patient data at a single site and exchange those with other members involved to guarantee a complete depiction.

Facilitating policy and effective environment: Healthcare directives require being favorable to support novelty in the market, but provisional enough to guarantee facility quality, fortification of confidentiality, and a lofty criterion of treatment. Real-time research records and novel changes in case of mHealth are essential to guide supervisors and educate policy-makers. The outlook of mobile health applications shall rest on the utilization of a decisive knowledge and substantiation podium which will allow health officers and law staters to deliver enhanced guided decisions concerning the question that how to endow refrained wellbeing assets in techniques as stated by Mechael.

9.12 RECOMMENDATION FOR BOLSTERING MHEALTH

Recommendations for bolstering mHealth (Tomlinson et al., 2013):

1. Present principles for exploration must be reassessed in bid to present assistance since when bolstering is fitting.
2. The concept of mHealth intrusions ought to be assisted in relation to a credible theory of behavior alteration and must utilize not less than two procedures determining on the beleaguered actions.
3. There is a necessity to set up an unlatched mHealth framework related to a vigorous podium with guidelines for application progress that would ease ascendible and sustainable wellbeing communication structures.
4. Executing plan, for example product design to check the various characteristics of intrusions must be discovered in bid to avail the significant confirmation base.
5. Bolstering mHealth in other revenue countries except those with high incomes generally is led by efficiency and usefulness of examinations as a result of which they are deciphered on a fitting facts base.
6. Different players such as governments, resource providers, and organizations should help to formulate principles to generate an autonomous commercially feasible bionetwork for improvement.

KEYWORDS

- **mobile apps**
- **text messaging**
- **smartphones**
- **mobile tablet computers**
- **mobile health (mHealth)**
- **telemedicine**
- **healthcare**
- **evaluation**
- **regulation and certification**
- **quality**

REFERENCES

Akter, S. and Ray, P. (2010). mHealth–An ultimate platform to serve the unserved". *IMIA Yearbook of Medical Informatics*, pp. 1–7.

Kotz, D. (2011). "A threat taxonomy for mHealth privacy". *IEEE Third International Conference on Communication Systems and Networks*, Bangalore, India, 4–8 January.

Labrique, A. B., Vasudevan, L., Kochi, E., Fabricant, and R., Mehl, G. (2013). "mHealth innovations as health system strengthening tools: 12 common applications and a visual framework".*GlobalHealth:SciencePractice*,vol.1,no.2,160–171.http://dx.doi.org/10.9745/GHSP-D-13-00031.

Martin, T. (August 2012). "Assessing mHealth: opportunities and barriers to patient engagement". *Journal of Healthcare for the Poor and Underserved*, vol. 23, 935–941

Mechael, P. N. (2009). "The case for mHealth in developing countries". *MIT Press Journal*, vol. 4, no. 1, 103–118.

Pimmer, C. and Tulenko, K. (2016). "The convergence of mobile and social media: Affordances and constraints of mobile networked communication for health workers in low- and middle-income countries". *Mobile Media & Communication,* vol. 4, no. 2, 252–269. DOI:10.1177/2050157915622657.

Tomlinson, M., Rotheram-Borus, M. J., Swartz, L. and Tsai, A. C. (2013). "Scaling up mHealth: Where Is the Evidence?" *PLOS Medicine*, vol. 10, no. 2, e1001382, www.plosmedicine.org.

Ventola, C. L. (2014). "Mobile devices and apps for healthcare professionals: Uses and benefits". vol. 39, no. 50, 356–364.

Vital Wave Consulting. (2009). "mHealth for Development: The Opportunity of Mobile Technology for Healthcare in the Developing World". Washington, D.C. and Berkshire, UK: UN Foundation-Vodafone Foundation Partnership.

Whittaker, R. (2012). "Issues in mHealth: Findings from key informant interviews". *Journal of Medical Internet Research*, vol. 14, no. 5, e129 URL: http://www.jmir.org/2012/5/e129/ doi:10.2196/jmir.1989 PMID:23032424.

World Health Organization. (WHO, 2011a). *Global Observatory for eHealth series–Volume 3*, https://www.who.int/goe/publications/goe_mhealth_web.pdf

World Health Organization. (WHO, 2011b). "mHealth: New horizons for health through mobile technologies: Second global survey on eHealth". *Global Observatory for eHealth Series*, vol. 8, 102, ISBN 978-92 4 156425 0 (NLM classification: W 26.5).

Yeh, F. Yeh, S.-T. and Fontenelle, C. (2012). "Usability study of a mobile website: The Health Sciences Library, University of Colorado Anschutz Medical Campus, experience". *Journal of the Medical Library Association*, vol. 100, no. 1, 64–68.

CHAPTER 10

Energy-Efficient Network Design for Healthcare Services

AMIT SEHGAL[1*], T. L. SINGAL[2], RAJEEV AGRAWAL[1], and SWETA SNEHA[3]

[1]Sharda University, Plot No 32–34, Knowledge Park 3, Greater Noida, Uttar Pradesh 201310, India

[2]Chitkara University, Rajpura Campus, Punjab 140401, India

[3]Michael J. Coles College of Business, Kennesaw State University, Kennesaw, GA 30144, USA

*Corresponding author. E-mail: amitsehgal26@gmail.com

ABSTRACT

The Internet of things (IoT) is a system of interrelated computing devices having unique identifiers that enable to transfer data over a network without requiring human-to-computer or human-to-human interaction. With the rapid growth in embedded wireless computing devices with high-speed Internet connectivity, body area networks comprising of interconnected several tiny-powered, wearable wireless biosensors provide an effective way of collecting vital health-related data. The emerging paradigm of the IoT in the smart healthcare system requires a specialized secure framework in order to enable real-time health monitoring, reliable diagnostics, effective treatment processes, and many other related aspects of the healthcare system. The network framework for the IoT-based healthcare system should cater to upgraded microcontroller units, IoT gateway devices, different web and wireless technologies for the IoT, variety of biosensors and data collectors, secure communication protocols, etc. These devices are continuously engaged in computation, processing, and transmission of data, which is a high-power consumption activity. On the contrary, most of these devices are battery driven, and thus, there is a strong requirement to minimize the consumption of power, thus making it an energy-efficient network. In this chapter, various aspects of energy consumption in the IoT framework for healthcare services are discussed.

10.1 ICT IN HEALTHCARE

The term "Smart Cities" may have different meaning to the people from diverse geographic and socioeconomic conditions. It may include modernization of education, infrastructure, communication, transport, public utilities and amenities, sustainable economy, energy, and many more parameters providing better quality of life through managed services. In addition to these, one of the most important and basic necessities of every citizen or resident of a city is better and easily accessible healthcare services. Undoubtedly, with growing urbanization, the access to healthcare services has become easier. Still, in a developing countries such as India, where majority of the population lives in rural areas or small towns, access to specialty healthcare is associated with long traveling hours and waiting queues (Strasser et al., 1994; Boulle, 1997; McFarlane et al., 2000; Strasser, 2003; Rao et al., 2011; Krishna and Ananthpur, 2013). The cost of such services at private hospitals forces people with economic limitations to move to multispecialty government hospitals, where best quality diagnosis and treatment is available at minimal cost. This further adds to the long waiting period at such hospitals for getting an appointment for diagnostic procedures such as radiology-based scans or treatment procedures such as surgery. This chapter addresses the challenges faced by the current healthcare system governed by the state and center governments, and a unified solution to these challenges is presented taking benefits of information and communication technology (ICT), Internet of things (IoT), and other related technologies.

Healthcare is an amalgam of multiple services rendered to individuals and communities by healthcare professionals of trained agents responsible for delivery of medical care services. The overall healthcare sector includes various entities such as concepts, for example, health parameters and diseases; ideas, for example, diagnostic techniques; objects, for example, healthcare centers and hospitals; and persons, for example, trained healthcare staff and clinical experts. These entities support, control, and interact with each other to make a complete system (Gulliford et al., 2002). The challenges faced in achieving the goal of affordable healthcare for a smart city are dominated by:

- shortage or absence of infrastructure for specialty healthcare;
- paucity of manpower (doctors, nurses, and trained paramedic staff);

- low public expenditure on health and its inefficiencies;
- inaccessibility to diagnostic services in rural areas.

These challenges are more severe in rural areas (Reddy et al., 2011).

With the development of ICT-based technologies such as IoT (Chase, 2013), machine learning/artificial intelligence, etc., continuous efforts are being made to develop a framework that will overcome the aforementioned challenges (Islam et al., 2015; Deo, 2015; Chung et al., 2016). The IoT-based framework for healthcare is one such solution (Chiuchisan et al., 2014; Pasha and Shah, 2018). Similar to the multilayered healthcare system of any country, this framework is also based on a layered architecture and supports several domains of the healthcare service sector. Deployment of an IoT framework in integration with the existing healthcare system can provide features of smart healthcare, as mentioned in Table 10.1. Starting from telemedicine to e-health and m-health (Silva et al., 2015), utilization of ICT is increasing and offering more and more services to the healthcare sector (Eysenbach, 2001; Istepanian et al., 2006; Veeramuthu et al., 2011; Postolache et al., 2012; Flodgren et al., 2015). Devices have been developed to offer IoT-based services such as ambient-assisted living (Rodrigues et al., 2015), remote monitoring for chronic diseases (Rojahn et al., 2016), smart ambulance to provide patient monitoring during mobility (Yamada et al., 2004; Beri et al., 2016; Pol et al., 2016; Udawant et al., 2017), and many more. Most of these applications are based on the sensors that record biosignals from the human body and transmit them to a data-aggregating unit. The data is then processed at the same unit or sent to a separate centralized data processing unit to generate clinical inferences regarding health state of the patient.

Techniques such as machine learning are also being used to suggest the future course of action for the patient (Impedovo and Pirlo, 2019). However, these devices and techniques are not mature enough to completely replace the traditional methods of diagnosis and patient monitoring and must work in close cognition with the clinical experts. Wearable sensors are available, which can acquire physiological data with high degree of accuracy without any direct intervention of human being. These data vary from a simple case of body temperature and pulse rate to capturing electrocardiography (ECG) and electroencephalography (EEG) signals. The data from these sensors is stored locally in a data aggregator or in remote database. This transfer of data from the sensors can be through a wired or wireless network. Access to these data is further provided to the users through different network access techniques depending upon the type of application or user devices. Thus, network plays a very important role in overall functioning of an ICT-based healthcare system.

Due to the wide diversity in the type of data and random in the placement, mobility, and ambient conditions of both the sensors or their bearers and the end users, the desired characteristics for such networks are quite different from many other commonly used communication systems. Similar to any other IoT system, the data generated in healthcare systems is also very large due to the extremely large number of users whose health status and clinical treatment act as source of data. Moreover, unlike many other IoT systems that generate text or numeric data (except those including imaging devices), the healthcare data includes high-resolution images made from pathological sample slides and radiology equipment. In addition, the data such as ECG or EEG is continuously generated and needs to be transmitted seamlessly in case of remote monitoring system of IoT-enabled intensive or critical care units. The quality of service (QoS) or performance parameters are much more demanding in terms of network resources with stringent accuracy and security. The two most crucial network resources are bandwidth and power.

TABLE 10.1   IoT Applications for Various Healthcare Services

Healthcare Service	IoT Application
Preventive alerts	Routine checkup and medication reminder, Immunization, guidelines for secondary prevention from disease (pop-up alert, SMS, e-mail, task list, detailed preventive guidelines)
Diagnosis	Suggested investigation report of clinical tests, information on patient condition, trigger notes/alerts in case of medical emergency
Treatment Plan	Treatment/medication plan based on diagnosis report and knowledge base similar patients, dosage recommendation, guidelines on possible drug reaction as per patient's medical records
Patient follow-up	Alerts/reminders for follow-up checkup or immediate consultation in case of emergency, monitoring of medication plan
In-patient management	Care management through previous records, planning for duration of hospitalization through estimation of patient's recovery rate, avoid redundant tests, respond to actions taken by care giver

The IoT networks are intelligent networks and require sensors and network devices, which should not only be smart but low cost also. These devices are continuously engaged in computation, processing, and transmission of data, which is a high-power consumption activity. On the contrary, most of these devices being battery driven, there is a strong requirement to minimize the consumption of power, thus making it an energy-efficient network. The demand for seamless connectivity with best possible QoS in the case of healthcare applications restricts the network and application planners to put the devices in sleep mode or adopt energy-efficient methods, which are more common in several other not-so-critical applications.

10.2 NETWORK ARCHITECTURE FOR HEALTHCARE

Based on the scale of deployment and coverage area, networks are categorized into personal area network (PAN), local area network (LAN), metropolitan area network (MAN), and wide area network (WAN). A PAN generally comprises of sensors, which are placed in a small geographic area with almost similar terrain profile (Li et al., 2005; Zhao and Viehland, 2009). These sensors communicate with a locally present coordinator device or data aggregator through single-hop or multiple-hop communication. The network among these sensors can follow a dynamic ad hoc architecture or a static client–server-based architecture. In the case of mobile devices and users, dynamic architecture is preferred, whereas in the case of static devices, both dynamic and static architectures can be followed. Beyond data aggregator, the network could be any one of LAN, MAN, and WAN or even combination of these. A three-layered architecture for the IoT framework (Sethi and Sarangi, 2017) is a common approach followed in many IoT-based healthcare systems. Figure 10.1 presents one such architecture.

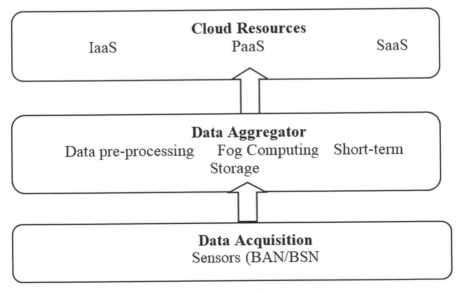

FIGURE 10.1   Three-layered architecture of an IoT framework.

The data acquisition layer comprises of sensors that are connected to create a PAN, collecting various physiological parameters from the patient (Castillejo et al., 2013; Agrawal, 2017). The network of such devices is known as body area network (BAN) or body sensor network (Chen et al., 2011; Filipe et al., 2015). These sensors connect with a data aggregator, which could be a smartphone connected to sensors using Bluetooth or a locally placed data server connected through WiFi. Other commonly used technologies enabling BAN connectivity are ZigBee, radio frequency identification (RFID), and ultrahigh frequency. The middle layer—data aggregator and processing—is responsible to collect the data from various sensors and process it to provide clinical inferences to the patient and send to the upper data storage layer. The data storage layer includes cloud-based storage and is used to keep the data for long duration such as few months to several years. In addition, the data that require more storage space and high computing and processing resources are also sent to the cloud so that the resources at the middle layer are kept simple and low cost with less energy requirement. However, techniques of fog computing are implemented at the middle layer to reduce the flow of data to and from cloud storage. This can be in the form of processing the data and sending generated inferences to the patient and caregiver and removing redundant data or the one with little relevant information from being sent to the cloud. Access to the data stored at middle layer or cloud and the corresponding user interfaces also requires network connectivity along with flow of data across three layers. Including these additional communication, storage, processing, and end-user applications, the overall network architecture of most of the IoT applications, such as smart home and city, smart grid, smart health, and industrial machine-to-machine and device-to-device is based on the seven-layered reference network model given in the IoT World Forum (Hakim, 2018). Figure 10.2 presents this network model.

In this reference model, the lower three layers—devices, network access, and edge computing—represent the real-time aggregation and processing of the data generated by real-time events. The top most three layers—data abstraction, application, and collaboration and processes—represent query-based events and computing in non-real-time data aggregation for long-term interfaces for user interaction and responses to the user. The middle layer between these two groups represents aggregation of data generated by both these layers and facilitates the flow of data among these groups.

The devices and processes used in all these layers have different energy requirements, thus having varying impact on the overall energy efficiency of the network. For example, the power requirement of devices in the upper group is much higher due to the high-end computing, huge storage, and other power hungry resources. Therefore, these devices use the main power line as the source of energy and not battery operated. The devices used in lower group of layers are generally battery operated, and thus, energy is a more precious resource in these devices. Thus, the challenges in terms of energy utilization are different for higher and lower layer devices. Since transmission of information is the most energy hungry activity, any technique used to reduce the flow of data across different layers and among the network and user will make the overall system more energy efficient. In this chapter, we focus on various techniques and methodologies, which can be used at lower layers across the IoT framework to minimize the energy consumption/requirement, and this makes it more energy efficient. The context of application has been restricted, primarily, to healthcare services keeping the generalization, wherever applicable.

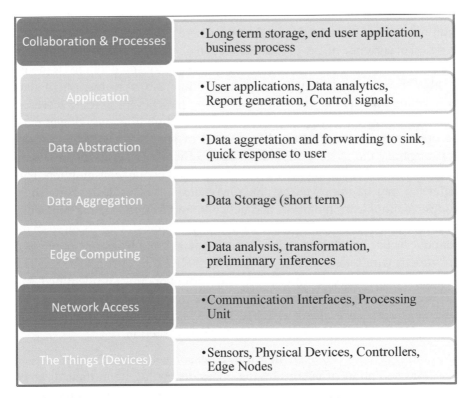

FIGURE 10.2 Seven-layered network model as per the IoT World Forum.

10.3   ENERGY CONSTRAINTS IN IOT NETWORKS

The lower layers of an IoT network include devices (RFID tags, biosensors, ambience sensors, smart dust, etc.), which are battery-operated and network interfaces providing a low-power radio link (Vasseur and Dunkels, 2010). The challenges at device level include size, cost, and energy consumption, whereas the network-level challenges include seamless connectivity, bandwidth, range of communication, and transmit and receive signal strength. The radio links used in IoT networks (IEEE802.11, IEEE802.15.4, etc.) are highly unstable and lossy with low reliability due to strong interference and weak signal strength (Ko et al., 2011). For better energy efficiency, both the devices and radio links are low power and contribute to the energy constraints for device and network designers. The constraints become more critical for applications where uninterrupted monitoring is required, demanding for devices to be in active state and continuous transmission of data across various layers.

The networks deployed for healthcare services are responsible to send health condition of the patients continuously to the clinical experts. This is required in case of preventive healthcare, where a person is being monitored to detect occurrence of any prehospitalization clinical emergency and also for the patients who are under treatment during or posthospitalization (Redondi et al., 2013). Any discontinuity in acquisition and transmission of data may be life threatening in case of monitoring patients for chronic diseases. Since these devices are battery driven, the utilization of battery power must be optimized for long battery life. Instead of simply reducing the power consumption, the system should be made efficient in terms of providing reliable and secure communication with minimum energy consumption. This efficiency can be improved by applying energy-efficient designs in sensor nodes, communication devices and network architecture, routing protocols, and data processing units. Most of the physiological sensors use smart, adaptive technology to transmit and receive data through any one or more of the various wireless standards such as IEEE802.11x and IEEE802.15.x. The parameters that affect energy efficiency of the network must be identified, and techniques should be applied for its improvement. Some of the commonly observed factors are given in Table 10.2 with their cumulative effect on battery consumption and described further in this section.

- *Energy hole problem:* In wireless sensor networks, there is uneven consumption of energy by the nodes depending upon their distance from the data sink or the aggregator node. The nodes that are closer to the sink act as aggregators for the nodes that do not have sink in their range directly and thus transfer their data to the other nodes in multihop mode. This results in early drain-out of energy for the near nodes due to the large amount of data transmission activity, thus making them unavailable soon. The far nodes, though have sufficient battery life available, cannot send data to the network due to the broken link. This condition is called energy hole (Boukerche, 2008). Several techniques have been proposed and tested to reduce the network failure due to this reason. In case of networks used for healthcare services, the energy holes may occur for a common wireless sink that is being used for several patients present at different locations within a hospital of in remote/rural areas, where direct connectivity to the cloud is not available for all the patients.

TABLE 10.2 Factors Affecting Energy Consumption in a Network

Sr. No.	Energy Consuming Activity	Cumulative Battery Power Consumption						
1	Energy hole		▓	▓	▓	▓	▓	▓
2	Data retransmission			▓	▓	▓	▓	▓
3	Collision of data				▓	▓	▓	▓
4	Idle-listening					▓	▓	▓
5	Overhearing						▓	▓

- *Retransmission of data*: Most of the networks operate in hand-shake mode to ensure error-free delivery of data. A threshold is set to decide the failure of transmission or error beyond acceptable limit, which initiates retransmission of data (Rajendran et al., 2003). This could be due to poor quality link having severe propagation loss, fading, and strong interference or failure of intermediate nodes. As mentioned earlier, transmission is the most energy-consuming activity for a sensor network; several techniques have been proposed and tested to reduce retransmission of data.

- *Collision of data:* In a sensor network, multiple nodes send data to a common data aggregator or sink node using similar network access technology such as ZigBee, BLE, or WiFi. This results in increased chances of collision of data during the multihop or at the sink node (Jones et al., 2001). Collisions must be avoided since they not only affect the performance of the network but also demand for retransmission of data, which adds to the energy consumption overhead on the already constrained battery. Prediction and prevention of collision is a major power-saving activity for sensor networks used in mission-critical application of healthcare.

- *Idle-listening:* A sensor node can be configured to operate in any of the several modes at an instant of time such as sleeping, sensing, active, and routing. Since most of the sensor networks operate in the multihop mode of data transfer, the nodes are configured to both transmit and receive data. In case of low-power networks, receive operation also consumes significant amount of power similar to transmit operation and thus need to be minimized to increase battery life and make the network more energy efficient (Kuntz, 2010). When sensors are used for critical monitoring applications, they need to listen continuously to detect occurrence of an event and thus remain in active state. In such conditions, the battery life of the nodes decreases much below the expected value as per design specifications, thus reducing energy efficiency of the network.

- *Overhearing:* It refers to the unwanted reception of data by sensor nodes, data aggregator, and other network devices (Kuntz, 2010). In case of multihop transmission, data from a distant node may be received by multiple intermediate nodes before it reaches the destination data aggregator or sink node. Such multiple and redundant receiving activity increases the battery consumption of the nodes compared to the conditions where overhearing is minimized.

The aforementioned and many other factors affect the energy efficiency of the network and thus challenge their suitability for critical applications related to healthcare services. To increase the uninterrupted lifetime of the network, the energy consumption needs to be reduced so that the same battery can provide power to the network for longer duration of time. Several techniques have been proposed to balance the effect of the factors mentioned in this section. This chapter focuses on the issues related to network design with an objective to make it more energy efficient.

10.4   ENERGY CONSUMPTION MODELS

While designing a sensor network for healthcare or any other application, components at various levels of the decided architecture are selected based on the factors such as cost, size, energy consumption, and acceptable value for performance parameters related to transmission and reception of data, computing power, delay, data rate, etc. For the battery-operated devices, energy consumption needs to be calculated before a device can be put to use in a particular application. The edge devices, including sensor nodes, are the most constrained devices, and suitable energy models must be followed during design, development, and implementation so that a correlation exists between all the modules of the node leading to minimum energy consumption and maximum lifetime of the node. The basic blocks that constitute architecture of a sensor node are power supply with suitable converter and regulator, sensor/actuator and analog-to-digital/digital-to-analog converter, data processing unit, and communication (transceiver) unit. As mentioned in Section 10.2, the challenges and requirements of sensor networks used for healthcare are quite different from general WSNs. Design and implementation of BANs based on traditional models of energy consumption and optimization may not produce the desired results in terms of lifetime and overall network performance. These models are based on theoretical estimation of energy consumption, generalized to various existing modules and platforms. For more accurate analysis of power consumption and lifetime, the models based on practical/real-time measurements done on actual hardware nodes should be followed. One limitation with such models is that they can be used only for the nodes that have hardware and protocols similar to the one used for measurement and testing of the model. Thus, it is required to develop models that provide an optimum balance between generalization and application-specific needs.

10.4.1 ENERGY PROFILE FOR SENSOR NODES

For a battery-operated device, the fundamental criterion to be followed while developing the energy model for a device is that the energy consumed by the device for all its operations within a time interval should be less than or equal to the energy stored in the device. This can be written as

$$E_{st} \geq \int_{t1}^{t2} P_{consumed})dt \tag{10.1}$$

where E_{st} is the energy stored in the device at time instant $t1$ and $P_{consumed}$ is the power consumed during the time interval $(t2 - t1)$. In case a renewable energy source is available, which provides power P_{supply} during time interval $(t2 - t1)$, the energy model is modified as

$$E_{st} \geq \int_{t1}^{t2} P_{consumed} - P_{supply})dt. \tag{10.2}$$

For estimation of lifetime of the device, the energy profile of the device is prepared, which represents consumption of power during its various states of operation. Figure 10.3 shows one such energy profile diagram for a device that operates in three modes—active, sleep, and standby. The average energy consumed by the node can be calculated as

$$E_{avg} = a * T_{active} + b * T_{standby} + s * T_{sleep} \tag{10.3}$$

where E_{avg} is the calculated average energy consumption of the device, T_{active}, $T_{standby}$, and T_{sleep} are the time durations for which the device is in active, standby, and sleep modes, respectively, and a, b, and s are the rate of occurrence of active, standby, and sleep states, respectively, over the averaging period.

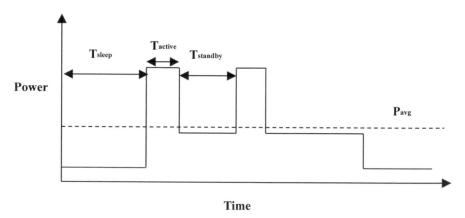

FIGURE 10.3   Energy profile of a sensor node.

Similar to most of the physical sensors, in case of biosensors as well, the physiological data acquired from the body need to be processed and converted to a form suitable for transmission. Many healthcare monitoring devices have computing and processing capabilities embedded in them so that the patient can see the monitored parameters, and some preliminary inferences can also be made regarding the clinical state of the person being monitored. The controllers and other data processing modules used for this purpose also consume a significant amount of energy. The controllers used to perform these functions in the sensor device also work in different modes of operation to conserve power when they are not actually processing the data or computing some inferences. Similar to the energy profile of the device, a profile of energy consumption by the controller module is also prepared. For a total time "t," which is the sum of transition time from state i to state j, $(T_{tr,i\text{-}j})$ and duration for which the controller remains in state j, $(T_{st,j})$, the energy consumed as a function of time $(E_{cp}(t))$ is the sum of energy consumed during transition from i to j $(E_{tr,i\text{-}j}(t))$ and energy consumed when operating in state j $(E_{st,j}(t))$

$$E_{cp}(t) = E_{tr,i\text{-}j}(t) + E_{st,j}(t) \tag{10.4}$$

$$t = T_{tr,i\text{-}j} + T_{st,j}. \tag{10.5}$$

For "n" number of states which a controller can go into, the probability that the controller remains in state j for a duration $T_{st,j}$ is $p_{st,j}$ and the probability of transition from state i to j is $p_{tr,i\text{-}j}$. The total energy consumed can be calculated as

$$E_{cp}(t) = \sum\nolimits_{j=1}^{n} E_{st,j}(t) * p_{st,j} + \sum\nolimits_{\substack{i=1 \\ i \neq j}}^{n-1} E_{tr,i-j}(t) * p_{tr,i-j}. \tag{10.6}$$

Similarly, the energy consumed can be calculated for the communication module, which, as mentioned earlier, is responsible for maximum energy consumption compared to all other modules of the sensor device. This is, primarily, because of the absence of high computing and graphics processing units in these sensor devices. If required, cloud-based resources are used for such processing, and the communication modules become active for flow of data between the device and the cloud.

10.4.2 ENERGY MODELS FOR DATA TRANSMISSION

Based on various components of energy consumption and available battery power for the sensor node and other network devices, the device and network lifetime of the overall network can be calculated. Network lifetime is a crucial metric used to define quality of a WSN. It depends on several factors and design parameters of the network such as network architecture and topology, protocols at various layers, channel characteristics, modes of operation and transition between them, data transmission techniques, etc. Various definitions of network lifetime are available in the literature (Chang and Tassiulas, 2004; Ehsan et al., 2012; Jaleelet al., 2013; Hajiaghayi et al., 2010; Huang et al., 2008). Taking key parameters from these definitions, a more generalized definition of network lifetime has been framed and given below.

Definition: "Network lifetime is the maximum time interval during which the minimal required sensor nodes and intermediate network devices have energy level above the minimum required threshold to ensure end-to-end network connectivity with desired value of QoS parameters."

Each layer in the network protocol stack has its own contribution in the overall energy consumption and thus network lifetime. Figure 10.4 shows some of the important factors at various layers, which affect the energy consumption and lifetime. Table 10.3 briefly introduces the related energy consumption network parameters.

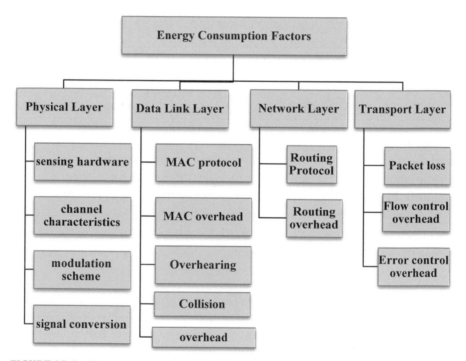

FIGURE 10.4 Energy consumption parameters at various network layers.

Various energy models have been proposed in earlier research (Azhari et al., 2017; Elsersy, 2013; Chepkwony et al., 2015; Amin et al., 2017). Some of the more important energy consumption parameters used in these models have been briefly described in this section.

The power consumption rate at the ith sensor node i, P_i, is given by

$$P_i = \sum_{j:(i,j)\in L} x_{ij} p_{ij}^t + \sum_{j:(j,i)\in L} x_{ji} p_{ji}^r \tag{10.7}$$

where p_{ij}^t denotes the energy consumption per second for transmitting one unit of data over link (i, j), p_{ji}^r denotes the energy consumption per second per unit data at receiver over link (i, j), L represents the directed link set, and $(i, j) \in L$ means that sensor node i can transmit data to sensor node j.

TABLE 10.3 Energy Consumption Parameters for a Sensor Network

Parameters	Description
Transmit power	Energy consumed per second per unit data transmitted by a node
Receive power	Energy consumed per second per unit data received by a node
Sensing energy	Energy consumed to sense one bit of data
Data rate	Average flow of data in bits per second between two nodes
Physical Layer overhead	Redundant bits in Physical Layer packet
Collision	Number of data bits lost due to collision causing retransmission or packet loss
Overhearing	Node in receiving mode for the redundant or unwanted data
MAC layer overhead	Overhead bits in MAC layer packet
Sleep mode power	Power consumed when the node is in sleep mode
Standby mode power	Power consumed when the node is in standby mode
Mode transition power	Power consumed during transition of the node from one state/mode to another

A routing variable x_{ij} is associated with each sensor node i $(i, j) \in L$. $x_{ij} = 0$ means that the sensor node i selects the link (i, j) to forward the data to sensor node j, and $x_{ij} = 0$ means that the link (i, j) is not selected.

The energy consumption at node i is given by

$$E_i = \sum_{j \in S_i} e_{ij}^t \sum_{c \in C} q_{ij}^{(c)} + \sum_{j:i \in S_i} e_{ji}^r \sum_{c \in C} q_{ji}^{(c)} \tag{10.8}$$

where e_{ij}^t denotes the per-unit data energy consumed at node i for transmission to its neighboring node j, e_{ji}^r denotes per-unit data energy consumed at node i for receiving from its neighboring node j, $q_{ij}^{(c)}$ denotes the transmitting rate c from source node i to destination node j, S_i is the set of all nodes within the communication range of node i, and C is the commodity defined by a set of source and destination nodes.

The *energy per useful bit* (EPUB) defines a way of computing the energy consumed at transmitter and receiver units and takes care of the energy consumed during the control packet data bits. It is given by

$$EPUB = \left(\frac{B_D + B_P}{B_D}\right)(P_{TX} + \xi.P_{RX})T \qquad (10.9)$$

where B_D represents the average number of data bits in a packet, B_P represents the average number of preamble bits in a packet, P_{TX} is the transmitter power in Watts, P_{RX} is the receiver power in Watts, including the associated electronic circuitry, and T is the bit time in seconds. The constant ξ denotes the ratio of the average time in the receive mode and the average time in transmit mode and is determined by the medium access control (MAC) layer scheme used. However, this expression does not consider other factors such as sensing and signal processing power, signal loss due to channel estimation, and feedback.

The bit energy consumption at physical layer can be expressed as

$$E_b = E_{elec}^{trans} + \beta d^{\alpha} + E_{elec}^{rec} \qquad (10.10)$$

where E_{elec}^{trans} is energy consumption at the transmitter that takes into account overheads of transmitter electronics circuitry (phase-locked loops, voltage-controlled oscillators, bias currents, and so on) and digital processing, E_{elec}^{rec} is energy consumption at the receiver that takes into account the overhead of receiver electronics, and the term βd^{α} takes care of per-bit radiated power to transmit over a distance d from the source, where α represents path loss whose value ranges from 2 to 5 and β is constant [expressed in J/(bit m$^{\alpha}$)].

Cross-layer energy consumption parameters have also been used for analysis of network lifetime in some research works (He et al., 2012; Karvonen et al., 2015; Correa-Chica et al., 2016). Physical, MAC and network layer energy models are analyzed in unison for more accurate estimation of energy consumption and thus network lifetime for a particular application. Not much effort in this direction has been done for analysis of networks used in healthcare services, thus offering tremendous scope for further research.

10.5   ENERGY-EFFICIENT BAN

BANs consist of a set of sensing nodes that are battery powered. These nodes could be wearable of implantable. To increase the lifetime and reliability of these networks, it is required to maximize the battery lifetime by reducing energy consumption of sensing nodes. Since transmission of data consumes maximum amount of energy, continuous efforts are being made to develop intelligent and adaptive BANs within the constraints of minimum power consumption and without making any impact on performance parameters such as seamless connectivity, security, real-time data acquisition and processing, high throughput with error-free communication, etc. In this section, techniques to optimize the energy consumption in BANs have been discussed, leading to an energy-efficient healthcare system.

For an energy-efficient network, the device-level power constraints must be considered while achieving a balance between cost and performance of the device. A standard architecture of a biosensor device includes a sensing unit acting as a transducer for the measured physical parameter, a processing unit, and a communication unit having signal processing circuits and antenna for transmission and reception of the signals. The performance of all these units of the device must be maintained individually and in integrity while keeping the energy consumption to a lower level for a longer lifetime. Optimum selection of resources such as sensitivity and resolution of sensing unit, computing power of the processing unit, and transmit power and receiver sensitivity is required, which will make the device not only cost effective but energy efficient as well. Efficient device operation and service provisioning methods are also implemented through embedded software modules to reduce the power consumption without any impact on device performance.

10.5.1 TECHNIQUES AT PHYSICAL DEVICE LEVEL

It has been well established in many research works that more than 70% energy consumption for a device is accounted by the communication unit. Techniques to regulate data transmission and flow of data across different layers of the network architecture have shown significant improvement in energy efficiency of the network. At the physical device level, efficient node placement methods are considered to implement low-power networks. Most of the IoT networks operate in many-to-one mode, where multiple sensor nodes send the data to a common data aggregator node or sink in single or multiple hops. The flow of data and number of hops can be optimized using node placement techniques for a balance between energy and performance. This not only balances the uneven flow of data but also reduces congestion in the network. Some of the popular algorithms used for node placement are— genetic algorithms (Norouzi and Zaim, 2014; Zorlu, and Şahıngöz., 2017), bioinspired algorithms (Kulkarni et al., 2009; Tamizharasi et al., 2013), particle swarm optimization (Shunyuan et al., 2016), optimized artificial fish swarm algorithm (Yiyue et al., 2012), artificial bee colony, and territorial predator scent marking algorithm (Abidin and Din, 2013).

In case of healthcare applications, we do not have much control on the node placement since the biosensors must be placed at the specific place on the body so as to measure the desired parameter. Moreover, in case of out-patient monitoring, the location of the patients having biosensors (wearable or implantable) also cannot be controlled for optimum node placement. It is, therefore, recommended to apply node placement techniques on data aggregator nodes or intermediate relay nodes. The purpose is to balance the flow of data to avoid any congestion at aggregator or relay node.

Since effective and efficient transmission of data is crucial not only for energy efficiency of the network but also for maintaining seamless connectivity, several research work is being done in the field of the front-end transmit and receive module, that is, antenna. The objective of such research work is to optimize the antenna design in terms of maximum gain, minimum losses, high sensitivity and selectivity, and minimum size. These parameters along with the type of material used are more critical in case of implantable health monitoring devices. Since antenna design is not in the scope of this chapter, the related research work has not been discussed in detail.

10.5.2   ENERGY EFFICIENCY AT DATA LINK LAYER

In a wireless network, various protocols at the data link layer (DLL) provide the functionality of data framing, MAC, and implementation of error control techniques. In context to energy efficiency, MAC sublayer of DLL is responsible for implementation of scheduling and power control techniques. In healthcare applications of the IoT, various biosensors are configured to form a BAN, and scheduling techniques are applied to optimize the flow of data from sensors to aggregator or sink nodes. Each node transmits data in its allotted time slot. Channel allocation techniques are applied for efficient sharing of the radio spectrum, which not only improves bandwidth utilization but also reduces the congestion or collision in the channels. Such scheduling techniques improve the energy efficiency of the network by reducing retransmission of data, overhearing, and idle listening, thus increasing the lifetime of battery-operated devices. In addition to traditional scheduling techniques, that is, frequency-division multiple access, time-division multiple access (TDMA), and code-division multiple access (CDMA), recent research studies have proposed more efficient scheduling techniques such as self-scheduled and distributed MAC, self-distributive MAC, distributed hybrid slot scheduling, QoS-aware scheduling, etc. Another MAC layer technique to improve energy efficiency of the networks is power control and power-off mechanisms. To overcome limitations of TDMA (wasted time slots) and CDMA (collision in case of heavy data traffic), other MAC protocols have been proposed. Energy FDM is one such protocol, which is based on CSMA and uses power control for better energy efficiency. However, this protocol was observed to suffer from high collision rate similar to CDMA. Hybrid protocols such as OPWUM have also been attempted with hybrid wake-up schemes at the receiver end to reduce energy consumption. The complex frame structure caused degradation in performance of the transmitter due to inefficient utilization of resources. Another multihop MAC protocol CEE based on the cross-layer transmission scheme was proposed to reduce energy consumption at during transmission. However, it suffered from poor throughput due to inefficient channel allocation model resulting in high collision rate. To fulfill the demand for more and more energy-efficient network design, a MAC protocol (TCH-MAC) based on integration of TDMA and CDMA has been proposed recently. This protocol has a TDMA-based scheme, which is traffic adaptive to handle problems due to heavy burst of traffic and an efficient CDMA-based scheme along with adjustable power control for the transmitter. This hybrid scheme has been shown to improve energy efficiency of the network while maintaining throughput and losses due to collision to desired levels. For detailed study of this MAC protocol.

In addition to these hybrid schemes, several power control schemes have been used, individually or in integration with other schemes, to control the transmit power depending upon the requirement for coverage area and signal strength. Such schemes are more suitable for contention-based topologies and implemented using protocols such as power-controlled multiple access, common power protocol, power controlled dual channel, etc. In addition to power control for the transmitter, the operation of receiver of a low-power device also needs to be optimized. As discussed earlier in Section 10.3, idle listening is also major reason affecting energy efficiency of a low-power network. It is, therefore, recommended that the device should be kept in sleep mode when it is not actually receiving any data but simply waiting for an event to occur or valid data to be received. Several power-off schemes have been proposed to implement this power-saving feature and thus improve the energy efficiency of the network. The examples of commonly used efficient power-off schemes are MACA protocol, power management using multisleep states, power-aware multiaccess with signaling, pico node multichannel MAC, etc. In addition to using these specially designed power-control and power-off protocols, fine tuning of transmit and receive power of antenna and using smart directional antenna have also been explored.

10.5.3   *ENERGY EFFICIENCY AT NETWORK LAYER*

The network layer is responsible for routing of data from source to destination. The simplest technique for routing is known as flooding, in which data received by a node are forwarded to all the neighboring nodes via broadcast. This technique is quite inefficient in terms of energy efficiency and also suffers from several other disadvantages such as implosion, overlap, gossiping, etc. Several modified forms of flooding have been proposed by researchers to overcome its shortcomings and make the network more energy efficient, reliable, and perform better in terms of other QoS parameters. Routing techniques have been developed to solve the problems, which result in uneven and random increase in energy consumption by the edge nodes and other network devices. This includes balancing uneven flow of data, reducing retransmission of data, eliminating redundant data transmission, lower end-to-end latency, and many more. Such routing protocols decide the most reliable path to transmit data not only with minimum packet loss and maximum throughput but also with minimum energy consumption. The routing protocols designed for various applications of sensor networks are categorized into five types—content or attribute based, flat based, geographical, hierarchical, and multipath routing. However, similar to physical and network layers, few additional challenges must be considered while designing a routing protocol for BANs. These are briefly introduced as follows.

- *Dynamic topology:* In the BAN, the sensors are placed either on (wearable) or inside (implantable) the human body. Since these sensors send their data through a wireless channel (wireless BAN or WBAN), their orientation with respect to the data aggregator or sink node is directly dependent on the movement of human body. This makes the channel conditions more random and dynamic, except for the case of a bed-ridden patient whose movement is restricted. The effect of multipath fading and shadowing due to the surroundings of the patient and change in channel characteristics due to movement from indoor to outdoor and vice versa further make the channel estimation more complex and random. The routing techniques for such random and dynamic network conditions should be sufficiently adaptive.
- *Energy efficiency:* Similar to any battery sensor network with battery-operated nodes, sensors in the BAN are also energy constrained. Though both wearable and implantable sensors must have long battery lifetime for uninterrupted service, it is more important to have much

longer lifetime for the implantable sensors since complex surgery is required to implant them. Furthermore, their size is generally very small, and this limits the battery power that can be embedded into them, thus demanding for minimum possible energy consumption. The routing protocol should, therefore, be designed to minimize energy consumption of the sensor nodes.

- *Device temperature:* During sensing, computing, and communication, sensor nodes may generate heat resulting in rise in temperature of their outer surface. This could be a critical issue for the nodes, which are in direct contact with the human body, especially for implantable sensors. Any effect of the routing protocol, which can cause heating of the nodes, must be considered while designing and deploying such protocols.

- *Desired QoS:* Reliability of a network is analyzed in terms of various QoS parameters, which indicate overall performance of the network. The network layer routing protocols decide the routing path and data forwarding, which affect several QoS parameters such as throughput, delay, jitter, etc. In case of BANs, network layer routing schemes should be designed to maximize the performance of the network in terms of QoS parameters.

Various classifications of network layer routing protocols have been presented in the literature based on different criteria such as mobility, cross-layer architecture, QoS, and energy efficiency. Similar classification has been done for the protocols used in the BAN. Figure 10.5 presents one such classification. However, since this chapter is focused on energy-efficient networks, a detailed classification and description of routing protocols for BAN based on energy efficiency is presented in further sections.

10.5.4 *ENERGY EFFICIENCY AT TRANSPORT AND APPLICATION LAYER*

Similar to the network layer, the protocols and data flow management schemes applied at transport layer also affect the energy efficiency of the network in addition to overall network performance. The major function of transport layer protocols is to ensure reliable data transmission with minimum packet loss and minimum retransmission due to link failure or network congestion parameters. Versions of transmission control protocol have been developed to provide reliable and energy-efficient end-to-end data transmission.

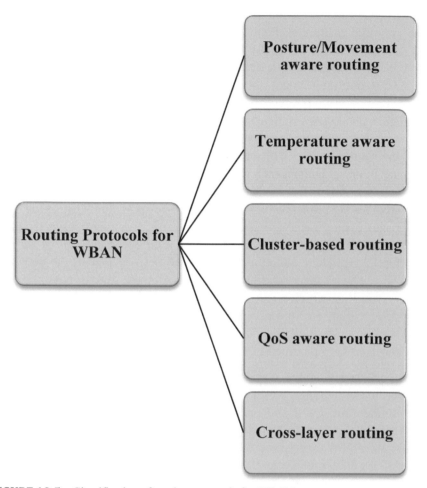

FIGURE 10.5 Classification of routing protocols for WBAN.

At the application layer, the operating system (OS) or the middleware is responsible for implementation of techniques that increase the performance of the device and overall network and also affect energy consumption. In case of healthcare applications, most of the BAN devices are kept in terms of processing capabilities, and the OS or middleware used also has limited functionalities. Techniques to predict the switching of device between various modes such as active, standby, sleep, and to perform this switching are used to make them more energy efficient.

It can, therefore, be concluded that combination of techniques is applied at various levels of the overall network architecture to improve the energy efficiency. The healthcare applications introduce challenges in addition to those of general sensor networks used for various other applications which must be addressed while designing a network architecture to provide remote healthcare services in the form of e-health, m-health, telemedicine, etc. More detailed description of such techniques is presented in further sections of this chapter.

10.6 ENERGY-EFFICIENT ROUTING PROTOCOLS

Energy efficiency in IoT-based healthcare networks is of utmost importance because of battery-constrained biosensor devices used in wireless BANs. Energy efficiency can be improved by various means such as adjusting physical parameters of communication technology, designing less power consuming devices, and developing energy-efficient routing protocols. Routing protocols are mainly designed for data aggregation and many-to-one transmission. The adoption of energy conserving routing protocols by monitoring the energy levels of the nodes and balanced energy utilization approaches is the major challenging issue in low-power healthcare systems (Yating, 2019).

In energy-efficient routing protocols, the route request (RREQ) packet having energy data is transmitted in energy-efficient reliable path of the network. It is followed by receiving the control data (route reply (RREP) packet). This whole process is known as flooding. With an increase in flooding, the packet overhead also increases. This may lead to huge consumption of energy. Therefore, there is a need to avoid overflooding situation for efficient design of energy-efficient routing protocols (Sarwesh, 2017a, b). Currently, there are several routing protocols that address not only the energy efficiency issue but also the reliability and QoS issues. For example, prediction-based secure and reliable routing protocol offers reliable and secure routing as well.

In order to support the energy efficiency of the healthcare network, an IoT-based routing protocol should dynamically move from one step to another according to the power on/off state of the IoT device. It necessitates the monitoring and logging-in of the generation and consumption of energy through communication networks. In WBANs, sensor nodes have limited energy associated with its lifetime. They do not produce much heat as nodes are directly implanted in the human body. All paths are well defined for data routing and must be energy aware. The main issue concerned with energy-efficient routing protocols is the implementation of complex algorithms. There are several efficient routing protocols, but they do not consider on different aspects such as delay tolerant, postural information, temperature rise, etc.

10.6.1   CLASSIFICATION OF ROUTING PROTOCOLS

Broadly, energy-efficient routing protocols can be categorized as follows.

- *Attribute-based routing protocols:* The sensor nodes transmit the content-based data packets to the neighboring nodes. The major attribute-based routing protocols include energy-aware data-centric in which each node decides either to forward or drop the received data packet for improving the energy efficiency at network level (Sarwesh, 2017). However, the major concern is possibility of overflooding, which needs to be avoided.
- *Flat-based routing protocols:* A large number of nodes having the same configuration and features collect the data together and transmit them to the destination. Initially, the data is stored in the routing tables of different nodes. Based on this information, the source node selects the intermediate nodes and then transmits the data to the desired destination. There are several parameters, including energy level, received signal strength, and hop count of intermediate nodes, which determine the operation of flat-based routing protocols (Sarwesh, 2017). These are preferred due to improvement in energy efficiency.
- *Geographical routing protocol:* The data is transmitted from the source node to the destination node taking the shortest distance path based on the location information. This improves the overall energy efficiency of the network in addition to reduction in the packet overhead with improved network lifetime.
- *Hierarchical routing protocol:* This is the most energy balancing efficient routing protocol. In this protocol, a number of sensor nodes constituent a cluster. One of the sensor nodes in a cluster is designated as the cluster head. Different sensor nodes collect the data and transmit them to their cluster head. The data is aggregated by the cluster head and then retransmitted to the base station (another sensor node in the network). The most widely used hierarchical routing protocol is low-energy adaptive clustering hierarchy (Yating, 2019).
- *Ad-hoc on-demand distance vector (AODV) routing protocol:* In the AODV routing protocol, the route selection is done by the destination node based on signal-to-noise ratio (SNR) and hop count metrics which are usually used for estimating the link quality. A modified data packet RREQ, which includes the SNR information, is used for route discovery. On receiving the control data (RREQ) by the destination

node, it sends the RREP data packet to the source. The network is energy efficient based on its network lifetime with higher throughput (Sarwesh, 2017; Youngbok, 2018).

- *Multipath routing protocol:* Additional control data are generated in case the route fails in single path routing protocol. This requires data retransmission, which results in increased overhead data in the network. To overcome this situation, multipath routing protocols such as meshed multipath routing are employed, which not only reduces the overhead of the system but also improves the energy efficiency and reliability of the network.

- *Routing protocol for low power (RPL) algorithm-based mobility supported routing protocol:* The frequent change in the network topology due to mobility of the nodes might result in deterioration in link quality, packet delivery delay, packet collision, or other inconsistencies. The RPL algorithm-based routing protocols provide energy efficiency while considering the mobility of sensor nodes (Lazarevskal, 2018; Al-Shammari, 2018). They make smart decisions that increase the network lifetime by estimating the energy consumption of the sensor nodes. There is significant improvement in end-to-end delay and packet delivery ratio while maintaining low packet overhead in the dynamic RPL networks.

- *Energy aware wearing routing protocol:* This protocol is primarily an energy-aware and QoS-aware routing protocol for communication devices used in the healthcare network. This results in reduced energy consumption and the traffic load (Elias, 2012; Bhanumathi, 2017).

10.6.2 STARATEGIES FOR ENERGY-EFFICIENT ROUTING PROTOCOLS

In wireless body area sensor networks, the multihop routing protocol reduces the number of retransmissions, which enhances the network lifetime, reduces overheads, lowers energy consumption per data packet, decreases end-to-end delay, and reduces the complexity. Using multihop routing protocols, the data are sent with higher confidence in terms of network lifetime, stability period, delay, and throughput, as well as minimum energy consumption. As an instance, the IM-SIMPLE protocol is a mathematical multihop model, which uses short packets for communication employing TDMA mechanism (Awan, 2016). A forwarder node is selected based on the distance from the destination node as well as its residual energy. This results in considerable reduction in energy consumption with increased throughput. There are several strategies in different routing protocols that specifically focus on energy efficiency. Some of them are briefly described as follows.

- *Relay nodes:* A relay node is introduced in the network, which enables balancing the load as well as reducing the energy consumption. The location of the relay node is selected in such a way that it reduces the probability of data packet drops with an increase in the delivery rate of data packets to the destination node. Data from multiple nodes is combined by the relay node to form a unified data packet prior to forwarding it with maximum energy efficiency. A two-hop extension routing protocol can also be deployed in order to send data packets directly for further reduction in the energy consumption.

- *Leader selection method:* A relay node has the capability to amplify the data prior to forwarding it to neighboring relay nodes. This leads to overall improvement in network performance in addition to conservation of energy.

- *Packet size optimization method:* Data bit errors may occur due to large size packets and retransmission requirements in WBANs. Very small size data packets pose limitations in more overheads and higher energy per packet. Therefore, there is a need of optimizing the packet size considering energy efficiency and packet error rate.

- *Cloud computing method:* Using cloud computing, a mobile health monitoring service is about 10 times more energy efficient than a standard one. This method is approximately 20 times faster in storing, analyzing, processing, delivering, distributing, and securing critical healthcare data. Integrating cloud computing with WBANs offers a convenient remote health monitoring method (Sarwesh, 2017), although it poses major challenges in providing security and authentication.

- *Restricted tree topology protocol:* There are number of relay nodes located between different nodes and the destination node. A star topology using opportunistic and dynamic relays is deployed, which results in higher reliability with minimum energy consumption under high propagation loss conditions. The link performance metric used is the received signal strength indicator (RSSI) (Lazarevskal, 2018).

- *Critical data routing:* Only the critical data is sent by the source nodes to two intermediate nodes, which have minimum transmission path loss. This method offers energy efficiency alongwith reduced propagation loss, improved network lifetime, enhanced stability period, and higher throughput (Al-Shammari, 2018).

- *Co-LAEEBA protocol:* Different nodes in the network use collaborative learning by sharing each other's resources. This results in effective communication among these nodes, and data packets are received successfully by them. The destination node combines the received data packets using the fixed-ratio combining method. This protocol uses the shortest-path routing algorithm based on minimum hop count in order to yield better residual energy, higher throughput, and greater stability period (Bhanumathi, 2017).
- Adaptive multihop routing *(AMR) protocol:* Adaptive multihop routing (AMR) is basically an adaptive tree-based with multiple hops, in which fuzzy logic evaluates routing metrics such as residual energy, hop count, and RSSI (Bhanumathi, 2017). This results in better load balance and higher network lifetime and energy efficiency.
- *Energy-aware peer routing:* In this method, the peer node is discovered, and the data packets are exchanged between them. Without employing a fully centralized system, the display unit is discovered dynamically in real time, thereby improving patient mobility and privacy. This results in enhanced performance with respect to reducing traffic load and overall energy consumption (Awan, 2016). This method offers real-time indoor healthcare monitoring services.
- *Cross-layer opportunistic MAC routing:* In this protocol, any node may serve as either a sensor node or a relay node. It is based on the use of appropriate handshake mechanism such as RTS/CTS alongwith ACK. Relay node is selected having highest residual energy and located nearer to the destination node. Thus, this strategy offers higher energy per bit, more network lifetime, reduced end-to-end delay, and higher energy efficiency.

10.7 ENERGY HARVESTING

As described in previous sections of this chapter, several techniques are being developed and tested to make the sensor networks more and more energy efficient. Another approach in this direction is to make the network self-sustained in terms of its energy requirement. Energy harvesting (EH) is one of the most widely explored techniques in this context and is being used since several decades under the umbrella of renewable energy to develop nonconventional sources of energy such as wind, water, solar, etc. With the development of battery-operated devices and their use in various applications of communication networks, a strong need was felt to provide source of energy, which can be used to recharge the battery so that the time to replacement of battery can be prolonged, thus increasing the uninterrupted lifetime of the network. Generation of electric energy from solar energy is one such technique that has widest utilization in terms of electric energy generated, that is, from a few milliwatts to several thousand watts. The recent development in the field of EH is to extract energy from ambient sources, which are occurring not only naturally but man-made as well. Generalizing such techniques, EH can be defined as "a process or method to obtain energy from the natural sources of energy such as wind, water, solar, etc., or man-made sources such as radio frequency (RF) signals, vibrations, pressure, etc., for the purpose of providing operational power to the devices, either directly or through charging of a battery." Such networks having devices powered through EH techniques are also called green networks, since they do not depend on the conventional or nonrenewable sources of energy. The IoT applications are a strong supporter of EH-based devices, and critical applications such as healthcare services strongly demand for implementation of EH with the objective of making the supporting network not only more energy efficient but more reliable in terms of seamless connectivity with longer lifetime.

10.7.1   ENERGY HARVESTING IN BANS

The sensor nodes in BANs continuously acquire and transmit data to provide monitoring of clinical state of the patient. To increase the network lifetime, the following three methods of EH are being used to provide energy to the sensor nodes, thus reducing the need to change the battery.

- *Energy from human body:* Human body, with its actions and movements, acts as a source of energy in different forms, which can be converted to electric energy and thus provide power to the biosensors.
- *Energy from surrounding environment (natural sources):* Several renewable energy sources such as solar energy, wind, heat, light, etc., are present in the environment, which can be harnessed and converted by the sensors as power source.
- *Energy from surrounding environment (man-made sources):* Electromagnetic waves (RF signals) are present almost everywhere in our surrounding environment due to several man-made wireless communication systems. This energy can be harvested by the sensors as a source of power.

For sensors used in healthcare applications, the natural sources of energy present in environment may not always be present since the person wearing the sensors could be present indoor where sufficient wind or solar energy is not available to generate enough electrical energy. Harvesting energy from the human body is also not reliable since the movement of the patient is generally restricted and cannot act as source of energy. Any extra device or component to store and amplify these weak or sparsely available energy sources will add to the discomfort in wearing the device, thus making it less user friendly. Since most of the sensors rely on wireless communication for connectivity, RF energy is expected to be present and can be used as a source of energy for the sensors. The channel connecting the sensor and its network access device, that is, data aggregator or sink node, carries both the RF energy and data between the two. This RF channel is one prime source of energy since there is continuous supply of energy from the network access device. Moreover, the device is designed and configured to operate in the same frequency band as that of RF channel, thus simplifying the design of the EH module for the sensor. Resource allocation schemes have been proposed in literature to utilize the same channel for sending additional energy signal to the sensor, which can be used as power source. In addition to this source, any other RF energy available in close proximity to the device can be used for EH.

KEYWORDS

- **energy efficient network**
- **energy efficient routing**
- **energy model**
- **Internet of things**
- **smart healthcare**
- **network**

REFERENCES

Abo-Zahhad, M., (2014). Survey on energy consumption models in wireless sensor networks. *Open Transactions on Wireless Communications*, vol. 1, no. 1, pp. 1–17.

Abidin, H. Z. and Din, N. M., (2013). Sensor node placement in wireless sensor network based on territorial predator scent marking algorithm. *ISRN Sensor Networks*, vol. 2013, Art. no. 170809.

Agrawal, D. P., (2017). Personal/body area networks and healthcare applications. In: *Embedded Sensor Systems*. Springer, Singapore.

Al-Shammari, H. (2018). Energy efficient service embedding in IoT networks. In *27th Wireless and Optical Communications Conference*, 1–5.

Amin, B., Ullah, N., Ahmed, S., Taqi, M., Hanan, A., (2017). Path-loss and energy efficient model (PLEEM) for wireless body area networks (WBANs). In *International Symposium on Wireless Systems and Networks*, pp. 1–6.

Awan, K. (2016). Wireless body area networks routing protocols: A review. *Indonesian Journal of Electrical Engineering and Computer Science*, vol. 4, no. 3, pp. 594–604.

Azhari, M. E., Moussaid, N. E., Toumanari, A., and Latif, R., (2017). Equalized energy consumption in wireless body area networks for a prolonged network lifetime. *Wireless Communications and Mobile Computing*, vol. 2017, Art. no. 4157858.

Beri, G., Ganjare, P., Gate, A., Channawar, A., and Gaikwad, V., (2016). Intelligent ambulance with traffic control. *International Journal of Electrical, Electronics, and Computer Systems*, vol. 4, pp. 43–46.

Bhanumathi, V. (2017). A guide for the selection of routing protocols in WBAN for healthcare applications. *Journal on Human-Centric Computing and Information Sciences*, vol. 7, no. 24, pp. 1–19.

Boukerche, A., (2008). *Algorithms and Protocols for Wireless Sensor Networks*. Wiley-IEEE Press, New York, NY, USA.

Boulle A., (1997). Rural healthcare and rural poverty—Inextricably linked—Policy in progress, HST Up-Date 1997; 28: 6–7.

Castillejo, P., Martinez, J., Rodriguez-Molina, J., Cuerva, A., (2013). Integration of wearable devices in a wireless sensor network for an Ehealth application. *IEEE Wireless Communications*, vol. 20, pp. 38–49.

Chang, J.-H., and Tassiulas, L., (2004) Maximum lifetime routing in wireless sensor networks. *IEEE/ACM Transactions on Networking*, vol. 12, no. 4, pp. 609–619.

Chase, J., (2013), The Evolution of Internet of Things. Texas Instruments, white paper.

Chen, M., Gonzalez, S., Vasilakos, A., Cao, H., and Leung, V. C., (2011). Body area networks: A survey. *Mobile Networks and Applications*, vol. 16, no. 2, pp. 171–193.

Chepkwony, R. C., Gwendo, J. O., Kemei P. K., (2015). Energy efficient model for deploying wireless body area networks using multihop network topology. *International Journal of Wireless and Mobile Networks*, vol. 7, no. 5, pp. 47–64.

Chiuchisan, I., Costin, H., and Geman, O., (2014). Adopting the Internet of Things technologies in healthcare systems. *International Conference and Exposition on Electrical and Power Engineering*, pp. 532–535.

Chung, K., and Boutaba, R.; Hariri, S., (2016). Knowledge based decision support system. *Information Technology and Management*, vol. 17, pp. 1–3.

Correa-Chica, Camilo, J.; Botero-Vega, Felipe, J., Gaviria-Gómez, N., (2016). Cross-layer designs for energy efficient wireless body area networks: A review. *Revista Facultad de Ingeniería*, no. 79, pp. 98–118.

Deo, R. C., (2015). Machine learning in medicine. *Circulation*, vol. 132, pp. 1920–1930.

Ehsan, S., Hamdaoui, B., and Guizani, M., (2012). Radio and medium access contention aware routing for lifetime maximization in multichannel sensor networks. *IEEE Transactions on Wireless Communications*, vol. 11, no. 9, pp. 3058–3067.

Elias, J., (2012). Energy-aware topology design for wireless body area network. In *IEEE International Conference on Communications (ICC)*, pp. 3409–3413.

Elsersy, M., (2013) "Balancing energy consumption and average end-to-end delay for optimum routing protocol in wireless sensor networks," 2013.

Eysenbach, G., (2001). What Is e-Health. *Journal of Medical Internet Research*, vol. 3, no. 2, Art. no. e20.

Filipe, L., Fdez-Riverola, F., Costa, N., and Pereira, A., (2015). Wireless body area networks for healthcare applications: Protocol stack review. *International Journal of Distributed Sensor Networks*, vol. 2015, Art. no. 1.

Flodgren, G., Rachas, A., Farmer, A. J., Inzitari, M., Shepperd, S., (2015). Interactive telemedicine: Effects on professional practice and healthcare outcomes. *Cochrane Database Systematic Reviews.* vol. 2015, no. 9, Art. no. CD002098.

Gulliford, M., Figueroa-Munoz, J., Morgan, M., Hughes. D., Gibson, B., Beech, R., and Hudson, M., (2002). What does 'access to healthcare' mean? *Journal of Health Service Research and Policy*, vol. 7, no. 3, pp. 186–188.

Hakim, A. E., (2018). Internet of Things (IoT) system architecture and technologies, White Paper.

Hajiaghayi, M., Dong, M., and Liang, B., (2010). Maximizing lifetime in relay cooperation through energy-aware power allocation. *IEEE Transactions on Signal Processing*, vol. 58, no. 8, pp. 4354–4366.

He, S., Chen, J., Yau, D. K., and Sun, Y., (2012). Cross-layer optimization of correlated data gathering in wireless sensor networks. *IEEE Transactions on Mobile Computing*, vol. 11, no. 11, pp. 1678–1691.

Huang, W.-J., Hong, Y.-W., and Kuo, C.-C., (2008). Lifetime maximization for amplify-and-forward cooperative networks. *IEEE Transactions on Wireless Communications*, vol. 7, no. 5, pp. 1800–1805.

Impedovo, D., and Pirlo, G., (2019). eHealth and artificial intelligence. *Information*, vol. 10, no. 3, p. 117.

Islam, S. M. R., Kwak, D.; Kabir, M. H., Hossain, M., Kwak, K., (2015). The Internet of Things for healthcare: A comprehensive survey. *IEEE Access*, vol. 3, pp. 678–708.

Istepanian, R., Laxminarayan, S., and Pattichis, C. S., (2006). *M-Health: Emerging Mobile Health Systems, (Topics in Biomedical Engineering)*. Springer, New York, NY, USA.

Jaleel, H., Rahmani, A., and Egerstedt, M., (2013). Probabilistic lifetime maximization of sensor networks. *IEEE Transactions on Automatic Control*, vol. 58, no. 2, pp. 534–539.

Jones, C. E., Sivalingam, K. M., Agrwal, P., Chen, J. C., (2001). A survey of energy efficient network protocols for wireless networks. *Wireless Networks*, vol. 7, pp. 343–358.

Karvonen, H., Iinatti, J., and Hämäläinen, M., (2015). A cross-layer energy efficiency optimization model for WBAN using IR-UWB transceivers. *Telecommunication Systems*, vol. 58, no. 2, pp. 165–177.

Ko, J., Terzis, A., Dawson-Haggerty, S., Culler, D. E., Hui, J. W., Levis, P., (2011). Connecting low-power and lossy networks to the Internet. *IEEE Communications Magazine*, vol. 49, no. 4, pp. 96–101.

Krishna, A. and Ananthpur, K., (2013). Globalization, distance and disease: Spatial health disparities in rural India. [Online]. Available: http://www.sites.duke.edu/krishna/files/2013/10/

Kulkarni, R. V., Venayagamoorthy, G. K., and Cheng, M. X., (2009). Bio-inspired node localization in wireless sensor networks. In *Conference Proceedings - IEEE International Conference on Systems, Man and Cybernetics*. pp. 205–210.

Kuntz, R., (2010). Medium access control facing the dynamics of wireless sensor networks. Ph.D. dissertation, University of Strasbourg.

Lazarevskal, M., (2018). Mobility supported energy efficient routing protocol for IoT based healthcare applications. In *IEEE Conference on Standards for Communications and Networking*, pp. 29–31.

Li, J., Bose, A., and Zhao, Y. Q., (2005). The study of wireless local area networks and wireless personal area networks. In *Canadian Conference on Electrical and Computer Engineering*, Saskatoon, SK, USA., pp. 1415–1418.

McFarlane, S., Racelis, M., Muli-Musiime, F., (2000). Public health in developing countries, *Lancet*, vol. 356, pp. 841–846.

Norouzi, A. and Zaim, A. H., (2014), "Genetic algorithm application in optimization of wireless sensor networks," *The Scientific World Journal*, vol. 2014, Art. no. 286575.

Pasha, M. and Shah, S. M. W., (2018). Framework for E-Health systems in IoT-based environments. *Wireless Communications and Mobile Computing*, vol. 2018, Art. No. 6183732.

Pol, S., Gupta, P., Rahatekar, D., and Patil, A., (June 2016). Article: Smart ambulance system. In *IJCA Proceedings on National Conference on Advances in Computing, Communication and Networking*, vol. 6, pp. 23–26.

Postolache, G., Girão, P. M., and Postolache, O., (2012). Requirements and barriers to pervasive health adoption. In *Pervasive and Mobile Sensing and Computing for Healthcare—Technological and Social Issues*, Springer, New York, NY, USA.

Rajendran, V., Obraczka, K., Garcia-Luna-Aceves, J. J., (2003). Energy-efficient collision-free medium access control for wireless sensor networks. In *1st International Conference on Embedded Networked Sensor Systems*, pp. 181–192.

Rao, M., Rao, K. D., Kumar, A. K. S., Chatterjee, M., Sundararaman, T., (2011). Human resources for health in India. *The Lancet*, vol. 377, pp. 587–598.

Reddy, K. S., Patel, V., Jha, P., Paul, V. K., Kumar, A. K., Dandona, L., et al., (2011). Towards achievement of universal healthcare in India by 2020: A call to action. *Lancet*, vol. 377, pp. 760–768.

Redondi, A., Chirico, M., Borsani, L., Cesana, M., and Tagliasacchi, M., (2013). An integrated system based on wireless sensor networks for patient monitoring, localization, and tracking. *Ad Hoc Networks*, vol. 11, pp. 39–53.

Rodrigues, J., Misra, S., Wang, H., and Zhu, Z., (2015). Ambient assisted living communications. *IEEE Communications Magazine*. vol. 53, pp. 24–25.

Rojahn, K., Laplante, S., Sloand, J., Main, C., Ibrahim, A., Wild, J., Johnson, K. I., (2016). Remote monitoring of chronic diseases: A landscape assessment of policies in four European Countries. *PLoS One*, vol. 11, no. 5, Art. no. e0155738.

Sarwesh, P., (2017a). Energy efficient network architecture for IoT applications. In *Beyond the Internet of Things*, Springer International Publishing, New York, NY, USA, pp. 119–144.

Sarwesh, P., (2017b). Energy efficient network design for IoT healthcare applications. In *Internet of Things and Big Data Technologies for Next Generation Healthcare*, Springer International Publishing, New York, NY, USA, pp. 35–61.

Sethi, P. and Sarangi, S. R., (2017). Internet of Things: Architectures, protocols, and applications. *Journal of Electrical and Computer Engineering*, vol. 2017, Art. no. 9324035.

Shunyuan, S., Quan, Y., and Baoguo, X., (2016). A node positioning algorithm in wireless sensor networks based on improved particle swarm optimization. *International Journal of Future Generation Communication and Networking*, vol. 9, no. 4, pp. 179–190.

Silva, B. M., Rodrigues, J. J., de la Torre Díez, I., López-Coronado, M., Saleem, K., (2015). Mobile-health: A review of current state in 2015, *Journal of Biomedical Informatics*, vol. 56, pp. 265–272.

Solanas, A., Patsakis, C., Conti, M., Vlachos, I., Ramos, V., Falcone, F., Postolache, O., Pérez-Martínez, P., Pietro, R., Perrea, D., and Ballesté, A., (2014). Smart health: A context-aware health paradigm within smart cities. *IEEE Communications Magazine*. vol. 52, pp. 74–81.

Strasser R., (2003). Rural health around the world: Challenges and solutions. *Family Practice*, vol. 20, pp. 457–463.

Strasser, R. P., Harvey, D., and Burley, M., (1994). The health service needs of small rural communities. *Australian Journal of Rural Health*, vol. 2, pp. 7–13.

Tamizharasi, A., Arthi, R., and Murugan, K., (2013). Bio-inspired algorithm for optimizing the localization of wireless sensor Networks. In *2013 Fourth International Conference on Computing, Communications and Networking Technologies*, Tiruchengode, India, pp. 1–5.

Udawant, O., Thombare, N., Chauhan, D., Hadke A., and Waghole, D., (2017). Smart ambulance system using IoT. In *2017 International Conference on Big Data, IoT and Data Science*, Pune, India, pp. 171–176.

Vasseur, J.-P., Dunkels, A., (2010). *Interconnecting Smart Objects with IP*. Elsevier, Amsterdam, The Netherlands.

Veeramuthu, V., Murali, P. K., Vaithayanathan, V., Chelliah P. R., (Sep. 2011). An ambient healthmonitor for the new generation healthcare. *Journal of Theoretical and Applied Information Technology*, vol. 31, no. 2, pp. 91–99.

Yamada, Y., Usui, S., Kohn, M., and Mukai, M., (June 2004). A vision of ambulance telemedicine services using the Quasi-Zenith satellite. In *Proceedings of the 6th International Workshop on Enterprise Networking and Computing in Healthcare Industry*, Odawara, Japan. pp. 161–165.

Yating, Q., (2019). A survey of routing protocols in WBAN for healthcare applications. *Journal on the Science and Technology of Sensors and Biosensors*, vol. 19, no. 7, pp. 1–24.

Yiyue, W., Hongmei, L., and Hengyang, H., (2012). Wireless sensor network deployment using an optimized artificial fish swarm algorithm. In *Proceedings of the International Conference on Computer Science and Electronics Engineering,* Hangzhou, China, vol. 2, pp. 90–94.

Youngbok, C. (2018). Energy efficient IOT based on wireless sensor networks for healthcare. In *IEEE International Conference on Advanced Communications Technology*, pp. 294–299.

Zhao, F., and Viehland, D., "Key Applications for Success of Personal Area Networks," 2009 Eighth International Conference on Mobile Business, Dalian, 2009, pp. 227–232.

Zhou, C. (2018). A wireless sensor network model considering energy consumption balance. *Mathematical problems in Engineering*, pp. 1–8.

Zorlu, O., and Şahıngöz, Ö. K., (2017). Node placement with evolutionary algorithms for maximum coverage of heterogeneous WSNs. In *2017 25th Signal Processing and Communications Applications Conference*, Antalya, Turkey, pp. 1–4.

CHAPTER 11

Applying Data Mining to Detect the Mental State and Small Muscle Movements for Individuals with Autism Spectrum Disorder (ASD)

RASHBIR SINGH[1], PRATEEK SINGH[2], and LATIKA KHARB[2,*]

[1]*Department of Information Technology, Amity University, Noida, Uttar Pradesh 201301, India*

[2]*Jagan Institute of Management Studies, Sector 5, Rohini, New Delhi, Delhi 110085, India*

Corresponding author. E-mail: latika.kharb@jimsindia.org

ABSTRACT

Technology is the need of every hour, and our motive is to make use of technology for the benefit of the autism spectrum disorder (ASD) patients. We verify which technique of data mining (*K*-nearest neighbor, decision tree, neural networks, and naive Bayes) would provide us with the most accurate prediction and classification of mental state of mind (i.e., excited, not excited, and relaxed) and small muscle movements (i.e., eyes open and eyes closed) using electromagnetic brainwave signals generated in our brain neurons (i.e., alpha, beta, theta, gamma, and delta) and using this application with electroencephalogram to detect different abilities the person has and situations or environment that make them hyperactive and propose the real-time solution for people with ASD.

11.1 INTRODUCTION

It is known that brains reply increases to the demand made by the humans. Stress can be defined as the state of tension, which results due to increase in demand in certain circumstances. In recent year, more than one-third of the population in the world has been reported to suffer from stress and stress-related diseases. Stress defines one's overall health, and this fact is not hidden. However, the question arises is: Can stress actually change the physiology of one's brains? There are various research works conducted to understand whether stress actually changes the physiology of one's brain. Not every type of stress is harmful; it also depends on the profundity, cure, and time period. As stress takes up various forms, it can happen due to fight between a person and his/her loved ones, failure when one is expecting success, change in environment, or sudden change in his/her day-to-day habit. Definition of stress varies from age groups and genders. For example, a student gets stressed if he does not secure good score in exam or adults tend to get stressed due to work pressure or household-related problems. According to physiologists, stress can change our brain in four ways:

- Chemical change, which is triggered by stress, can cause irritation.
- High intensity of stress can even shrink one's brain.
- A stressful event or action can even kill brain cells.
- Stress can distort and disturb one's memory by triggering one's brain threat response to an event.

While cortisol (stress hormone) reduces the working of the hippocampus (brain part that is used to command many functions of the body, located in the medial temporal lobe), it will increase the scale and activity of the corpus amygdaloideum, the brain's main center for emotional responses and motivation. The corpus amygdaloideum is answerable for a certain process that threats perception and also toward fight-or-flight response.

The increasing volume of data is exceeded the ability of health organizations to process it for improving clinical and financial efficiencies and quality of care (Carvalho et al., 2019). Brainwaves are electric signals generated in the neurons. The electrical changes among the neurons inside the brain causes change in electric potential, which is produced across different parts of the mind. The difference generated between the electric potential levels is recorded and used for various detection applications, including stress, relaxation, and small muscle movements. These brain signals are categorized as electroencephalogram (EEG) signals. The condition of brain changes due to this change in electric potential in the neurons inside the brain. Thus, different brainwave values correspond to different mental states Lahane et al. (2016).

Most EEGs are used in order to analyze and get results on screen for the seizure brain issues. EEGs can also similarly used for reasons, which can cause diverse inconveniences; these incorporate rest issues and changes in conduct. They are once in a while used to assess mind interest after an extraordinary head hurt or sooner than a heart transplant or liver transplant (http://neurosky.com/f etched on 06/11/2017). The motivation behind this chapter is to grab the continuous records of various feelings of anxiety, little muscle moves, and enthusiastic range utilizing the EEG headgears such as Neurosky mind wave and blending it with a miniaturized scale controller such as Arduino to catch the data and change them into alpha, beta, gamma, delta, and theta cerebrum waves.

As an individual experiencing autism spectrum disorder (ASD) has been observed to have diminishing alpha brainwave values, high beta brainwave values in ASD patient is seen to promote aggressive behavior. Gamma brainwaves can be used to detect an individual's skills and abilities. High theta values induce the characteristics of impulsivity and unpredictability.

11.2 LITERATURE SURVEY

The enlarging volumes of information emerging by the progress of technology and the growing individual needs of data mining make classification of very large scale data a challenging task (Zhou et al., 2012). To understand the objective in the above paragraph and to know the uniqueness and how each brainwave contributes to one's physiological activities, the following areas are extensively studied.

Brainwaves: These are the waves generated in an electromagnetic fashion by our brain, which are categorized into five categories: alpha, beta, theta, gamma, and delta. EEG is the technology used to capture the electric potential differences generated inside one's brain and read these brainwaves, which can then be used for analysis of treatment in medical fields. In this research work, we use this for analyzing different mental and physical states with the help of data mining.

EEG: An EEG is used to discover inconveniences related to an electric movement of the brain. An EEG tracks and insights and mind wave fashion. Little metallic plates (electrodes) with small electric wires are placed above the head of the user; the amplifier amplifies the electromagnetic brainwaves, captures them, and plots a real-time graph of the electric movements inside the brain. The graph shows us the events and impacts happened inside the brain. A person's day-to-day activity and his interest create an electric brainwave into a recognizable pattern. Through an EEG, therapeutic specialists can scan and anticipate the seizures and different issues. He/she will give you the recommendation changes in lifestyle/medication to help the person.

Alpha: Alpha brainwaves are in range of 8–13 Hz (see Table 11.1 and Figure 11.1). Alpha waves are unique kind of brainwaves, and it is noted that electric potential of alpha waves increases, which can be recorded by EEG or magnetoencephalography. These waves are originated from the occipital lobe of brain as soon as a person begins to gain relaxation with his eyes closed while staying awake. The alpha waves have the following features.

TABLE 11.1   EEG Information and Their Ranges

Waves	Frequency	Short Definition
Alpha	8–13 Hz	Alpha brainwaves deliver a trademark quiet, inventive, "sense redress" state while we close our eyes and start to pull back from outside tactile incitement. It is the scaffold among waking and sleeping
Beta	13–20 Hz	Beta brainwaves come into place dominate our customary waking cycle of attention. Beta waves are "quick" generated in an activity, like when we are attentive, alert, occupied with inconvenience tackling, judgment, decision-making, or concentrating on our mental hobby. Beta brainwaves are additionally isolated into three groups
Lo-Beta/Beta1	Beta1, 12–15 Hz	They are "rapid" and deep
Beta/Beta2	15–22 Hz	Activities with high involvement that makes sense to us
Hi-Beta/Beta3	22–38 Hz	They are said to be the unnecessary beta generated during activities involving high tension and excitement level
Theta	4–8 Hz	Theta brainwave is our scope for picking up information inside, memory, and one's instinct. Theta brainwaves generate in most when a person is asleep yet additionally are overwhelming in profound contemplation
Gamma	20 Hz	It has been associated with better learned working, self-consciousness, selfmanage, issue settling, dialect change in children, memory, and loads of components of increased consideration and idea
Delta	1–4 Hz	Delta brainwaves are created in rest and private reflection. They are mild, low recurrence, and profoundly entering just like a drum beat

- These waves reduce with state where mind is tired, open eyes, and when a person is sleeping.
- Waves generated during the activity of eyes closed while the person is awake are said to be the strongest alpha brainwaves.

- They are evaluated with the help of quantitative EEG by using opensource free tools, comprising of EEGLAB and/or the Neurophysiological Biomarker Toolbox.
- Alpha waves are absent till three years of age.

Every activity requires the involvement of these waves. Therefore, it is noted that different activities comprise different frequency requirements such as waves generated during movement of arm will be different than that of movement of legs, or when a person is meditating or listing to music. These waves reduce when a physical movement occurs or the intention of movement takes place.

11.2.1   HOW ARE ALPHA BRAINWAVES USED IN OUR RESEARCH?

In case of ASD, people with ASD have observed to have diminishing alpha electric waves in brain areas, which are related to motor movement and senses. This might explain why people with ASD have some difficulties in performing tasks properly for what they are instructed about. Alpha waves may be proven to be helpful in keeping subjects with ASD calm, aware, and relaxed.

Beta: Beta brainwaves vary from 13 to 20 Hz (see Table 11.1 and Figure 11.1). Beta electric waves in brain neurons are the highest frequency brainwaves, which are generated when we feel attentive, focused, and have high intensity of alertness. Lack of these brainwaves is often related to the problem of attention level, the person faces difficulty in carrying out a certain task for a longer consecutive period of time, disability in learning, and injured brain cells. The brain mapping of ASD patients has also been exposed to the fact that patients have both highly fast and slow brainwave activity in the frontal lobe of the brain, which might suggest lack of interconnection between the frontal lobe and the back area of the brain neurons.

11.2.2   HOW ARE BETA BRAINWAVES USED IN OUR RESEARCH?

Beta blockers: These are the medicines that are practiced to block one's beta receptors that help in improving one's blood flow, managing heart abnormality, and, in case of ASD patients, managing aggressive behavior in autistic adolescents, and adults' beta blockers greatly reduce aggressive behavior (Ratey et al., 1987). Beta states arc the states that are identified with common waking cognizance. Furthermore, beta waves are divided into three different parts, as shown in Table 11.2.

TABLE 11.2   Categories of Beta Waves

Category Name	Description
Low Beta Waves	12.5–16 Hz, "Beta 1"
Mid Beta Waves	16.5–10 Hz, "Beta 2"
Unnecessary beta waves/Hi-Beta	20.5–28 Hz, "Beta 3"

Gamma: Gamma brainwaves are not similar to gamma radiation waves. Gamma mind waves are the electric brainwaves, which are generated between the brain neurons that vary between 25 and 100 Hz, with the cycle of about 40 Hz; this is the normal healthy human being, and in general range, it is always >20 Hz (see Table 11.1 and Figure 11.1).

Gamma waves are implicated in creating a harmony of conscious observation. The existence of gamma brainwaves was completely unknown before the invention of advanced digital EEG recorders, because the conventional analog EEG was unable to record such high-frequency brainwaves in the human brain (as the minimum spectrum of these waves is at 25 Hz).

11.2.3   HOW ARE GAMMA BRAINWAVES USED IN OUR RESEARCH?

If we somehow manage to know about the biofeedback generated from hobbies, games, and other activities that motivate the development of spectrum of gamma brainwaves around the neurons and its network around the brain, then, for individuals with an ASD, it can help in detecting what skills and abilities an individual ASD patient has. We can use this concept to promote enhanced learning and teaching among the students with ASD, which will help them sustain on their own and not to be dependent on other's income. Social skill is useless if one does not have a proper understanding about the society. If we can develop a way to know about how the brain is "wired up" in case of patient with ASD, then we can work for them and help the society in educating about the personality of the person with ASD like who the person is and what are their individual skill sets are. This will eventually benefit an individual's self-esteem who is suffering from ASD by making him more aware about his individuality and potentially that can develop a positive future for them (Lawson, 2013).

Theta: The frequency range of theta brainwaves varies from 4 to 8 Hz (see Table 11.1 and Figure 11.1). These waves are often called "suggestible waves" because of prevalence during the state of trace or hypnotism. Theta brainwaves are unique as they exist between one's sleep and daydreaming, which results in making us feel more relaxed with an open mindset. Feeling of raw and deep is often related to theta brainwaves as they are the main reason because of which we are experiencing that. An excessive amount of theta generation exposure may often lead to make people defenseless in some situations of despairing. Theta brainwaves have their own impact as they are the main reasons of helping in enhancement of our innovative thinking and impulse, which make us feel more natural. It, moreover, helps with the restoration of sleep from stressful conditions. As long as the time period of theta exposure is large or the volume is high, it is much more helpful for our brain and overall personality.

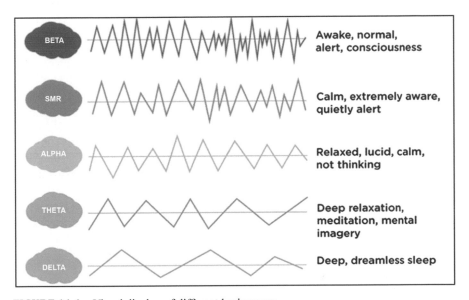

FIGURE 11.1 Visual display of different brainwaves.

Some of the key points to note about theta brainwaves are the following.

- An excess amount leads to impulsivity, hyperactivity, attention-deficit/hyperactivity disorder, carelessness, and sorrow (how are theta brainwaves used in our research?)
- Too little amount of it may result in tension, poor enthusiastic acknowledgment, and pressure.
- Most reasonable amount of it leads to the development of instinct, creativity, unwinding, and passionate association.

The electric potential adequacy is in the vicinity of 20 and 100 (http://www.brainworksneurotherapy.com/what-are-brainwaves).

EEG uses distinct brainwaves (delta, theta, alpha, beta, and gamma) generated by different parts of the brain for detecting distinct emotional spectrum such as stress, small muscle movements, feeling of joy, sadness, relaxation, the wink of the eye, movement of the neck, level of attention, mediation a person has, and so forth. Different research studies use a combination of distinct brainwaves to prove their studies. Therefore, this literature survey includes research papers from 1989 to 2017.

This literature survey is the most important step in detecting which of the waves are more extensively used and interacted by the researchers, which will help in the development of technique, in prioritizing exceptional waves, and in determining which wave should be used in this research. There occurred quite a few studies in past years.

11.2.4   CLASSIFICATION TECHNIQUES

K-nearest neighbor (KNN): A KNN calculation, regularly condensed KNN, is a way to deal with information order that gauges how likely an information point is to be an individual from one gathering or the other relying upon what bunch the information guides closest toward it (http://itsusync.com/different-types-of-brain-waves-delta-theta-alpha-beta-gamma fetched on 06/11/2017).

Decision tree: A decision tree is a graph that uses a branching method to illustrate every possible outcome of a decision. It assigns monetary/time or other values to possible outcomes so that decisions can be automated.

Neural network: A neural network, for the most part, includes an enormous number of processors working in parallel and masterminded in levels. The main level gets the crude information data—practically equivalent to optic nerves in human visual handling. Each progressive level gets the yield from the level going before it, instead of from the crude info—similarly neurons further from the optic nerve get signals from those nearest to it. The last level creates the yield of the framework.

Naive Bayes: A naive Bayes classifier is an algorithm that uses Bayes' theorem to classify objects. Naive Bayes classifiers assume strong, or naive, independence between attributes of data points. Popular uses of naive Bayes classifiers include spam filters, text analysis, and medical diagnosis. These classifiers are widely used for machine learning because they are simple to implement.

KNN: The KNN method is a popular classification method in data mining and statistics because of its simple implementation and significant classification performance (Zhang et al., 2018).

KNN can be utilized for both classified as well as unclassified categories of data management and prediction systems. It is the most vastly used as a part of an arrangement issue in the business. For the assessment of any strategy, we have to look upon three viewpoints:

- ease to interpret output;
- calculation time;
- predictive power.

KNN calculation looks over all parameters of contemplations. It is regularly utilized for its simplicity of elucidation and low count time.

TABLE 11.3 Research Papers Using KNN for EEG Classification

Sr.No	Research Name	Year	Author
1	Brain Computer	2002	Blankertz et al.
2	Sleep recognition system with EEG using k-means	2010	Güneş et al.
3	EEG-based Emotion Recognition	2010	Khosrowabadi et al.
4	Imagined speech	2010	Brigham et al.
5	Emotion Recognition	2010	Petrantonakis et al.
6	EEG correlates for chronic mental stress	2011	Khosrowabadi et al.
7	EEG and KNN classifier.	2011	Sulaiman et al.
8	Tensorial treatment of EEG estimates	2013	Dimitriadis et al.
9	Detection of sleep stages	2017	Amjadzadeh et al.
10	Machine Learning Methods as a Test Bed	2017	Mohanchandra et al.

Result: From Table 11.3, we can conclude that KNN is the best suitable algorithm as it serves the best classification prediction. Although KNN is simple but can predict even the most complex outputs and in our research, it gave the highest accuracy in all the iterations as compared to other three algorithms. Hence, the KNN fulfills the requirements for our high accuracy algorithm.

Table 11.4 includes the list of research papers being analyzed, and the results obtained are shown in the form of bar charts in Figure 11.2, representing which brainwaves were being used by the researches the most. Figure 11.3 represents the contribution of different brainwaves in predicting the emotional spectrum, Figure 11.4 represents the contribution of different brainwaves in predicting small muscle movements, and Figure 11.5 represents the contribution of different brainwaves in predicting attention and meditation.

TABLE 11.4　EEG Data are Generally Labeled According to the Frequency Ranges

Sr. No.	Author	Year	Brain Waves	δ	Θ	α	ß	γ
1	Vanitha V and Krishnan P.	2016	Emotional Spectrum (Stress) / Small Muscle movement / Attention and Mediation			✓	✓	✓
2	Subhani AR et al.	2012	Emotional Spectrum (Stress) / Small Muscle movement / Attention and Mediation	✓	✓			
3	Sulaiman N et al.	2011	Emotional Spectrum (Stress) / Small Muscle movement / Attention and Mediation			✓	✓	
4	Ssang-Hee, Seo	2010	Emotional Spectrum (Stress) / Small Muscle movement / Attention and Mediation				✓	
5	Prashant Lahane et al.	2016	Emotional Spectrum (Stress) / Small Muscle movement / Attention and Mediation			✓	✓	
6	Rosler et al.	2013	Emotional Spectrum (Stress) / Small Muscle movement / Attention and Mediation	✓	✓	✓	✓	✓
7	T. Jeyase elan et al.	2017	Emotional Spectrum (Stress) / Small Muscle movement / Attention and Mediation					
8	Hu, Bin, et al	2015	Emotional Spectrum (Stress) / Small Muscle movement / Attention and Mediation	✓	✓			
9	Zheng Yali, et al	2015	Emotional Spectrum (Stress) / Small Muscle movement / Attention and Mediation			✓	✓	
10	Marzbani, Hengam eh et al.	2016	Emotional Spectrum (Stress) / Small Muscle movement / Attention and Mediation	✓		✓		✓
11	Marzbani, Hengam eh et al.	2015	Emotional Spectrum (Stress) / Small Muscle movement / Attention and Mediation	✓	✓			
12	Sulaiman, Norizam, et al	2012	Emotional Spectrum (Stress) / Small Muscle movement / Attention and Mediation			✓	✓	

TABLE 11.4 *(Continued)*

Sr. No.	Author	Year	Brain Waves	δ	Θ	α	ß	γ
13	Peniston Eugene G. et al.	1991	Emotional Spectrum (Stress) Small Muscle movement Attention and Mediation			✓	✓	
14	Fahrion, Steven L. et al.	1992	Emotional Spectrum (Stress) Small Muscle movement Attention and Mediation	✓	✓			
15	Hamid Noor Hayatee Abdul et al.	2010	Emotional Spectrum (Stress) Small Muscle movement Attention and Mediation				✓	✓
16	Sulaiman, Norizam, et al	2009	Emotional Spectrum (Stress) Small Muscle movement Attention and Mediation					✓
17	Norhazman, H. et al.	2012	Emotional Spectrum (Stress) Small Muscle movement Attention and Mediation				✓	
18	Hess, Ch W. et al.	1987	Emotional Spectrum (Stress) Small Muscle movement Attention and Mediation				✓	
19	Swingle, Paul G. et al.	2007	Emotional Spectrum (Stress) Small Muscle movement Attention and Mediation					✓
20	Tyson Paul D	1987	Emotional Spectrum (Stress) Small Muscle movement Attention and Mediation				✓	
21	Graap Ken, and David Freides	1998	Emotional Spectrum (Stress) Small Muscle movement Attention and Mediation	✓	✓			
22	Peniston, Eugene G., and Paul J. Kulkosky	1989	Emotional Spectrum (Stress) Small Muscle movement Attention and Mediation	✓	✓	✓		
23	Park Kwang Shin et al.	2011	Emotional Spectrum (Stress) Small Muscle movement Attention and Mediation	✓	✓			
24	Kim Seon Soo et al.	2013	Emotional Spectrum (Stress) Small Muscle movement Attention and Mediation				✓	

TABLE 11.4   *(Continued)*

Sr. No.	Author	Year	Brain Waves	δ	Θ	α	ß	γ
25	Van Berkum, Jos JA	2008	Emotional Spectrum (Stress) Small Muscle movement Attention and Mediation					✓
26	Heraz Alicia	2009	Emotional Spectrum (Stress) Small Muscle movement Attention and Mediation	✓	✓	✓		✓
27	Saidatul, A. et al.	2011	Emotional Spectrum (Stress) Small Muscle movement Attention and Mediation				✓	✓
28	Hamid Noor Hayatee Abdul, et al.	2015	Emotional Spectrum (Stress) Small Muscle movement Attention and Mediation				✓	✓
29	Chavan Deepika R. et al.	2016	Emotional Spectrum (Stress) Small Muscle movement Attention and Mediation				✓	✓
30	Bell Martha Ann, and Kimberly Cuevas	2013	Emotional Spectrum (Stress) Small Muscle movement Attention and Mediation			✓	✓	
31	Halliday, David M. et al.	1998	Emotional Spectrum (Stress) Small Muscle movement Attention and Mediation				✓	✓
32	Abdulka der, Sarah N. et al.	2015	Emotional Spectrum (Stress) Small Muscle movement Attention and Mediation			✓	✓	
33	Woodman, Geoffrey F	2013	Emotional Spectrum (Stress) Small Muscle movement Attention and Mediation				✓	
34	Teplan, Michal	2002	Emotional Spectrum (Stress) Small Muscle movement Attention and Mediation				✓ ✓	

Result from Table 11.4: Objective is to determine which of the brainwaves from alpha, beta, gamma, theta, and delta are the most important and prominent in determining the characteristics of the working of brain and the state in which the mind is and what is the contribution each wave have in order to decide the prediction attribute for the research work. This research work classifies different states of whether the person is relaxed or not, excited or not, stressed or not, etc.

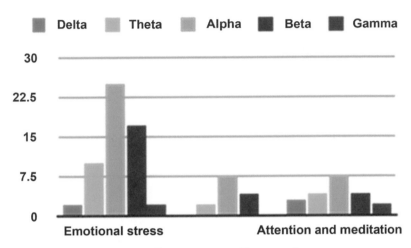

FIGURE 11.2   Comparison of different waves used by researches.

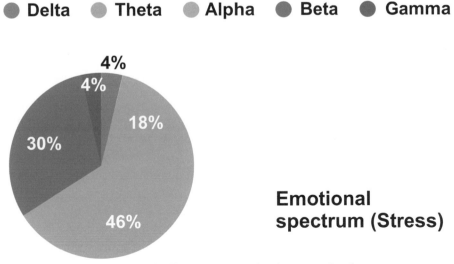

FIGURE 11.3   Comparison of different waves used to detect emotional spectrum.

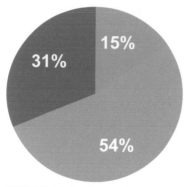

Small Muscle Movement

FIGURE 11.4   Comparison of different waves used to detect small muscle movement.

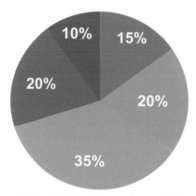

Attention and mediation

FIGURE 11.5   Comparison of different waves used to detect attention and meditation.

From the literature survey in Table 11.4, we concluded that for exceptional criteria emotional spectrum (pressure, happiness, sadness, and henceforth) delta (4%), theta (18%), alpha (45%), beta (30%), and gamma (4%) are utilized by the researchers in their research, and alpha has the best utilization and beta has the second highest utilization.

For small muscle movements (blink of an eye and motion of the neck), delta (0%), theta (15%), alpha (54%), beta (31%), and gamma (0%) are utilized by the researchers in their research, and alpha and beta have the highest utilization.

For attention and meditation, delta (15%), theta (20%), alpha (35%), beta (20%), and gamma (10%) are utilized by the researchers in their research, and here as well, alpha and beta are the two maximum used brainwaves by way of the researchers in their studies.

On the basis of the above data, Table 11.5 has been constructed showing percentage of contribution of different waves in generating different results, and hence, priority is decided.

By this, we resolved that the alpha have the priority as one, beta has the priority as two, theta has the priority as three, and gamma having unique contribution even after having priority as five. Therefore, for our prediction model and methodology, this research work will be adopting alpha, beta, theta, and gamma for the classification model in data mining.

TABLE 11.5   Percentage of Contribution of Different Waves

Type	Delta	Theta	Alpha	Beta	Gamma	Result
	4	18	45	30	4	Emotional spectrum (stress)
	0	15	54	31	0	Small muscle movement
	15	20	35	20	10	Attention and mediation
Priority	4	3	1	2	5	

The literature survey was conducted using more than 70 research paper and web links (articles) (few are listed in Tables 11.3 and 11.4); it is concluded that alpha, beta, theta, and gamma are the most important brainwaves considered, while from Table 11.3, it was understood that KNN is the widely used technique and pilot study was also conducted for the same; the study is explained in detail in methodology.

11.3   METHODOLOGY

Methodology steps are detailed in Figure 11.6.

- The dataset will be fetched from online sources (Andrzejak et al., 2001; Dharmawan, 2007).
- The data obtained from the first source (Andrzejak et al., 2001) are in raw format so the appropriate feature extraction method is applied on to the raw data.
- After applying the feature extraction, the data are being stored into excel/text format to make it readable.
- The readable datasets are then classified on the basis of different values of alpha, beta, gamma, and theta.
- The classified datasets are then divided into the test dataset and the training dataset.

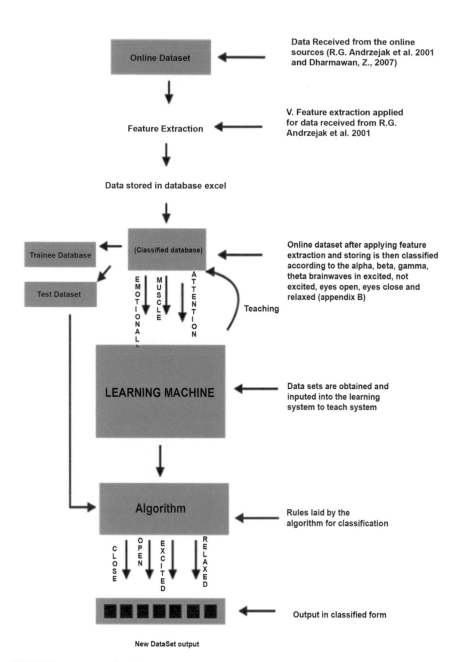

FIGURE 11.6   Methodology.

- Training data are used for training of the learning machine.
- The test dataset is used for testing the accuracy of the machine.
- Then, an appropriate algorithm from decision tree, KNN, naive Bayes, and neural networks is tested for their accuracy.
- The most accurate algorithm (KNN) is then used for training the machine and making predictions.
- The resulting data will be sent to the learning machine for the purpose of creating reliable machine learning systems.
- The machine learning system will teach the processed dataset and verify its leaning.
- This learning system will give more specific information about whether the user is relaxed, excited, not excited, eyes open, or eyes closed.
- This will create the classified dataset.
- Therefore, the desired solution will be outputted, and the system will again analyze the user's mind with data.

For the purpose of analysis, we have analyzed five algorithms:

- Decision tree
- KNN method
- Neural Networks
- Naive Bayes

Figure B1(a) in Appendix B shows the training dataset that is processed with read excel in the rapid miner tool with the classified information with data of 800 sets as relaxed, excited, not excited, eyes open, and eyes closed. This excel is connected with the cross validation with two parts training and the test is done on various algorithm models (deep learning, decision tree, KNN, neural networks, and naive Bayes (see Figure A1 in Appendix A) and performance is judged with percentage accuracy of different models. Following is the percentage accuracy of four different models on the training dataset (see Figure A1(a) in Appendix A).

- *Decision tree with 96.25% accuracy* (see Figures A1(a) and A2(a) in Appendix A).
- *KNN method with 97.50% accuracy* (see Figures A1(b) and A2(b) in Appendix A).
- *Naive Bayes with 96.25% accuracy* (see Figures A1(c) and A2(c) in Appendix A).
- *Neural networks with 78.75% accuracy* (see Figures A1(d) and A2(d) in Appendix A).

In Appendix A, Figure A1 shows the algorithms and Figure A2 shows the percent accuracy of the respective algorithms.

From Table 11.6, we arrived to the conclusion that KNN is the best appropriate algorithm, which served with the 97.50% accuracy for our prediction machine. Presently, we have taken a mixed dataset to be utilized as a section with the training dataset to predict the classified information of little muscle movements with classification as eyes open and eyes closed and the mental state of the person with classification as excited, not excited, and relaxed comprising of 100 certainties everything about estimations of gamma, theta, alpha, and beta.

TABLE 11.6   Accuracy Comparison of Different Algorithms

Sr. No	Algorithm	Accuracy (%)
1	Decision Tree	96.25
2	KNN Method	97.50
3	Neural Net	78.75
4	Naive Bayes	96.25

Working of KNN: For example, here, we are taking a basic case to demonstrate in this calculation. Following is a spread of red circled and green squares; we are using RC to denote red circles and GS for green squares [see Figure 11.7(a)].

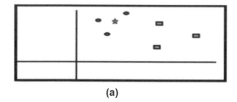   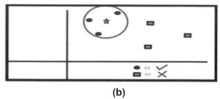

(a)   (b)

FIGURE 11.7   *K*-NN example.

As you can see [see Figure 11.7(a)], we have blue star (BS). It can either be categorized as red circle or green square. The "*K*" value in the KNN model is calculation of the closest neighbor we wish to take votes from. Suppose we take value of *K* as 3. Then, we will create a circular boundary around the blue star and create a circle as large as by keeping focus on blue star and similarly capture just three data points on the plane [see Figure 11.7(b)].

The three nearest neighbors around the blue start came up to be all red circles. Thus, with great certainty level, we can state that the blue star should have a place within the red circle class label. Here, the decision turned out to be extremely evident as the possible three neighbors to the blue star came out to be red circles. The selection of the value of K in KNN is exceptionally important in order to perform calculations. Next, we will discuss more about the components to be taken into consideration for the best possible selection for the value of K. As the value of K increases, the graph becomes more smother.

The two parameters that we need to access in KNN are the training error rate and the validation error rate [see Figure 7(a)].

From Figure 11.8, we can conclude that the error rate at value of K as one is constantly zero for the training test. Any data point is closest to itself hence gives the 100% accuracy. This being said, the KNN with K value as 1 will predict the constantly same exact value. In the event where validation error curves are similar, we would choose value of K as 1 [see Figure 11.8(b)].

This makes the understanding of KNN all the more clear. At $K = 1$, we were exceeding the upper bound. Thus, the error rate at first reduces and approaches to a minimum point in the graph. After the minimum point, it then increases with the increase in the value of K. To get the ideal estimation of K, you can isolate the training and validation from the initial stage dataset.

Presently, plot the validation error curve to get the ideal estimation of K. This estimation of K should be utilized for all predictions.

Figure B2 in Appendix B shows the prediction made by the KNN under third column with label as prediction on the basis of the inputs from alpha, beta, theta, and gamma (columns 9–12). The confidence level shows how certain an expectation is. The confidence of a classification shows the states how certain the model is.

The cost of confidence, that is, 1 and 0, can be defined with the help of the following if–else condition:

if(confidence(1) > threshold)
then 1
else
0

Subsequently, the prediction is made and may be actually visible within the prediction column of Figure B2 in Appendix B, classified as eyes open, eyes closed, excited, not excited, and relaxed.

Figure B1(b) in Appendix B indicates the dataset used for training the prediction machine with attributes as gamma, theta, alpha, and beta with

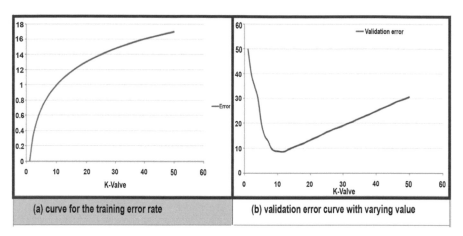

| (a) curve for the training error rate | (b) validation error curve with varying value |

FIGURE 11.8   *K*-NN graphs.

the label, which classifies the idea of various values of gamma, theta, alpha, and beta small muscle actions (eyes open/eyes closed), and state of mind (excited/not excited/relaxed).

This research work has used $K = 5$ (percent nearest neighbors) for determining the classified output and for making predictions, and the performance accuracy obtained is 97.50%.

11.4   DATA

To be clinically and commercially relevant, the algorithmic complexity of feature extraction methods must be such that they can be easily and quickly computed, with minimal processing and power consumption demands (Phinyomark and Scheme, 2018).

11.4.1   DATA ACQUIRING

The training dataset is from Andrzejak et al. (2001). The dataset has five sections: dataset A discussed as Z, dataset B discussed as O, dataset C discussed as N, dataset D discussed as F, and dataset E discussed as S, each containing set of EEG fragments with a recording of the electromagnetic movement of a healthy person for 23.6 s. Datasets A and B are having data related to EEG chronicles from healthy volunteers with categorization as eyes open and eyes closed, individually.

The second dataset characterized by Dharmawan (2007) included healthy people who volunteered and analyzed under EEG to collect the data as playing particular PC computer games with a class as excited, not excited and relaxed on the basis of the various different values of the alpha, beta, theta, and gamma.

11.4.2 DATA EXTRACTION

Ambiguous data are removed and are polished/refined to get more refined information for unique groups differently. The element utilized here is categorized underneath the graph. The trapezoidal rule can be used to find the area under the graph, which is formed in the dataset from the first source, which is in raw graphical form. On numerical examination, the trapezoidal governs (likewise alluded to as the trapezoid control or trapezium run) a strategy for approximating the particular imperatively

$$\int_{a}^{b} f(x)\,dx \tag{11.1}$$

$$\int_{a}^{b} f(x)\,dx = (b-a)\big((f(a)+f(b))/2\big). \tag{11.2}$$

Equation (11.1) shows the differentiation with the upper bound as (b) and lowers bound as (a). The working of the trapezoidal rule can be understood by approximating the region underneath the diagram of the element $f(x)$ as a trapezoid and computing its locale.

With this, we can derive the different values for different waves. It takes after the district of the recurrence groups (delta, theta, alpha, and beta) is ascertained for every EEG section.

11.5 CONCLUSION

We are able to predict patient's small muscle movements and categorize them as eyes open, eyes closed, and mental state by categorizing as excited, not excited, and relaxed with the help of our prediction system, and we were able to identify the most accurate algorithm, which can be used in our research, which is KNN, which have 97.50% accuracy rate. In Appendix C, Figure C1 shows (a) pie chart and (b) bar graph of the classified data, and there is weighing in the dataset, while Figure C2 shows the histogram of (a) gamma, (b) theta, (c) alpha, and (d) beta with the x-axis as frequency and y-axis as different values.

11.6 FUTURE SCOPE

This methodology can be used with a microcontroller with the algorithm coded in simple C/C++, a programming language that will eventually work as a direct connection between the EEG headgear and the computer. The microcontroller attached to the EEG headgear used by a patient will apply the required feature extraction onto the data raw, data received, and separate different brainwaves (alpha, beta, theta, and delta) and will give the solution using the technology of Internet of things to solve the cause of the issue.

For example, a patient is hyperactive due to the loud noise; then, the microcontroller will communicate with the environment and use the noise cancellation techniques to lower the brainwaves that cause the patient to turn hyperactive and will monitor the brainwaves in real time and will give the solution for the problem in real time. This is the only one example application, the possibilities are endless, and the patient will get the real-time solution and a hardware communicating to him in real time; the hardware will be cheap and affordable and hence can also lower the cost of expensive treatments from the neurologist.

KEYWORDS

- **hyperactivity**
- **brainwaves**
- **neurophysiological**
- ***K*-nearest neighbor (K-NN)**
- **neural networks**

REFERENCES

Andrzejak, R. G., Lehnertz, K., Mormann, F., Rieke, C., David, P., and Elger, C. E., (2001). Indications of nonlinear deterministic and finite-dimensional structures in time series of brain electrical activity: Dependence on recording region and brain state. Physical Review E, vol. 64, no. 6, Art. no. 061907.

Carvalho, J. V., Rocha, A., Vasconcelos, J., and Abreu, A., (2019). A health data analytics maturity model for hospitals information systems. *International Journal of Information*

Management, vol. 46, pp. 278–285Dharmawan, Z., (2007). Analysis of computer games player stress level using EEG data. Master of Science Thesis Report, Faculty of Electrical Engineering, Mathematics and Computer Science, Delft University of Technology, Delft, The Netherlands.

Lahane, P., Vaidya, A., Umale C., Shirude S., and Raut A., (2016). Real time system to detect human stress using EEG signals, *International Journal of Innovative Research in Computer and Communication Engineering.*, vol. 4, no. 4.

Lawson, W., (2013). Sensory connection, interest/attention and gamma synchrony in autism or autism, brain connections and preoccupation. *Medical Hypotheses*, vol. 80, no. 3, pp. 284–288.

Phinyomark, A. and Scheme, E., (2018). Novel features for EMG pattern recognition based on higher order crossings. In *2018 IEEE Life Sciences Conference (LSC)*, Montreal, QC, Canada, pp. 263–266.

Ratey, J. J., Mikkelsen, E., Sorgi, P., Zuckerman, S., Polakoff, S., Bemporad, J., Bick, P., and Kadish, W., (1987). Autism: The treatment of aggressive behaviors. *Journal of Clinical Pharmacology*, vol. 7, pp. 35–41.

Zhang, S., Li, X., Zong, M., Zhu, X., and Wang, R., (May 2018). Efficient kNN classification with different numbers of nearest neighbors. *IEEE Transactions on Neural Networks and Learning Systems*, vol. 29, no. 5, pp. 1774–1785.

Zhou, L., Wang, H., and Wang, W., (2012). Parallel implementation of classification algorithms based on cloud computing environment. *Indonesian Journal of Electrical Engineering*, vol. 10, pp. 1087–1092.

Index